GunDigest®
Book of the

REMINGTON

870

NICK HAHN

Published by

Gun Digest® Books, an imprint of F+W Media, Inc.
Krause Publications • 700 East State Street • Iola, WI 54990-0001
715-445-2214 • 888-457-2873
www.krausebooks.com

To order books or other products call toll-free 1-800-258-0929
or visit us online at www.gundigeststore.com

ISBN-13: 978-1-4402-3211-4
ISBN-10: 1-4402-3211-3

Edited by Jennifer L.S. Pearsall
Cover Design by Al West and Sharon Bartsch
Designed by Sharon Bartsch

Printed in China

PREFACE

The Remington Model 870 Wingmaster pump-action shotgun is the best-selling and the most popular shotgun in North America, and possibly the entire world. No other shotgun—ever—has seen such widespread use as the Remington Model 870. In the English-speaking world, it is simply referred to as the "eight-seventy." Its numerical model designation has become so entrenched in the worldwide shotgunners' vocabulary that, in the Spanish-speaking world, it is commonly called *ocho setenta*. I have even heard it referred to in Russian as *vosyem-semdyisyat*, and in Japanese as *hachi-nanaju*, each iteration a literal translation of "eight seventy" in their respective languages.

It wasn't always so. When the Model 870 first appeared, in 1950, it caught the eye of many shooters, but it still had a steep hill to climb to catch up with the reigning pump gun of the period, the Winchester Model 12. I well remember when I got my first Model 870, as a kid in the mid 1950s. At that time, it was more commonly called by its model name, the "Wingmaster" and not by the numerical model designation. I was quite proud of my Remington Wingmaster, despite the fact that my hunting buddy Larry and my older brother, Jim, both preferred the Winchester Model 12. But, even as a kid, I was struck by the simplicity and robustness of my gun's design and parts. It was simple to take down—I could remove the trigger group by punching out two pins and remove the barrel by unscrewing the magazine cap. No other pump gun offered such simple and easy take-down operation. My brother and friend Larry, with their Winchester Model 12s, could not remove their trigger groups that easily, nor could they remove the barrel from the attached magazine tube and pump handle. I definitely derived a sense of satisfaction and a childish feeling of superiority from having a more easily disassembled pump gun, whenever we cleaned our shotguns after a hunt.

The Remington Model 870 brought the pump shotgun into the modern world in more ways than just easy disassembly. It was quite slick looking, with a streamlined, smooth-sided receiver, and it was also considerably lighter than most of the competition. The basic Model 870 AP, with a corn cob pump handle and a plain buttstock, weighed, on the average, 6¾ pounds in a 12-gauge with a rib-less 28-inch barrel. Only the Ithaca Model 37 weighed about the same, or perhaps a tad less. The Winchester Model 12, on the other hand, weighed at least a ½- to ¾-pound more at 7½ pounds in the same configuration.

The 870 was way ahead of its time, when it came to pump gun design. Small wonder, then, that the Remington Model 870 has lasted unchanged for more than a half century Indeed, it is the only pump gun to remain mechanically unchanged! The Ithaca Model 37 has been in production longer than the Model 870, albeit as a Remington Model 17 initially. As an actual Ithaca-branded gun, its production has been interrupted from time to time, and that famed bottom-ejecting pump gun has had numerous mechanical changes through the years. Not so with the Model 870. It has had cosmetic changes, sure, and usually for the better, I might add, but mechanically it has remained the same. That speaks volumes for the gun's design.

This book has been written as a tribute to the remarkable Remington Model 870 more than anything else. It is certainly not a technical work, nor is it meant to be a definitive study of this gun mechanically, historically, or otherwise. The work is meant to be more of a montage, if you will, of stories and information related to this wonderful and ageless gun. To be sure, it does contain technical information, as well as a historical chronology of the production of different versions of this model. But, overall, it is meant to show how widespread and diversified this shotgun is in its use throughout the world. This work is meant to entertain and inform at the same time; it is not an academic study of the Remington Model 870, but rather a tribute composed of bits and pieces of information, anecdotes, and personal accounts about a remarkable shotgun that has now surpassed its production beyond 10 million. It is about a shotgun that is found in all corners of the world and in the hands of the rich and the poor. It is about *everybody's* shotgun.

—Nick Hahn, Litchfield Park, Arizona, March 2012

ACKNOWLEDGEMENTS

The idea to write a book about America's best selling and most popular shotgun was not something that I had developed on my own and decided to pursue. It was Jim Schlender, Publisher at F&W Media, and his editor, Jennifer L.S. Pearsall, who proposed it to me and shepherded the project until it was completed. I am most grateful to Jennifer and to Jim, who have been extremely supportive and helpful during this project from beginning to end. I am thankful to them both for their help and support.

Three members of the Freedom Group Family of Companies, the umbrella organization that now owns Remington, were instrumental in providing information that was needed to complete this project. Jessica Kallam, Press Relations Manager at Remington, sent the most current information that was available for this project. Lisa Walters, Historian, answered countless questions and directed me toward more resources I could use. Michael Haugen, Director International Military/Law Enforcement Sales, took the time from his busy schedule to answer my questions, while he was on an overseas trip. Michael also sent me photographs and information immediately upon his return from the trip, on his own time and on a weekend! *De oppresso liber,* Michael! The Freedom Group Family of Companies is fortunate to have Jessica, Lisa, and Michael representing its interests. Any organization would be extremely lucky to have such people working for them.

Finally, I wish to acknowledge and thank an individual who provided me with the bulk of the material for this project, including photographs, articles, catalogs, and other bits of information that were crucial for putting together this book, Roy Marcot, of the Remington Society. Very simply put, without the material provided by the Remington Society, this book could not have been written. I am most indebted to Roy for his help and for allowing me the use of the material for this book. Much of the information contained in the chronological history of the 870 was gleaned from Roy's article entitled "A Guide to Collecting Remington Model 870 Shotguns," which was published in the Society's semi-monthly publication, *The Remington Collector's Journal*.

Although my name appears as the author of this work, in reality, all of the people that I have mentioned should be listed as co-authors.—*Nick Hahn*

4

CONTENTS

CHAPTER ONE

REMINGTON ARMS COMPANY —
A BRIEF HISTORY

E. Remington and Sons factor in
Ilion, New York - circa 1874

ALTHOUGH THIS IS a book about one particular gun, specifically the Remington Model 870, a short discourse on the history of the Remington Arms Company that makes this gun is necessary. It is necessary so that the reader can better understand how and why this giant of an American arms company came to make the remarkable Model 870 pump-action shotgun.

Legend has it that, in 1816, a young man by the name of Eliphalet Remington, Jr., was dissatisfied with the available rifles at the time. The best were all imported from Europe and were very expensive. Remington could not afford these expensive rifles, so he made a rifle for himself. He was reputed to have been a mechanical genius, and the rifle he made was far superior to anything being produced by any of the other American gunmaker at the time. He took his new rifle to a local shooting match and won first place with it. Everyone who saw the rifle wanted one, and that is how, according to the legend, Remington Arms Company, the oldest surviving American arms maker, made its beginning.

Hounded by popular demand, Remington started making rifles for his living. Soon his reputation had spread everywhere, and the Remington Arms Company quickly became an estab-lished arms maker. The Remington Arms Company factory made rifles in its upstate New York facility for the first couple decades, though with modest production numbers and no particular gun on large scale. These first firearms were, of course, muzzleloaders. But Remington was very innovative and constantly looked for better ways to make guns. Remington also welcomed the intellect of individual inventors, who frequently came to the factory regularly bringing new ideas, new ways to make guns better. The orders for Remington rifles were steady, and the reputation of the company continued to grow.

It wasn't until the war with Mexico, in 1846, when Remington received a government contract for rifles, that the company received a large influx of money and the gunmaking improved radically. Because the government contract required a much larger output, Remington had to find ways to be more efficient and expedient in making large quantities of firearms. This was something that was to become the trademark of Remington, a feat repeated time and time again through the years.

A second government contract was awarded a few years later, when the American Civil War broke out. At that

ELIPHALET REMINGTON, JR.
October 28, 1793
- August 12, 1861.
Founder of the Remington Arms Company. This man was a true innovator when it came to firearms, a reported mechanical genius of his era.

point, Remington had diversified its firearms making and gone on to manufacture cap-and-ball revolvers, which soon became quite popular. Clearly, America's wars and government contracts were helping Remington the company to grow. At the same time, realizing that a better and more efficient method must be continually developed to deal with these large government contracts, Remington the man became one of the leaders in the development of precision mechanics and other innovative methods of making better firearms.

The end of American Civil War brought about a dramatic change in firearms. Muzzleloading firearms became obsolete, with the introduction of self-contained metallic cartridges and breechloading firearms. Remington didn't miss a beat, becoming one of the fore-

It was Remington's famous breechloading Rolling Block rifles that earned the company its initial fine reputation, with sales to foreign countries far outpacing those in the U.S.

most producers of these types of new arms.

Remington breechloaders became much in demand, not just in America, but abroad. At the same time, Remington also continued its handgun development and production, now making cartridge revolvers and small, two-shot handguns that came to be known as "derringers." Remington's handguns were extremely popular and, out on the Western frontier, some famous gunmen were reputed to have favored Remington revolvers. But it was the breechloading rifle that really gave Remington a boost. Remington started selling its breechloaders, the famous Remington Rolling Blocks, to France, Denmark, Sweden, and other countries in Europe, as well as Egypt. At first the numbers were modest. Distribution began with 200 breechloaders to France, then increased to 10,000 to Denmark, 12,000 to the U.S. Navy, 85,000 to Spain, 30,000 to Sweden, 50,000 to Egypt, and on and on. Before long, the numbers had *skyrocketed*. France ordered 145,000 rifles, Spain 130,000, and even an American sporting goods house, Hartley & Graham, ordered 144,000 rifles, the majority of which they then sold to China! All in all, Remington sales of its breechloading rifles ran well over one million units.

Unfortunately, the excellent Remington revolvers didn't fare as well as the company's breechloading rifles had. By this time in America's history, the Colt's Firearms Company had a near-monopoly on cartridge-firing revolvers, thanks to its famous single-action revolver, the legendary Colt Model 1873. Smith & Wesson was running a weak second to Colt's, and that put Remington, despite its excellent product, out of the running. The vagaries of gun manufacture and popularity are such that, in many cases, a good or even a superior product doesn't survive.

Then, in the late 1800s, the foreign orders stopped. The world of firearms had changed again. New firearms designs seemed to pop up every day, and repeating rifles had become the new standard. Not only were the repeating rifles the new weapons in demand, but the nature of ammunition had changed from blackpowder to the more powerful smokeless powder. Remington didn't have a repeating rifle design of its own, although several designs were attempted. For instance, from 1886 to 1904, Remington produced the Remington-Lee bolt-action rifle. Unfortunately, the reception for this rifle was lukewarm, although Remington did manage to get a contract to sell some to the U.S. Navy.

Struggling against the tide of Colt's and S&W, Remington found relief with an order from Russia, for manufacture of the Russian service rifle, the Model 1891 Mosin-Nagant bolt-action. Remington made an enormous number of these rifles, and although not all of them were delivered, as Russia was undergoing a revolution and a change in regime, Remington was able to sell these rifles to other countries. Part of this excess sell-off went to the U.S. Government, which supplied these rifles to the U.S. Expeditionary Force that journeyed into Russia during that country's civil war. Meanwhile, on the home front, Remington had captured a significant portion of the sporting shotgun market in America with its Browning patent Remington Model 11 autoloader, and the company received U.S. Government contracts to manufacture the U.S. Enfield Model 1917 and the U.S. Springfield Model 1903, both of which were used by U.S. troops in World War I. All was definitely not lost.

Clearly, Remington had a history of producing arms for foreign governments going back

REMINGTON FACTORY

A bird's-eye view of the Ilion, New York, Remington factory. We took the original photograph from more than a few decades ago (right) and color-enhanced it (top) to bring it back to life.

to its early years. During World War I, besides making rifles for the U.S. Government and the Russian regime, Remington made Enfield Model 1917s chambered in the .303 British for the British Army. Remington also produced the U.S. Model 1911 Automatic Pistol for the U.S. Government. (These are not to be confused with the later Remington Rand-produced 1911A1s during World War II, which were made by a different company.) The Model 1911s that were made during World War I were Remington pistols made in their Ilion, New York factory. Remington also diversified during this period, and though there were several new sporting arms made, some might say that the company stretched itself a bit too thin with its forays into making typewriters, cash registers, locks, bicycles, ammunition, and even clothing.

The Depression Era hit everyone very hard. Remington had its problems, but still managed to stay afloat and even absorb some other companies that were in financial trouble, most notably Parker Brothers, famed makers of double-barrel shotguns. Remington bought out Parker Brothers in 1934, but Remington's financial wellbeing was mainly tied to the fact that, during the 1930s, a major interest in the Remington Arms Company was acquired by DuPont. DuPont was one of the largest, if not *the* largest, chemical company and a major producer of explosives and gunpowder in the United States.

World War II brought about another shot in the arm to Remington. During the war years, Remington supplied the U.S. Government not only

with rifles, but ammunition, as well. Remington had founded the Union Metallic Cartridge Company shortly after the end of the Civil War, and then acquired Peters Cartridge Company in the intervening years. With DuPont being the majority owner of the company, Remington became a major ammunition manufacturer, something it still is, of course, to this day. By the end of the first year of WWII, Remington had supplied the U.S. Government with one million rifles. By the end of the second year, two million rifles had been produced by Remington for the United States Government, mostly the Springfield 1903A1 rifles that the U.S. government sent over to England under the Lend Lease Act. In 1944, Remington was one of the companies (the other was Springfield Armory), chosen by the U.S. Government to produce a selective-fire version of the M1 Garand. This was the Remington T22, which, after the war in the 1950s, evolved into the M14. Needless to say, Remington had been a major contributor to the war effort, supplying several million rifles and millions upon millions of rounds of ammunition in various calibers for U.S. military use.

It was the aftermath of World War II that generated a new burst of production of modern firearms for sportsmen, including both rifles and shotguns by Remington. Utilizing technology and materials developed during the war years, Remington led the field in new, modern sporting arms in America. Thus came about the birth of the shotgun that is the subject of this book, the Remington Model 870.

Today, Remington is bigger than it ever has

The Remington headquarters in Ilion, New York, are as active and productive as ever, perhaps even more so, as the company is part of the larger concern known as the Freedom Group Family of Companies. This umbrella entity also owns Marlin Firearms, DPMS Panther, H&R/NEF, Dakota Arms, Bushmaster, Parker Guns, Para USA, and several other firearms-related companies.

been before. Its ultra-modern manufacturing facility is located in Ilion, New York, the same place where it has been operating since its beginning. The company continues to make the newest and the best firearms that modern technology and ingenuity can produce. Remington produces a dizzying array of rifles and shotguns and recently started producing a pistol, the Remington 1911R1, something the company has not done since World War I. Remington had made other modern-day pistols, including a small pocket automatic, the Model 51, in the 1930s, and a single-shot bolt-action, the venerable XP100, which was made from the 1960s until the 1980s.

But there hadn't been anything since the XP100 (which was essentially a cut-down single-shot bolt-action rifle; its action was used to develop the Model 600 and Model 660 carbines), and, so, the 1911R1 is the first true pistol since the Model 51. Today, aside from all the guns that are produced in America, Remington also now imports rifles and shotguns from abroad, most notably Italy and Russia, and markets them under its brand name.

Remington now, of course, is a part of a much larger concern, one that finds it under the umbrella of the Freedom Group Family of Companies, which also owns Marlin Firearms Company, a company that is almost as old as Remington itself (Marlin was founded in 1836), as well as Harrington & Richardson, another old firearms company, originally founded in 1871. Several other companies are also under the same Freedom Group umbrella, including Parker Guns, L.C. Smith, and some of the newer arms companies like Dakota Arms, NEF (New England Firearms), Bushmaster Arms Company, and DPMS Panther Arms. It is now, as much as ever, a titan of the firearms industry.

CHAPTER TWO

REMINGTON PUMP SHOTGUNS —
THE EARLY YEARS

Remington®

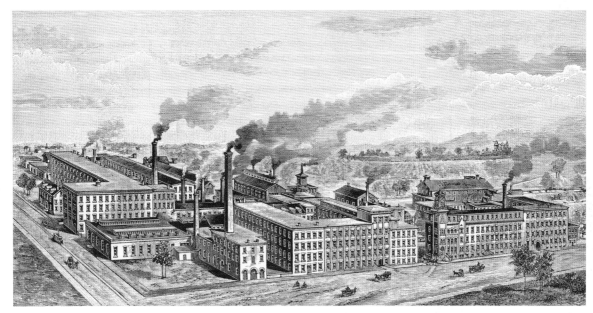

Remington Arms Company - Ilion, New York
- circa 1890 -

THE PUMP- OR SLIDE-ACTION shotgun has long been considered the "all-American" shotgun. In fact, the term "all-American" has been applied to this type of shotgun more often and by more gun writers through the years so that it's come to a point where most Americans believe that it is indeed an American invention. But beliefs aren't facts. In fact, the earliest version of a pump-action firearm was first experimented with and produced abroad, when an English gunsmith by the name of Alexander Baine patented the first pump-action, in 1854.

England, as it turns out, is the origin of most modern shotgun innovations, especially those in the area of double guns. Shotgun gauge sizes were established by the English, and most, if not all, were first made in England. The 28-gauge, often attributed by

American gun writers to Parker Brothers of America, was actually developed in England decades before Parker made its first 28-gauge, in 1910. The invention of choke boring is also often credited by some American gun writers to an Illinois duck hunter by the name of Fred Kimble. But records show that an English gunsmith named W.R. Pape was truly the first to come up with the concept of choke boring, at least several years before Kimble had his version recognized.

But back to the Baine pump-action for a minute. Subsequent to this Englishman's design, there were several versions of pump-action firearms produced in both England and France. None of them were commercially successful. In general, the guns were full of bugs and failed to function reliably. In the end, these

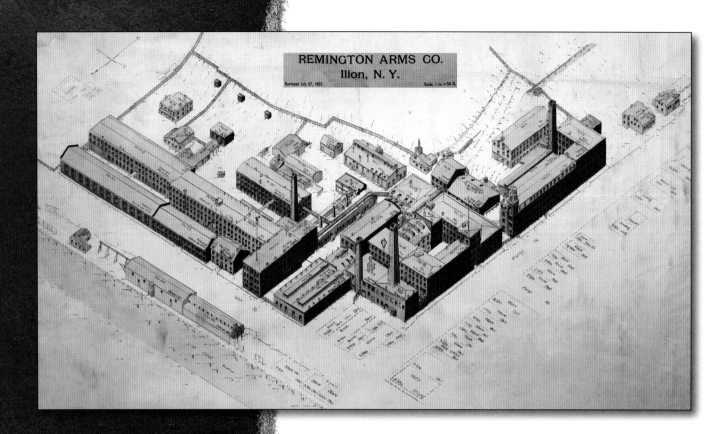

REMINGTON ARMS CO.
Ilion, N. Y.

Surveyed July 27, 1907.   Scale, 1 in.=50 ft.

ARTIST'S RENDERING

This sketch, an overhead view of the Ilion, New York, Remington manufacturing facility, was produced July 27, 1907, according to the company label at the top. Compared to the current-day pictures of the facility in Chapter 1, it's not hard to see that the original designers were visionary. While the machinery inside has surely changed with the decades, the overall appearance of the structures has changed little. It is a wonderful blending of old and new that seems much in keeping with the firearms themselves—especially the Model 870 pump-action.

not-so-all-American pumps were considered novelties in an era where mechanical inventions were popping up almost daily.

An American was the next up to tackle the slide-action shotgun design, that undertaking done by one Christopher Spencer, who designed the first pump shotgun recognizable as a red-white-and-blue invention, in 1882. Though it was leaps and bounds beyond its English and French ancestors, Spencer's pump gun was still far from perfect and had its share of problems. Spencer made improvements and debuted the Model 1885, which was still not all that reliable in function, though it was expensive and beautifully made, with fancy checkering and engraving in the higher grades. The gorgeous gun certainly raised interest among American gun enthusiasts. Of particular curiosity was that it was a hammerless gun, quite unlike the later Winchesters and Marlins that featured exposed hammers and which proved to be popular and commercially successful. Yet, despite the fact that Spencer's 1885 pump was of a *hammerless* design, it wasn't exactly streamlined in appearance, especially when compared to the modern pump guns of today. It loaded and ejected from the top of the receiver, and it had a conglomeration of strange angles and curves common to nineteenth century firearms designs.

The Spencer pump shotgun was not a commercial success, partly because it was expensive, and partly because, despite improvements over previous versions, it still failed to be all that reliable. The company, as one would expect, went bankrupt. Spencer's business was purchased by New York arms dealer Francis Bannerman, who tried to revive sales of the Model 1885, the attempt failed. The product just had not been refined to a point where it could be counted on and, of course, it was just too pricey. Eventually, it was the American inventor John M. Browning who would refine Spencer's pump design to come up with the first truly commercially successful version of a pump-action shotgun, the Winchester Model 93. This gun, in turn, spawned the Winchester Model 97, which firmly established the pump-action shotgun as a permanent fixture in gun culture.

Be that as it may, this is not about who invented the 28-gauge or choke boring, and it's not even actually about who invented the pump shotgun. In America, like the rest of the world, the shotgun scene was dominated by the side-by-side shotgun in the nineteenth century. During the breechloading era of the latter half of the 1800s, initially it was the rabbit-eared hammer gun that was made by just about all the major gun makers in America. Later, the hammerless shotgun became the standard. Indeed, the classic double gun was in its heyday in the late nineteenth century U.S., a trend continuing on through the turn of the century; American shotgun enthusiasts are familiar with names such as the Parker Brothers, L.C. Smith, Ithaca, A.H. Fox, LeFever, and many other somewhat lesser-known makers. Remington produced some of the finest American doubles ever made. But just a couple years before the twentieth century kicked in, pump-action shotguns made their first successful appearance. American shotgunning would never be the same.

As I've said, the Spencer pump came first, and though it was unreliable and failed to thrive commercially, it evolved through John Browning into the Winchester Model 93, and then the Model 97. This second version of Browning's became an immediate, runaway success and

the game was on. A year after the Model 97's appearance, Marlin came out with its own pump gun to compete with Winchester, the Marlin Model 98. The two pump guns were not only one digit apart in model designation, but looked remarkably similar in appearance.

Up until this point in time, Marlin had been Winchester's only competition in the lever-action rifle arena. Now it seemed the companies were going to compete in the pump-action shotgun field, as well. But it was not to be. Marlin never caught up with Winchester in pump shotguns and eventually gave up, only periodically attempting to re-enter the arena with a new design or a new import from time to time. Remington, meanwhile, had continued to stick to building double-barrel shotguns. But with the continued success of the Model 97, the writing was on the wall, and it quickly became quite apparent to everyone associated with firearms manufacture that the pump gun was going to be the shotgun of the future in America.

One might be tempted to say that the popularity of the new pump was that it held more rounds than the side-by-sides Americans had been going afield with for so long. Although that undoubtedly played a part in the design's success, the much bigger advantage was that a quality pump shotgun could be made and sold for much less than what it cost to make a comparable double gun. Yes, at the time there were always cheap double guns, both American-made and imports. Some, in fact, were priced even lower than the pumps. But they were just that, cheaply made guns that did not last long. So, both Winchester and Marlin were doing brisk business selling their new pump-action repeaters that were proving immediately to be both reliable and durable.

Remington's first attempt at making the pump shotgun took place 10 years after the appearance of the Winchester Model 97. That invention was the Model 10, a slick-looking, bottom-ejecting, hammerless pump gun with a streamlined receiver. Both the Winchester Model 97 and Marlin Model 98 were exposed-hammer guns, a factor that gave them a distinctly dated look in the first decade of the twentieth century. The

REMINGTON ARMORY
ILION N.Y. 1854.

Remington had a tough row to hoe on its way to the Model 870. High on the list was competitin from Winchester's famous Model 12, rightly dubbed the "Perfect Repeater" at its introduction in 1912.

Remington, being hammerless, looked more streamlined and much more modern compared to the other two. Still, despite its "modern" looks, with its debut having come a decade after the appearance of the other two, the Remington Model 10 had a hard time competing. Additionally, the design had flaws, and the gun wasn't proving to be as reliable as the Winchester Model 97. Remington was struggling a bit with its new creation.

Then, in 1912, Winchester came out with what is now the legendary Model 12, the so-called "Perfect Repeater," as Winchester liked to advertise. It was very well designed, a hammerless and streamlined gun that was beautifully put together. It was Winchester's first pump shotgun *not* designed by John Browning who had, by that time, broken his ties with Winchester and given Remington the rights to produce a version of his tremendously successful autoloader, which became known as the Remington Model 11. Winchester had no autoloader

THE CITY WITHIN

A vintage 1930s-era shot at the entrance to the Remington compound. Remington certainly aimed to keep its employees happy and productive, with laundromats, lunch counters, and more daily conveniences close at hand for its busy factory workers.

to compete with Remington's Model 11, but they did have the new pump gun Model 12, and it was proving to be a smashing success.

The Winchester Model 12 first appeared as a light, slender 20-gauge, later to be followed up with bigger 12- and a 16-gauge versions and, still later, a smaller 28-gauge variant. In response to Winchester's big hit, in 1921, Remington came out with its Model 17, also a 20-gauge. This was a John Browning-designed—basically, what Browning did was improve upon the earlier Remington Model 10 design, then turned around and sold the manufacturing rights to Remington—bottom-ejection pump gun that was just as light and slender as its Winchester competitor.

Unfortunately, despite Browning's genius in gun designing, he did have a tendency to sometimes make things overly complicated. This was the case with the Model 17. It was an excellent gun, but a bit complex and, ultimately, it proved to be no competition to the Winchester Model 12.

By the 1920s, every shotgun maker in America wanted to come up with a successful repeater. It was quite clear that the repeater was the shotgun of the future in America. The design was cheaper and faster to make and better adapted to assembly line production, while the double-barrel was much more labor intensive and, in some cases, required complicated hand assembly. In 1929, Remington came out

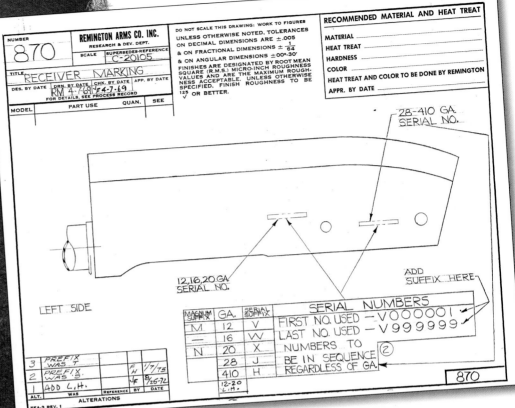

As genius as John Browning was, sometimes his designs were *too* complex. Early model Remington pumps such as the Models 17 and 29 proved too expensive to make and still couldn't compete with Winchester's Model 12. Remington designers scrambled to find a pump to beat its biggest competitor.

with a slightly modified 12-gauge version of the Model 17 and called it the Model 29. It was a stop-gap measure; the company needed a 12-gauge gun to compete on the market, and the best it could do at the time was to make a "newer" and bigger version of the Model 17. It was a good gun, but it was still far too complicated, in fact, even *worse* than Remington's Model 10. Remington designers had to avoid John Browning's various patent rights on the Model 17 and, in doing so, made the mechanism even *more* complicated. Additionally, it proved expensive to manufacture, and it still proved no challenge to the unyielding popularity of the Winchester Model 12.

Then, in 1931, Remington unveiled its Model 31, a beautifully made and extremely smooth operating, side-ejection pump-action shotgun—and it was every bit as well made as the very popular Winchester Model 12. In fact, many considered it a better gun than the Winchester, particularly its action, which quickly developed a reputation for being the smoothest pump-action around. Remington used the Madison Avenue hype and called it the "ball bearing action" in response to Winchester's claim that their Model 12 was the "perfect repeater." Remington discontinued the Model 17 and Model 29 in 1933, two years after the appearance of the Model 31. The Model 31 was made in 12, 16 and 20, and even in a lightened version with an alloy receiver. Remington's Model 11 autoloader was a best seller, so the decision makers at Remington didn't feel a need to keep more pump guns around to compete with Winchester's Model 12. No doubt they felt that the Model 31 would be enough. Remington sold the manufacturing rights for the nifty but complicated Browning-designed model 17 to Ithaca, who was in desperate need of a repeater to bolster its sagging double-gun sales. The rest is history, of course. Ithaca came out with its Model 37, which quite literally saved the company, and that gun has been in production, albeit with periodic interruptions and renaming—it was called the Model 87 for a while—to this day. Browning resurrected the bottom-ejection design as its Model BPS pump shotgun, in 1977.

The great world economic depression that began around 1929 and lasted through the late 1930s (actually until the start of World War II), had a profound effect on the gunmakers in America as it did in the rest of the world. Most of the great double-gun companies in America had either folded or were barely hanging on when the Depression ended. The only shotgun makers that survived were the ones that were able to produce and sell the less expensive and more popular repeaters, the pump shotguns in particular.

Winchester's shotgun department survived on the sales of the old Model 97 and the very popular Model 12, as well as its economy version, solid-frame (no take-down) Model 25, which was born during the Depression. Winchester hoped to lure prospective buyers to it who found the Model 12 too expensive. Its marquee double gun, the Model 21, survived, but only because the president of the company insisted that it be kept. The Model 21 lost money for Winchester during its entire lifetime with that company.

Parker Brothers, A.H. Fox, and other double makers all folded or were absorbed by bigger companies. Parker Brothers was bought by Remington, while A.H. Fox was purchased by Savage. L.C. Smith hung on for its dear life until shortly after World War II ended and it was bought out by Marlin. Others disappeared completely. The

message to shotgun makers in [...] clear, since only companies t[...] Great Depression and World [...] that made repeating shotguns, not d[...] survived because of the Model 37 pump g[...] its doubles disappeared after the war. Remington's excellent Model 32 over/under lasted only a short time after World War II. (Actually, post-war Model 32s were assembled with parts that were made before the war, they were really not new guns.) Remington dropped the Model 32 from its line and later, in the 1950s, the manufacturing rights were sold to a German company, Krieghoff. Remington's repeating shotguns, however, both the Model 11 autoloader and the Model 31 pump gun, continued to be manufactured during the war, as well as after the war, until 1949.

So, even before the outbreak of World War II, the pump shotgun became firmly established in America. It was the most popular shotgun in America for a variety of reasons, the main one being that a quality pump gun still cost less than a comparable autoloader, and especially less than a double gun; the rest of the world, especially England, was totally committed to double guns and building them the old fashioned way, by hand, and there's never been anything inexpensive about that. Most of the Old World gun makers sneered at American pump guns as mechanical contraptions unsuitable for "sport." It seems that only the Italians were interested in repeaters, autoloaders in particular, and the French did produce some pump guns, as well. The French though, have always been innovative when it comes to gun design. After all, it was the French who invented breechloading guns. But despite the French proclivity for tinkering with new mechanical gun designs, they were still more interested in double guns, producing sliding-breech and other innovative doubles. Repeaters were simply not on their priority list.

America became the only place where the pump guns' popularity continued to grow. Many today may not realize this, but the pump gun was the most popular shotgun for *all* shotgunning, including skeet, from around the 1930s until the 1960s. If you look at outdoor and shooting magazines

HARD AT WORK
Remington was a maker of fine double guns, back in the day. This nineteenth-century photo shows a factory floor crowded with white-aproned craftsmen hard at work on the bench assembling and finishing dozens of doubles.

from those periods, you will find that the majority of shotgunners posing in game fields or on trap and skeet ranges are armed with pump guns. That makes perfect sense. Other than the economically priced single-shot and the occasional bolt-action shotgun, the pump gun was and still is the most affordable of shotguns on the market.

With the economy beginning to boom after World War II ended, shotgun makers in America knew there would be more and more demand for inexpensive, but well made, repeating shotguns. Former servicemen returning from the Great War all wanted a piece of that American dream—a car, a house with a picket fence (if they were married), and, for those interested in the outdoors, a shotgun for bird hunting and a rifle for big game. These returning servicemen, whether they'd been overseas only a couple years or for the entire four-year duration, had become accustomed to the semi-automatic weapons. The standard U.S. infantry rifle was the semi-automatic M1 Garand, as was the M1 Carbine. So, it is a small wonder that the returning servicemen preferred repeating shotguns over double guns and, thus, the popularity of repeating shotguns, a trend that had already begun before the war, simply continued.

Although many may have preferred the auto-loading shotgun, the selection for these was very limited at that time, in fact, just a few models, including the Belgian-made Browning Automatic (the A-5), the Remington Model 11, or Savage Model 720. All three guns, although cheaper than a quality double, still cost more than a well-made pump gun. Add to that the fact that prices for shotguns in general had risen sharply since the end of the war. Prior to the outbreak of World War II, the Browning A-5 autoloader cost around $60 with a plain barrel, and Remington's Model 11 cost about the same. The Winchester Model 12 was about $50 in its standard grade, with the Remington Model 31 was priced almost the same. After the war, though, these prices increased dramatically, so much so that, in some cases, they had doubled in less than a decade. By 1950, five years after the end of the war, the standard model Browning autoloader with a plain barrel cost $109, and the standard grade, plain barrel Winchester Model 12 pump gun cost $84.95, cheaper than the Browning autoloader, but not by too much. Still, being cheaper it was the pump gun that was the biggest seller, and that made that action design the one most chose for their shotgunning.

Consumers kept pace. There was new prosperity after the war, and an increased number of hunters afield coincided with this. More cars were being made, and more Americans were buying them. As a result, hunters became much more mobile and were able to go to places they hadn't been able to before. In the old days, going long distances for hunting usually required railway travel. After the war, it was travel by car. And naturally, the increase in interest in hunting brought about an increase in demand for sporting arms.

After the war demand, for repeating shotguns was so great that Browning could not keep up with the production of its Belgian-made guns, so it contracted Remington to make the autoloader for them for a period of four years, from 1947 until 1951. Remington's own Model 11 sold as fast as they could leave the assembly line. But, Remington knew that it could not sit back on its laurels and continue indefinitely with its Model 11. The Model 31 pump sold well enough, but it was still no competition for the Winchester Model 12, which had really captured the American shooters' fancy as the "perfect repeater," a great job by Madison Avenue! Remington had to come up with something new, something that was not only less expensive to manufacture than the Model 11 and Model 31, but something that was better and more modern.

The Model 31, like its competitor Winchester Model 12, was expensive to make, although it was less expensive than making a double gun. Additionally, the Model 31 was made in three different series. The first series were made from 1931 to 1936. The second series were produced from 1936 to 1940 and were different in that they lacked the barrel collar of the first series guns. The third series was built from 1941 until 1949, when the model was discontinued altogether. The third series guns were different from the first two in many ways. The barrel lock mechanism was smaller and the guns had a much larger safety button. Additionally, there were internal differences like the hammer, extractor, action bar lock, and several other parts, including the trigger housing. This difference in the series didn't help matters, since the parts were not interchangeable and there were essentially three different versions, not counting the alloy framed model, in the span of 18 years. On top of that, the Model 31 required extensive milling operations, since all parts were machined, with no stamped or cast components. Like the Winchester Model 12, it was a beautifully made pump gun, but not an economically feasible product.

Remington realized that something had to be done. The company's internal memos from the era clearly show that it was concerned with the fact that it was not very competitive in the pump gun market. So, in January 1947, Remington authorized the amount of $2,000 for use by the Machine Development Section to initiate a preliminary study, a feasibility study, in fact, for development of a new pump-action gun. Apparently the study showed that the development of a new pump gun was something that would market well to the American public and, so, in February of 1948, an additional $20,000 was authorized to develop a basic new design that would fit into a "family of guns" that had a relationship with the Model 11-48 autoloader. Ultimately, the much larger amount of $790,000 was authorized for the development of tooling for the new pump-action gun.

Remington focused on making a new gun, a design that was cheaper and easier to make than the pumps that had come before it, yet one that was better and also more modern. The engineers and designers went to work, and what they came up with was a shotgun that was modern, strong, and reliable, yet inexpensive enough that it could be purchased by just about everyone. In other words, a Model T version of a shotgun—everybody's shotgun! This, many believe, Remington accomplished with the introduction of the Model 870.

the NEW SHOTGUNS

THE MODEL 870 —
THE FIRST 30 YEARS

EVEN BEFORE WORLD WAR II, there were plans in place to make different, more modern autoloader and pump guns. But the exigencies of war, including Remington's involvement with producing rifles and ammunition for the U.S. Government, precluded any chance for the company to develop new designs for sporting shotguns. Of course, Remington wasn't alone in this situation. Other American gun manufacturers were also involved in produc-

ing war materials, everything from rifles, pistols, machine guns, and ammunition to components for other weapons systems.

When the war ended, Remington almost immediately launched into producing a newly designed, "modern" autoloader. Work on the new design began in 1946, the year after the war ended. In 1948, only three years after the end of the second war to end all wars, Remington announced the introduction of a

THE NEW REMINGTON "Wingmaster" MODEL 870   CUSTOM BUILT WITH GOLD INLAY

The 1970s were a boon for the Model 870, with the introduction of truly scaled-down 28-gauge and .410-bore models, something no other pump-gun maker had done. Remington also debuted a 20-gauge lightweight that was available with a 3-inch chamber, a combination gun scribes of the era swooned over.

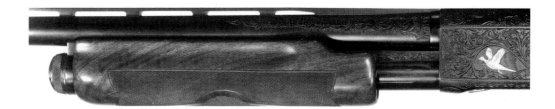

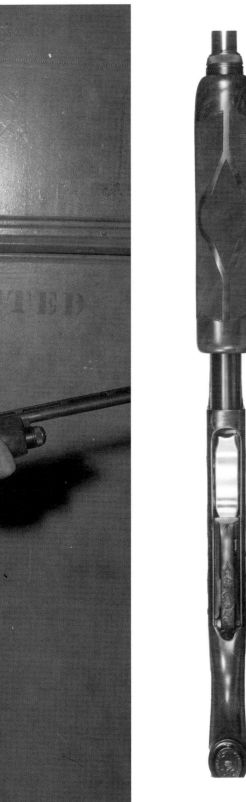

new, streamlined autoloader, the Model 11-48. As the first two numbers indicate, it was mechanically based (although modified) on the old Model 11 and utilized the Browning long recoil system. The second set of numbers indicated the year the gun's design was completed. In 1949, Remington dropped both the Model 11 and the Model 31 from its production lines, and the new autoloader Model 11-48 began to appear on dealers' racks. It was an immediate success, and Remington quickly followed up, in 1950, with the release of a new pump gun that was, for all intents and purposes, a by-product of the 11-48.

WITH THE WAR OVER ...

Work on the new pump shotgun had begun three years earlier, in 1947, as the design for the 11-48 had actually already been completed (and even though 1948 was designated as the year of design completion and the year that firearm was introduced to the public). The Remington designers and engineers who were involved in the creation of the 11-48, L. Ray Crittendon, Phillip Haskell, Ellis Hailston, and G. E. Pinckney, developed the new pump gun design by using the receiver, the trigger housing group, and other common parts from the 11-48. With the design completed, in January of 1950, Remington announced the launch of its new pump-action shotgun, the Remington Model 870 "Wingmaster."

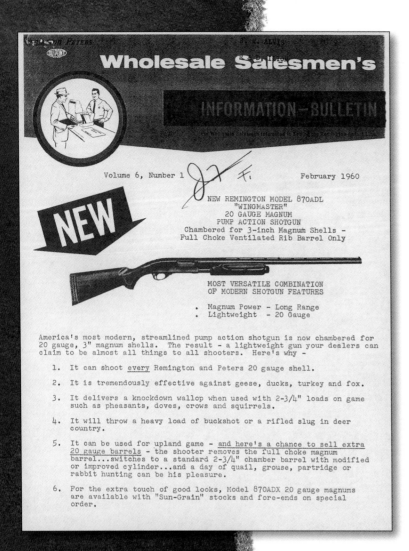

Wholesale Salesmen's
INFORMATION—BULLETIN

Volume 6, Number 1   February 1960

NEW

NEW REMINGTON MODEL 870ADL
"WINGMASTER"
20 GAUGE MAGNUM
PUMP ACTION SHOTGUN
Chambered for 3-inch Magnum Shells -
Full Choke Ventilated Rib Barrel Only

MOST VERSATILE COMBINATION
OF MODERN SHOTGUN FEATURES

· Magnum Power - Long Range
· Lightweight - 20 Gauge

America's most modern, streamlined pump action shotgun is now chambered for 20 gauge, 3" magnum shells. The result - a lightweight gun your dealers can claim to be almost all things to all shooters. Here's why -

1. It can shoot <u>every</u> Remington and Peters 20 gauge shell.

2. It is tremendously effective against geese, ducks, turkey and fox.

3. It delivers a knockdown wallop when used with 2-3/4" loads on game such as pheasants, doves, crows and squirrels.

4. It will throw a heavy load of buckshot or a rifled slug in deer country.

5. It can be used for upland game - <u>and here's a chance to sell extra 20 gauge barrels</u> - the shooter removes the full choke magnum barrel...switches to a standard 2-3/4" chamber barrel with modified or improved cylinder...and a day of quail, grouse, partridge or rabbit hunting can be his pleasure.

6. For the extra touch of good looks, Model 870ADX 20 gauge magnums are available with "Sun-Grain" stocks and fore-ends on special order.

THE 20-GAUGE LW MAGNUM

This internal memo addressed to Remington's wholesale sales force announced the debut of the Model 870 20-gauge in a lightweight version with a 3-inch Magnum chamber. The fine print urges the salesmen to tout this version as a gun that can be "almost all things to all shooters."

Interestingly, according to Remington's own internal memos, the Remington designers chose the 16-gauge receiver of the 11-48 to use as the receiver for the Model 870 12-gauge. The designers had wanted to make the new pump gun as light and as slender as possible. Since the Model 11-48 autoloader was basically made in three sizes—the 12-gauge receiver, the 16-/20-gauge receiver, and the later, smaller, 28-gauge/.410-bore receiver—the new Model 870 12-gauge was, therefore, a bit slimmer than the 11-48 in 12-gauge. It was also considerably lighter than most of the competition from other manufacturers.

This new Model 870 12-gauge used a standard 16-gauge 11-48 receiver for both the 12-gauge and 16-gauge models and, like the 11-48, a bit smaller, "shaved" 16-gauge receiver for the 20-gauge offering. In reality, for all practical purposes, it was really just one receiver size that was used for all three gauges, albeit, shaved a bit for the slightly smaller 20-gauge.

The new pump gun was very different from existing designs. It utilized components that were easy to make, as many parts were stamped and cast. Yet these same parts were made strong and durable, so that they wouldn't break down easily and also so they could be shared with the Model 11-48 autoloader. It was obvious that Remington had learned well from its war-time experiences in making weaponry; it had learned how to make parts inexpensively, yet parts that were strong and durable.

With this mention of inexpensive parts, stamped and cast parts, etc., one might think that, perhaps, Remington cut corners and used cheap material to put together this new pump gun. That was not the case at all. For all critical components, only the best material was used. The receiver was machined from a solid chunk of high-grade carbon steel, and the barrels were made of the best steel Remington could find. All other critical components, such as the breech block, were made of the best, highest grade carbon steel. Only the non-critical components were made of stamped metal,

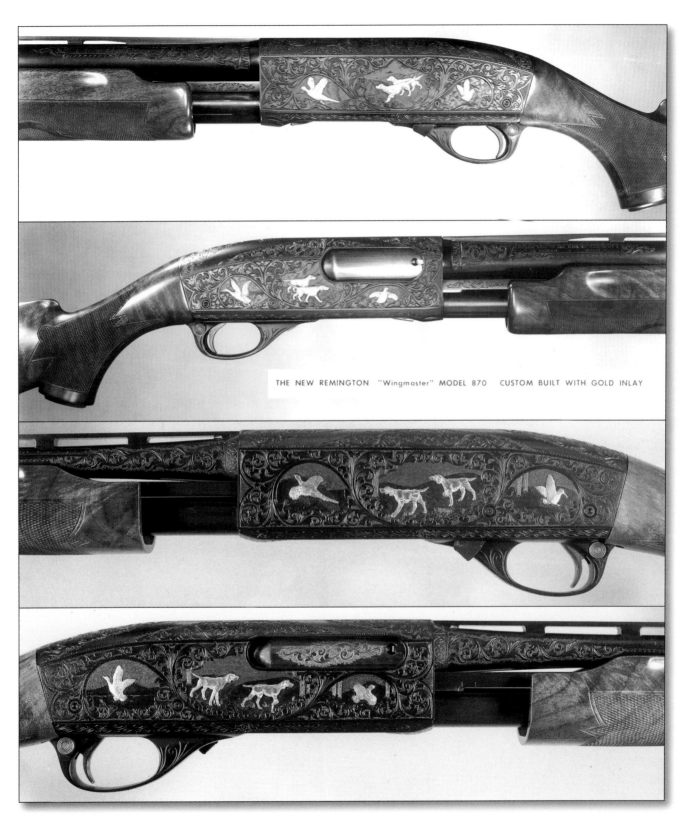

The New Remington "Wingmaster" Model 870 Custom Built with Gold Inlay

LIMITED BY IMAGINATION ONLY
The stunning engraving and inlay work on these Remington custom shop Model 870s clearly demonstrates that what a customer orders is limited only by their imagination.

Remington
DUPONT

PUMP ACTION SHOTGUN
Wingmaster ®

5 - SHOT • 12 - 16 - 20 Gauge
4 - 5 SHOT • 28 - 410 Gauge

MODEL 870

INCLUDING 3 INCH MAGNUM MODEL • 12 - 20 GAUGE

INSTRUCTION FOLDER and PARTS PRICE LIST

(Vent Rib Shown)

HOW TO PUT GUN TOGETHER — Your gun comes to you taken down. To put together is a simple operation. Here is all you need to do:

Important: Do not pump action or pull trigger with barrel removed.
Remove rust preventive coating from all metal parts, including bore of barrel, with a soft cloth. Unscrew magazine cap, remove cardboard packing ring, press action bar lock (if gun is cocked), move fore-end half way back. Put barrel extension into front end of receiver, magazine ring guide over magazine tube; slide barrel rearward. Screw on magazine cap. Make sure magazine cap is tight. Do not jam barrel against ejector when assembling barrel to receiver.

Caution: Before firing make sure barrel bore is clean and free of any grease, heavy oil or obstruction.

SAFETY (Fig. 1) — Before loading or unloading your gun, push safety across rear of trigger to ON SAFE position. Red band on safety **will not show.**

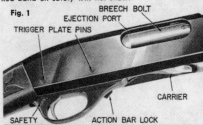

Fig. 1
BREECH BOLT
EJECTION PORT
TRIGGER PLATE PINS
CARRIER
SAFETY
ACTION BAR LOCK

FIRE POSITION — Push safety across to FIRE position. Red band marking **will show.** Trigger can then be pulled to fire gun.

TO SINGLE LOAD— Push safety ON SAFE. Pull fore-end fully to rear. If gun is cocked and action locked closed, press in action bar lock (Fig. 1). Place shell into open ejection port upon downthrust carrier. Then slide fore-end towards muzzle to load shell into barrel and lock action closed.

TO MAGAZINE LOAD — Push safety ON SAFE. Slide fore-end completely forward to close action. Turn gun bottom upward and press shell against carrier then forward FULLY into magazine. Make sure that rim of shell snaps past shell latch to avoid shell sliding back over carrier. Should this occur, forcefully open action or, if necessary, remove trigger plate assembly to remove shell.

TO LOAD BARREL from MAGAZINE — Shells can be fed from loaded magazine by simply pumping fore-end. Press in action bar lock (Fig. 1) if gun is cocked. Then pump fore-end back and forth to open and close action.

TO UNLOAD GUN — Push safety ON SAFE. Press in action bar lock; pull fore-end slowly rearward until front end of shell from barrel is even with ejection port in receiver. Then lift front of shell outward and remove from ejection port. Continue pulling fore-end back fully until next shell releases from magazine. Roll gun sideways to allow released shell to drop from ejection port. Then close action by pushing forward on fore-end. Continue this same method until magazine and gun are empty.

TO UNLOAD BARREL only — Push safety ON SAFE. Press in action bar lock; pull fore-end rearward until front end of shell from barrel is even with front end of ejection port. Then lift front end of shell from receiver as described above.

CAUTION: Open action and check shell chamber in **breech of barrel** and **magazine** to make sure no rounds remain in gun.

STANDARD MODEL (12-16-20 GA.) — Barrel is chambered for 2-¾ inch shells in light or heavy modern factory load or 2-¾ inch magnum. Gun capacity of five shells includes 4 in 2-¾ inch magazine. Each gun is equipped with wood magazine plug for reducing magazine capacity to 2 shells. To increase gun capacity to 5 shells, remove plug as follows: Unscrew magazine cap. Remove magazine spring retainer from front of magazine tube by placing screw driver under inside rim of retainer and prying free. Remove carefully. Retainer is under compression of spring. Remove wood plug. Reassemble spring and retainer into tube. **IMPORTANT — Place retainer into magazine tube, cup inward, and tap firmly until flat on end of tube.**

3 INCH MAGNUM MODEL — Barrel is chambered for 3 inch [...] Magnum model will also shoot standard length 2-¾ inch shell.

"VARI-WEIGHT" [...] or 12 Gauge Standard model. "Va[...] gun weight. This steel magazine plug [...] fore assembling steel plug into front [...]. Remove magazine spring retainer [...] above). Open action. Compress magaz[...] hole in magazine tube (at front) with [...]

NOTE: [...] ce barrel and magazine cap.

HAND [...] visible "spots" of moisture can cause [...] m of each metal part. additional [...]

BELOW [...]ove lubrica[...]car[...] from co[...]barrel [...] MAINTE[...] any ne[...]

REMING[...]

30

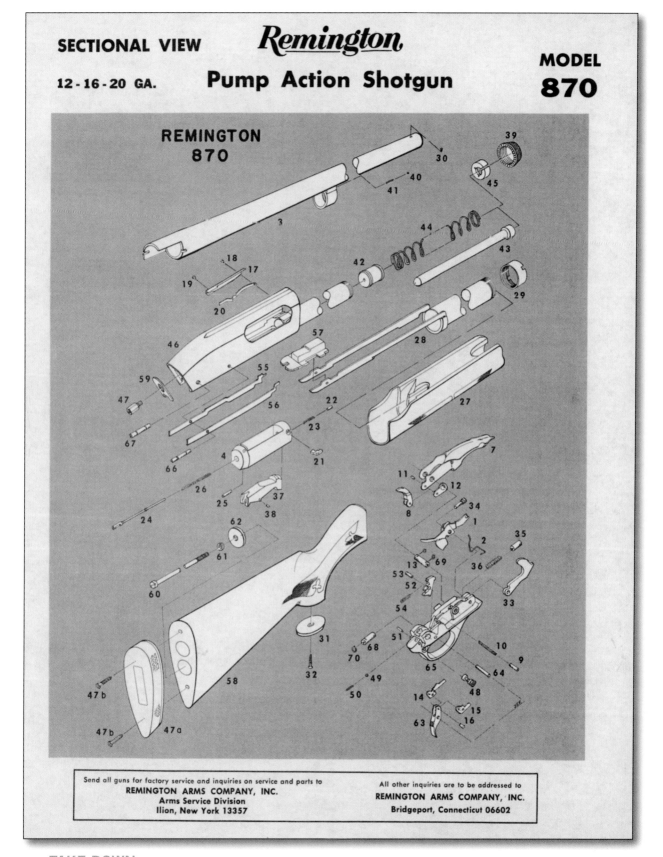

Remington

Pump Action Shotgun

REMINGTON
870

Send all guns for factory service and inquiries on service and parts to
REMINGTON ARMS COMPANY, INC.
Arms Service Division
Ilion, New York 13357

All other inquiries are to be addressed to
REMINGTON ARMS COMPANY, INC.
Bridgeport, Connecticut 06602

TAKE-DOWN

An instruction manual, parts and price list, and take-down schematic for the Model 870 from yesteryear. Note that these documents support all the gauges and chambers, a sure telling of simplicity that is the hallmark of this gun.

_MINGTON ARMS COMPANY, INC.
INTER-DEPARTMENTAL CORRESPONDENCE

Remington   _PETERS_

"CONFINE YOUR LETTER TO ONE SUBJECT ONLY"_____

April 4, 1978

TO: H. ALBAUGH

FROM: L.K. GOODSTAL

3 MILLIONTH M/870 SHOTGUN

The 3 millionth M/870 shotgun is forecasted to be shipped sometime during the first week of May, 1978.

It is suggested that we manufacture a special 3 millionth M/870
to symbolize this historic manufacturing feat; this gun should
be maintained by the Company, the same as our 2 millionth M/870,
as a museum item.

Larry Goodstal

LKG:tpp

2,000,000th MODEL 870

REMINGTON SHOTGUN

Bob Hall (right) Remington Arms Co. - Ilion, Plant Manager and
Larry Goodstal - Museum Curator are placing the 2,000,000th
Remington Model 870 shotgun on display. This special Model 870
is highly engraved and inlayed with gold. It has a selected high
grade American Walnut Stock and is stamped with serial number
2,000,000. It's purpose is to commemorate Remington's completion
of 2,000,000 Model 870 shotguns. - October 1973

Remington, America's Oldest Gun Makers, was founded in 1816 when
Eliphalet Remington II, built his first rifle. Business expanded and
by 1826 the Remingtons moved to their present location, Ilion, N.Y..
They had access to the Erie Canal and soon became leading American
firearm and barrel makers.

The Remington shotgun business dates before our Civil War. These
pioneer Remington shotguns were muzzle loading percussion lock type.
Remington first offered a breech loading (cartridge) shotgun during the
advent of the famous Remington - Rider Rolling Block Action. This first
breech loading (cartridge) shotgun was called Remington - Rider No.1
and was introduced in 1867. The Rider No.1 paved the way for nearly
two dozen more Remington shotgun models.

The famous model 870 (as pictured) was introduced in 1950 and soon
became one of the most popular repeating shotguns in the world. It is
currently being offered in the following types: "Wingmaster" field gun
(Right and Left Hand) 12 and 20 gauge. Standard Field 12, 16 and 20
gauge. 3" Magnum - Duck Gun. "Brushmaster" Deer Gun. Special
"Lightweight" offered in 20, 28 and 410 Ga., 3" 20 Gauge Magnum.
High grade "All American" Trap - "TB" Trap (Right and Left Hand).
"TC" Trap and "SA" Skeet.

LKG:b
5/6/74

Remington Arms Company, Inc.

BIG NUMBERS
Above are Remington press releases announcing the second and third million 870s produced.

and the trigger housing was cast from alloy. In short, all the major components were made from top-grade materials. There were no sacrifices made, when it came to components that would affect the reliability and durability of function. Yet, because Remington used more modern and efficient manufacturing methods, combined with less expensive parts for the none-critical areas, the new guns, the Model 11-48 autoloader and its sister Model 870 pump gun could be produced at a considerably lower cost than experienced with its previous guns, such as the Model 11 autoloader and the Model 31 pump gun.

The Model 870 pump gun was a part of what Remington called its "family of guns," sharing an impressive 60 parts with the Model 11-48 autoloader! There were, additionally, numerous parts that, although not identical, could be made to work for one model or the other with slight modification. Remington later expanded on this "family of guns" concept, introducing the Model 760 pump-action rifle (1952) and Model 740 auto-loading rifle (1955), which likewise shared parts with the 870 and the 11-48, making its firearms truly a "family." Obviously, the use of common parts reduced the cost factor considerably, and the number of different parts declined from a total of 93 for the Model 31 to 20 fewer, just 73, for the new Model 870. But the greatest cost savings were to be found in the machining operation. The old Model 31 required 586 separate machining operations to be performed, while the Mode 870 required approximately 150. It was quite a reduction in time and, therefore, significant cost savings, when you consider that the machining time is one of the most, if not _the_ most, expensive operations in gunmaking.

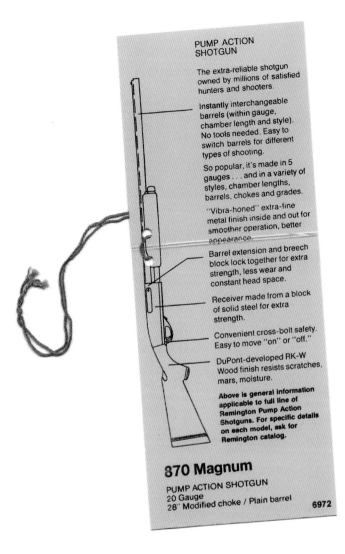

PUMP ACTION SHOTGUN

The extra-reliable shotgun owned by millions of satisfied hunters and shooters.

Instantly interchangeable barrels (within gauge, chamber length and style). No tools needed. Easy to switch barrels for different types of shooting.

So popular, it's made in 5 gauges . . . and in a variety of styles, chamber lengths, barrels, chokes and grades.

"Vibra-honed" extra-fine metal finish inside and out for smoother operation, better appearance.

Barrel extension and breech block lock together for extra strength, less wear and constant head space.

Receiver made from a block of solid steel for extra strength.

Convenient cross-bolt safety. Easy to move "on" or "off."

DuPont-developed RK-W Wood finish resists scratches, mars, moisture.

Above is general information applicable to full line of Remington Pump Action Shotguns. For specific details on each model, ask for Remington catalog.

870 Magnum
PUMP ACTION SHOTGUN
20 Gauge
28" Modified choke / Plain barrel
6972

Remington
PUMP ACTION SHOTGUN
MODEL 870
Wingmaster

THE ONE GUN FOR ALL TYPES OF SHOTGUN SHOOTING

Extra barrels of different chokes and lengths instantly interchangeable.

Double action bars.

Breech block lock, for longer life and more constant head space.

5-shot, chambered for 2¾" shells.

also: Model 870 Magnum —chambered for 3" shells

RETAIL
A small sampling of Remington "Wingmaster" 870 retail hang tags from over the years. Everything's collectible!

Model_____
Grade_____
Gauge_____
Barrel Lgth._____
Choke_____
Price_____

Barrel manufacture was also simplified. The barrels were made to be completely interchangeable within each gauge, without any fitting necessary, and all could be removed by simply unscrewing the magazine cap. The barrels also had a long extension into which the bolt locked in. The fire-control mechanism was fitted into the trigger housing which, as already mentioned, was cast alloy. It could be easily removed by knocking out two pins from the side of the receiver. This made cleaning a snap, something that was not quite so easily done with other pump guns of the era. In fact, it was the only pump gun with such a simple trigger housing removal system for a long time before other makers started to do the same.

The new pump gun had double, or twin, action bars, something that hadn't previously existed in a pump gun design. The two bars prevented any possible binding of the action, something that could happen with a single bar, if there was any twisting of the fore-end or other issues. All these features were firsts in a pump gun. Remington made sure that the prospective customers

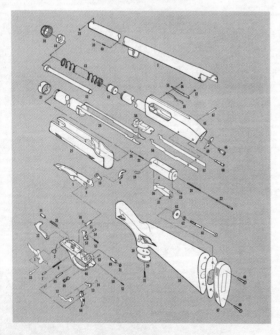

SOUTHPAWS

Instruction manual and parts list for the Model 870 in its left-hand version. Remington was the first to produce a true and dedicated pump-action for Southpaws.

were made aware of this, with advertising that continually pointed out these features.

Aside from the mechanical innovations, the new Remington pump gun just *looked* more modern than its competition. It was streamlined and smooth in appearance and bore none of the hangovers from the early twentieth-century styling that the pump guns from other manufacturers seemed to possess. For one, the new Remington pump gun had a very successful stock design. It seemed to fit everyone who shouldered it. At the same time, the gun was exceptionally well balanced. Too, there was no unnecessary sculpting of curves or dips, just a completely smooth receiver with no protrusions or any other bump or hitch to disrupt the smooth lines. Best of all, the smooth lines of the receiver were much easier to machine than those that had angles and curves, therefore making the gun even cheaper to make! This was one of the many areas where cost reduction took place. All the gun writers of the era marveled at the simplicity of 870's design and the smooth, clean appearance of the gun.

It is interesting to note that the internal memos of the period stressed the fact that the new pump gun was going to be the platform for a new gas-operated autoloader. What's interesting about that? One would think that a new autoloader would be derived from the autoloading Model 11-48. But no! It was this new pump gun, which was slightly smaller and lighter, that would be the foundation! Small wonder then that, when Remington did come out with its legendary Model 1100 gas-operated autoloader, it, too, had a stock that seemed to fit everyone and a slim, streamlined receiver.

The Model 870 was a bit more nose-heavy than the Winchester Model 12, but the weight-forward balance made it an immediate hit with the clay target shooting crowd. Its overall weight was less than that of just about all of its competition; with the exception of the Ithaca Model 37, which weighed around 6½ pounds in the 12-gauge field grade, there were no other pump guns that were as light or lighter than the new Remington Model 870. The light weight also made it popular with field shooters, especially pheasant hunters. (To this day, the Model 870 is probably the most popular pheasant gun in North America, although today's 870s are heavier than the original, owing to the thicker barrel walls employed to accommodate the use of Rem Chokes, and thicker fore-arm wood. Also, today everyone seems to prefer guns with ventilated ribs, which add anywhere from a quarter- to a half-pound of weight to the gun, depending on barrel length. Coupled with a thick, one-inch recoil pad weighing at least another ¼-pound, standard on all 870s today, these additions have caused the gun to gain about a pound over the original plain Jane Model 870 AP.)

Right from the start, the new pump gun was offered in 12-, 16-, and 20-gauge in the standard Model 870AP, as well as in the deluxe Model 870 ADL. It was also offered in skeet models in 12-, 16-, and 20-gauge, and in trap versions in standard and TC grades. There was also the Model 870 R, an AP model with a 20-inch barrel and marketed as a "riot" gun meant for the police market. All standard AP guns were stocked in good, straight-grained American walnut. The ADL guns and trap and skeet grades, which came as ADL configurations, had a better grade of wood, which Remington described as "select" grade.

All 12-gauge guns came with what Remington called its "Vari-Weight," a steel plug that weighed ¾-pound and could be put into the magazine tube to increase weight. A standard AP model with a plain barrel and that weighed 6¾ pounds could increase its weight to 7½ pounds with this plug. The 12-gauge trap or skeet gun with a ventilated rib was advertised at 7½ pounds, and the Vari-Weight would increase that to 8¼ pounds. Many owners of the new Remington Model 870 liked the Vari-Weight plug concept and would switch it around, adding and subtracting weight from their guns. Others felt it was just a gimmick and used their guns without the Vari-Weight plug—very successfully, I might add.

From its initial appearance, in 1950, the Model 870 was available, basically, in two grades, the standard AP and the deluxe ADL with its trap and skeet grades. In 1955, a 12-gauge 3-inch Magnum version appeared and, in 1959, a 12-gauge

barrel with rifle sights was introduced. Of course, there were always the custom shop high grades like the Peerless, F Grade, and so on, but these basic initial offerings remained unchanged for years.

Then, in 1962, a Model 870 "Brushmaster" deer gun wearing a 20-inch barrel with rifle sights and a recoil pad made its first appearance. Also, a 20-gauge Magnum Model 870 was introduced. In 1963, the standard AP model was dropped, and all Model 870s became available in the deluxe ADL version only. This move wasn't really surprising. Internal memos from the time indicated that the Remington front office was concerned with the "good looks" feature of the gun. Many felt that the plain-Jane AP model was unappealing and, perhaps, was losing sales for Remington. It had to go. The AP was to be no more.

For the next six years, there were no major changes or developments in the 870 line. In fact, through the first 20 years of its existence, the Model 870 didn't see too many changes at all. It sold very well and, by the early 1960s, had become the best-selling pump-action shotgun in America. Remington was in an enviable position. The 1960s saw the company more involved with the development of another great Remington shotgun, an autoloader that became known as the legendary Model 1100. However, as popular as the Model 1100 was and still is, it never caught up to the Model 870.

The Model 870 stayed the same for the two decades, from its birth in 1950 until 1969. There were no changes in design or models. After all, why should Remington change anything, when the Model 870 sold so well and had no other pump guns for competition?

Although the Winchester Model 12, the Model 870s biggest competitor, was still a better seller in the early 1950s, it began to lose ground to the Remington Model 870 in the mid-1950s. There were two reasons for this. One was the lower price of the Remington, and the other was the lighter weight of the Model 870AP compared to the Winchester

Model 12. The 870AP tipped the scales around 6¾ pounds, while the Model 12 averaged a solid 7½ pounds, for a difference of ¾-pound. Winchester tried to solve that problem by introducing a lightened version of the Model 12 in 1960. The new Winchester Model 12 Featherweight, as it was called, was advertised at 6½ pounds for a 12-gauge, although it actually weighed closer to 6¾ pounds, just like the Remington Model 870. But the Winchester Model 12 Featherweight was made only in 12-gauge and it was discontinued after just three years, a year before the entire Model 12 line was discontinued. Even with reduced weight, the Model 12 just couldn't compete with the Remington Model 870. It was obvious that, by the 1960s, the Remington Model 870 was firmly established as the No. 1 pump shotgun in America!

In addition to the looks and feel of the gun that made the 870 so appealing, price was a crucial factor in its popularity. Initially, in the 1950s, when Winchester Model 12 was able to provide very stiff competition to the Remington Model 870, the price difference hadn't appeared to be that great. But, as time went on, the finely machined Winchester couldn't really keep up with the Remington in price. In 1950, when the Model 870 first hit the market, it was priced at $69.95 for the plain, standard AP model. The Winchester Model 12 in its comparable version sold for $84.95, a difference of $15. That may not seem like much today, but, in 1950, it was a considerable amount. When Winchester introduced its "Featherweight" version of the Model 12, it was priced at $94.95, but the Remington Model 870 cost $89.45, still less than the Winchester! By 1963, a year before Winchester discontinued its Model 12, the 870 had gone up in price to $89.95 while the Model 12 had risen to $104.95, breaking that magical hundred mark, something that most gun makers in America desperately tried to avoid in pricing their basic models in that era. The difference between the two was still only $15.00, but, even in 1963, that was a significant amount. Indeed, in 1963, there were several single-shot .22 rifles that

were priced around $15! The cheaper .22s, like the J.C. Higgins sold by Sears, and other economy models sold by Montgomery Wards, cost under $15.00! Considering the price difference, it is easy to see how the Remington Model 870 was able to catch up, and pass the Winchester Model 12 in popularity. After all, why pay over a hundred dollars for a Winchester Model 12 when you could get a "modern" Remington Model 870 for less and get a single-shot .22 for your kid to boot!

Winchester made a big mistake when it dropped the Model 12 and replaced it with the cheaply made Model 1200. Unfortunately, for Winchester, it was something it had to do, since it just cost too much to make the Model 12, as, unlike the Remington Model 870, it didn't utilize any stamped or cast parts. Everything on the Model 12 was machined, and it cost money to do all that machining. Still, despite the fact that the Model 12 had lost its No. 1 standing as the best seller, it was still considered a top choice of many. So, when Winchester dropped the Model 12 altogether, the company completely lost its standing in the pump-gun arena.

Desperate to regain ground, Winchester slated its new Model 1200 as the answer to its absence from the pump-gun scene—or, at least that's what the bean counters in Winchester management thought. The Model 1200 had an alloy receiver and cheaply made stamped parts—and it was a *disaster*, one that simply increased the popularity of the Remington Model 870 even more. In fact, the poor quality of the Model 1200 made everyone aware of just how much better the Model 870 was made. Those wishing to purchase a new pump gun flocked to the Remington, unless they absolutely had to save money—or simply didn't know much about guns.

Before the outbreak of World War II, Remington had been playing catch up with Winchester, trying to come up with a pump gun that could compete with the Model 12. Remington had finally been able to compete, at least to some extent, when it came out with the finely made Model 31, 19 years after the appearance of the Model 12. But now, in the mid-1960s, the

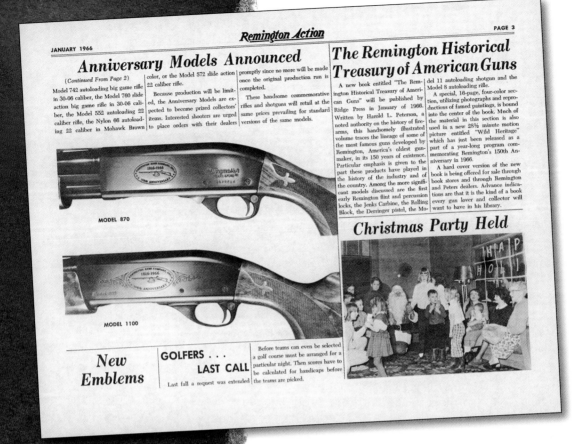

JANUARY 1966

Anniversary Models Announced

(Continued From Page 2)

Model 742 autoloading big game rifle in 30-06 caliber, the Model 760 slide action big game rifle in 30-06 caliber, the Model 552 autoloading 22 caliber rifle, the Nylon 66 autoloading 22 caliber in Mohawk Brown

color, or the Model 572 slide action 22 caliber rifle.

Because production will be limited, the Anniversary Models are expected to become prized collectors' items. Interested shooters are urged to place orders with their dealers

promptly since no more will be made once the original production run is completed.

These handsome commemorative rifles and shotguns will retail at the same prices prevailing for standard versions of the same models.

MODEL 870

MODEL 1100

The Remington Historical Treasury of American Guns

A new book entitled "The Remington Historical Treasury of American Guns" will be published by Ridge Press in January of 1966. Written by Harold L. Peterson, a noted authority on the history of firearms, this handsomely illustrated volume traces the lineage of some of the most famous guns developed by Remington, America's oldest gunmaker, in its 150 years of existence. Particular emphasis is given to the part these products have played in the history of the industry and of the country. Among the more significant models discussed are the first early Remington flint and percussion locks, the Jenks Carbine, the Rolling Block, the Derringer pistol, the Mo-

del 11 autoloading shotgun and the Model 8 autoloading rifle.

A special, 16-page, four-color section, utilizing photographs and reproductions of famed paintings, is bound into the center of the book. Much of the material in this section is also used in a new 28½ minute motion picture entitled "Wild Heritage" which has just been released as a part of a year-long program commemorating Remington's 150th Anniversary in 1966.

A hard cover version of the new book is being offered for sale through book stores and through Remington and Peters dealers. Advance indications are that it is the kind of a book every gun lover and collector will want to have in his library.

Christmas Party Held

New Emblems

GOLFERS . . .
LAST CALL

Last fall a request was extended

Before teams can even be selected a golf course must be arranged for a particular night. Then scores have to be calculated for handicaps before the teams are picked.

A LOOK BACK

A page from a yesteryear Remington employee newsletter. Christmas party fun, an exposé on a Remington Historical Society firearms collection, and oh! Anniversary Model 870s and 1100s. Lots to celebrate!

roles were reversed. Remington had capitalized on interchangeable parts and efficient production methods, while Winchester had been slow to realize that a less expensive method of manufacture was necessary to stay competitive in that new age. Too, the Winchester Model 1200 appeared 15 years after the introduction of the Remington Model 870. So, not only was it was an inferior product, it was also far too late. By 1966, the one-millionth Model 870 had been produced, and that was the year that coincided with Remington's one hundred-fiftieth anniversary. To celebrate, a special 150th Anniversary Edition Shotgun was produced. No other shotgun was able to accomplish what the Model 870 had done—*one million guns in just 16 years*! It wouldn't be a stretch to say that, when it came to pump-action shotguns, the last half of the twentieth century belonged to the Remington Model 870.

It was also during the 1960s that the Remington Model 870 began to make inroads in another area, one outside of the sporting field. Many law enforcement agencies throughout the country had started to look for replacements for their aging Winchester Model 97s and Model 12s, as well as Ithaca Model 37s, Remington Model 31s, and Stevens pump guns,

STYLING

The sketches may have become photographs over the years, but the heart of the Model 870's owner manual has remained virtually unchanged since the gun's inception, because the gun itself is unchanged.

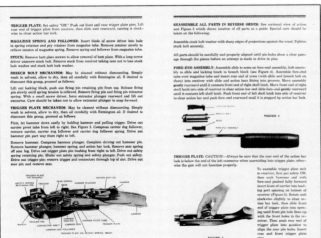

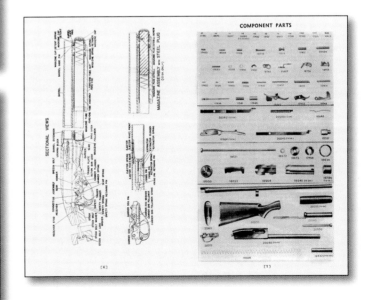

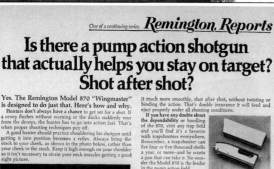

the so-called riot or police shotguns. In the early days, these models were nothing but standard grades with chopped off barrels. There were no rifle sights, no synthetic stocks or any of the other tactical features that you find today.

Winchester and other makers, of course, tried to compete in this market, and though some agencies initially bought other pump guns (mainly because they were cheaper), they soon abandoned them and replaced them with Remington Model 870s. Today, of course, just about all law enforcement agencies use the Remington Model 870, with only a small percentage choosing to use other makes.

WELCOME TO THE '70S!

The decade of the 1970s was an important one in the Model 870's history. In 1969, Remington introduced the scaled-down 28-gauge and .410-bore Model 870s. Prior to the appearance of these, there had been no truly properly scaled-down small-framed pump guns in those gauges and bore sizes, with just a couple exceptions. High Standard's solid-framed (i.e, not a takedown) Flite-King had been introduced, in 1966, as a 28-gauge. (High Standard also had a .410 Flight-King, which had been introduced in 1961, but was dropped four years later, in 1965, due to lack of sales.) Mossberg was the other exception, offering a scaled-down .410-bore, the Model 500E, which came out in the mid-1960s, after the initial appearance of that company's 12-, 16-, and 20-gauge versions of the Model 500. But no one had both a 28-gauge and a .410-bore on a scaled-down frame, only Remington.

The new Remington Model 870 28-gauge and .410-bores were initially offered as a matched pair of skeet guns, adding a little caché to them. To reduce weight, Remington stocked these guns with Honduran mahogany, a wood that has a reddish tint and is said to be lighter than American walnut. Mechanically, these little Model 870s were identical to their bigger brothers. They were just scaled to a smaller sized receiver, making them appear very slender and slick. Remington initially thought that these would be more or less specialized guns, mostly used by skeet shooters as had happened in the past with the scaled-down versions of the autoloader Model 11-48 in 28-gauge and .410-bore. No doubt, Remington was surprised at the reception received by its new guns, which sold far beyond just skeet shooters. As a result, the following year, 1970, Remington started to sell these guns individually, instead of just as matched pairs. At the same time, it started producing field versions. The little pumps in 28-gauge with a plain barrel were listed at 5½ pounds with a ventilated rib model at six. These guns made for delightful upland guns that could be carried all day without much problem.

In 1971, Remington accomplished another "first," with the introduction of true left-handed versions of the Model 870, these available in 12-, 16-, and 20-gauge. A year later, Remington announced the new Model 870 LW 20, a "light-weight" version of the 20-gauge 870 in 2¾-inch, as well as 3-inch Magnum chambers. Before the appearance of the LW 20, all 20-gauge 870s were essentially built on a lightened 12-gauge receiver; some said that they were 16-gauge receivers. Whatever the case may be, the 20-gauge "standard" Model 870 receivers hadn't been all that much smaller than the 12-gauge receiver. The new "lightweight" versions had, just like the 28-gauge and .410, truly scaled-down receivers and, therefore, thinner barrels at the chamber area, which also reduced weight. The new receivers were slightly bigger than the 28-gauge and .410-bore versions, but significantly smaller and lighter than the old "standard" receivers. Needless to say, the new scaled-down guns, also with mahogany wood, were an immediate hit.

The timing had been perfect. The early 1970s saw a tremendous increase in the popularity of the 20-gauge, a growth in favoritism that would eventually eclipse the 16-gauge. Every gun writer of the period lauded the 20-gauge with its 3-inch chambering as the next best thing to sliced bread—a "wonder gauge," declared by all to be the perfect all-around gun. And, so, the small-framed 20-gauge Model 870s became best sellers. Even today, they are still one of the more popular versions of the Model 870. The original plain barrel version was listed at 6 pounds, while

the ventilated rib guns came in at 6¼ pounds. Today, the plain barrel versions are no longer available, and the barrels themselves are thicker and heavier to accommodate the interchangeable Rem Chokes. The current Model 870 20-gauge will weigh around 6½ pounds.

In 1972, Remington brought out a special, limited-production model that was called the Model 870 "All American." It was a fancy grade trap gun, extensively roll engraved and with exhibition quality wood. Not exactly everyone's cup of tea, but it was a special gun that attracted some buyers.

The twenty-third year of the Model 870's production, 1974, was yet another historic year for the gun, for this was the year when the two-millionth Model 870 rolled off the assembly line. No other shotgun of any type or any make had ever reached that number in production in such a short time! Heck, most models didn't even last that long!

For America's Bicentennial Year, 1976, Remington came out with a limited production of the special Model 870 Bicentennial Commemorative models, which were produced in 12-gauge only and in SA skeet and TB trap models. They were lavishly decorated with rolled engraving and fancy wood.

Only four short years after the two-millionth Model 870 came off the assembly line, the three-millionth Model 870 was announced by Remington! It was clear to see by everyone that the Model 870 was a roaring success. No sporting gun had ever reached the three-millionth mark in production in such a short time.

One other change occurred at this time. In 1979, Remington stopped using mahogany wood for the lightweight 20-gauge and the 28-gauge and .410-bore models. All Model 870s hence forth were to be stocked in American walnut.

It should be plain to see that the 1970s were probably the most significant years, in many ways, for the Model 870. Completely new, small-framed models had been introduced, as well as left-handed versions. These left-handed Model 870s were the first true left-handed version production pump guns ever made.

THE MODEL 870 —
THE FIRST 30 YEARS
ADVERTISEMENTS

DOLLARS

There are more than a few who wish the prices today
looked like the hang tags in these long-ago advertisements.
Still, the Model 870, even at today's prices, continues to
be an affordable scattergun for everyone.

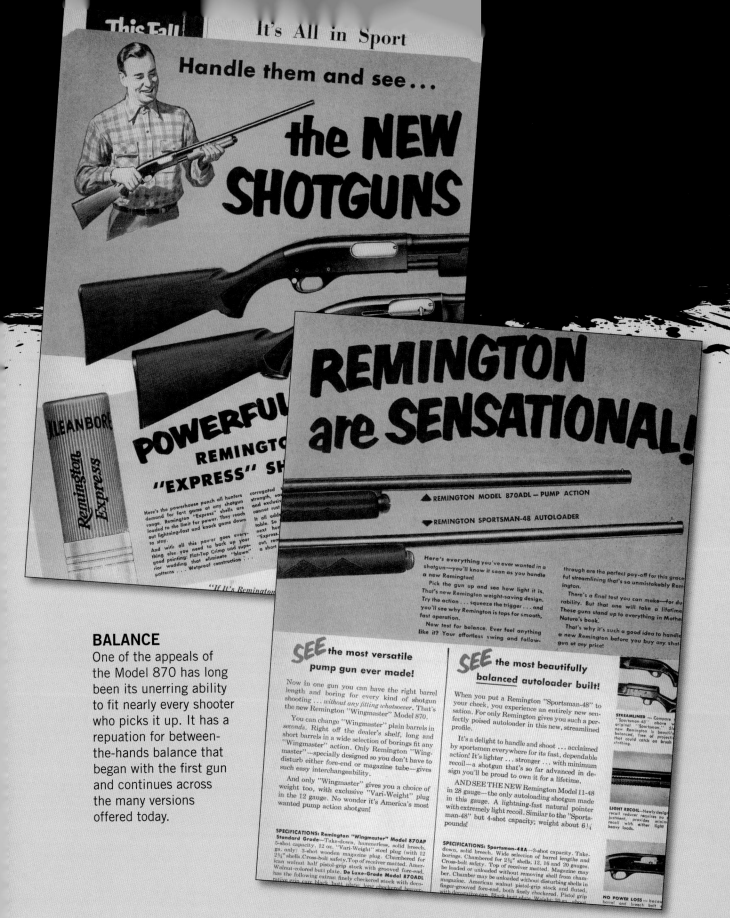

BALANCE

One of the appeals of the Model 870 has long been its unerring ability to fit nearly every shooter who picks it up. It has a reputation for between-the-hands balance that began with the first gun and continues across the many versions offered today.

Your new shotgun was tested at the factory with Remington-Peters shotgun shells.

For best results, we recommend you use these shells in your new Remington shotgun.

Great guns deserve great ammunition.

We Make Both.

Remington.
PETERS
DU PONT

For complete information on all Remington-Peters products, write for your free color catalog:
Remington Arms Company, Inc.
Department GOG
Bridgeport, Conn. 06602

Printed In U.S.A.

Form RD 5648
Rev. 9-71

GUN OWNER'S GUIDE

Remington Model **870**
DU PONT

12, 16, 20, 28
and 410 Gauges

PUMP ACTION SHOTGUN

TO ASSEMBLE GUN — Gun is shipped taken down. Before assembling, clean lubrication from metal parts and bore of barrel. Remove magazine cap and cardboard packing ring. If gun is cocked press action bar lock and slide fore-end half way back.
CAUTION: Do not pump action or pull trigger with barrel removed. Place barrel into receiver with barrel guide ring over magazine tube. Seat barrel firmly into receiver. Do not jam barrel against ejector. Replace and tighten magazine cap.
SAFETY (Fig. 1) — Before loading or unloading gun, push safety to ON SAFE position. Red band on safety will not show.
FIRE POSITION — Push safety to FIRE position. Red band marking will show. Trigger can be pulled to fire gun.
TO SINGLE LOAD — Push safety ON SAFE. Pull fore-end fully to rear. If gun is cocked and action locked closed, press in action bar lock (Fig. 1). Place shell in open ejection port upon carrier. Slide fore-end forward to load shell and lock action.
TO MAGAZINE LOAD — Push safety ON SAFE. Slide fore-end completely forward to close action. Turn gun bottom upward and press shell against carrier then forward FULLY into magazine. Make sure that rim of shell snaps past shell latch to avoid shell sliding back over carrier. Should this occur, forcefully open action or, if necessary, remove trigger plate assembly to remove shell.
TO LOAD CHAMBER from MAGAZINE — Shells can be fed from loaded magazine by pumping fore-end. Press-in action bar lock (Fig. 1) if gun is cocked. Pump fore-end back and forth to open and close action.
CAUTION: Before firing make sure barrel bore is clean and free of any grease, heavy oil or obstruction.
TO UNLOAD GUN — Push safety ON SAFE. Press in action bar lock; pull fore-end slowly rearward until front end of shell from latch is even with ejection port in receiver. Lift front of shell outward and remove from ejection port. Continue pulling fore-end back fully until next shell releases from magazine. Roll gun sideways to allow released shell to drop from ejection port. Close action. Continue until magazine and gun are empty.
STANDARD MODEL (12—16—20 GAUGE) — Barrel is chambered for 2¾" shells in light or heavy modern factory loads or 2¾" MAGNUM.
(28—410 GAUGE) — Barrel is chambered for 2¾" shell in 28 ga. and 3" and 2½" shell in 410 ga.
3 INCH MAGNUM MODEL — Barrel is chambered for 3 inch Magnum shell.
NOTE: 3" MAGNUM shells cannot be fired in standard guns designed for 2¾" shells.
CAPACITY — Gun capacity is five shells — one in chamber and four in magazine. When using 3" shells, capacity of 410 ga. is reduced to 4 shells. Each gun is equipped with wood magazine plug for reducing magazine capacity to 2 shells. To increase gun capacity to 5 shells, remove plug as follows: Unscrew magazine cap. Remove magazine spring retainer from front of magazine tube by placing screw driver under inside rim of retainer and prying free. Remove carefully. Retainer is under compression of spring. Remove wood plug. Reassemble spring and retainer into tube. **IMPORTANT** — Place retainer into magazine tube, cup inward, and tap firmly until flat on retainer is flush with end of tube.

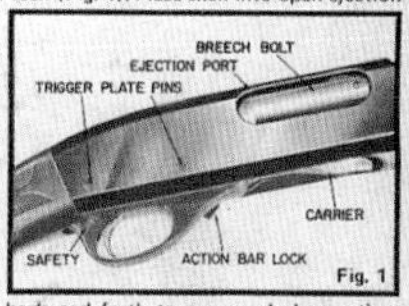

BREECH BOLT
EJECTION PORT
TRIGGER PLATE PINS

CARRIER
SAFETY **ACTION BAR LOCK** **Fig. 1**

REMINGTON ARMS COMPANY, INC.   ILION, NEW YORK, U.S.A.

"VARI-WEIGHT" MAGAZINE PLUG (Steel) — Can be assembled to Magnum model or 12 Gauge Standard model. "Vari-Weight" plug will limit magazine capacity to 2 shells and add ¾ lbs. to gun weight. This steel magazine plug is supplied with small retaining screw at front end. Remove this screw before assembling steel plug into front of magazine tube. When assembling plug, remove magazine cap and barrel. Remove magazine spring retainer from front of open magazine tube. (See wood plug removal instructions above). Open action. Compress magazine spring and push steel plug into front of tube. Align retaining screw hole in magazine tube (at front) with screw hole in assembled steel plug. Insert screw, tighten to steel plug.
NOTE: Magazine spring retainer is not replaced if steel plug is used. Replace barrel and magazine cap.

BARREL CLEANING — Push safety ON SAFE. Open action and make certain no shells remain in chamber or magazine. Unscrew magazine cap and remove barrel. Replace magazine cap to end of magazine tube. Clean barrel with cleaning rod and lightly oiled cloth. If necessary, scrub bore with powder solvent. Wipe clean and re-oil very lightly.

ACTION CLEANING — A petroleum solvent can be used. Take necessary precautions. Action mechanisms remain clean much longer after shooting if lubrication is used sparingly.

DISASSEMBLY of Model 870 for cleaning or service of action parts should be done as follows:

TRIGGER PLATE ASSEMBLY (Fig. 2) — Push safety ON SAFE. Open action and make certain no shells remain in chamber or magazine. Cock action. Tap out front and rear trigger plate pins. Lift rear of trigger plate from receiver, then slide rearward to remove from gun. If necessary to clean, brush with solvent. Clean as a unit. Wipe dry and re-oil very sparingly. To replace trigger plate assembly, close action and carefully insert assembly (carrier first) into receiver. Adjust until trigger plate is aligned in opening. Push downward on rear of trigger plate until assembly enters receiver freely. Adjust to align holes and tap in front and rear trigger plate pins. Open action and push up carrier until action bar lock is visible. Top of action bar lock should ride along and not over-ride bottom edge of action bar.

NOTE: Do not allow hammer to snap forward with trigger plate assembly removed from gun. In reassembling trigger plate mechanism, always be sure that end of action bar lock is below end of connector, left. Otherwise, gun will not function properly (Fig. 2).

FORE—END ASSEMBLY UNIT — Push safety ON SAFE. Open action and make certain no shells remain in chamber or magazine. Close action and remove magazine cap and barrel. Reach into bottom of receiver and press left shell latch inward. Slide fore-end off magazine tube. NOTE: Top right edge of slide may bind on bottom front of ejection port in receiver. To free slide, push front end of bolt downward.

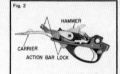

Fig. 2
HAMMER
CARRIER
ACTION BAR LOCK

After fore-end assembly is removed from gun, breech bolt parts and slide may be lifted from ends of action bars. Not necessary to disassemble bolt parts. Brush with solvent to clean.
NOTE: Gun must be cocked when reassembling fore-end parts. During reassembly of fore-end assembly unit, place slide in correct position on ends of double action bar. Place breech bolt assembly (includes attached locking block assembly) over slide on bars. Insert end of action bars into matching receiver grooves. Move fore-end gently rearward into receiver until contact is made with front end of right shell latch (See exploded view). Press front of right shell latch into side of receiver. Move fore-end past right shell latch until contact is made with left shell latch. Press front of left shell latch inward to allow fore-end assembly to pass and reassemble freely into receiver. Reassemble barrel and tighten firmly with magazine cap.

BELOW FREEZING WEATHER — Special attention should be taken that oil is removed from action parts. If a lubricant is desired — use dry graphite or similar non-congealing lubricant. Take care to prevent rusting from condensation and wetness (cold weather to warm room temperature) on action parts and barrel bore, barrel chamber.

HANDLING — Outside of gun should be wiped with oil to prevent rust. Invisible "prints" of moisture can cause rusting unless removed. Exposure to unfavorable weather or moisture from condensation also require additional care.

MAINTENANCE — Gun should be checked periodically by a competent gunsmith to ensure proper inspection and any necessary replacement of worn or damaged parts.

IMPORTANT — Remington firearms are designed, manufactured and proof tested to standards based on factory loaded ammunition. Improperly loaded handloads can be dangerous. Remington Arms Company, Inc., cannot assume responsibility for damages or injury caused by handloads or reloaded ammunition.

STOCK END GRAIN SEALING — To seal open end grain of stocks that have been cut to a shorter length use "Du Pont Penetrating Oil Finish". This product is available in most all Du Pont paint outlets.

MODEL 870
PUMP ACTION SHOTGUN

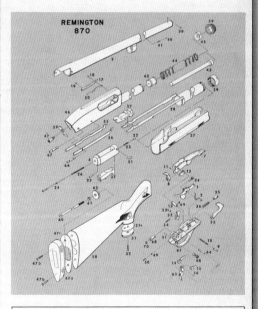

REMINGTON
870

Send all guns for factory service and inquiries on service and parts to
REMINGTON ARMS COMPANY, INC. •
Arms Service Division
Ilion, New York 13357

All other inquiries are to be addressed to
REMINGTON ARMS COMPANY, INC.
Bridgeport, Connecticut 06602

MODEL 870
PUMP ACTION SHOTGUN

PARTS LIST

NOTE: SEE INSTRUCTIONS FOR ORDERING PARTS.

View No.	Part No.	NAME OF PART	List Price
NOTE	18849	Field Grade 12, 16, 20 Gauge listed below. See added page for other grades.	
1	18849	Action Bar Lock	$ 1.75
2	19622	Action Bar Lock Spring	.30
NOTE:		All Barrels (some gauge) interchangeable without adjustment. Prices furnished upon application. Also give choke needed.	
3	20000	Barrel Assembly, 12 Ga. PLAIN, 30" (includes Barrel, Barrel Guide Ring, Barrel Guide Pin, (Steel), Magazine Cap Detent, Front Sight Spring)	
	20003	Barrel Assembly, 12 Ga., PLAIN, 28"	
	20004	Barrel Assembly, 12 Ga., PLAIN, 26"	
	20001	Barrel Assembly, 16 Ga., PLAIN, 28"	
	20005	Barrel Assembly, 16 Ga., PLAIN, 26"	
	20002	Barrel Assembly, 20 Ga., PLAIN, 28"	
	20006	Barrel Assembly, 20 Ga., PLAIN, 26"	
	20740	Barrel Assembly, 12 Ga., VENT RIB, 30" (includes Barrel, Barrel Guide Ring, Barrel Guide Pin, Front Sight (Steel), Front Sight Retaining Pin, Magazine Cap Detent, Magazine Cap Detent Spring)	
	20741	Barrel Assembly, 12 Ga., VENT RIB, 28"	
	20742	Barrel Assembly, 12 Ga., VENT RIB, 26"	
	21250	Barrel Assembly, 16 Ga., VENT RIB, 28"	
	21251	Barrel Assembly, 16 Ga., VENT RIB, 26"	
	21255	Barrel Assembly, 20 Ga., VENT RIB, 28"	
	21256	Barrel Assembly, 20 Ga., VENT RIB, 26"	
4	18545	Breech Bolt, 12 Ga.	5.95
	20015	Breech Bolt, 16 Ga.	5.95
	20016	Breech Bolt, 20 Ga.	5.95
	22860	Breech Bolt Assembly, 12 Ga. (includes Breech Bolt, Extractor, Extractor Plunger, Extractor Spring, Firing Pin, Firing Pin Retractor Spring, Locking Block Assembly)	
	22861	Breech Bolt Assembly, 16 Ga.	10.80
	22862	Breech Bolt Assembly, 20 Ga.	10.80
7	18584	Carrier	10.80
	20060	Carrier Assembly, (includes Carrier, Carrier Dog, Carrier Dog Pin, Carrier Dog Washer)	1.80
8	15480	Carrier Dog	2.55
10	17416	Carrier Dog Follower	1.10
	17415	Carrier Dog Follower Spring	.30
11	18781	Carrier Dog Pin	.30
12	18760	Carrier Dog Washer	.30
13	17417	Carrier Pivot Tube	.30
14	17419	Connector, Left	.45
15	17551	Connector, Right	.45
16	17420	Connector Pin	.30
17	25431	Ejector, 12 Ga.	.30
	24446	Ejector, 16 Ga.	1.10
	24447	Ejector, 20 Ga.	1.10
18	18646	Ejector Rivet, Front	1.10
19	18647	Ejector Rivet, Rear	.30
20	18648	Ejector Spring	.30
21	16176	Extractor	.30
22	17432	Extractor Plunger	.30
23	17433	Extractor Spring	1.80
24	17436	Firing Pin	.30
25	18623	Firing Pin Retaining Pin	1.00
26	17437	Firing Pin Retractor Spring	.30
	20088	Fore-end (Wood only) 12 Ga.	.45
	20089	Fore-end (Wood only) 16 - 20 Ga.	9.00
27	27552	Fore-end Assembly, 12 Ga. (includes Fore-end, Fore-end Tube Assembly, Fore-end Tube Nut)	9.00
	27553	Fore-end Assembly, 16 - 20 Ga.	12.75
	20065	Fore-end Tube Assembly (includes Action Bar, Left, Action Bar, Right, Fore-end Tube)	12.75
28	18634	Fore-end Tube Nut	5.00
29	18673	Front Sight (Plain Barrel)	.85
30	15660	Front Sight (Vent Rib) Steel Bead	.30
	18752	Front Sight Retaining Pin (for use on Vent Rib Steel Sight)	.30

View No.	Part No.	NAME OF PART	List Price
31	18015	Grip Cap	
31a	14943	Grip Cap Spacer	$ .50
32	25380	Grip Cap Screw	.30
33	18749	Hammer	.30
34	16600	Hammer Pin	1.20
	15809	Hammer Pin Washer	.30
35	17465	Hammer Plunger	.30
36	19014	Hammer Spring	.30
37	22325	Locking Block Assembly (includes Locking Block, Locking Block Stud)	.40
	24075	Locking Block Assembly (oversize)	1.20
39	25375	Magazine Cap	3.25
40	17451	Magazine Cap Detent	3.25
41	16791	Magazine Cap Detent Spring	1.20
42	32350	Magazine Follower, 12 - 16 - 20 Ga.	.30
43	18097	Magazine Plug, 3-Shot, Wood	.30
	18690	Magazine Plug Retaining Screw	.85
44	19479	Magazine Spring	.30
45	16949	Magazine Spring Retainer	.30
46	20030	Magazine Tube, 12 Ga. (includes Receiver, Ejector, Ejector Rivet, Front; Ejector Rivet, Rear; Ejector Spring, Magazine Tube, Barrel Support)	.45
	20031	Receiver Assembly, 16 Ga.	25.05
	20032	Receiver Assembly, 20 Ga.	25.05
47	18551	Receiver Stud	25.05
47a	14620	Recoil Pad	.40
	14543	Recoil Pad Screw	3.60
	14944	Recoil Pad Spacer	.30
48	25115	Safety	.30
49	23223	Safety Detent Ball	.45
50	17514	Safety Spring	.30
51	17515	Safety Spring Retaining Pin	.30
52	18750	Sear	.30
53	17463	Sear Pin	.30
54	17518	Sear Spring	.30
55	20040	Shell Latch, Left, 12 Ga.	.30
	20041	Shell Latch, Left, 16 Ga.	1.65
	20045	Shell Latch, Left, 20 Ga.	1.65
56		Shell Latch	1.65
	20046	Shell Latch	
	20047	Shell Latch	
57		Slide Assembly	
58	14577	Stock Assembly	
		Stock Assembly Screw	
59	19993	Stock Bearing Plate	
60	18571	Stock Bolt	
61	18572	Stock Bolt	
62	18573	Stock Bolt	
63	25370	Trigger	
	20610	Trigger Assembly, connector	
64	17533	Trigger Plate	
65	25035	Trigger Plate	
	22985	Trigger Plate	
66	20601	Trigger Plate	
67	17541	Trigger Plate	
68	25410	Trigger Plate	
69	17539	Trigger Plate	
70	17540	Trigger Plate	

DELIVERIES ARE F.O.B. ILION, N.Y.

PRICES AND PA...

MODEL 870
PUMP ACTION SHOTGUN

PARTS LIST

NOTE: SEE INSTRUCTIONS FOR ORDERING PARTS.
See 12, 16, 20 Gauge List For Parts Not Listed Below.

Part No.	NAME OF PART	List Price
18849	Action Bar Lock	$ 1.75
19622	Action Bar Lock Spring, 28 Ga.	.30
14706	Action Bar Lock Spring, 410 Ga.	.30
29805	Barrel Assembly, 28 Ga., 25", Plain	
	Please list choke needed	
30020	Barrel Assembly, 28 Ga., 25", Vent Rib	
30025	Barrel Assembly, 410 Ga., 25", Vent Rib	
14439	Breech Bolt, 28 Ga.	5.95
14440	Breech Bolt, 410 Ga.	5.95
30040	Breech Bolt Assembly, 28 Ga.	10.80
30041	Breech Bolt Assembly, 410 Ga.	10.80
20615	Butt Plate	1.05
25410	Butt Plate Screw (2)	.30
15387	Butt Plate Spacer	.30
14741	Carrier, 28 Ga.	1.80
30130	Carrier, 410 Ga.	1.80
30131	Carrier Assembly, 28 Ga.	2.55
14280	Carrier Assembly, 410 Ga.	2.55
14452	Ejector, 28 Ga.	1.10
14721	Ejector, 410 Ga.	1.10
14678	Ejector Rivet	.30
14441	Ejector Rivet, Front, 410 Ga.	1.80
31730	Extractor 28 Ga.	.30
	Extractor 410 Ga.	
14742	Extractor Plunger 410 Ga.	
14806	Extractor Spring 410 Ga.	.30
14297	Firing Pin Retaining Pin	.30
15702	Firing Pin Retractor Spring	.30
30050	Fore-end (Wood Only), 28 Ga.	.45
30051	Fore-end (Wood Only), 410 Ga.	9.00
29810	Fore-end Assembly, 28 Ga.	9.00
29811	Fore-end Assembly, 410 Ga.	12.75
29815	Fore-end Tube Assembly	12.75
14276	Fore-end Tube Nut	5.00
27731	Front Sight, 28 Ga., (for Plain Barrel)	.85
27732	Front Sight, 410 Ga., (for Plain Barrel)	.30
18796	Front Sight (for Vent Rib) Steel Bead	.30
15660	Front Sight Retaining Pin (for Vent Rib Steel Sight)	.30
14295	Hammer	.30
29920	Locking Block Assembly	1.20
14279	Magazine Cap	3.25
14961	Magazine Follower, 28 Ga.	1.20
14960	Magazine, 410 Ga.	.85
90497	Magazine Plug (3-Shot Wood) 28 Ga.	.85
14878	Magazine Plug (3-Shot Wood) 410 Ga.	.30
17496	Magazine Spring, 28 Ga.	.30
14901	Magazine Spring, 410 Ga.	.45
17501	Magazine Spring Retainer	.45
		.30

Part No.	NAME OF PART	List Price
30081	Receiver Assembly, 28 Ga.	$25.05
30080	Receiver Assembly, 410 Ga.	25.05
20041	Shell Latch, 28 Ga., Left	1.65
20046	Shell Latch, 28 Ga., Right	1.65
20043	Shell Latch, 410 Ga., Left	1.65
20048	Shell Latch, 410 Ga., Right	1.65
30140	Slide Assembly	2.75
30085	Stock Assembly (includes Butt Plate, Butt Plate Screw (2), Grip Cap, Grip Cap Screw, Stock)	16.15
31280	Trigger Plate, R.H.	4.50
29930	Trigger Plate Assembly, 28 Ga.	11.90
29931	Trigger Plate Assembly, 410 Ga.	11.90
20602	Trigger Plate Pin, Front	.30
20607	Trigger Plate Pin, Rear	.30

ACCESSORY (Added Cost)

Part No.	NAME OF PART	List Price
31285	Match-Weight Skeet Cap	$ 9.95

The Match - Weight Skeet Cap is adjustable to suit individual shooters. Weight of cap will vary from eleven ounces when empty to one pound two ounces when filled with the maximum amount of shot.

To adjust, unscrew and remove from gun and remove magazine cap. Loosen lock nut and turn rod counter clockwise to increase depth of shot chamber. Fill with number 8 or 9 shot and tighten lockout. Replace magazine cap and reassemble Match - Weight Skeet Cap to gun.

SKEET GRADE

NOTE: For Parts Not Listed, see Field Grade, 28 & 410 Gauge.

Part No.	NAME OF PART	List Price
31285	Match-Weight Skeet Cap Assembly, 28 and 410 Ga. (includes below)	
31255	Adjustable Skeet Weight	
17451	Magazine Cap Detent	
16791	Magazine Cap Detent Spring	
14719	Skeet Weight Follower	
14723	Skeet Weight Lock Nut	
14718	Skeet Weight Rod	
30615	Barrel Assembly, Skeet Grade, 28 Ga., 25", Vent Rib	
30616	Barrel Assembly, Skeet Grade, 410 Ga., 25", Vent Rib	
31675	Fore-end Assembly, 28 Ga. SA Grade	$12.75
31676	Fore-end Assembly, 410 Ga. SA Grade	12.75
31590	Stock Assembly, 28 & 410 Ga. SA Grade	16.15
30715	Trigger Plate Assembly, 28 Ga. (includes same as Field Grade except)	
19465	Action Bar Lock	13.90
14560	Hammer	1.75
19037	Sear	1.20
30716	Trigger Plate Assembly, 410 Ga.	1.20
		13.90

DELIVERIES ARE F.O.B. ILION, N.Y.

PARTS AND PRICES SUBJECT TO CHANGE WITHOUT NOTICE

BIGGER FAMILY

Note the plug for Peters ammunition and the DuPont chemical insignia in the top left page of this owner's manual. Cross-marketing was in full force even back then.

THE 1980s AND INTO THE NEW CENTURY

THE 1980S WERE, perhaps, just as important as the preceding decade, at least in some ways. There were some new technological changes in the form of the Rem Chokes, and new models were introduced. At the same time, some older models were dropped.

It began with the introduction of new stock styling, in 1980. The checkering on the Model 870 had been, for 30 years, of the so-called "impressed" variety, i.e., it was not cut. However, Remington introduced a new machine checkering process that actually rivaled that of a hand-checkered pattern. At the same time, the stock finish changed from the glossy RKW finish (a high-gloss creation of Remington's parent company DuPont), to the more satiny appearing, almost oil finish-like application. It made for a much more attractive looking stock to many, though, to be sure, there were those who lamented the passing of the glossy finish and the *fleur de lis* pattern of the old impressed checkering.

In 1981, the Model 870 Competition Trap model was introduced, along with a Model 870 Limited 20-gauge lightweight with a 23-inch barrel and a short, 12½-inch stock (which today would qualify it as a youth or women's gun). The following year, the SA Skeet Grade in all gauges was discontinued, as well as the TB Trap Grade in both right- and left-hand versions. One year later, in 1983, a special 12-gauge 3-inch magnum Model 870 Ducks Unlimited Commemorative edition was produced, as was a 12-gauge left-hand deer gun.

The year 1983 also saw the introduction of the Model 870 Special Field in 12- and 20-gauge. This was a gun that Remington made for the upland hunter, and it was radically different from other pump-action guns on the market. It had a short, stubby, 21-inch ventilated rib barrel choked Improved Cylinder, Modified, or Full, and its stock was straight gripped— "English-style," as Remington called it. At the same time, the Limited model that had been introduced a year earlier was renamed the Youth Gun, and its barrel was shortened to 21 inches, matching the Special Field model.

For the next five years there weren't any major changes to the Remington 870 lineup, except for the introduction of the Model 870 SP Special Purpose Magnum, which featured either a 26- or 30-inch barrel choked Full, with dully finished metal and a sheenless hardwood stock. This variant debuted in 1985, designed specifically for waterfowl and turkey hunters. Then, in 1986, Remington restyled the Model 870 with a new checkering pattern and introduced the Rem Chokes. Some of Remington's literature lists 1988 as the year of Rem Choke introduction. However, Rem Chokes were actually available earlier, in 1986. This inconsistency in the reporting of the Remington lineage is a bit odd as, from a technological standpoint, 1986 was an important year for the company. Up until that point, Remington had been behind the curve with regards to its two major competitors, at least when it came

Above is the economical version of the Model 870, the plainly finished Express version. Move up to the Enhanced Wingmaster, below, and you get a high-polished blue receiver with fine line engraving, and a stock with both better wood and a nicer finish to show off the grain.

Perhaps the biggest technological advance for the Model 870 occurred in 1992, with the reveal of the light-contour barrels. These helped knock back the ounces the gun had gained when Rem Chokes and their thicker barrels were first introduced.

to screw-in chokes. Browning had offered its Invector Chokes for several years already, and Winchester had actually pioneered screw-in chokes in America with its Versalite Chokes, all the way back in 1959 (these were later renamed Winchokes).

The same year, Remington finally saw the light in the world of screw-in chokes, it also introduced the Model 870 Special Purpose Deer Gun, which was, basically, the earlier introduced Model 870 SP Special Purpose with a shorter barrel and rifle sights. A year later, Remington came out with the Model 870 Express, an economy version of the regular 870 Wingmaster. The Express had matte-finished metal and a hardwood stock. The following year, the Model 870 Express was offered in a combo version, with a 20-inch slug barrel and a 28-inch ventilated rib barrel. The Model 870 TC Trap Grade got a new stock with different dimensions and an overbored 31-inch barrel with a choice of Rem Chokes or a plain Full choke. Next up, again one year later, the Model 870 Special Purpose's wood was upgraded from hardwood to American walnut, and a cantilever scope mount option was offered for the 12-gauge Model 870 Deer Gun line.

Little by little, Remington continued to expand its offerings of different versions of the Model 870 through the 1990s. In fact, this period could be classified as the "special version" era, one in which Remington churned out numerous specialized versions of its already very popular Model 870. By the end of the 1990s, with the old century turning into the new, Remington had produced an incredible number of Model 870 varietals.

To start, in 1991 alone, the economy Model 870 Express line was expanded to include the Model 870 Express Turkey, Model 870 Express Cantilever Super Mount Deer Gun, Model 870 Express Rifle Sighted Deer Gun, Model 870 Express Small Gauge, and the Model 870 Express Youth Gun. Remington also introduced the Model 870 SPS Express Special Purpose Synthetic and the Model 870 SPS-T Special Purpose Synthetic Turkey.

Remington began to roll out new, specialized versions almost yearly, at this point. In 1992, it introduced the Model 870 Marine Magnum Security Gun wearing a seven-shot extended magazine, 18-inch barrel, synthetic stock, and electroless nickel-plating on the metal hardware, a hardiness solution for use in marine environments. Remington also added a 12-gauge rifle-barrel Deer Gun and a .410-bore version of the Model 870 Express. Another specialized model, the Model 870 SP Camo, in Mossy Oak Bottomland, appeared at the same time.

Perhaps the more important technological change introduced in 1992 was the light-contour barrels for the Model 870 shotguns. As mentioned earlier, the addition of the Rem Choke system required an increase in barrel thickness which, in turn, added weight to the gun overall. The Rem Choke guns were noticeably heavier in the nose, more forward balanced than those without Rem Chokes. There were many who complained, finding disfavor with the newer, more heavily barreled guns, enough so that many of those who took umbrage made it a point to search for the older barrels without the Rem Choke system. Apparently Remington listened to the complaints, coming out with what it considered to be the solution, its light-contour barrels. These barrels are, as you would infer, lighter than the original Rem Choked barrels, and guns fitted with light-contour barrels come closer to feel and balance of the older versions of the Model 870.

In 1993, Remington announced the production of its six-millionth Model 870 shotgun! This was something that had never happened to any shotgun ever produced by any company! And it took less than 50 years! With that milestone in place, Remington introduced even more kinds of specialized versions of the Model 870, such as the Model 870 SPS BG-Camo gun with a synthetic stock, camo finish, 20-inch barrel, and rifle sights, as well as the Model 870 SPS Deer with a fully rifled barrel and synthetic stock.

Indeed, it seemed as if Remington could not come up with enough versions of the Model 870. Each year, at least one new version would pop up. In 1994, a barrel bearing a cantilever scope mount was introduced on the Model 870 Wingmaster in 12- and 20-gauge. At the same time, a Model 870 SPS with the cantilever scope mount on the barrel and with the gun wearing a synthetic stock in a Monte Carlo style, as did another barrel variation with Rem Choke. Also, a Model 870 Express Small Gauge shotgun in 28-gauge appeared, and a 20-gauge Model 870 Express Youth Gun with or without Deer barrel was added to the Express line.

The year 1995 was unusual, in that only a single new version of the Model 870 was introduced. This was the Model 870 Express HD (Home Defense) shotgun with an 18-inch Cylinder-choked barrel and checkered synthetic stock. The gun was obviously designed for one purpose, that for which its name explains fully.

The seven-millionth Model 870 shotgun came off the assembly line, in 1996. This was the year Remington decided to reintroduce some of the models that had been discontinued previously. To that end, the Model 870 TC Trap gun with the option of a straight comb or a Monte Carlo arrangement was reintroduced. Remington also brought back the Model 870 Express Small Gauge gun in 20-gauge, 28-gauge, and .410-bore. These had been made on and off over the years, but they now became a regular part of the line. Remington next added a custom touch to the Model 870 Wingmaster Field, Target, and Deer Gun shotguns, by giving them fine line engraving on the receiver panels.

In 1997, Remington added the Mossy Oak Break-up Pattern to the Model 870 Magnum SPS Gun, and the Model 870 Turkey Gun received the Realtree X-Tra Brown camo. Two additional Model 870 Express Combos—each came with a 26-inch ventilated rib barrel and a 20-inch fully rifled Deer barrel—in 12- and 20-gauge were added to the Express line.

The year 1998 saw a bunch of new additions, mostly in the area of special purpose guns. There were four new versions of the Model 870 Express Super Magnum shotguns chambered for 3½-inch 12-gauge shotshells. The standard variant had a hardwood stock with a 28-inch Rem Choke barrel; the Synthetic Super Magnum had a black synthetic stock and a 26-inch Rem Choke barrel; the Synthetic Turkey Camo gun had a synthetic stock with Advantage Camo design and a 23-inch, Extra Full Rem Choke barrel, as well as an extra 20-inch fully rifled Deer barrel; and, finally, there was the Model 870 Express Turkey Camo shotgun with Advantage camo-covered synthetic stock in 12- and 20-gauge. Youth Turkey Gun versions were introduced, both with 21-inch Rem Choke barrels, and Remington also offered a Model 870 Express 12-gauge with a 28-inch Rem Choke barrel in a left-handed version. Additional touches to the line included the inclusion of fine line receiver engraving on the Model 870 Wingmaster 28-gauge field gun.

In the final year of the twentieth century, Remington continued to add to the already large selection of specialized Model 870s in its line. In 1999, it introduced five more "special purpose" types of Model 870s and expanded the Model 870 Wingmaster line, its premier gun, with the addition of 28-gauge and .410-bore versions. The Model 870 SPS "Super Magnum" Camo Shotgun and the Model 870 SPS-T "Super Magnum" Camo Shotgun, both with 12-gauge 3½-inch chambers made their appearances. Remington also brought out the Model 870 SPS "Super Slug" Deer Gun, which featured a 23-inch, fully rifled, modified-contour barrel fitted with a barrel-mounted cantilever scope mount, and a black synthetic stock. The Express line was also further expanded with the Model 870 Express Super Magnum Turkey Gun, a 12-gauge with 3½-inch chamber 23-inch barrel with extra full Rem Choke and black synthetic stock. There was also the Model 870 Express Synthetic Deer Gun, with a 20-inch, fully rifled barrel wearing adjustable rifle sights, a matte black finish on the metal work, and a black synthetic stock.

It is without doubt that the 1990s were busy years for the Remington Model 870. Camouflaged waterfowl guns and short-barreled turkey guns became standard equipment for waterfowlers and gobbler hunters everywhere. Deer guns were also no longer simply rifle sighted, short-barreled versions of the standard bird gun. Instead, now the barrels were fully rifled, and many were fitted to address the demand that the guns should be easily adapted for use with scopes. Remington met all of these demands and more!

The start of the new century coincided with the fiftieth anniversary of the Model 870, and Remington commemorated the event with a Model 870 50th Anniversary Classic Trap Gun. This gun had a 30-inch barrel with Rem Chokes and fancy American walnut stock and fore-end wood. Remington also started producing the Model 870 Wingmaster Super Magnum with 28-inch barrel and Rem Chokes, but now the gun could handle 2¾-, 3-, and 3½-inch shells. The same year also saw the introduction of the Model 870 SPS-T RS/TG Shotgun with fully adjustable TruGlo rifle sights, 20-inch Rem Choke barrel, black matte finish on the metal, and black synthetic stock and fore-end. Remington also brought out the Model 870 SPS-T Super Magnum Camo CL/RD Shotgun, with a 23-inch Rem Choke barrel hosting a Leupold/Gilmore Red Dot sight and accompanied by the Mossy Oak Break-up camo finish on the metal and the synthetic stock and fore-end. In looking back over the decade that came before it, it seems that, since the start of the 1990s, Remington had introduced camo versions of the Model 870 at the rate of four to one against non-camo versions.

Remington began the new century with the introduction of the Model 870 SPS-T Super Magnum Camo CL/RC Shotgun with a cantilever scope mount on a 23-inch Rem Choke barrel, and a Model 870 SPS-T Synthetic Camo RS/TG Shotgun with a 20-inch Rem Choke barrel and TruGlo sights. There was also the Model 870 SPS Super Magnum Camo Shotgun with a 26-inch ventilated rib Rem Choke barrel and Mossy Oak Break-up finish on the metal and synthetic stock and fore-end. One final entry in the "special purpose" category was a Model 870 SPS-T Youth

RS/TG Synthetic Turkey Camo Shotgun with a 20-inch Super Full Rem choke barrel, TruGlo fiber-optic sights, and Mossy Oak Break-up finish on all metal and the synthetic stock and fore-end. The lone non-camo, non-special purpose shotgun was the Model 870 Classic Trap shotgun with a 30-inch ventilated rib Rem Choke barrel, a high-polish blued finish on the metal, and a semi-fancy American walnut stock and fore-end.

In 2002, Remington took a break from the SPS Camo versions and increased its Express line offerings, as well as adding another to the Wingmaster line. It began with a Model 870 Wingmaster and a Model 870 Express in 16-gauge, a blatant move to cash in on the newly regenerated interest in the 16-gauge that had other manufacturers introducing shotguns in that chambering. In addition to the 870 Express 16-gauge, the Model 870 Express Synthetic and the Model 870 Express Synthetic Youth Shotgun were introduced. Remington also put the Model 870 Express in 28-gauge and .410-bore into its lineup as regular offerings. These had been produced before in limited numbers, and now they were cataloged as a perpetual standards.

In 2003, Remington went back to the drawing board with the SPS line, introducing the Model 870 SPS-T, a 20-gauge gun with a camo pattern and TruGlo fiber optic sight. Remington also started to offer the Express line in camo, to include the Model 870 Express Super Magnum Turkey Camo, a Model 870 Express Turkey Camo, and a Model 870 Express Youth Turkey Camo.

The following year, 2004, saw the introduction of only one new 870 product in the sporting field, that being the Model 870 SPS Deer Shotgun, a fully cantilevered 20-gauge gun. This lack of attention to the hunting crowd can be viewed as somewhat necessary, as Remington was making its first real foray into the fast growing "tactical" field, with guns such as the new Model 870 TR (Tactical Response), a gun designed strictly for police work.

The year 2005 saw the appearance of some special editions and another "first." Remington began with the introduction of the Model 870 Wingmaster Jr. and the very special Model 870 Wingmaster Dale Earnheart Limited Edition gun with fine line engraving. As for the "first," that could be the announcement of the Model 870 SP-T Super Magnum Thumbhole stock shotgun, a stock configuration previously unheard of in the Remington

BIG GREEN

Another classic hang tag from "Big Green" Remington. Akin to John Deere green, this color is still the hallmark of this powerhouse American gun maker.

lineup of shotguns. Also, a Model 870 Express Super Magnum Fall Flight gun and a Model 870 Express Super Magnum Synthetic with a 28-inch barrel made their debuts. The offerings for the year ended with another special edition, a Model 870 Express Jr. NWTF (National Wild Turkey Federation) Edition shotgun.

Passing the decade half-way mark, in 2006, Remington introduced the Model 870 Special NRA Edition. There were also the additions of new camouflage patterns to existing models. These included the Model 870 SPS Super Magnum MAX Gobbler Edition in Realtree All Purpose HD camo with a 23-inch Super Full Turkey choke tube and Williams Firesights fiber optic sights. The top of the receiver was drilled and tapped for a Weaver-style scope base for optics use, and the synthetic stock was adjustable for length of pull.

Three new additions also appeared in the Express line in 2006, beginning with the Model 870 Express Super Magnum Waterfowl in Mossy Oak Duck Blind camo. Then there was the Model 870 Express Combo, a 12-gauge 3-inch magnum chambering with a 21-inch barrel and Turkey Extra Full choke tube, along with a 23-inch fully rifled barrel wearing a cantilever scope mount. Next came a Model 870 Express 20-gauge that could hold seven rounds, and 2006 was also the first year that Remington made the Model 870 into a "black gun." The Model 870 Tac-2 SpecOps Stock has an 18-inch barrel with a two-shot magazine extension, along with a synthetic pistol grip stock that had an adjustable length of pull from 12 to 16 inches. The Model 870 Tac-3 hosted a 20-inch barrel with a three-shot magazine extension. Both models were also made available with a stock that folded over the top of the receiver.

By 2007, Remington's "tactical" versions of the Model 870 had grown like the SPS models! The camouflage pattern offerings were no longer confined to just a couple or even a half-dozen. There were all sorts of exotic offerings, everything from a Desert Recon pattern to one called the Digital Tiger! A sampling of the various Model 870 TR versions ranged from the standard model to the FBI, Patrol, Border Patrol, K-9, Urban Sniper, Louis Awerbuck, Expert, Professional, Entry, Compact, and SWAT variations. In addition, there were the SpecOps and Desert Recon Tac versions, as well as many variations of all these models! Without doubt, by 2007, Remington had jumped into the tactical shotgun field with both feet, and that commitment to the genre is astounding, considering that, just a decade earlier, there were, perhaps, maybe two "police" versions of the Model 870.

At this point, and as this book goes to press in 2012, there are so many sporting and tactical variations of the Model 870 that it is almost impossible to keep up with them. Each year some of the models are tweaked, with something added or upgraded. No doubt I have left out mention of some of the models that were introduced in the intervening years. Suffice it to say that the Remington Model 870 has appeared and will continue to appear in a dizzying array of model variations. How could it not? Today, 63 years after its birth, the Remington Model 870 is available in just about every conceivable variation—and then some! But the large selection aside, perhaps the biggest news in the last five years or so has been that, in 2010, the ten-millionth Model 870 came off the assembly line at Remington. This unprecedented accomplishment is lavishly engraved and gold inlaid, and the stock and fore-end are made of exhibition-grade American walnut. Of all the special-edition anniversary guns, beginning with the two-millionth, this one is, by far, the fanciest Model 870 ever.

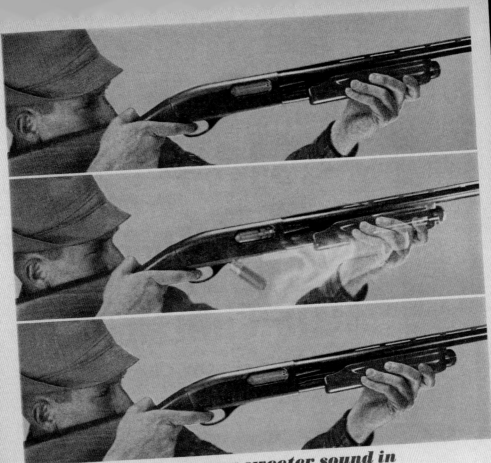

CHAPTER FOUR

Is there any sweeter sound in the whole wide world than the smooth sliding action of a Remington 870?

Shoulder a Remington 870 "Wingmaster". Work the cat-smooth action . . . and hear the soft "shuck-shuck" that tells you the empty shell is long gone and there's a fresh load in the chamber. A sweet sound if ever there was one!

Solid. There's no clatter and rattle with a Remington 870. That's because it has precision-built double action bars that prevent twisting and binding. Shooters tell us that an 870 action feels as if it slides on ball bearings.

Strong. The receiver is machined from a solid block of steel. The breech block locks solidly into the barrel. All the parts of the action mechanism are made for each other . . . work together as a team.

Smooth. It doesn't make a bit of difference what kind of fodder you feed a Remington Model 870. Whether you're pumping a second load of No. 4's for a wide-flaring mallard or sliding home a powerful rifled slug to down a big buck . . . it's smooth and quick.

By the way, the Remington 870 is still at prices that won't make you flinch . . . as low as $99.95*. It's tailored for your particular type of shooting—with over 49 barrel, choke and gauge combinations. Interchangeable barrels, too. Write for free Guns and Ammunition catalog to Dept. MB-9, Remington Arms Co., Inc.

Remington (DUPONT)

"Wingmaster" is Reg. U. S. Pat. Off. by Remington Arms Company, Inc., Bridgeport, Conn. 06602. In Canada: Remington Arms of Canada Limited, 36 Queen Elizabeth Blvd., Toronto, Ont. *Fair Trade retail prices in states having Fair Trade laws. Prices subject to change without notice.

MADISON AVENUE

This collection of ads from the early 1980s demonstrates the transition from the earlier days of artist's renderings to photographs in Remington's marketing material. Still, the gun remains the same, steadfast, reliable, always "America's Favorite Pump Gun."

Before you buy... be sur

REMINGTON

It's easy to see why Remington "Wingmaster" Model 870 is America's most wanted pump action shotgun. No other is so adaptable to so many different kinds of shooting. No other gives you such big value, superior quality, exclusive features . . . for such a moderate price.

And speaking of exclusive features, the "Wingmaster" is the *only* shotgun for which you can buy extra plain barrels—*any time*—and combine them with your "Wingmaster"

action, *in seconds* . . . with no special fitting whatsoever!

Your Remington dealer will be glad to show you other "Wingmaster" exclusives, like the "Vari-Weight" plug in 12 gauge that gives you two weights in one gun . . . the double action bars that prevent binding, make your pump stroke smooth and positive.

Before you buy, see *all* that's new in the Remington "Wingmaster."

ONLY REMINGTON "Wingmaster" HAS ALL THESE FEATURES

A gliding stroke is assured by these twin action bars. They divide the force of your pump stroke, preventing binding and twisting.

No tools needed for take-down. You just unscrew magazine cap and lift barrel off. Extra plain barrels require no fitting.

¾-pound steel "Vari-Weight" plug, light wood plug or no plug give three guns in one. Steel plug in 12 ga. only.

Breech block locks into barrel extension—gives longer life, less wear, constant head space . . . another "Wingmaster" exclusive.

For extra safety, the "Wingmaster" is so designed that it will not fire if the trigger is pressed while the action is being closed.

"EX

It's POWER yo you get with These smashi fast game at why:

They're *loa* Progressive-b power *all alon* bricated wad work. And F way for all perfect patter

But speed,

Perfect p

Heading for a pe ton Flat-Top Cri column. And tight *behind* the pellets

o see the sensational

ngmaster MODEL 870

and don't forget...

power-packed

REMINGTON
ESS" SHELLS

and POWER
n "Express."
on shells drop
range. Here's

mit for power.
der builds up
rrel. Tight, lu-
l the power to
mp opens the
to deliver a
ch and pattern

are only part of the story. Remington shells are the *only* shells with famous "Kleanbore" priming that can't corrode or rust a gun barrel.

Only Remington shells are corrugated . . . for greater strength, for easy feeding and extraction, for non-slip handling when your fingers are cold or wet.

So be specific next time you buy shells. Pick power-packed Remington "Express." If your dealer is temporarily out, remember, the best is well worth a short wait.

... smashing power!

Proof of Power . . . See how a #4 pellet goes clear through a ⅞-inch pine plank at 30 yds; penetrates .593" at 40 yds, .432" at 50 yds!

cause Reming-
uct the shot
eep the power
wn" patterns!

1816—The Oldest Gunmakers in America Present the Newest Guns—195

Remington DUPONT

"Wingmaster," "Express" and "Kleanbore" are Reg. U.S. Pat. Off. by Remington Arms Company, Inc., Bridgeport 2

REASSEMBLE ALL PARTS IN REVERSE ORDER: See sectional view of action and Figure 3 which shows location of all parts as a guide. Special care should be taken on the following:

Assemble stock bolt washer with sharp edges of projections against the wood. Tighten stock bolt securely.

All parts should be carefully and properly aligned until pin holes show a clear passage through the pieces before an attempt is made to drive pins.

FORE-END ASSEMBLY: Assemble slide to bars on fore-end assembly. Assemble locking block to bolt assembly and assemble breech bolt to the slide (see Figure 4). Assemble fore-end tube over magazine tube and insert rear end of arms (with slide and breech bolt on them) into receiver with slide and action bars fitting into grooves. Move assembly **gently** rearward until it contacts front end of right shell latch. Move front end of right shell latch into side of receiver to clear action bar and slide fore-end **gently** rearward until it contacts left shell latch. Push front end of left shell latch into side of receiver to clear action bar and push fore-end rearward until it is stopped by action bar lock.

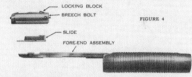

LOCKING BLOCK
BREECH BOLT
FIGURE 4
SLIDE
FORE-END ASSEMBLY

TRIGGER PLATE: CAUTION!—Always be sure that the rear end of the action bar lock is below the end of the left connector when assembling into trigger plate; otherwise the gun will not function properly.

To assemble trigger plate unit to receiver, first put safety ON, then cock hammer and with fore-end pushed fully forward insert front of carrier into loading port opening on bottom of receiver (Figure 5). Rotate unit clockwise slightly to clear action bar lock, then slide front end of trigger plate into opening until front pin hole lines up with the front holes in the receiver. Then push rear end of trigger plate into position to align the rear pin holes. Insert rear and front trigger plate pins.

FIGURE 5

[5]

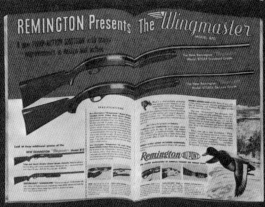

INCENTIVE

It's not like anyone needs an incentive to buy an 870, but from time to time Remington has offered rebates on its famous scattergun. These are surely a bonus to anyone, even when the gun and its many versions are some of the most affordably priced firearms around.

TRAP AND SKEET SHOTGUNS

THE REMINGTON MODEL 870 WINGMASTER first caught the shooting public's attention when, in the same year of its introduction, 1950, a young man by the name of Rudy Etchen shot the first 100 straight in handicap trap doubles at the Grand American with one. Etchen, who was employed by Remington as a professional shooter, actually shot one of the very first Model 870s to come off the assembly line. With his success at the Grand, it didn't take long for others to acquire the new Remington pump gun and try to emulate Etchen's accomplishment. In a sport where the copycat syndrome is part of the culture, a gun that's associated with a champion, especially one that breaks a new record, automatically becomes the next Holy Grail for aspiring champions. Trap shooters are notorious for constantly looking for that "perfect" gun, and the Model 870 quickly became a hot new item.

Initially, Remington came out only with the Model 870 TC, the basic trap model, which had a semi-beavertail fore-arm and a higher comb on the buttstock. The wood was a fancy grade and well checkered, a detail that Remington referred to as being "finely checkered." The gun sported a 30-inch ventilated ribbed barrel that was choked Full, but it could be purchased with a 28-inch barrel choked either Full or Modified. This latter was the gun Rudy Etchen took with him to the Grand and with which he broke the handicap doubles record.

It didn't take long for Remington to follow up with the "Tournament Grade," which had even fancier wood and nicely hand checkered stock and forearm. There were, of course, the Premier Grades and F Grades, all very fancy versions with exhibition wood, fine engraving, and gold inlays. But it was still the basic Model 870 TC that became the best seller among trap shooters. Still, the Model 870 TC wasn't cheap, as far as pump guns went in those days. In the first year of production it sold for $159.95, when the basic Model 870 AP cost less than half that, at $69.95! So, while trap shooters bought the pricey 870 TC, it didn't break any sales records—and it didn't take a genius to figure out what to do about that.

Obviously, the Model 870 trap gun was a very popular version, but, in its TC version, was just too expensive for some shooters. Indeed, many trap shooters chose to buy the plain ADL model with a long barrel and used it to play the game. Remington's attempt to fix the problem was to introduce, in 1955, the Model 870 TB, a slightly different and less expensive variant of the Model 870 TC. Remington followed up the TB,

FANCIFIED

This press release announced the All American edition of the 870 trap gun, in 1972. Mechanically the same as all the other 870s, the All Americans sported "customized features" without customers having to special order the gun.

REMINGTON ARMS COMPANY, INC.
PUBLIC RELATIONS DIVISION
BRIDGEPORT, CONNECTICUT 06602

Remington DUPONT *Peters*

News Release

FOR RELEASE **JANUARY 3, 1972**

NEW REMINGTON MODEL 870
ALL AMERICAN TRAP GUN
OFFERS CUSTOM FEATURES

Pride of ownership is probably a more significant factor for trap guns than for any other type of shotgun. Most trap shooters use their trap guns on the clay target ranges only and nowhere else. And no other shotguns are inspected, compared, admired and publicly displayed as much as trap guns. As a result, trap shooters, over the years, have come to expect more in the beauty of stock wood, special engraving and fine details of checkering and finish that appear on their guns.

Traditionally, however, the finest quality guns have been available only on a special order basis and at a cost of over a thousand dollars. Now, an American pump action trap gun whose inherent design and operational dependability have stood the test of time, Remington's Model 870, is being offered in a handsome, customized version that will be directly available without special order at an attractive price.

The new Remington Model 870 All American trap gun will warm the pride of every shooter who owns one and evoke the envy and admiration of those who do not. The stock and fore-end are carved from blocks of fine, richly colored, beautifully grained American walnut. The inherent beauty

- MORE -

New Rem. M/870
All American Trap Gun

of the wood is protected and furthe[r]
exclusive rugged RK-W finish. Cust[...]
raised diamonds decorates the stoc[k...]

Both sides and the top o[f...]
the trigger guard and the breech [...]
engraved in a delicately cut scro[ll...]
shield embossed with a three-dime[nsional...]
eagle and containing the descrip[tion...]
Trap Gun" in gold lettering agai[nst...]
background is located on the le[ft...]
Finally, a gold plate for perso[nalization...]
into the pistol grip cap.

The new Model 870 All American trap gun will be available with standard trap stock dimensions in regular trap or Monte Carlo versions. Barrels will be full choke in 30" length.

Appropriately for such a fine gun, the cost will include a hard, luggage type, foam-lined carrying case with snap closures and lock.

Remington Model 870 All American trap guns will be available starting in April, 1972.

-30-

REMINGTON MODEL 870 MATCHED PAIR
PUMP ACTION SKEET GUNS IN 28 & 410 GAUGES
WITH SPECIAL CARRYING CASE

REMINGTON ARMS COMPANY, INC.
PUBLIC RELATIONS DIVISION
BRIDGEPORT, CONNECTICUT 06602

Remington DUPONT *Peters*

News Release

FOR RELEASE   JANUARY 3, 1972

REMINGTON OFFERS 34-INCH BARRELS FOR MODELS 1100 AND 870 TRAP GUNS

Trap shooters are devotees of the long sighting plane. A majority of them prefer the smoother, more deliberate swing of longer length barrels for their version of the clay target games, particularly at handicap yardages.

While the 30-inch, full choke barrel is most common, many trap shooters have indicated their preference for even longer barrels.

In order to meet this demand, Remington has announced the availability of extra long, 34-inch barrels for its popular Model 1100 autoloading and Model 870 pump action trap grade shotguns. These will be standard trap barrels, in full choke only, with ventilated ribs and regular trap beads. They will be sold as extra barrels only and will not be available as part of a complete gun.

Since these barrels will also interchange on regular 12 gauge Models 1100 and 870 field guns, they should also answer the need of waterfowlers who prefer the more deliberate pointing characteristics of extra long shotguns for pass shooting.

New, 34-inch full choke trap barrels for 12 gauge Models 1100 and 870 shotguns will be available starting in February, 1972.

-30-

CASED SETS
Sub-gauge skeet guns in 28-gauge and .410-bore were first offered as matched pairs, in 1969.

LONG BARRELS
Trap shooters l-o-v-e *love* long barrels for their extended sight radius advantage. Remington responded well to demand for this feature with a 34-inch barrel offering, announced in the press release to the left.

in 1959, with the Model 870 TX, yet another less costly trap gun. The TX variant had all the basic ingredients of the pricier model, and the TC model was quietly phased out.

Remington Model 870 trap guns became more or less a common sight on trap ranges across the country in a very short space of time. With the appearance of the All American edition of the trap gun, in 1972, Remington would periodically produce a gussied-up version of its popular trap gun as a

Though the double-barrel over/under is the top choice for today's trap shooters, for the admirable contingent who still prefer the pump, the Remington 870 trap models, now a half-century since its introduction, *dominate* any other brand of pump on the tournament line.

CLASSIC GOOD LOOKS
High gloss stocks, better wood, a high cheek-piece on the stock, and the nicely contrasting red buttpad with its white line spacer define the classic good looks of Remington 870 competition trap models.

commemorative issue. There were several such versions through the years, such as the 50th Anniversary Commemorative issue in 2000, the Classic Trap Model.

Today, well more than a half-century after the original introduction of the first production Remington 870 trap gun, trap fields are dominated by over/unders and many specialized single-barrels and autoloaders. Yet, when it comes to those who prefer pump guns, to this day the Remington Model 870 outnumbers all other makes and models in those shooters' hands. For one, it has always had a nose-heavy feel, especially with longer barrels, and many trap shooters find the balance on the Model 870 to be much better suited for trap shooting than other pump guns on the market. In fact, the gun was still popular enough for a time that, in 1981, Remington brought out the Model 870 Competition Trap gun with a 30-inch barrel and special recoil absorbing integral piston. But it couldn't compete with the overall slump in popularity of the pump-action for use in the sport, and the action's growing absence from competitive trap fields brought about the discontinuance of the Model 870 TB (in both its right- and left-hand models), in 1982. Today,

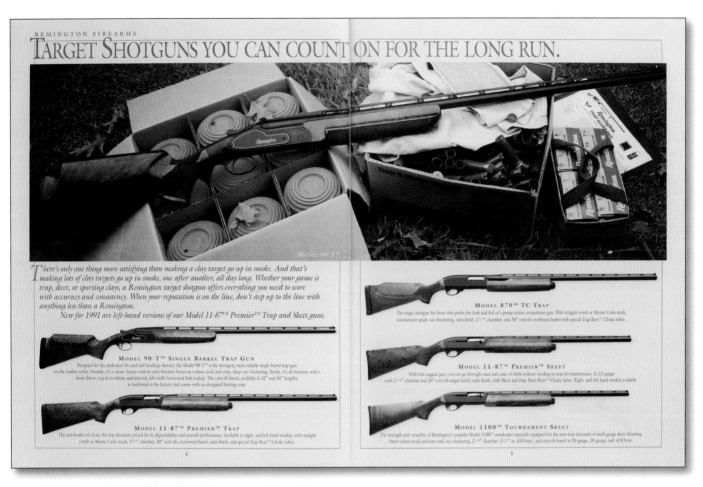

1991—A DIFFERENT TREND?

With the pump gun losing ground as a favorite action choice among clay shooters in the early 1990s, Remington sashayed away from its famous pump for a while and devoted some its focus to specialized single-shots and its semi-autos.

the Model 870 Classic Trap is still in production, although it appears to be the only regular production Model 870 trap gun in Remington's lineup, perhaps more a remark about the popularity of the sport itself—especially when compared to the all-things-tactical craze that continues to grip America and not the gun.

When it comes to skeet guns, the pump gun as a whole hasn't fared so well in the recent decades. Now, prior to World War II and on into the early 1960s, the pump gun was quite popular as a tool for the game of skeet, and the Remington 870 as one of the most favored of the breed. The most common version was, of course, the Model 870 SA, basically the Model

Target Shotguns: A Winning Tradition.

Using a Remington in competition has been an easy choice for a lot of shooters for a lot of reasons, and here are just a few: <u>Balance</u> – it's between your hands where you want it in the skeet guns, and a little farther forward in the trap guns. That's what gives Remington target guns the amazing pointability that so many shooters talk about. When you bring a Remington up to your shoulder, something magical happens: the gun seems to transform into an extension of your body, so you can concentrate totally on the target. <u>On-person performance</u> – a Remington target gun won't beat you up. The great balance and ergonomic design make these the softest-shooting family of target guns on the market today. And <u>value</u> – you won't find a competition trap, skeet, or sporting clays gun with as much quality and performance, priced as comfortably as a Remington. So there are plenty of reasons, but a lot of champions put it simply: "My Remington just makes it easier for me to break targets." And that's what it's all about.

New for 1992 is our lightning-fast "Sporting Clays" version of the dependable Model 11-87™ Premier™.

MODEL 11-87™ SPORTING CLAYS

1992
While the 1991 catalog (previous page) rather left out the 870 as it related to clay shooters, the next year it was back again, spotlighted in the middle of the catalog page as the TC Trap iteration.

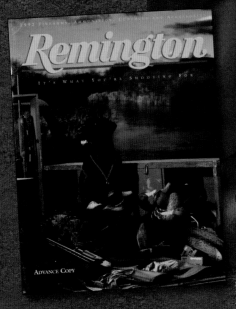

MODEL 11-87™ PREMIER™ SPORTING CLAYS

Just another 11-87™? Look again. It starts with a target-grade, cut checkered, American walnut competition stock that's 14 3/16" in length of pull and has a 1 1/2" drop at the comb, and 2 1/4" drop at the heel to lock in your sight picture. The butt pad is radiused at the heel and rounded at the toe to slide smoothly on to your shoulder as you mount the gun. The top of the receiver, the barrel, and the rib have a fine matte finish to eliminate any reflections from the blueing that could distract your eyes as you track the target. Swing it. Feels quick, because we've taken almost 3/4 lb. out of the front end and moved the center of balance back between your hands - where you want it. We did it by designing a new light contour barrel and shortening the magazine tube and fore-end. The barrel has a lengthened forcing cone for pattern uniformity and reduced recoil, and carries a medium-height, 5/16" wide rib with stainless mid-bead and ivory front bead sights. The competition trigger pulls clean, with no creep, and breaks crisply. For the variety of patterns sporting clays demands, we've included five choke tubes to select from as you tune the gun to each station: Skeet, Imp. Skeet, Imp. Cyl., Mod., and Full. These special tubes are also designed for quick, no-wrench field changes, because we've extended the tube beyond the muzzle and knurled the end for a good grip. Each tube is also clearly marked on the outside, eliminating the need to remove the tube to check its identification. Comes in our new two-barrel, custom-fitted hard case. Note: Like other Model 11-87™ Premier™ target guns, the Model 11-87™ Sporting Clays has a 2¾" chamber, is not pressure compensated, and is set up to handle target and light field loads only.

MODEL 90-T™ SINGLE-BARREL TRAP GUN

Designed for the dedicated 16-yard and handicap shooter, the Model 90-T™ is the strongest, most reliable single-barrel trap gun on the market today. Its great balance gives the Model 90-T™ a fluid feel and pointability that's uncanny: it moves like an extension of your body. And perceived recoil is comparable to gas operated autoloaders! Outside, it's a classic beauty with its satin-finished American walnut stock and crisp, deep-cut checkering. Inside, it's all business, with a short-throw, top-lever release and internal, full-width horizontal bolt lockup. The vent rib barrel, available in 32" and 34" lengths, is overbored at the factory and comes with an elongated forcing cone. For more information on additional available options for the Model 90-T™, see your local Remington dealer.

MODEL 870™ TC TRAP

The target shotgun for those who prefer the look and feel of a pump action competition gun. With straight comb or Monte Carlo stock, tournament-grade cut checkering, satin finish, 2¾" chamber, and 30" vent rib overbored barrel with special Trap Rem™ Choke tubes.

MODEL 11-87™ PREMIER™ TRAP

The autoloader of choice for trap shooters, prized for its reliability and smooth, low-recoil performance. In fact, we believe it's the softest shooting trap gun on the market. Available in right- and left-hand models, with straight comb or Monte Carlo stock, 2¾" chamber, 30" vent rib, overbored barrel, satin finish, and special Trap Rem™ Choke tubes. Note: Model 11-87™ Premier™ target guns have 2¾" chambers, are not pressure compensated, and are set up to handle target loads only.

MODEL 1100™ TOURNAMENT SKEET

The strength and versatility of Remington's popular Model 1100™ autoloader specially equipped for the non-stop demands of small-gauge skeet shooting. Satin walnut stock and fore-end, cut checkering, 2¾" chamber (2½" in .410 bore), and vent rib Rem™ Choke barrel in 20-gauge, 28-gauge, and .410 bore have fixed skeet choke.

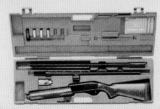

NEW! TWO-BARREL, TAKE-DOWN SHOTGUN HARD CASE

Now included when you buy certain models of our shotguns, is a custom-formed, high-strength, two-barrel, fitted gun case. Inside, there's room for two barrels, six Rem™ Chokes, the magazine plug, a choke wrench, and all sorts of accessories like Rem™ Oil, shooting glasses, etc. The outside of this FAA-approved case is made of a high-strength, lightweight, impact-resistant synthetic that will protect your gun during shipping and incorporates a sturdy padlock lug for security. A great value, and it's *free* when you buy a Model 11-87™ Sporting Clays, Model 11-87™ Premier™, or Model 870™ Wingmaster® with our new light contour barrel.

REMINGTON TARGET GUNS. TOTAL CONFIDENCE AVAILABLE IN PUMP, BREAK ACTION, AUTO, AND LEFT- & RIGHT-HAND VERSIONS.

There are a lot of reasons to use a Remington in competition, and here are just a few: *Great balance* – it's between your hands where you want it in the Skeet and Sporting Clays guns, and a little forward in the Trap guns. *Low recoil* – a Remington target gun won't beat you up. The great balance and ergonomic design make these the softest-shooting family of target guns on the market today. *Value* – you won't find a competition Trap, Skeet, or Sporting Clays gun of the same level of quality and performance priced as comfortably as a Remington.

MODEL 90-T™ SINGLE-BARREL TRAP GUN

Designed for the dedicated 16-yard and handicap shooter, the Model 90-T™ is the strongest, and most reliable single-barrel trap gun on the market today. Perceived recoil is the lowest of any break action gun due to its unique distribution of mass. Satin-finished American walnut stock and crisp, deep-cut checkering is standard. The short-throw, top-lever release actuates an internal, full-width horizontal bolt. The 32″ or optional 34″ vent rib barrel is overbored at the factory and has an elongated forcing cone. Choke is fixed full. New for 1993 is an adjustable high-rib version of the Model 90-T™ for shooters who prefer a more open target picture and higher head position.

MODEL 870™ TC TRAP

The trap gun for those who prefer the traditional look and feel of a pump action target gun. With straight comb or Monte Carlo stock, tournament-grade cut checkering, satin wood finish, 2 3/4″ chamber, and 30″ vent rib overbored barrel with special Trap Rem™ Choke tubes.

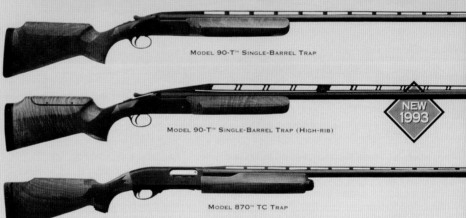

MODEL 90-T™ SINGLE-BARREL TRAP

MODEL 90-T™ SINGLE-BARREL TRAP (HIGH-RIB)

NEW 1993

MODEL 870™ TC TRAP

12

Remington
IT'S WHAT YOU'RE SHOOTING FOR.

The pump has never been the predominant action for the faster game of skeet, but it's never been absent for high-house/low-house work, either. Remington's first skeet pump was the 1950s 870 SA, which featured a 26-inch barrel for more nimble handling.

MODEL 11-87™ PREMIER®
SPORTING CLAYS

◀ This Model 11-87™ features a target-grade, cut checkered, American walnut stock set up for Sporting Clays that's 3/16" longer in length of pull and 1/4" higher at the heel. The butt pad is radiused at the heel and rounded at the toe for smooth mounting. The receiver top, barrel, and rib have a fine matte finish on the blueing. The new light contour barrel has a lengthened forcing cone, and carries a medium-high, 8mm wide rib with stainless mid-bead and Bradley-style front bead sight. Skeet, Imp. Skeet, Imp. Cyl., Mod., and Full Rem™ Choke tubes are supplied. Each tube is knurled at the end, and clearly marked on the outside. Comes in our new two-barrel, custom-fitted hard case.
Note: Like other Model 11-87™ target guns, the Model 11-87™ Premier® Sporting Clays has a 2 3/4" chamber, is not pressure compensated, and is set up to handle target and light field loads only.

MODEL 11-87™ PREMIER® TRAP

The autoloader of choice for trap shooters, prized for its reliability and smooth, low-recoiling performance. The softest-shooting trap gun on the market today. In right- and left-hand models, with straight comb or Monte Carlo stock, 2 3/4" chamber, 30" vent rib overbored barrel, satin wood finish, and special Trap Rem™ Choke tubes.
Note: Model 11-87™ Premier® target guns have 2 3/4" chambers, are not pressure compensated, and are set up to handle target loads only.

MODEL 11-87™ PREMIER® TRAP

MODEL 1100™
TOURNAMENT SKEET

The strength and versatility of Remington's popular Model 1100™ autoloader, set up for the non-stop demands of competitive small-gauge skeet. Satin walnut stock and fore-end, cut checkering, 2 3/4" chamber (2 1/2" in .410 bore), and twin-bead target-sighted vent rib barrel. In 20-gauge, 28-gauge, and .410 bore.

MODEL 1100™ TOURNAMENT SKEET

13

870 ADL having a 26-inch ventilated rib barrel with Skeet boring and two beads on the barrel. The stock itself was just a bit higher at the comb, but, basically, it was like the field model. The Model 870 SA appeared simultaneously with other basic models in 1950, when the 870 was first introduced. Shortly, high-grade versions followed, such as the Tournament Grade with its fancy wood and fine hand checkering. If you were willing to pay, you could always get one of the really fancy versions put out by the Remington Custom Gun Shop, such as the Premier Grade or F Grade with exhibition wood and intricate engraving with gold inlays. These options can be ordered today, as well.

When Remington decided to put out the scaled-frame versions of the Model 870 in 28-gauge and .410-bore, in 1969, the sub-gauges were first offered as a matched pair of skeet guns. These guns also came with weights that could be attached to the magazine cap to increase the forward weight of the gun as some skeet shooters prefer. These little skeet guns became very popular, despite the fact pump guns were beginning to lose favor on the skeet fields even before the introduction of these new guns.

Despite the pump gun's slipping popularity among skeet shooters, Remington continued to produce the Model 870 in skeet versions. In 1972, the 20-gauge lightweight version of the Model 870 was introduced with a smaller receiver. This gun also was offered as a skeet gun and became popular with those who continued to use pump guns in skeet.

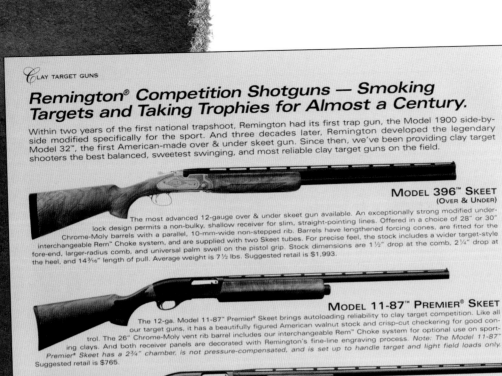

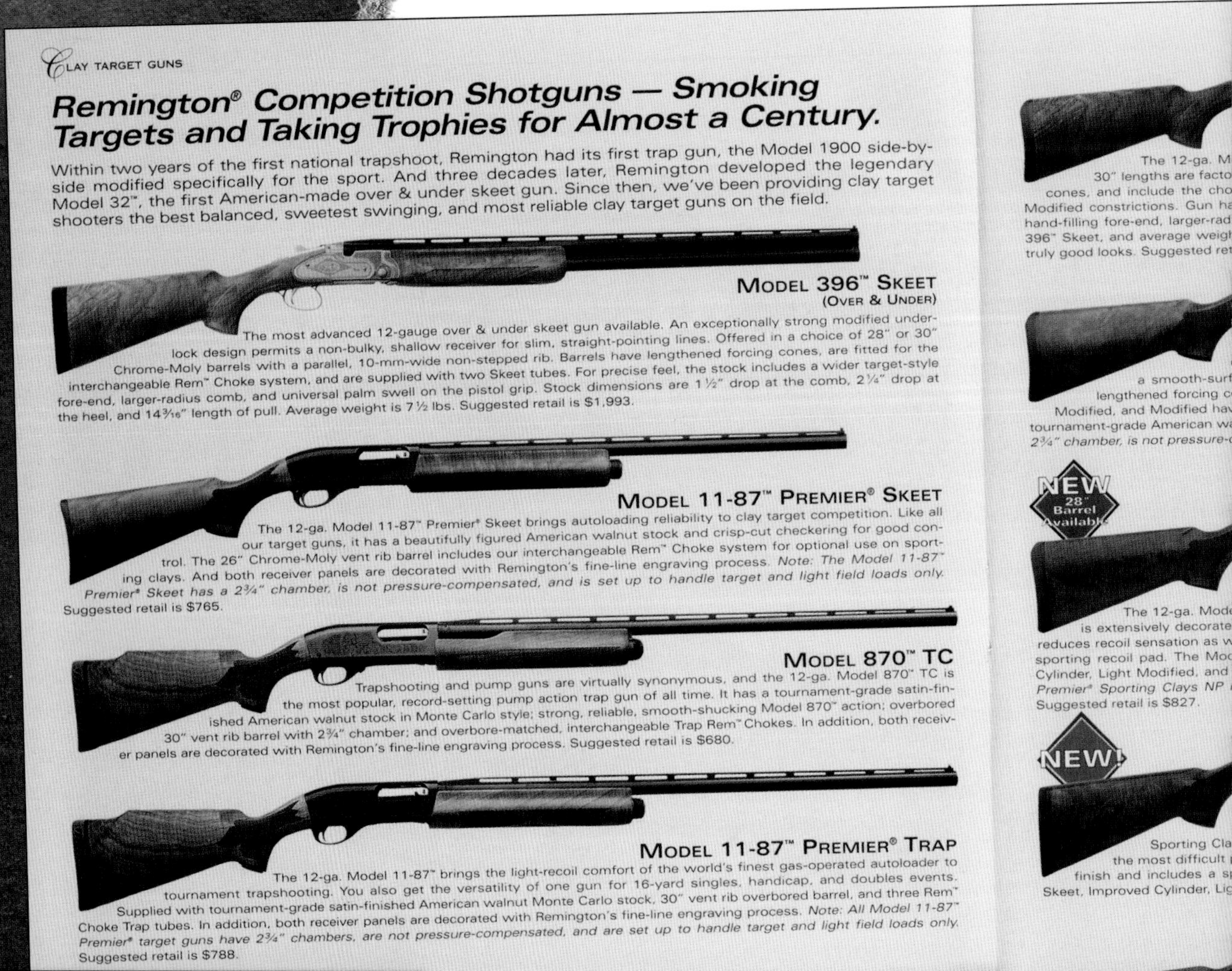

Remington® Competition Shotguns — Smoking Targets and Taking Trophies for Almost a Century.

Within two years of the first national trapshoot, Remington had its first trap gun, the Model 1900 side-by-side modified specifically for the sport. And three decades later, Remington developed the legendary Model 32™, the first American-made over & under skeet gun. Since then, we've been providing clay target shooters the best balanced, sweetest swinging, and most reliable clay target guns on the field.

MODEL 396™ SKEET
(OVER & UNDER)

The most advanced 12-gauge over & under skeet gun available. An exceptionally strong modified under-lock design permits a non-bulky, shallow receiver for slim, straight-pointing lines. Offered in a choice of 28" or 30" Chrome-Moly barrels with a parallel, 10-mm-wide non-stepped rib. Barrels have lengthened forcing cones, are fitted for the interchangeable Rem™ Choke system, and are supplied with two Skeet tubes. For precise feel, the stock includes a wider target-style fore-end, larger-radius comb, and universal palm swell on the pistol grip. Stock dimensions are 1½" drop at the comb, 2¼" drop at the heel, and 14³⁄₁₆" length of pull. Average weight is 7½ lbs. Suggested retail is $1,993.

MODEL 11-87™ PREMIER® SKEET

The 12-ga. Model 11-87™ Premier® Skeet brings autoloading reliability to clay target competition. Like all our target guns, it has a beautifully figured American walnut stock and crisp-cut checkering for good control. The 26" Chrome-Moly vent rib barrel includes our interchangeable Rem™ Choke system for optional use on sporting clays. And both receiver panels are decorated with Remington's fine-line engraving process. *Note: The Model 11-87™ Premier® Skeet has a 2¾" chamber, is not pressure-compensated, and is set up to handle target and light field loads only.* Suggested retail is $765.

MODEL 870™ TC

Trapshooting and pump guns are virtually synonymous, and the 12-ga. Model 870™ TC is the most popular, record-setting pump action trap gun of all time. It has a tournament-grade satin-finished American walnut stock in Monte Carlo style; strong, reliable, smooth-shucking Model 870™ action; overbored 30" vent rib barrel with 2¾" chamber; and overbore-matched, interchangeable Trap Rem™ Chokes. In addition, both receiver panels are decorated with Remington's fine-line engraving process. Suggested retail is $680.

MODEL 11-87™ PREMIER® TRAP

The 12-ga. Model 11-87™ brings the light-recoil comfort of the world's finest gas-operated autoloader to tournament trapshooting. You also get the versatility of one gun for 16-yard singles, handicap, and doubles events. Supplied with tournament-grade satin-finished American walnut Monte Carlo stock, 30" vent rib overbored barrel, and three Rem™ Choke Trap tubes. In addition, both receiver panels are decorated with Remington's fine-line engraving process. *Note: All Model 11-87™ Premier® target guns have 2¾" chambers, are not pressure-compensated, and are set up to handle target and light field loads only.* Suggested retail is $788.

1998

Remington.
COUNTRY

MODEL 396™ SKEET

(right column, partially visible)

The 12-ga. M... 30" lengths are facto... cones, and include the cho... Modified constrictions. Gun ha... hand-filling fore-end, larger-rad... 396" Skeet, and average weigh... truly good looks. Suggested ret...

a smooth-surf... lengthened forcing c... Modified, and Modified ha... tournament-grade American wa... 2¾" chamber, is not pressure-c...

NEW 28 Barrel Available

The 12-ga. Mode... is extensively decorate... reduces recoil sensation as w... sporting recoil pad. The Mod... Cylinder, Light Modified, and ... Premier® Sporting Clays NP ... Suggested retail is $827.

NEW!

Sporting Cla... the most difficult ... finish and includes a s... Skeet, Improved Cylinder, Lig...

stock has ... Choke tubes in ... both skeet and uplan...

Gun Di...

	Barrel Length
396" Skeet	30"
	28"
11-87" Premier' Skeet	26"
870" TC	30"
11-87" Premier' Trap	30"

SPORTING CLAYS HYPE

While the 870 continues to be produced in the TC trap version, the growing popularity of the game of sporting clays in the 1990s saw Remington producing more semi-automatics geared to better fit the inherent variety of that sport. This catalog spread is from 1998.

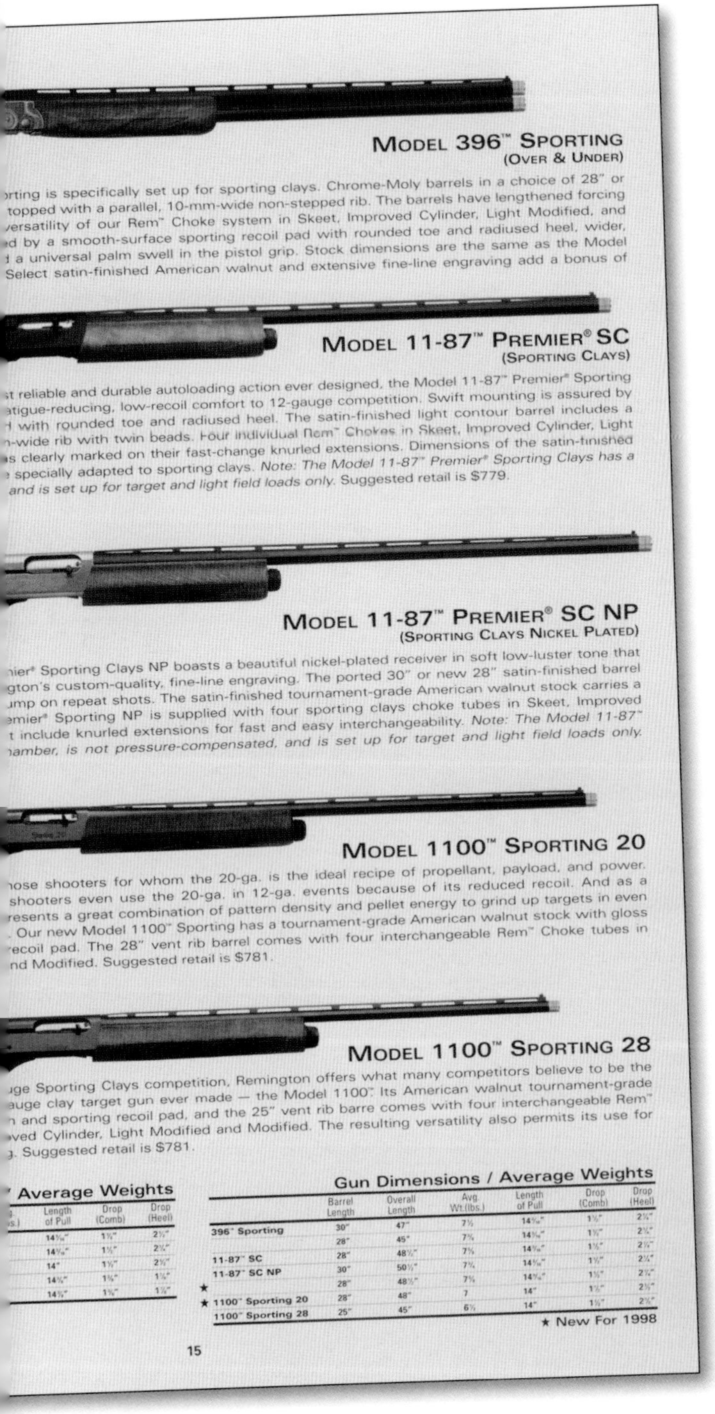
MODEL 396™ SPORTING
(OVER & UNDER)

orting is specifically set up for sporting clays. Chrome-Moly barrels in a choice of 28" or
topped with a parallel, 10-mm-wide non-stepped rib. The barrels have lengthened forcing
versatility of our Rem™ Choke system in Skeet, Improved Cylinder, Light Modified, and
ed by a smooth-surface sporting recoil pad with rounded toe and radiused heel, wider,
d a universal palm swell in the pistol grip. Stock dimensions are the same as the Model
Select satin-finished American walnut and extensive fine-line engraving add a bonus of

MODEL 11-87™ PREMIER® SC
(SPORTING CLAYS)

st reliable and durable autoloading action ever designed, the Model 11-87™ Premier® Sporting
atigue-reducing, low-recoil comfort to 12-gauge competition. Swift mounting is assured by
d with rounded toe and radiused heel. The satin-finished light contour barrel includes a
n-wide rib with twin beads. Four individual Rem™ Chokes in Skeet, Improved Cylinder, Light
as clearly marked on their fast-change knurled extensions. Dimensions of the satin-finished
e specially adapted to sporting clays. *Note: The Model 11-87™ Premier® Sporting Clays has a*
and is set up for target and light field loads only. Suggested retail is $779.

MODEL 11-87™ PREMIER® SC NP
(SPORTING CLAYS NICKEL PLATED)

nier® Sporting Clays NP boasts a beautiful nickel-plated receiver in soft low-luster tone that
gton's custom-quality, fine-line engraving. The ported 30" or new 28" satin-finished barrel
ump on repeat shots. The satin-finished tournament-grade American walnut stock carries a
emier® Sporting NP is supplied with four sporting clays choke tubes in Skeet, Improved
t include knurled extensions for fast and easy interchangeability. *Note: The Model 11-87™*
hamber, is not pressure-compensated, and is set up for target and light field loads only.

MODEL 1100™ SPORTING 20

hose shooters for whom the 20-ga. is the ideal recipe of propellant, payload, and power.
shooters even use the 20-ga. in 12-ga. events because of its reduced recoil. And as a
resents a great combination of pattern density and pellet energy to grind up targets in even
. Our new Model 1100™ Sporting has a tournament-grade American walnut stock with gloss
recoil pad. The 28" vent rib barrel comes with four interchangeable Rem™ Choke tubes in
nd Modified. Suggested retail is $781.

MODEL 1100™ SPORTING 28

uge Sporting Clays competition, Remington offers what many competitors believe to be the
auge clay target gun ever made — the Model 1100™. Its American walnut tournament-grade
n and sporting recoil pad, and the 25" vent rib barre comes with four interchangeable Rem™
oved Cylinder, Light Modified and Modified. The resulting versatility also permits its use for
g. Suggested retail is $781.

Average Weights

s.)	Length of Pull	Drop (Comb)	Drop (Heel)
	14⅜"	1½"	2½"
	14⅜"	1½"	2¼"
	14"	1½"	2½"
	14⅜"	1⅜"	1¾"
	14⅜"	1⅜"	1⅞"

Gun Dimensions / Average Weights

	Barrel Length	Overall Length	Avg. Wt.(lbs.)	Length of Pull	Drop (Comb)	Drop (Heel)
396™ Sporting	30"	47"	7½	14⅜"	1½"	2¼"
	28"	45"	7⅜	14⅜"	1½"	2¼"
11-87™ SC	28"	48½"	7⅝	14⅜"	1½"	2½"
11-87™ SC NP	30"	50½"	7¾	14⅜"	1½"	2¼"
★	28"	48½"	7⅝	14⅜"	1½"	2½"
★ 1100™ Sporting 20	28"	48"	7	14"	1½"	2½"
1100™ Sporting 28	25"	45"	6½	14"	1½"	2½"

★ New For 1998

15

Unfortunately, even though the Remington Model 870 is perhaps the world's most popular shotgun, its use on the skeet fields does not compare with its popularity elsewhere. That is no fault of the gun. It used to be that the vast majority of shotguns seen on a typical skeet field were pump guns. Just take a look at some of the old photos from the 1940s and '50s. A typical skeet squad would have more than half its shooters armed with pump guns. When I was a kid and started shooting skeet in the 1950s, there were just as many pump gunners as there were those who shot autoloaders. That, of course, is not the case today. There still may be shooting clubs in parts of America where the pump gun is a common sight, but, for the most part, it is the over/under and autoloader that have taken over the skeet fields in America.

Be that as it may, during the time when pump guns were popular with skeet shooters, the Remington Model 870 played a very big role, winning many championships from coast to coast. Just as with the trap guns, the Model 870 skeet guns tended to have a very good balance for the sport for which it was intended, especially given the American style of skeet, where the gun is premounted before the call for the bird. Although not quite as nose-heavy as the trap guns, the Model 870 skeet guns nevertheless had a much better balance for the discipline than many other pump-actions on the market. Still, the pump gun lost its popularity in the skeet fields and sales of the Model 870 SA and other models, such as the SX that came out in 1959, continued to drop. Remington finally decided to discontinue the Model 870 SA, in 1982.

As fated as the decline of the pump gun's popularity on clay target fields may have been, the action's demise also prevented the Model 870 from capitalizing on the tremendous growth in the arena of sporting clays. Although there are some brave souls who will tackle a sporting clays fields with a pump gun, by and large, this is a clay shooting sport confined to autoloaders and over/under shotguns. And, while the pump makes an appearance now and again as a side game in a clays tournament, no one would say this is a popular gun for the sport. For Remington, that means there are no sporting clays models of the 870. However, there is no reason why a pump gun could not be successfully used in this sport. Keep in mind that, in the 1930s, '40s, '50s, and possibly even into the 1960s, many a skeet tournament was won by

SKEET, TRAP & SPORTING CLAYS

RECORD-SETTING CLAY TARGET GUNS
THAT STAND THE TEST OF TIME

Whenever a clay target shooter refers to his shotgun as "Old Reliable," it's more than likely the shotgun is a Remington®. It may be one that's been used without interruption for thirty years, or one that has recently been rediscovered as still superior to a temporary replacement. That's not surprising. More clay target records have been set with currently available Remington shotguns than any others.

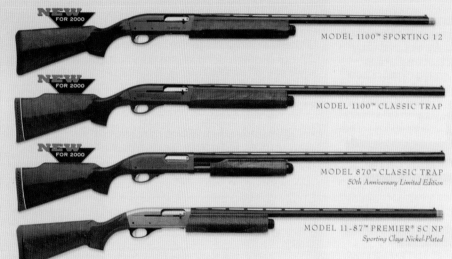

MODEL 1100™ SPORTING 12

MODEL 1100™ CLASSIC TRAP

MODEL 870™ CLASSIC TRAP
50th Anniversary Limited Edition

MODEL 11-87™ PREMIER® SC NP
Sporting Clays Nickel-Plated

32

No company has a richer tradition in the clay target sports, or has built more successful and widely acclaimed shotguns for them than Remington. When competitive trapshooting started, Remington shotguns were the first specifically made for the sport. And competitive skeet shooting actually began at our own gun club. Those early squads were always filled with Remingtons.

In fact, if the names of gun models were also listed, the record books would be filled with the name Remington. More competitive skeet records have been set with the light-recoiling, flinch-preventing Remington **Model 1100™** autoloader than any other shotgun. It's never gone away. Today, you'll find it showing up again in more and more championship shoot-offs.

Serious clay target shooters learn fast from experience. And that experience is unquestionably behind the trend back to autoloading actions in 12-gauge clay target competition — trap, skeet and sporting clays. These high-volume shooting sports require lots of practice and often, several hundred targets

BORN-AGAIN CLASSIC
Reintroduced in 2000 was the 870 Classic Trap, with its better wood and upgraded finish.

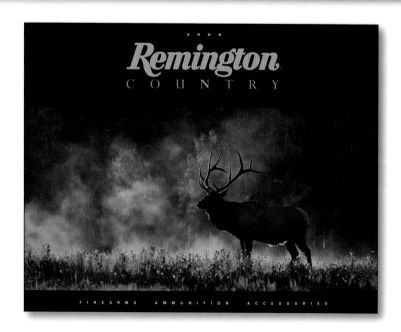

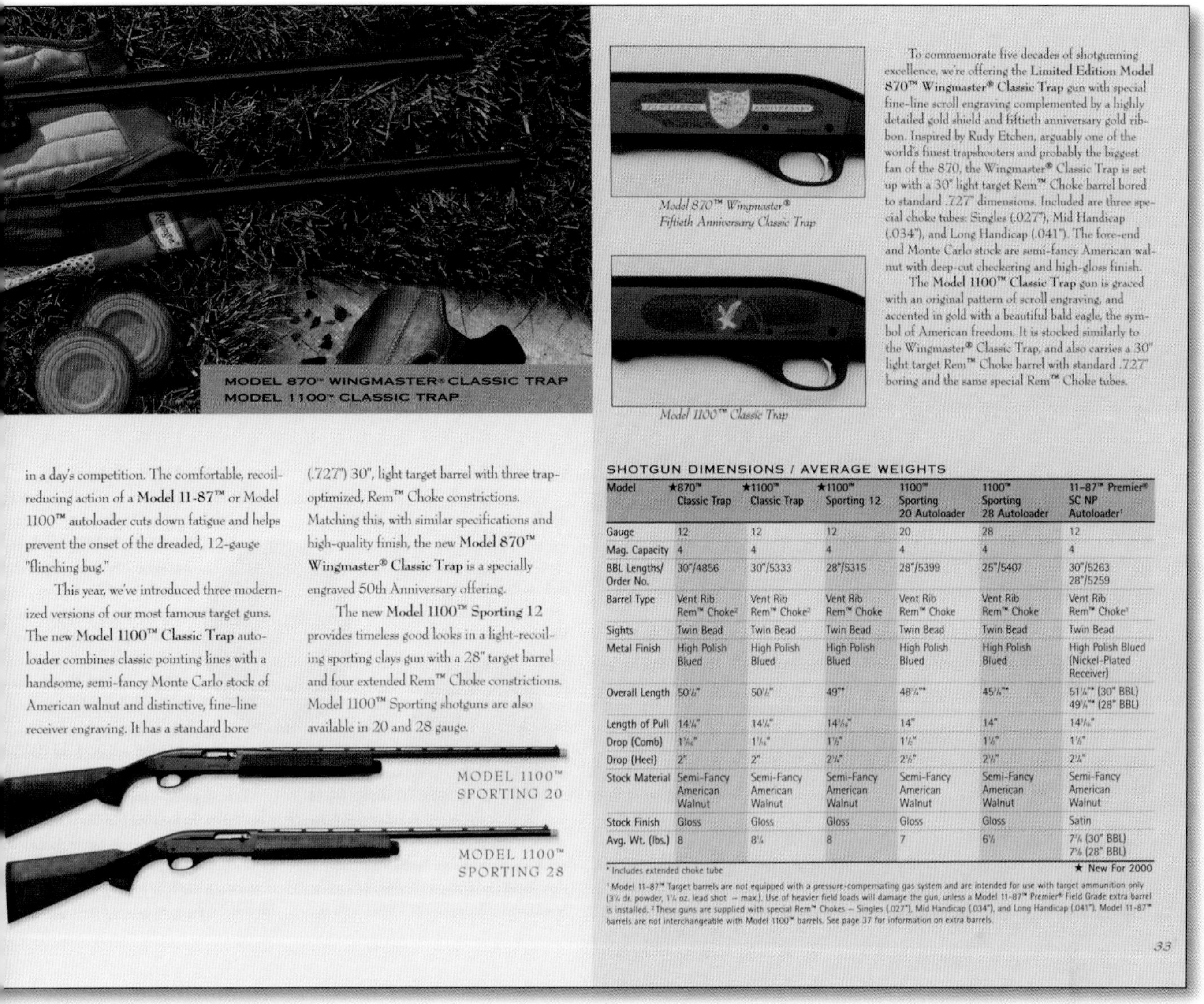

MODEL 870™ WINGMASTER® CLASSIC TRAP
MODEL 1100™ CLASSIC TRAP

Model 870™ Wingmaster® Fiftieth Anniversary Classic Trap

To commemorate five decades of shotgunning excellence, we're offering the **Limited Edition Model 870™ Wingmaster® Classic Trap** gun with special fine-line scroll engraving complemented by a highly detailed gold shield and fiftieth anniversary gold ribbon. Inspired by Rudy Etchen, arguably one of the world's finest trapshooters and probably the biggest fan of the 870, the Wingmaster® Classic Trap is set up with a 30" light target Rem™ Choke barrel bored to standard .727" dimensions. Included are three special choke tubes: Singles (.027"), Mid Handicap (.034"), and Long Handicap (.041"). The fore-end and Monte Carlo stock are semi-fancy American walnut with deep-cut checkering and high-gloss finish.

The **Model 1100™ Classic Trap** gun is graced with an original pattern of scroll engraving, and accented in gold with a beautiful bald eagle, the symbol of American freedom. It is stocked similarly to the Wingmaster® Classic Trap, and also carries a 30" light target Rem™ Choke barrel with standard .727" boring and the same special Rem™ Choke tubes.

Model 1100™ Classic Trap

in a day's competition. The comfortable, recoil-reducing action of a **Model 11-87™** or Model 1100™ autoloader cuts down fatigue and helps prevent the onset of the dreaded, 12-gauge "flinching bug."

This year, we've introduced three modernized versions of our most famous target guns. The new **Model 1100™ Classic Trap** autoloader combines classic pointing lines with a handsome, semi-fancy Monte Carlo stock of American walnut and distinctive, fine-line receiver engraving. It has a standard bore (.727") 30", light target barrel with three trap-optimized, Rem™ Choke constrictions. Matching this, with similar specifications and high-quality finish, the new **Model 870™ Wingmaster® Classic Trap** is a specially engraved 50th Anniversary offering.

The new **Model 1100™ Sporting 12** provides timeless good looks in a light-recoiling sporting clays gun with a 28" target barrel and four extended Rem™ Choke constrictions. Model 1100™ Sporting shotguns are also available in 20 and 28 gauge.

MODEL 1100™ SPORTING 20

MODEL 1100™ SPORTING 28

SHOTGUN DIMENSIONS / AVERAGE WEIGHTS

Model	★870™ Classic Trap	★1100™ Classic Trap	★1100™ Sporting 12	1100™ Sporting 20 Autoloader	1100™ Sporting 28 Autoloader	11-87™ Premier® SC NP Autoloader[1]
Gauge	12	12	12	20	28	12
Mag. Capacity	4	4	4	4	4	4
BBL Lengths/ Order No.	30"/4856	30"/5333	28"/5315	28"/5399	25"/5407	30"/5263 28"/5259
Barrel Type	Vent Rib Rem™ Choke[2]	Vent Rib Rem™ Choke[2]	Vent Rib Rem™ Choke	Vent Rib Rem™ Choke	Vent Rib Rem™ Choke	Vent Rib Rem™ Choke[1]
Sights	Twin Bead	Twin Bead	Twin Bead	Twin Bead	Twin Bead	Twin Bead
Metal Finish	High Polish Blued	High Polish Blued	High Polish Blued	High Polish Blued	High Polish Blued	High Polish Blued (Nickel-Plated Receiver)
Overall Length	50½"	50½"	49"*	48¾"*	45¾"*	51¼"* (30" BBL) 49¼"* (28" BBL)
Length of Pull	14¼"	14¼"	14 3/16"	14"	14"	14 3/16"
Drop (Comb)	1 7/16"	1 7/16"	1½"	1½"	1½"	1½"
Drop (Heel)	2"	2"	2¼"	2½"	2½"	2¼"
Stock Material	Semi-Fancy American Walnut	Semi-Fancy American Walnut	Semi-Fancy American Walnut	Semi-Fancy American Walnut	Semi-Fancy American Walnut	Semi-Fancy American Walnut
Stock Finish	Gloss	Gloss	Gloss	Gloss	Gloss	Satin
Avg. Wt. (lbs.)	8	8¼	8	7	6½	7¾ (30" BBL) 7⅝ (28" BBL)

* Includes extended choke tube ★ New For 2000

[1] Model 11-87™ Target barrels are not equipped with a pressure-compensating gas system and are intended for use with target ammunition only (3¼ dr. powder, 1⅛ oz. lead shot – max.). Use of heavier field loads will damage the gun, unless a Model 11-87™ Premier® Field Grade extra barrel is installed. [2] These guns are supplied with special Rem™ Chokes – Singles (.027"), Mid Handicap (.034"), and Long Handicap (.041"). Model 11-87™ barrels are not interchangeable with Model 1100™ barrels. See page 37 for information on extra barrels.

33

a pump gunner. And, in the 1950s and '60s, many skeet tournaments were won with the Model 870!

Shotgun popularity, like everything else, depends heavily on prevailing trends. In the last several decades, the pump gun has lost favor with clay target shooters. I believe that has more to do with trends and fashion than the actual usefulness of the slide-action shotgun. Some claim that the pump gun isn't fast enough, that an autoloader or an over/under is much faster for the second shot. That is very debatable. Going back to Winchester's exhibition shooter Herb Parsons and on to more recent times with Tom Knapp when he shot for Benelli using the Nova pump gun, both men proved that a pump gun could be just as fast if not faster than an autoloader. Also, keep in mind that the first 100 straight in trap doubles at the Grand American was accomplished by Rudy Etchen with his 870! So, a pump gun such as the 870 could be used very successfully, in skilled hands, for the game of sporting clays.

If Remington was ever to put together a neat sporting clays version of the 870, such as the ones it as in its autoloader Model 1100 and the Model 11-87, I believe the pump gun could re-enter the clay shooting world has a viable shotgun action. Unfortunately, I don't think that will ever happen. Remington is selling plenty of 870s as it is, so it is highly unlikely anyone could persuade the company to make a special and dedicated sporting clays version when you take into account that the pump gun is no longer considered a practical shotgun for the discipline. In my opinion, that's too bad.

CHAPTER SIX

UPLAND SHOTGUNS

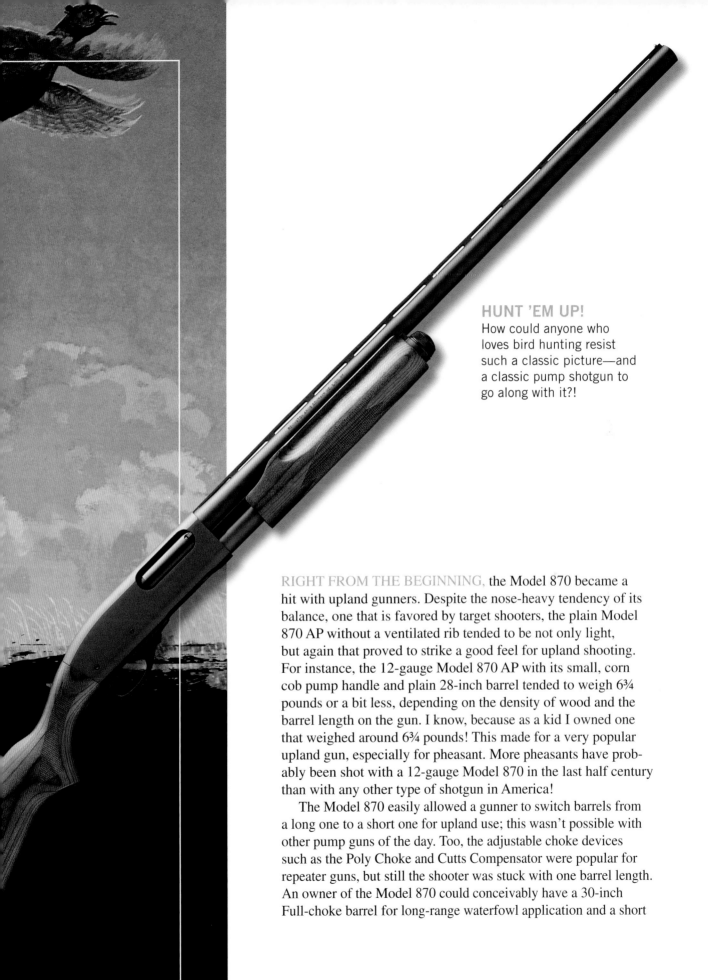

HUNT 'EM UP!
How could anyone who loves bird hunting resist such a classic picture—and a classic pump shotgun to go along with it?!

RIGHT FROM THE BEGINNING, the Model 870 became a hit with upland gunners. Despite the nose-heavy tendency of its balance, one that is favored by target shooters, the plain Model 870 AP without a ventilated rib tended to be not only light, but again that proved to strike a good feel for upland shooting. For instance, the 12-gauge Model 870 AP with its small, corn cob pump handle and plain 28-inch barrel tended to weigh 6¾ pounds or a bit less, depending on the density of wood and the barrel length on the gun. I know, because as a kid I owned one that weighed around 6¾ pounds! This made for a very popular upland gun, especially for pheasant. More pheasants have probably been shot with a 12-gauge Model 870 in the last half century than with any other type of shotgun in America!

The Model 870 easily allowed a gunner to switch barrels from a long one to a short one for upland use; this wasn't possible with other pump guns of the day. Too, the adjustable choke devices such as the Poly Choke and Cutts Compensator were popular for repeater guns, but still the shooter was stuck with one barrel length. An owner of the Model 870 could conceivably have a 30-inch Full-choke barrel for long-range waterfowl application and a short

The sport of trap may have paved the way for the Model 870, but it was hunters who flocked to the gun in droves, thanks to its utter reliability and a price point that fit almost every wallet. Today, this gun is as handsome as ever and still easy on the bank account.

In smaller gauges, the older fixed-choke Model 870s made for delightful upland guns. Receivers were shaved down from the 12-gauge model, and barrels were thinner, making them less nose-heavy and thus more responsive for use on pheasants, quail, and the like.

26-inch Improved Cylinder barrel for upland gunning. With a shorter barrel, the gun was lighter and faster to mount and swing, something that the fixed-barrel guns, even with their adjustable chokes, just could not offer.

In smaller gauges, the Model 870 made for even a better upland gun. In 16-gauge, it was listed as weighing 6½ pounds and, in many instances, especially in the plain AP model, it weighed even less. In 20-gauge, it was listed at 6¼ pounds, and just as with the 16-gauge, some 20-gauge models weighed less than the advertised weight. All in all, in smaller gauges, the Model 870 made for a delightful upland gun. The receivers of the 20-gauges were "shaved" and slightly smaller than the 12-/16-gauge receiver and, because the barrels were thinner, the guns tended to have less of a nose-heavy feel than the 12-gauges had. Although as a kid I lugged around the 12-gauge Model 870 AP that weighed 6¾ pounds, I would have cut my right arm off for a 16- or 20-gauge that weighed even less. I sure logged in a lot of miles carrying that 12-gauge gun over hills and whatnot.

When Remington came out with the scaled-down 28-gauge and .410-bore versions, in 1969, they first appeared as skeet guns. But almost right away, Remington realized these same guns could also be used for upland hunting use, and field versions appeared almost immediately. They were popular, especially in 28-gauge, but that chambering didn't quite have the following in the early 1970s that it has today, and no earth-shattering sales records were set in the field versions of the scaled-down Model 870s.

Remington, Reports

How much should you pay for a beginner's shotgun?

You can buy a cheap beginner's shotgun for next to nothing. But you may be doing yourself and the beginner a great disservice. We recommend our Model 1100 automatic or Model 870 "Wingmaster" pump action in either the 28 or 410 gauge. And there are a number of good reasons why—for you as well as for the beginner.

Our small-gauge Models 1100 and 870 are shotguns that any beginner will be comfortable with. Equally important, they're guns the beginner will not outgrow as proficiency increases. And they have a versatility that even the most experienced shooter will find challenging.

Our small-gauge shotguns are very easy to handle. One reason is their light weight and fine balance. The other reason is design. Both the 1100 and the 870 are made to fit you. The grip, for example, is thinner—so it's more comfortable.

In the 1100, the exclusive recoil-reduction system helps get you on the second shot quicker than any other automatic shotgun. Recoil sensation is kept to a minimum. You feel a gentle push instead of a punch. And there isn't a beginner around who won't appreciate that feature.

Another feature of the 1100 is its great reliability. It works beautifully—in any weather, under any firing conditions. In endurance/performance tests conducted by Remington engineers, malfunction rates for the 1100 were **less than one-half of one percent.** We think it's the world's most reliable shotgun. A lot of shotgun shooters evidently think so, too. It's the best-selling automatic made.

Our Model 870 "Wingmaster" is no slouch, either. This popular pump-action shotgun works smoothly and naturally for you. Recoil tends to force a barrel up and back. The 870's pump action

actually lets you make use of this force to help bring the fore-end back to eject the hull. Then, the forward motion of your hand, which chambers the next shell, helps bring the gun back on target, ready to shoot, with no wasted time. Thus, your natural reactions to recoil help keep your shotgun under constant control ...and ready for that second shot.

The small-gauge story. For someone just starting out, our 410 and 28-gauge shotguns are ideal. True, both these gauges have less shot in their shells than, say, the 12 or 20 gauges. But the range and percent of shot in the pattern are the same. And the shot hits just as hard. For small game such as rabbits, woodcock and squirrels, the 410 and 28 gauges are just right. And a shooter who becomes proficient in these gauges will do far better when shooting the 12 or 20. In short, learning on the 410 and 28 is excellent training for the beginner. It's also a great way for the experienced shooter to sharpen up his skills—in the field or at skeet.

Both the 1100 and the 870 are made with interchangeable barrels. So within gauge and chamber lengths you can select from a variety of chokes to suit different hunting and shooting needs.

Prices for the Model 1100 start at $199.95* for both the 28 and the 410 gauge. Prices for the Model 870 start at $144.95* for the 28 and 410 gauge. This might seem like a lot of money for a "first" gun for son or wife or daughter. But consider this. With any of these guns, you're getting the finest-quality shotguns we make. The receivers, for example, are solid steel, not aluminum as in some other shotguns.

In the long run, you'll save money by starting with the small-gauge 1100 and 870. Because they'll be used for more than just a couple of seasons. Besides, when the beginner is proficient enough to appreciate quality, he's going to want a Remington anyway. So it pays to start at the top.

And it pays to use Remington shotgun shells. They're the tops in reliable performance, too. Besides, they're the shotgun shells we use to test the Models 1100 and 870—so you know they're right for those guns.

"Remington Reports" are based on facts documented by the people who design and make our products. For more information, write for a free copy of our latest full-color catalog: Remington Arms Company, Inc., Dept. 119, Bridgeport, Connecticut 06602.

Remington. DUPONT

Great guns deserve great ammunition. We make both.

"Remington" and "Wingmaster" are trademarks registered in the United States Patent Office. *Suggested minimum price, subject to change without notice.

REMINGTON PUMP ACTION SHOTGUN

MODEL 870 "WINGMASTER"

Remington Model 870 Shotgun

In 1972, Remington announced the introduction of the scaled frame 20-gauge Model 870, the "Lightweight" LW in both 2¾-inch and 3-inch chamberings. The 20-gauge Model 870 LW was aimed directly at the upland gunners, and it succeeded. The Model 870 20-gauge LW was listed as being about 6 pounds with a ventilated rib, and under 6 pounds with a plain barrel. As the saying goes, it was a "natural," as an upland gun. It had all the right ingredients. It was light, slim, and easy to grasp when carrying, which is what upland gunners do a lot! It was quick to mount and fast to swing and shoot. For all practical purposes, as a pump gun, it was a perfect upland gun. In fact, Remington tried to capitalize on the small size and weight of the new 20-gauge model by advertising it as the "perfect upland gun." The ads of the period showed

a picture of a hunter struggling to carry a huge, oversized gun, with the caption reading, "You don't have to feel like this at the end of a long day." That 1972 advertisement starts with that caption, which then leads into a lengthy paragraph explaining the advantages of a lighter gun and claiming the weight of 5¾ pounds with a plain 26-inch barrel. It was an effective ad, and not a hard sell at all, and many upland gunners bought the new 20-gauge.

By 1972, Remington had dropped the Model 870 AP in its field guns, making it available only as a short-barreled police gun in 12-gauge that was called the Model 870 R. The new scaled-down 20-, like the earlier 28-gauge and .410-bore was, instead, made available in the Deluxe ADL version only, with a semi-beavertail fore-arm that, naturally, added weight. However, like

4
5
Special Purpose Shotguns
When extra stealth can mean the extra edge.
Model 870™ SP Cantilever Scope Mount Deer Gun
Model SP-10™ Special Purpose Shotgun

Remington Special Purpose Shotguns are designed for those hunting situations that require an extraordinary level of performance and concealment. The perfect choice for waterfowl, turkey and deer hunters.
All of the time-tested Remington autoloader and pump action design features are here. The receivers are machined from a solid billet of ordnance-grade steel for strength. The gas operating system is designed to function with a minimum of cleaning. The pump actions are built around Remington's famous twin action bars for fail-safe feeding and ejection. And the stocks and fore-ends are American walnut with deep cut checkering.
You'll never be given away by a Remington SP. The wood is coated with a special finish that protects against moisture but won't reflect light. The barrels and receivers have a non-reflective finish that resists rust and corrosion. And every Remington SP comes with a detachable camo sling made of tough Cordura® nylon.
All SPs use the Rem™ Choke system, providing you with just the right pattern, whatever your shooting needs. Available screw-in chokes include a "Turkey Extra Full," which gives you the extra-tight pattern that's ideal for turkey hunters.
MODEL SP-10™
This Special Purpose 10-gauge is the ultimate autoloader for today's waterfowler. The devastating power of the SP-10 enables you to make shots with lead or steel at ranges that would be marginal for other guns. The SP-10 will put one-third more shot into the pattern at 40 yards than most 12-gauge guns.
But this extra power doesn't mean extra recoil. The SP-10's unique stainless steel gas operating system, in which the cylinder moves instead of the piston, spreads out and softens recoil so you can stay on target for a second and third shot.

SP-10™ MAGNUM AUTOLOADING SHOTGUNS
Gauge	Barrel Length & Choke	Overall Length	Avg. Wt. (lbs.)	Order Numbers
10	30" Rem™ Choke	51½"	11	4808
	26" Rem Choke	47½"	10¾	4812
Gun supplied with Full, Mod. and Turkey Extra Full (lead shot only) choke tubes. Important Note: Critical components—including the barrel, bolt assembly and trigger plate assembly of the Remington SP-10 and other 10-gauge shotguns—are not interchangeable with previously manufactured autoloaders.
Nominal stock dimensions: 14" length of pull, 1½" drop at comb, 2½" drop at heel.

MODEL 11-87™ SPECIAL PURPOSE SHOTGUNS
Gauge	Barrel Length & Choke	Overall Length	Avg. Wt. (lbs.)	Order Numbers 3" Chambers[1]
12	28" Rem™ Choke (Vent Rib)	48¼"	8¼	9905★
	26" Rem Choke (Vent Rib)	46"	8⅛	9906
	21" Rem Choke Deer Gun[2] w/cantilever scope mount, rings[‡]	41"	8½	9839
	21" Rem Choke Deer Gun[2] w/rifle sights[‡]	41"	8	9837
Nominal stock dimensions: 14" length of pull, 1½" drop at comb, 2½" drop at heel.
Nominal stock dimensions: (Cantilever Deer Guns): 14⅜" length of pull, 1⅛" drop at comb, 1¾" drop at heel.

MODEL 870™ SPECIAL PURPOSE SHOTGUNS
Gauge	Barrel Length & Choke	Overall Length	Avg. Wt. (lbs.)	Order Numbers 3" Chambers[1]
12	28" Rem™ Choke (Vent Rib)	48½"	7⅜	4866★
	26" Rem Choke (Vent Rib)	46½"	7¼	4862
	20" Rem Choke Deer Gun w/cantilever scope mount, rings[‡]	40½"	8	4877
	20" Rem Choke Deer Gun w/rifle sights[‡]	40½"	7¼	4875
[‡]All 12-gauge Rem Choke deer shotguns supplied with a Rifled choke tube and Imp. Cyl. tube. [1]All 3" chambers handle 2¾" shells. [2]These barrels are not equipped with a pressure compensating gas system. **Scope not included. ★New for 1990.
Nominal stock dimensions: 14" length of pull, 1½" drop at comb, 2½" drop at heel.
Nominal stock dimensions: (Cantilever Deer Guns): 14⅜" length of pull, 1⅛" drop at comb, 2" drop at heel.

Model 870™ SP's
CANTILEVER SCOPE MOUNT 870™ DEER GUN
Designed for those deer hunting conditions that call for the moderate range of a shotgun and the sighting advantages of a scope. The cantilever mount locks the scope to the barrel to insure greater accuracy. Comes with Rifled and Imp. Cyl. Rem Choke Tubes.
RIFLE SIGHTED 870™ SP DEER GUN
20" Barrel. Dull finish for concealment. Rifled and Imp. Cyl. Rem Choke Tubes for flexibility.
VENT RIB 870™ SP
The positive feel of a pump with 26" or 28" Vent Rib barrels.
Model 11-87™ SP's
CANTILEVER SCOPE MOUNT 11-87™ DEER GUN
Autoloading performance with the sight-enhancing characteristics of a barrel-mounted scope for accuracy. Rem Chokes for slugs or buckshot. Scope rings included.
RIFLE SIGHTED 11-87™ SP DEER GUN
A 21" barrel with Rifled and Imp. Cyl. Rem™ Chokes.
VENT RIB 11-87™ SP
The most versatile autoloader ever. Its exclusive pressure-compensating (PC) gas system handles any shell, from 2-3/4" field loads to 3" magnums in any combination. Available with 26" or 28" barrels.
Model 870™ SP Deer Gun
Model 870™ SP Vent Rib
Model 11-87™ SP Cantilever Scope Mount Deer Gun**
Model 11-87™ SP Deer Gun
Model 11-87™ SP Vent Rib

870s EVERYWHERE
By 1990, Remington was showing its depth, churning out Model 870s in a huge array of task-specific variations.

Remington
1990 Firearms & Ammunition Catalog

the smaller gauges, it was stocked in mahogany, a wood lighter than walnut. The early 20-gauges (without the Rem Choke barrels), often weighed less than the advertised 6 pounds. I've seen some with a plain barrel that were closer to 5¾ pounds. The current guns stocked in walnut and with Rem Chokes tend to weigh around 6½ pounds.

Because of its light weight, the 20-gauge LW in the 3-inch chambering became quite popular with pheasant hunters, although the 2¾-inch chambered gun was more than adequate for normal pheasant hunting, especially over a dog. So, the 20-gauge LW was an undeniable hit with upland hunters, but, at the time it came out, the 12-gauge still ruled the roost—just as it does today. Back in the day, the 12-gauge was even more dominant. Heck, it was considered almost *unmanly* for a grown man to be afield with a 20-gauge, despite the strong push by the manufacturers and gun writers of the era. So, the 20-gauge LW was more or less relegated to young shooters and women. Meanwhile, those knowledgeable upland gunners without ego snatched up the little pump

guns and happily carried them in the uplands, totally ignoring the popular trends.

In 1984, Remington came out with a Model 870 Special Field in 12- and 20-gauge, a radically different approach to the traditional pump gun. The Special Field models had short, 21-inch barrels and, harkening back to early twentieth century, a straight, English-grip stock. The magazine tube was also shortened and the forearm slimmed down some, so that the gun overall had a much more muzzle-light feel. In fact, many complained that the gun was too whippy up front and failed to provide enough weight for a smooth swing. Whatever the case may be, there were those who loved the new abbreviated versions and swore by these stubby pump guns.

By this time, Remington had developed a machine checkering system that provided the Special Field models with very nice cut checkering, eliminating what many had come to consider the "tacky looking" impressed *fleur de lis* pattern that Remington had used for many years. Also, the glossy RKW finish was abandoned on the Special Field models and the wood on these guns was given a satin look a lá an oil finish. Naturally, because of the shortened magazine tube and shorter barrel, as well as the slimmed down wood, the Special Field models weighed less than the regular models.

I've met several people through the years who absolutely loved the Special Field. I knew one fellow who had one, when I was in Ecuador, from 1984 through 1986. He worked for AID and was stationed with the Embassy in Quito and hunted mostly *perdiz*, the close-flushing South American tinamou that is quite abundant in that area. He loved his stubby-barreled Special Field. However, had he been stationed in Guayaquil, in the lowlands where I was, I think he would have had different thoughts about it. In the lowlands, we shot mostly dove, pigeon, and duck, all three species that required some barrel length for a smooth swing. Clearly, the Special Field models weren't everyone's answer to a dedicated upland pump gun.

With the introduction of the Rem Choke system, the barrel walls became thicker and the

Introduced in 1984, the Special Field 870 had a short, 21-inch barrel and a straight, English-style grip. The magazine was proportionally shortened, as well. Many fell for this svelte little gun and swore by it as a hunting partner.

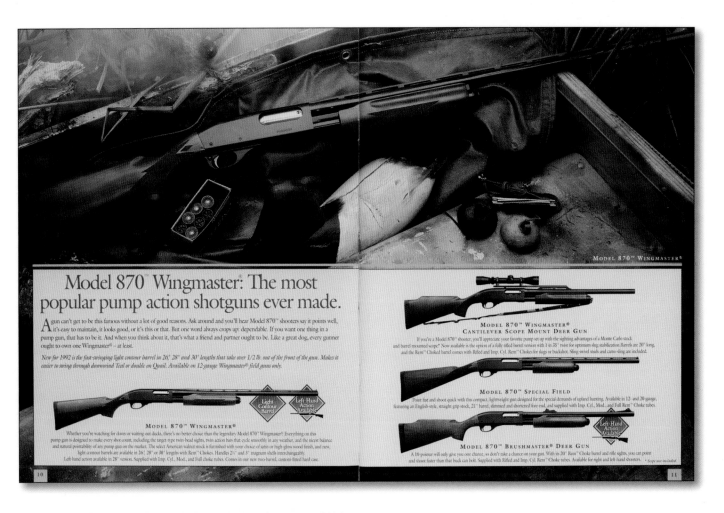

WHAT *CAN'T* YOU SHOOT WITH AN 870?

For the last couple decades, Remington has come up with an 870 nearly as fast as the thought for some new stock or barrel length or finish runs though a customer's head. Truly it seems there's no form of hunting this gun can't tackle.

Model 870 gained weight. Unfortunately it gained weight in the wrong place for an upland gun—up front! Although the Rem Chokes made the Model 870 much more flexible (no need to buy an extra barrel for different applications), it changed the overall balance of the gun. In reality, the increase in weight was minimal, but there were those who swore that they could feel the difference and didn't like the new versions.

More recently, Remington introduced the "Light Contour" barrels for the Model 870, as well as for its autoloader models. These

It's the change in the

air – that wonderful crispness that heralds the change of season. It's the colors of falling leaves and the smell of newly chopped corn. You can see the squirrels at harvest, and hear the first Canadas coming through. We know all the clues, but each time hunting season arrives, the same excitement is there anew. It's a rebirth, and it's why bird hunters and their dogs live so long. A tonic for the soul.

So what will it be this year? Run little Nell, or let her mother come along one more season? Ah, take 'em both...the youngster will learn the drill faster from her mother than you anyway...

What will you carry into the field this fall? We hope it will be your favorite Remington and plenty of green shells for good measure – an old recipe that's still an unbeatable combination. And we've got you covered when it comes to dressing for success afield.

2

EXPRESS™ SHOTGUNS. GREAT PERFORMANCE AT A GREAT PRICE.

The Model 870™ Express™ has all the important design and mechanical qualities of its Wingmaster® brother, but with features that allow us to offer it at a very easy-to-swing price. No company offers as much quality in American-made shotguns as Remington. And no American-made shotgun offers as much performance as the Express™.

The Express™ family includes a line-up of barrel configurations and gauges that is hard to beat, from vent rib wingshooters, to turkey guns and deer set-ups, and even small gauge, youth, and security models. So if you want to shoot a genuine Model 870™, but with no frills, you want to shoot a Model 870™ Express™.

MODEL 870™ EXPRESS™ COMBO (12- & 20- GA.)

The Model 870™ Express™ Combo packages are designed for shotgunners with a taste for venison. Includes a 20" rifle-sighted, Imp. Cyl. deer barrel in addition to a 28" vent rib barrel and Mod. Rem™ Choke tube.

MODEL 870™ EXPRESS™ TURKEY

The positive feel of Remington's legendary pump action with the concealment advantages of our Express™ line. In 12-gauge, with 21" vent rib turkey barrel and Extra-Full Rem™ Choke Turkey tube.

MODEL 870™ EXPRESS™ DEER GUN

The pump action deer gun for hunters who prefer open sights. Features a 20" fully-rifled barrel, quick-reading iron sights, and Monte Carlo stock. Also available with rifle-sighted, 20" Imp. Cyl. barrel.

MODEL 870™ EXPRESS™ COMBO (12- & 20- GA.)

MODEL 870™ EXPRESS™ TURKEY

MODEL 870™ EXPRESS™ DEER GUN

MODEL 870

MODEL 870

MODEL 870

14

FIREARMS · AMMUNITION · 1·9·9·3 · CLOTHING · ACCESSORIES

Remington

IT'S WHAT YOU'RE SHOOTING FOR.

MODEL 870™ EXPRESS™

◄ We're darn proud of our Express™ family of
shotguns because we know we're bringing shotgunners the very best value money can buy in an
all-American pump gun: solid steel receiver for
strength; 3" chambers; Wingmaster® fire control
and cross bolt safety; twin action bars for smooth,
non-binding cycling; vent rib, turkey, and deer
barrel choices; solid rubber butt pad; small gauge
versions; and a youth gun for beginners and
small-framed shooters.

With all these features – Wingmaster® guts, a
wide variety of configurations and great price, it's
no wonder that Express™ is the most popular
American-made shotgun on the market today.

*Note: All 12- and 20-ga. Express™ shotguns are
chambered for 2 3/4" and 3" shells. The .410 bore
Express™ is chambered for 2 1/2" and 3" shells.*

MODEL 870™ EXPRESS™
SMALL GAUGE

The ideal gun for shooters who want the light
weight and maneuverability of a .410 or 20-
gauge, with the concealment advantages of the
non-reflective metal and wood finish of our
Express™ line. The .410 comes with a 25" Full
choke barrel, and the 20-gauge is available with a
26" or 28" Rem Choke barrel with Mod. Rem™
Choke tube.

MODEL 870™ EXPRESS™
YOUTH GUN

The lightest and smallest Model 870™ Express™,
in 20-gauge with a 13" length of pull and 21" vent
rib barrel. It features a handsome hardwood
stock with low-luster finish, and comes with
Mod. Rem™ Choke tube.

MODEL 870™ EXPRESS™ SECURITY

The ideal choice for home defense. With 18 1/2"
Cylinder choke barrel and front bead sight.
*Note: the Model 870™ Express™ Security is intended
for personal protection, and will not accept law
enforcement accessories.*

18

DOVES AND PHEASANTS
AND QUAIL, OH MY!

The 1993 annual Remington catalog placed a firm
emphasis on the Model 870 as the perfect gun for
any upland hunting application.

barrels have a slimmed-down contour in none of
the barrel's critical areas and, therefore, are lighter
than the standard barrels. They therefore provide
a balance similar to what the Model 870 had prior
to the appearance of Rem Chokes. Today's 870s
with Light Contour barrels feel much livelier and
closer to the older guns. If Remington ever came
out with an 870 that had a slimmed-down pump
handle like the original corn cob style and paired it
with a Light Contour barrel, it would make a dandy
upland gun in any gauge.

In the 62 years of its existence, the Model 870
has probably been used in America's upland fields
more than any other pump gun. Whether it's the
old style, pre-Rem Choke version of the Model
870 or the newer, contour barrel with Rem Choke,
if you are a pump gunner, you'd be hard pressed
to find a better suited gun for the uplands. There
are some who claim that the pump gun is outmod-
ed, no longer a viable shotgun for the bird fields.
Indeed, not long ago, a well-known gun writer

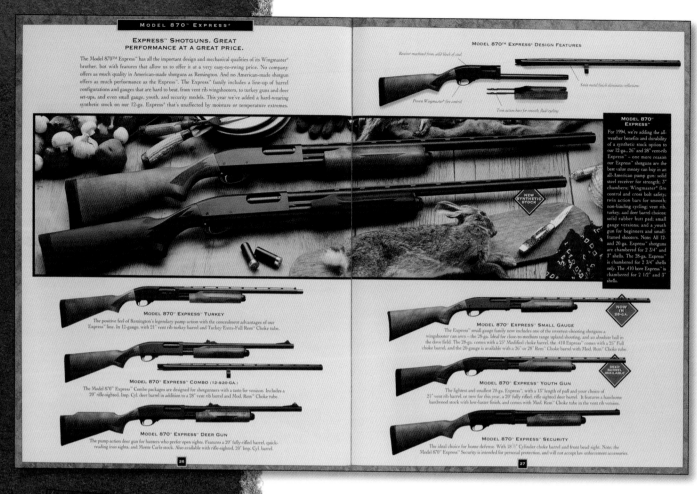

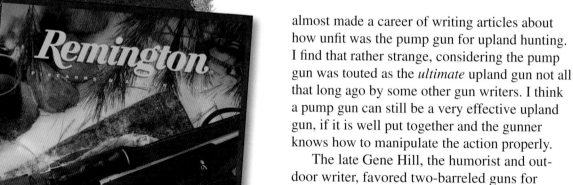

almost made a career of writing articles about how unfit was the pump gun for upland hunting. I find that rather strange, considering the pump gun was touted as the *ultimate* upland gun not all that long ago by some other gun writers. I think a pump gun can still be a very effective upland gun, if it is well put together and the gunner knows how to manipulate the action properly.

The late Gene Hill, the humorist and outdoor writer, favored two-barreled guns for most of his upland gunning. He had some very fine guns, including a favorite 16-gauge W.W. Greener side-by-side. Yet, he mentions in his book *Shotgunner's Notebook* that one of his favorite dove and quail guns was a 28-gauge Remington Model 870. Hill removed the pistol grip from the stock to more or less make it a Special Field style and generally slimmed down the buttstock and the forearm, making his little 28-gauge even thinner and lighter. He said the gun handled wonderfully. It is interesting to note that, despite having access to much finer, more expensive guns, it is not unusual at all to

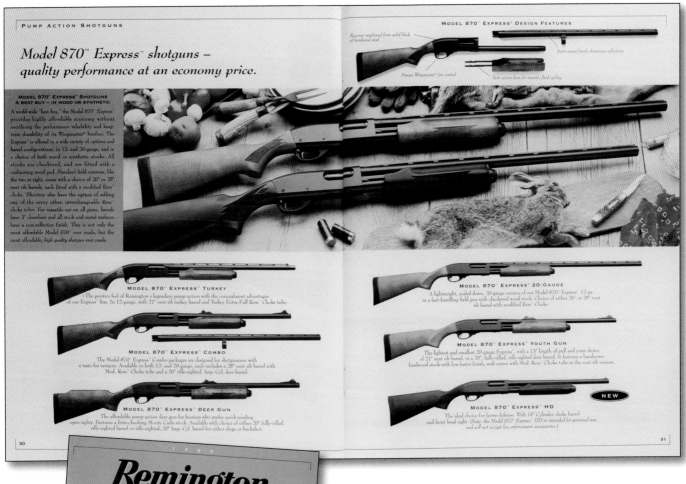

THE EXPRESS ROUTE
The 1994 catalog (left page) introduced the 870 Express in small gauges and a youth size, while the all-synthetic Express became available in 1995 (this page).

find upland gunners who reach for the 870. I might add that Hill did all his alterations before the appearance of the Special Field models which would have been similar, and of course the Special Field was never even made in 28-gauge so, in essence, Hill created his own!

I believe that a pump gun can be a very good upland gun, and the Remington 870 is one of the best for that role. Perhaps the 12-gauge 870 is a bit on the heavy side for all-around upland gunning, but it certainly has done its job in the field, particularly on pheasant! I am not alone in this opinion, as many other 870 admirers freely admit that the 12-gauge version is, perhaps, a touch too heavy. One gun writer even went so far as to voice the same feelings about the long discontinued 870AP, the original plain Jane model. He said that the older AP model was light (it averaged 6¾ pounds in 12-gauge), but that the newer 870s were a bit too heavy for the uplands. His solution was to use a 20-gauge for upland shooting. The 20-gauge version, especially the LW or LT models, can make for a wonderful, light upland gun. It is

The Model 870™ Express™ — The All-American Pump Gun That's All Business.

Our Model 870™ Express™ is an All-American pump gun that brings performance-oriented hunters the best of two worlds. Beneath its no-nonsense, ready-for-work exterior lies the same quality of materials, careful manufacture, and lifetime reliability of our standard Model 870™ Wingmaster®, the pump gun without peer. But it delivers this to shooters at a truly economical price. As a result, it is not only the "best-buy" version of the best-selling shotgun ever designed, it's the best buy of shotguns, period. And it earns this position with a variety of choices that span the spectrum of shotgun applications.

MODEL 870™ EXPRESS™ DESIGN FEATURES

Receiver machined from solid block of hardened steel

Satin metal finish eliminates reflections

Proven Wingmaster® fire control

Twin action bars for smooth, fluid cycling

PROVEN DEPENDABILITY AT AN AFFORDABLE PRICE

You can pay more for a pump gun, but for functional reliability and lifetime durability, you can't buy a better one than a Model 870™ Express™. The reason is simple. It's built on the basic action of the best-selling, most tested shotgun ever made, the legendary Model 870™ Wingmaster. It's the same gun, but a bit less fancy. Just as strong, just as reliable, and just as durable — with an action that cycles just as smoothly. Nor are your choices limited. It's offered with a wide selection of barrel configurations, a Rem™ Choke system, and in 12-, 20-, 28-ga. and .410 bore. All wood and metal surfaces have a non-reflective, non-revealing finish. The 12-gauge vent rib field gun is offered in both wood and synthetic stocked versions. You can count on it — today, tomorrow, and someday, in your grandson's hands.

MODEL 870™ EXPRESS™ TURKEY
A perfect turkey gun with the non-reflective, flat-finish concealment advantages on both stock and exposed metal of our Express™ line. Available in 12-gauge, with 21" vent rib turkey barrel that carries easily beneath overhanging branches and minimizes movement on a stand. A Turkey Extra-Full Rem™ Choke tube provides the exceptionally dense patterns needed for taking a wary Tom.

MODEL 870™ EXPRESS™ 20-GAUGE YOUTH GUN
Sized for smaller shooters with a 13" length of pull. Offered in a choice of a well-balanced 21" vent rib barrel with a Mod. Rem™ Choke for birds, or a 20" fully rifled, rifle-sighted deer barrel (pictured) to match up with the accuracy of our 20-gauge Copper Solid® Sabot Slugs. It features a handsome hardwood stock with positive checkering and low-luster finish.

MODEL 870™ EXPRESS™ HD
An ideal utility and home defense gun. With 18½" Cylinder choke barrel and single front bead sight. An excellent choice as a permanent camp shotgun or as a foundation for adding the versatility of additional extra barrels. Note: the Model 870™ Express™ HD is intended for personal use and will not accept law enforcement accessories.

MODEL 870™ EXPRESS™ COMBO
The Model 870™ Express™ Combo is a versatile cross-over package designed for both birds and deer. Available in either 12- or 20-gauge, each includes a 28" vent rib barrel with Mod. Rem™ Choke tube and a 20" rifle-sighted, Imp. Cyl. deer barrel.

MODEL 870™ EXPRESS™ DEER GUN
The affordable pump action deer gun for hunters who prefer adjustable open sights. Monte Carlo stock promotes fast sight alignment. Available with choice of either 20" fully rifled barrel for sabot or standard slugs, or 20" Imp. Cyl. barrel for either slugs or buckshot.

BACK for '96

MODEL 870™ EXPRESS™ SMALL GAUGE
There's no better buy in a lightweight, fast-handling field gun than these small-gauge versions of our Model 870™ Express™. Fully checkered wood stock with recoil pad. .410 bore and 28-gauge have 25" vent rib barrels and modified fixed choke. The 20-gauge version is offered with your choice of either 26" or 28" vent rib barrel with modified Rem™ Choke.

Note: See page 41 for Express™ shotgun specifications.

38

39

1996
Remington®
C O U N T R Y

FIREARMS • AMMUNITION • ACCESSORIES

YEAR OF THE EXPRESS
Remington devoted an entire spread of its 1996 catalog to nothing but Model 870s in their numerous Express variations.

light in weight, easy to carry, and has enough clout for all upland game. The smaller 28-gauge 870 can also make for a delightful upland gun, especially for the smaller birds and, in the hands of a good shot who knows his distances, the 28-gauge can be used for all upland game with success. Because of the LW and LT model 20-gauges and the smaller framed 28-gauge guns, the 870, in my opinion, is the best choice for upland gunning of all the pump guns on the current market. I know that there are some pump guns that are as light, perhaps even a bit lighter. But none are as solidly and as well built as the 870, and none can be considered more reliable than the time-tested Remington. Besides, the 870 not only balances and handles better than any other pump gun on the market today, it just plain looks better as well!

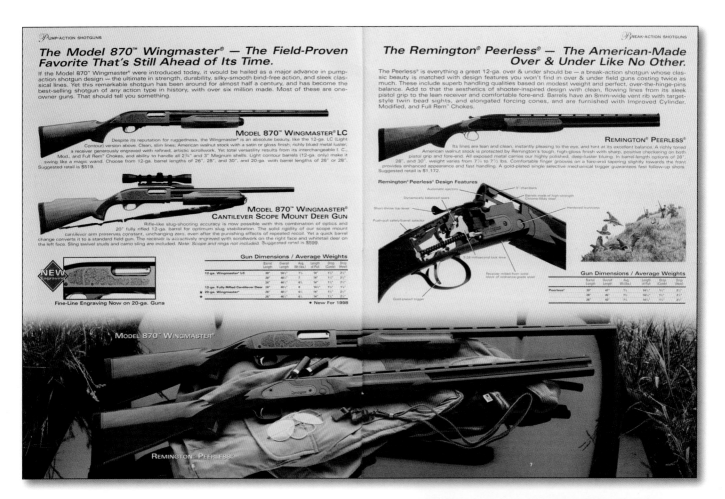

NEW IS OLD, OLD IS NEW

The model term "Wingmaster" was breathed back to life in 1998, and fine line engraving gussied up the 20-gauge models with their high-gloss stocks.

Today's gun culture seems to be somewhat "stuck" on the two-barreled shotgun, when it comes to upland gunning. Far more gun articles are written about double-barreled shotguns for bird hunting than any other type of shotguns. It seems to be almost a foregone conclusion today that a double gun, an over/under or side-by-side, is the way to go. The autoloader also seems to be acceptable, especially since there are so many lightweight versions on the market today. To that end, the pump gun has been more or less ignored of late. It wasn't so long ago that many gun writers touted the pump gun as one of the best choices for the uplands. Just read the shotgun literature from the past. You'd be amazed how many thought the pump gun was *the* gun to use in the uplands. Sadly, that is not the case

MODEL 870
EXPRESS

TOP-OF-THE-LINE PERFORMANCE
AT BOTTOM-LINE PRICES

The Model 870™ Express® gives you all the smooth-working reliability and durability of the best-selling, most highly regarded shotgun action ever made. But because it is dressed for work rather than show, it comes at a remarkably affordable cost. This "best buy" pump gun is offered in versions for every type of hunting, and in a variety of practical non-reflective or camo finishes.

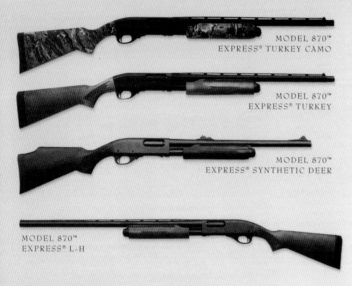

MODEL 870™
EXPRESS® TURKEY CAMO

MODEL 870™
EXPRESS® TURKEY

MODEL 870™
EXPRESS® SYNTHETIC DEER

MODEL 870™
EXPRESS® L-H

A wise old saying states, "There's a time and place for everything." Maybe the unknown author was a hunter, because, when it's time to go hunting, that's the place for a **Model 870™ Express®** — America's pump gun.

This is a shotgun that was totally conceived for hunting — hard hunting. Sure, there's a place for your glossy-stocked, brightly blued, scattergun beauties. But not in a sleet-spattered duck blind, thorny-thick grouse cover, or the stony-steep slopes of chukar country. That's when you leave the elegant guns behind, and pack a Remington® Express® pump gun in your pick-up. They both go with the territory.

There's a lot of ingenious practicality to any Model 870™ Express®. These are definitely "no frills" shotguns, without the extra embellishment of fancy finishes. That works for you in two ways. First, it cuts their cost, because when we eliminate the expense of American walnut and mirror-like polishing, we pass the savings back to you. Second, the finish on these shotguns is designed to deal with more appropriate factors — like wear and weather. And in the field it gives you the added benefit of reflecting nothing, except your good sense in owning such a shotgun. While all of our Express® shotguns have the right outside dress for the occasion, they also have the right stuff inside to do the job with the same unmatched durability and functional reliability of the legendary Model 870™ Wingmaster®. That's because beneath the

30

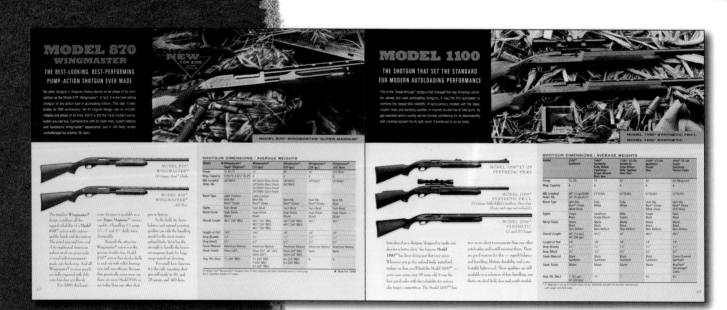

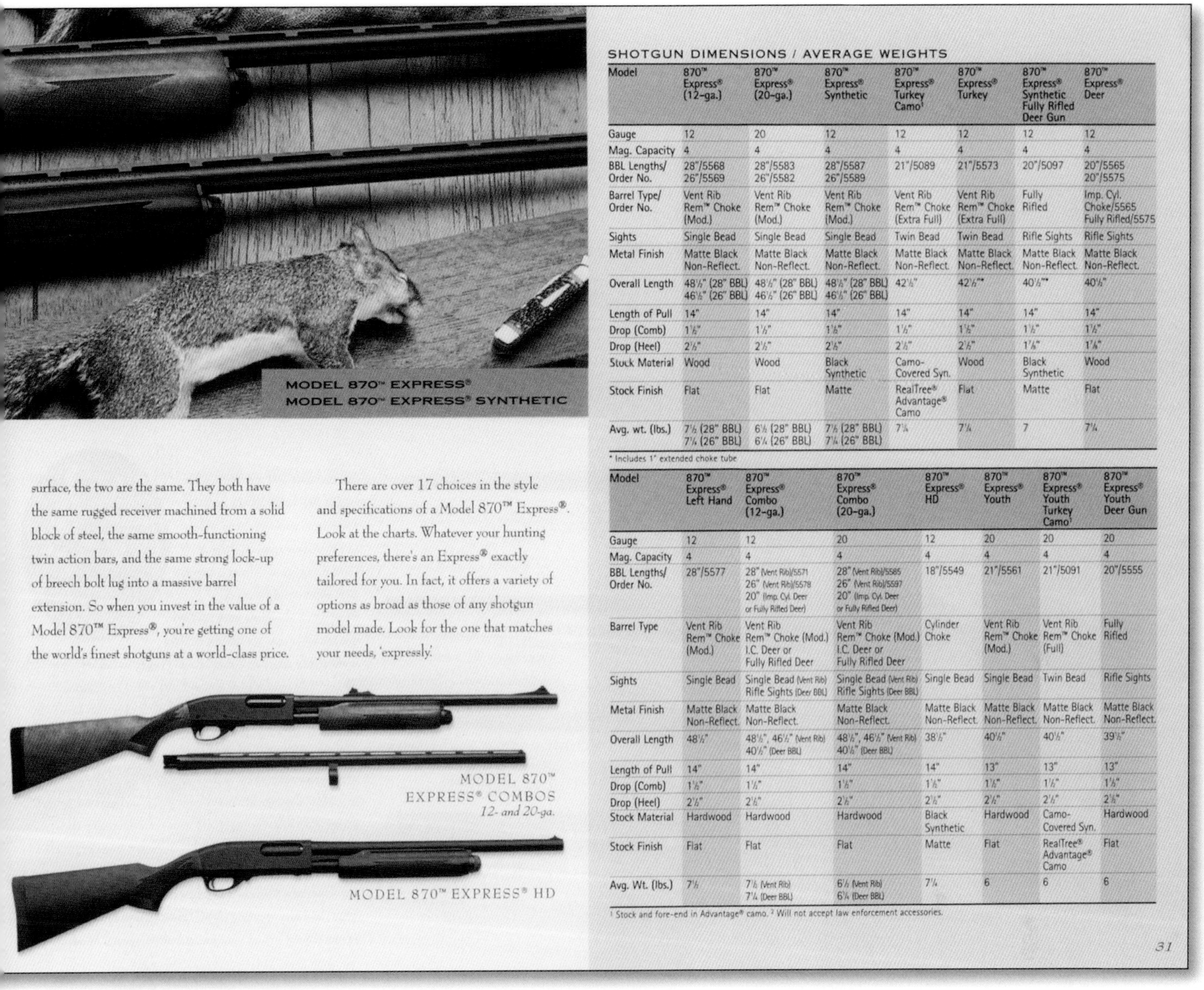

MODEL 870™ EXPRESS®
MODEL 870™ EXPRESS® SYNTHETIC

surface, the two are the same. They both have the same rugged receiver machined from a solid block of steel, the same smooth-functioning twin action bars, and the same strong lock-up of breech bolt lug into a massive barrel extension. So when you invest in the value of a Model 870™ Express®, you're getting one of the world's finest shotguns at a world-class price.

There are over 17 choices in the style and specifications of a Model 870™ Express®. Look at the charts. Whatever your hunting preferences, there's an Express® exactly tailored for you. In fact, it offers a variety of options as broad as those of any shotgun model made. Look for the one that matches your needs, 'expressly.'

MODEL 870™ EXPRESS® COMBOS
12- and 20-ga.

MODEL 870™ EXPRESS® HD

SHOTGUN DIMENSIONS / AVERAGE WEIGHTS

Model	870™ Express® (12-ga.)	870™ Express® (20-ga.)	870™ Express® Synthetic	870™ Express® Turkey Camo[1]	870™ Express® Turkey	870™ Express® Synthetic Fully Rifled Deer Gun	870™ Express® Deer
Gauge	12	20	12	12	12	12	12
Mag. Capacity	4	4	4	4	4	4	4
BBL Lengths/ Order No.	28"/5568 26"/5569	28"/5583 26"/5582	28"/5587 26"/5589	21"/5089	21"/5573	20"/5097	20"/5565 20"/5575
Barrel Type/ Order No.	Vent Rib Rem™ Choke (Mod.)	Vent Rib Rem™ Choke (Mod.)	Vent Rib Rem™ Choke (Mod.)	Vent Rib Rem™ Choke (Extra Full)	Vent Rib Rem™ Choke (Extra Full)	Fully Rifled	Imp. Cyl. Choke/5565 Fully Rifled/5575
Sights	Single Bead	Single Bead	Single Bead	Twin Bead	Twin Bead	Rifle Sights	Rifle Sights
Metal Finish	Matte Black Non-Reflect.	Matte Black Non-Reflect.	Matte Black Non-Reflect.	Matte Black Non-Reflect.	Matte Black Non-Reflect.	Matte Black Non-Reflect.	Matte Black Non-Reflect.
Overall Length	48½" (28" BBL) 46½" (26" BBL)	48½" (28" BBL) 46½" (26" BBL)	48½" (28" BBL) 46½" (26" BBL)	42½"	42½"*	40½"*	40½"
Length of Pull	14"	14"	14"	14"	14"	14"	14"
Drop (Comb)	1½"	1½"	1½"	1½"	1½"	1½"	1½"
Drop (Heel)	2½"	2½"	2½"	2½"	2½"	1⅞"	1⅞"
Stock Material	Wood	Wood	Black Synthetic	Camo-Covered Syn.	Wood	Black Synthetic	Wood
Stock Finish	Flat	Flat	Matte	RealTree® Advantage® Camo	Flat	Matte	Flat
Avg. wt. (lbs.)	7½ (28" BBL) 7¼ (26" BBL)	6½ (28" BBL) 6¼ (26" BBL)	7½ (28" BBL) 7¼ (26" BBL)	7¼	7¼	7	7¼

* Includes 1" extended choke tube

Model	870™ Express® Left Hand	870™ Express® Combo (12-ga.)	870™ Express® Combo (20-ga.)	870™ Express® HD	870™ Express® Youth	870™ Express® Youth Turkey Camo[1]	870™ Express® Youth Deer Gun
Gauge	12	12	20	12	20	20	20
Mag. Capacity	4	4	4	4	4	4	4
BBL Lengths/ Order No.	28"/5577	28" (Vent Rib)/5571 26" (Vent Rib)/5578 20" (Imp. Cyl. Deer or Fully Rifled Deer)	28" (Vent Rib)/5585 26" (Vent Rib)/5597 20" (Imp. Cyl. Deer or Fully Rifled Deer)	18"/5549	21"/5561	21"/5091	20"/5555
Barrel Type	Vent Rib Rem™ Choke (Mod.)	Vent Rib Rem™ Choke (Mod.) I.C. Deer or Fully Rifled Deer	Vent Rib Rem™ Choke (Mod.) I.C. Deer or Fully Rifled Deer	Cylinder Choke	Vent Rib Rem™ Choke (Mod.)	Vent Rib Rem™ Choke (Full)	Fully Rifled
Sights	Single Bead	Single Bead (Vent Rib) Rifle Sights (Deer BBL)	Single Bead (Vent Rib) Rifle Sights (Deer BBL)	Single Bead	Single Bead	Twin Bead	Rifle Sights
Metal Finish	Matte Black Non-Reflect.	Matte Black Non-Reflect.	Matte Black Non-Reflect.	Matte Black Non-Reflect.	Matte Black Non-Reflect.	Matte Black Non-Reflect.	Matte Black Non-Reflect.
Overall Length	48½"	48½", 46½" (Vent Rib) 40½" (Deer BBL)	48½", 46½" (Vent Rib) 40½" (Deer BBL)	38½"	40½"	40½"	39½"
Length of Pull	14"	14"	14"	14"	13"	13"	13"
Drop (Comb)	1½"	1½"	1½"	1½"	1½"	1½"	1½"
Drop (Heel)	2½"	2½"	2½"	2½"	2½"	2½"	2½"
Stock Material	Hardwood	Hardwood	Hardwood	Black Synthetic	Hardwood	Camo-Covered Syn.	Hardwood
Stock Finish	Flat	Flat	Flat	Matte	Flat	RealTree® Advantage® Camo	Flat
Avg. Wt. (lbs.)	7½	7½ (Vent Rib) 7¼ (Deer BBL)	6½ (Vent Rib) 6¼ (Deer BBL)	7¼	6	6	6

[1] Stock and fore-end in Advantage® camo. [2] Will not accept law enforcement accessories.

31

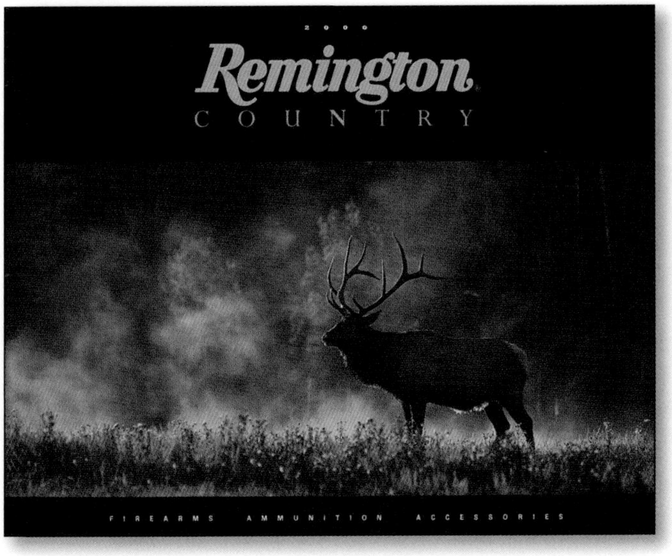

RABBIT TO SQUIRREL?

Take a close look at the top pic for the 2000 catalog spread on the 870 and the one a few pages back for the 1994 and '95 catalogs. Did the rabbit lose its ears and grow a long tail? Remington may be imaginative when it comes to its 870s, but in photo spreads for its catalogs, maybe not so much.

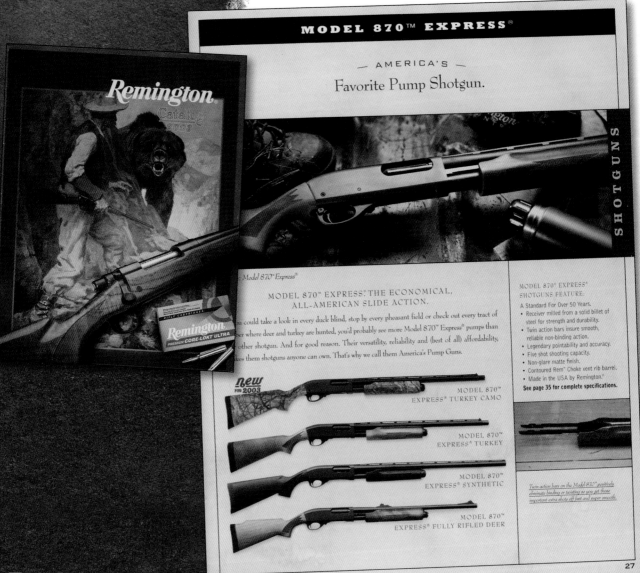

today. However, if a survey was to be conducted, I am convinced it would show that more hunters go afield after upland game with a pump gun than with any other type of shotgun. Furthermore, it would show that the vast majority of pump gun shooters are using the good old 870!

I have no doubt in my mind that the Remington Model 870 will lead the field as the most used shotgun in the uplands. It won't be the Special Field model, nor will it be the newer guns with light contour barrels. The most used shotgun in uplands will probably be the 12-gauge version of either the newer model with the Rem Chokes or the plain fixed-choke older models!

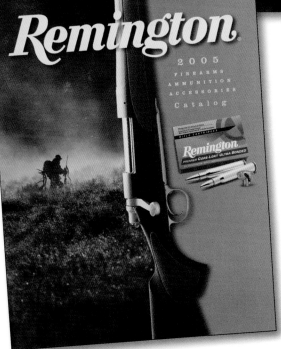

"NEW" WINGMASTER
The Wingmaster became all "new" again with a Dale Earnhardt limited edition profile in 2005.

Remington. **PETERS** **A**RMS and **A**MMO **Dealer Bulletin**

VOLUME 7, NUMBER 1

APRIL, 1971

Attention Remington Dealers:

HERE ARE NEW-FOR-1971 VERSIONS OF MODEL 1100, MODEL 870, MODEL 700 AND MODEL 580...TO HELP YOU MAKE MORE SALES AND PROFITS

This customer's buying "the lightweight 20 gauge magnum I've always wanted" . . . and the dealer's telling him he can have this new version of the Model 1100 in his choice of plain or ventilated rib barrel. Both have 3" chamber, 28" full choke barrel.

Today, there are growing trends to multi-gun ownership and to more selective shopping by shooters. Thousands of customers are ready to acquire their 2nd, 3rd or 4th shotgun, big game rifle or 22 rifle. Thousands more are looking for models and versions designed and styled to more precisely meet their needs and tastes.

To help you make sales in this more "choosy" market, Remington offers for 1971 a total of 19 NEW specifications. Here's a quick reference chart of the new versions . . . to help you help your customer select "the Remington I've been looking for" . . . guns made for fast sales in today's changing market.

MODEL 700 BDL

NEW! Bolt Action Deluxe Center Fire Rifle . . . now in hottest, fastest caliber on the market: NEW 17 REMINGTON.

MODEL 870

Pump Action Shotgun . . . now in true "mirror-image" versions with left-hand loading and ejection port, left-hand safety. **NEW!**

MODEL 580

NEW! 22 Rim Fire Bolt Action Single Shot Rifle . . . now in "Boy's Rifle" version with stock shortened 1" for young shooters.

NEW REMINGTONS FOR 1971

Model 700 BDL	Description			Barrel Length	Order Number
	17 Remington Caliber			24"	6046

Model 870	Barrel Style	Barrel Length	Choke	Order Number 12 Ga.	Order Number 20 Ga.
LEFT-HAND, Pump Action, 2¾" Chamber Field Guns	Plain	30	Full	5504	—
	Plain	28	Full	—	5522
	Plain	28	Mod.	5506	5524
	Plain	26	Imp. Cyl.	5508	5526
	Vent. Rib	30	Full	5510	—
	Vent. Rib	28	Full	—	5528
	Vent. Rib	28	Mod.	5514	5530
	Vent. Rib	26	Imp. Cyl.	5516	5566
Trap Guns	Vent. Rib	30	Full	5518	—
	Vent. Rib	30	Full	5520	(Monte Carlo)
3" Magnum Chamber Field Guns	Plain	30	Full	5494	—
	Vent. Rib	30	Full	5496	—

Model 1100	Barrel Style	Barrel Length	Choke	Order Number 12 Ga.	Order Number 20 Ga.
Lightweight 3" Magnum	Plain	28	Full	—	9656
	Vent. Rib	28	Full	—	9658

Model 580BR	Caliber	Description		Overall Length	Order Number
Boy's Rifle	22 R. F.	Bolt Action Single Shot		40"	5570

And here's news of a special money-making promotion no dealer will want to miss . . .

16 NEW "MIRROR-IMAGE" LEFT-HAND MODEL 870's HELP DEALERS BOOST SALES OF PUMP ACTION SHOTGUNS TO SOUTHPAW SHOOTERS

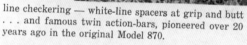

At dealers' requests, Remington in recent years has helped retailers do a more successful job of catering to the sizable market for left-hand firearms.

Currently, 24 Specifications in 4 guns give Remington dealers a bigger opportunity than ever to serve left-handed shooters, and the latest additions are sure to be popular with southpaw shotgunners.

Listed here (and on front page of this Bulletin) are the several latest versions of the famous Model 870 Pump Action Shotgun . . . the widest selection of left-hand pump action shotguns on the market.

True "mirror-image" left-hand guns, these southpaw 870's have loading and ejection ports on the left side of the receivers, and also have left-hand safeties.

Other well-liked features and advantages of the regular right-hand Model 870 remain: Solid steel receiver — super-smooth "vibra-hone" metal finish — scratch-resistant Du Pont RK-W finish on American walnut stock — rubber recoil pad — grip cap — fine-line checkering — white-line spacers at grip and butt . . . and famous twin action-bars, pioneered over 20 years ago in the original Model 870.

For left-handed shooters — and right-handed shooters who have left master eyes — these 16 new southpaw 870's will be welcome additions to Remington's famous line of pump action shotguns.

Left-hand 870 interchangeable barrels will not be available this year.

REMINGTON LEFT-HAND MODEL 870 PUMP ACTION SHOTGUNS

Chamber	Barrel Style	Barrel Length Inches	Choke	Index Number 12 Gauge	20 Gauge
2¾"	Plain	30	Full	5504	—
2¾"	Plain	28	Full	—	5522
2¾"	Plain	28	Mod.	5506	5524
2¾"	Plain	26	Imp. Cyl.	5508	5526
2¾"	Vent. Rib	30	Full	5510	—
2¾"	Vent. Rib	28	Full	—	5528
2¾"	Vent. Rib	28	Mod.	5514	5530
2¾"	Vent. Rib	26	Imp. Cyl.	5516	5566
2¾"	Vent. Rib	30	Full	5518	—
2¾"	Vent. Rib	30	Full	5520 (Monte Carlo)	—
3" Magnum	Plain	30	Full	5494	—
3" Magnum	Vent. Rib	30	Full	5496	—

If your customer's a left-handed trap shooter, be sure you tell him about #5518 and #5520 . . . the "TB" grade lefties he may have been waiting for!

DEDICATION

Left-handed people—and left-handed shooters, in particular—are always in the minority. But you wouldn't know it from the sales material issued to Remington's dealers in 1971. There are 16—sixteen!—reverse engineered, left-handed Model 870s offered. Now *that's* dedication to *all* the customer base.

MOST TWENTIES ARE TOO BIG FOR THEIR GAUGE.

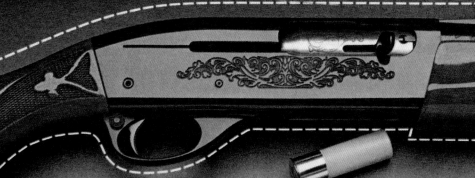

Model 1100 LT-20.

Model 870 20-ga. Lightweight.

If you're going to shoot 20-ga. shells, why lug a gun all day the size and weight of a 12-ga.? You don't have to.

When we built our 20-ga. autoloaders and pump-actions, we didn't cut corners. We did cut the size and weight, to make the Model 1100 and Model 870 the only 20-ga. shotguns in their action types that aren't just rechambered 12-ga. guns.

After thousands of man-hours spent on our drawing boards, in toolrooms and research labs, we came up with completely different lightweight 20s. We started with a 20-ga. shell and built the gun around it. Yet we built it without compromise. So the receiver is still solid ordnance steel. And we kept the solid action concepts proven in over 5 million Model 1100s and 870s.

The result: one of the lightest, most easily pointable and well-balanced 20s you'll find. Anywhere, at any price. But don't just take our word for it; go to your dealer's. Heft one of our lightweight 20s in one hand, and anybody else's in the other. If the competitor's gun is as light as ours, ask about its receiver. Chances are, it's

aluminum or a lightweight alloy. Not the ordnance-quality steel we use in ours.

Then check its stock. Is it the finest American walnut like ours or a lighter, softer wood, just made to look like it? On all too many guns today the only thing left that *is* American is the wood. With Remington, every single part on every shotgun and rifle is made and serviced in the U.S.A. And we're proud of it.

Our newest lightweight, the "Limited." For youthful shooters or smaller-framed adults, there's a new Remington 20-ga. lightweight to start with, and grow with. The Model 1100 LT-20 "Limited" has a stock 1" shorter and a compact 23" barrel. Yet in its action parts and in performance, it's all 1100.

See all the twenties that aren't too big for their gauge, but are very big in value. The Model 1100 and 870 lightweights. See your Remington dealer today; ask for our new catalog, or write us for one at the address below.

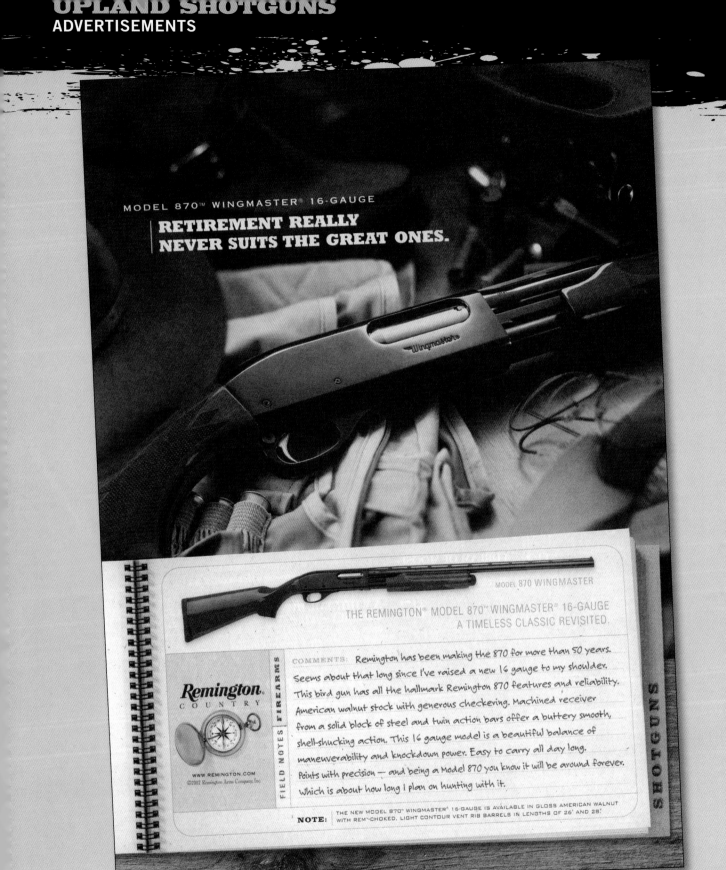

A Good Gun Should Come Up Fast As They Do.

There's not much time to think it over when a ruffed grouse or a covey of quail explodes at your feet.

That's when you need the Remington 1100 or 870 "Special Field," the first autoloading and pump action shotguns designed to shoulder in a wingbeat.

The innovative 21" barrel is ideal for mounting and swinging fast. The American walnut stock, with straight pistol grip, lets you shoulder it instinctively. The lighter weight makes for easier scrambling through brushy thickets.

The 12-gauge "Special Field" shotguns now come with new Rem™ Choke screw-in tubes to make them even more versatile. 20-gauge models have a choice of Full, Modified or Improved Cylinder choke barrels. Mechanically, "Special Field" shotguns are the same as America's favorites– the 1100 autoloader and 870 "Wingmaster" pump. Both deliver great shootability and long-term Remington value. And both are made in the U.S.A.

Whether you choose the softer recoil of the 1100 or the softer price of the 870, a "Special Field" will help contribute to your success, out there in Remington Country.

Call 1-800-THE-GUNS for your nearest Remington Pro Line™ Center. And, stop in for your free catalog from America's most experienced manufacturer of sporting arms and ammunition.

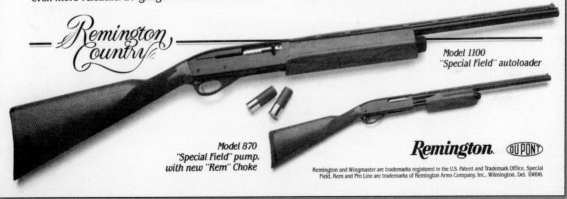

Remington Country

Model 1100 "Special Field" autoloader

Model 870 "Special Field" pump, with new "Rem" Choke

Remington. DUPONT

Remington and Wingmaster are trademarks registered in the U.S. Patent and Trademark Office. Special Field, Rem and Pro Line are trademarks of Remington Arms Company, Inc., Wilmington, Del. 19898.

CHAPTER SEVEN

WATERFOWL SHOTGUNS

NOWHERE IN THE WORLD is waterfowling such a major pursuit as it is in North America. There are more decoys, waders, hip boots, camouflage clothing, and other waterfowling paraphernalia sold in America than anywhere else. Naturally, then, more waterfowling guns are also made and sold in America than anywhere else.

The popularity of waterfowling in America dates back to the days when skies used to be darkened by passing waterfowl, and wild duck was a common and very popular fare on the menus of the best eateries in the country. To meet this demand, there were men who made a living off shooting ducks and geese and supplying them to the restaurants. These market hunters were probably the first who popularized the pump gun in this country. Later, despite the end of no-season, no-limit shooting and the three-shot gun capacity law, the pump gun's popularity among waterfowlers continued.

MODEL 870 WINGMASTER, FOR OVER 40 YEARS, THE MOST POPULAR PUMP ACTION SHOTGUNS IN THE WORLD.

TAKE 'EM!
The 1991 catalog placed a distinct emphasis on the Model 870 as a gun suitable for the harsh conditions often encountered in waterfowl hunting.

VARIETY IS THE SPICE
Today's Model 870 waterfowl guns come in a variety of camouflage options. They also have grip panels at fore-end and wrist, and some feature special recoil-reducing buttpads.

102

The Remington Model 870 is, perhaps, the quintessential waterfowl gun in America today. It is not only rugged and reliable and goes bang every time, but it is also a handsome shotgun that seems to fit any time period. When it first came out, in 1950, it was available in 2¾-inch chambering only, but it became popular with duck hunters immediately, so it didn't take long for Remington to come out with a 3-inch Magnum chambering for them. In 1955, Remington introduced the Model 870 Magnum in both the standard AP version, as well as the deluxe ADL, and, to borrow the old cliché, the rest is history.

As years went by, the Model 870 Magnum stayed the same. The plain AP model was eventually dropped and the ADL became standard, but otherwise, there was no change. Along the way, Remington also applied a more durable and shiny plastic-like finish that it called RKW to the gun, and the company also started to make its guns with the signature impressed checkering in *fleur de lis* style.

In 1960, Remington announced the 20-gauge 3-inch Magnum, a response to the rapidly rising popularity of this gauge

Terms and conditions of sale for these special guns are the
same as those outlined in our January 2, 1974 Wholesaler
Appointment Letter except that the Special Dating Plan
deadline date of May 1, 1974 has been extended to July 1, 1974.

This limited edition Model 870 will be highly prized
only by DU members, but non-members as well. Your Remington
representative will be talking with you soon about your
part...........this program. Additional catalog pages
......................equest.

Very truly yours,

C. W. Roney
Director of Sales

Remington PETERS

REMINGTON ARMS COMPANY, INC.

MANUFACTURERS OF
SPORTING FIREARMS, AMMUNITION

SPORTING FIREARMS, TRAPS, ILION, NEW YORK
AMMUNITION, BRIDGEPORT, CONNECTICUT
LONOKE, ARKANSAS
CABLE—PHARTLEY, BRIDGEPORT
TELEX: 964-201 STRATFORD, CONN.

TRAPS   TARGETS

BRIDGEPORT, CONNECTICUT 06602

PETERS CARTRIDGE DIVISION
BRIDGEPORT, CONNECTICUT
TARGETS, FINDLAY, OHIO
ADA, OKLAHOMA
ATHENS, GEORGIA

April 26, 1974

ANNOUNCING THE REMINGTON MODEL 870 DUCKS UNLIMITED

COMMEMORATIVE PUMP ACTION SHOTGUN

A LIMITED EDITION HONORING DUCKS UNLIMITED'S

37 YEARS OF EFFORT IN WATERFOWL PROJECTS

To Our Firearms Wholesalers

Gentlemen:

This year, in celebration of Ducks Unlimited's 37 years of
successful efforts in the funding and administration of waterfowl
programs, Remington will produce a special commemorative version
of the sportsman's favorite pump action shotgun, the Remington
Model 870 "Wingmaster."

As shown in the attached catalog page, this special gun will
incorporate all the great features of the Model 870 plus a
receiver fitted with a colorful commemorative medallion. In
addition, each gun will be serial numbered from a special
block of numbers. Special receiver scroll work and serial
numbers are distinctively gilded.

Here are the details of the program:

Specification	Order No.	Wholesaler Inc. Tax*
Model 870 DU Commemorative 12 gauge; 30" Full Choke Ventilated Rib Barrel	6996	

* Includes $18.00 donation to be forwarded t...
  by Remington.

Appropriate commemoration of a fine organization's many years of service.

Here is an opportunity to own a special, limited-edition version of the most popular gun Remington has ever made... while contributing to America's wildlife resources.

The purchase price of the "Ducks Unlimited" Commemorative 870 includes a contribution to "Ducks Unlimited", which will be forwarded to DU by Remington.

For 37 years, the intelligent, well-planned work of the organization known as "Ducks Unlimited" has been a model of foresight and effectiveness in the funding and administration of waterfowl propagation programs.

The Commemorative Model 870 selected to honor DU's 37 years of preeminence in its field is appropriately chosen.

The gun is offered with a 30" full choke, ventilated rib barrel, in 12 gauge, 2¾" chamber.

These shotguns will be consecutively numbered from a specially reserved group of serial numbers, each prefixed by the letters DU.

As shown in the illustrations, the quality of finish on the entire gun, and the detailing of the commemorative refinements, makes the "Ducks Unlimited" Remington Model 870 "Wingmaster" Pump Action shotgun, a possession any sportsman would prize.

Remington DUPONT

REMINGTON ARMS COMPANY, INC.
BRIDGEPORT, CONNECTICUT 06602

Form No. DU 87
Printed in U.S.A.

PUBLIC RELATIONS DIVISION

REMINGTON ARMS COMPANY, INC., BRIDGEPORT ...LETTER

S. W. Alvis
R & D Ilion

APRIL 1974

REMINGTON MODEL 870 SHOTGUN
IN SPECIAL DUCKS UNLIMITED
COMMEMORATIVE VERSION

REMINGTON ARMS CO.
RECEIVED
APR 29 1974
FIREARMS DESIGN

Remington Arms Company, Inc., has announced that its
Model 870 pump action shotgun will be produced in a special
Ducks Unlimited commemorative version in 1974.

The Model 870 DU commemorative will be made in 12 gauge
with a 30 inch full choke vent rib barrel. All Model 870 DU
commemorative shotguns will be serial numbered from a selected
block of numbers and will be followed by a DU suffix. Serial
numbers, as well as scroll work on both sides of the receiver,
will be gold colored. Centered in the scroll work on the left
side of the receiver will be a handsome Ducks Unlimited medallion
in red, white, blue and gold.

As a further, unique feature of the Model 870 DU commemorative, a portion of the purchase price paid for it by
individuals will become a contribution forwarded directly by
Remington to Ducks Unlimited.

The issuance of this commemorative shotgun combines
both support and recognition by Remington of the valuable work

---

...the past 37 years in restoring,
...owl habitat in North America.
...ive will not only have a hand-
...ne that provides visible
...ne conservation organization.
...Model 870 as a DU commemora-
...uced in 1949, the 870 has
...in production units. It is
...en ever made and one that is a
...rs throughout the country.
...utive year that Remington has
...shotgun. In 1973, the Model
...roduced in a special version
...booth wildlife project.
Commemorative shotguns and, particularly ones made by
Remington, are relatively rare, and the availability of the
Model 870 DU commemorative becomes a welcome event both for gun
collectors and those who simply appreciate the opportuni...
own and use a unique version of th...
numbers.

CONSERVATION-MINDED

In just one of the many special editions Remington has offered over the years, the conservation group Ducks Unlimited was highlighted. These guns can command a premium for collectors today, but only in new-in-box, unfired condition with all the original paperwork.

104

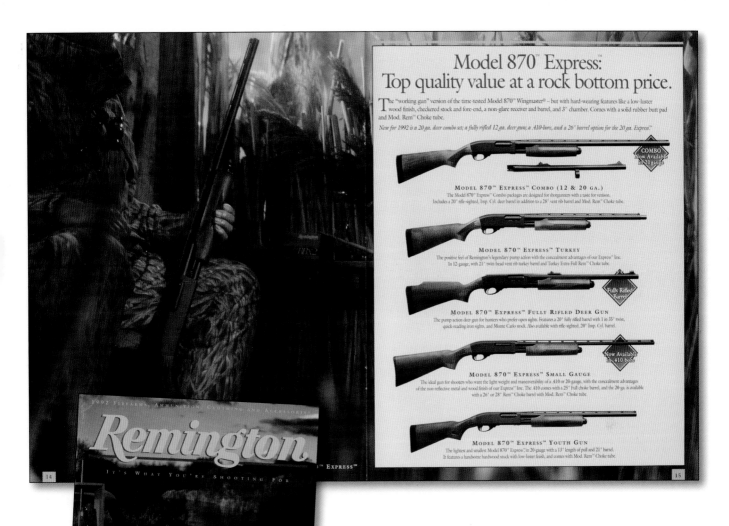

WATERFOWLING ROMANCE
Even as late as the 1990s, Remington paid homage to the romance that surrounds America's centuries-old sport of waterfowling, with classic pictorials of dogs and decoys, and even a modern hunter (notice the all-camo jumpsuit?) in paint, instead of photo. Oh, and always, always, the 870.

and chambering. Guns and ammo makers were eager to sell more guns and ammo, so the 3-inch Magnum 20-gauge became the new "wonder gun." Gun writers of the era didn't help matters. Just about all the outdoor journalists of the day promoted the pairing, claiming it was the "miracle gauge," the perfect "all-around" choice. There were even one or two writers who claimed that the 20-gauge 3-inch Magnum was superior to the 12-gauge for long-range shooting! Ironically, as quick as Remington was to capitalize on the rising popularity of the 3-inch Magnum 20-gauge, Winchester chose *not* to jump on the bandwagon. The Winchester Model 12, the Remington Model 870's only serious competitor, never did have this chambering and gauge pairing offered.

In 1972, when Remington came out with the scaled-down 20-gauge Model 870, it simultaneously announced that 2¾-inch and 3-inch chambered versions would be available. By that year, the popularity of the larger chambering was in full swing, and any new shotgun on the market that was chambered in 20-gauge just about had to have 3-inch chamber-

MANY WINGMASTERS HAVE BEEN PASSED ON TO A NEW GENERATION OF OWNERS...TWICE.

A gun doesn't become this sought-after without a lot of good reasons. Some Wingmaster® owners say it points well, it's easy to maintain, it looks good, or it's this or that. But one word always crops up: dependable. And if you want one thing in a shotgun, that has to be it. Wingmasters are so dependable, many of them are now being carried by a third generation of owners – proof enough of the mechanical durability and great design that has made these shotguns the wingshooter's favorite for over four decades. Sure, they probably have some blueing missing here and there, and maybe a few dents and dings in the wood, but when their owners reach for 'em, they're always ready to answer the call.

MODEL 870™ WINGMASTER® LC
LIGHT CONTOUR

The American walnut stock is furnished with satin or high-gloss finish, and new, light contour Rem™ Choke barrels in 26", 28" or 30" lengths. Handles 2 3/4" and 3" magnum shells interchangeably. Left-hand action available in 28" version. Supplied with Imp. Cyl., Mod., and Full choke tubes. *Light contour Wingmasters come in our new two-barrel, custom-fitted hard case.*

MODEL 870™ SPECIAL FIELD

You can point fast and shoot quick with this compact, lightweight gun designed for the special demands of upland hunting. Available in 12- and 20-gauge, featuring an English-style, straight grip stock, 21" barrel, slimmed and shortened fore-end, and Rem™ Choke tubes.

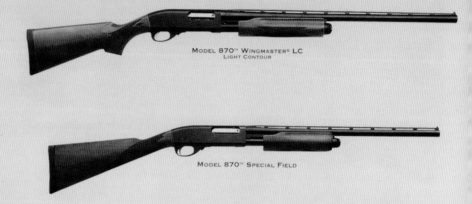

MODEL 870™ WINGMASTER® LC
LIGHT CONTOUR

MODEL 870™ SPECIAL FIELD

8

THE WINGMASTER PREVAILS

The 1993 catalog not only placed an emphasis on the classic Wingmaster, by placing a photo of it so prominently in the center of the catalog against a backdrop of duck camo and decoys, the company showed that this gun was no slouch in tough, wet conditions.

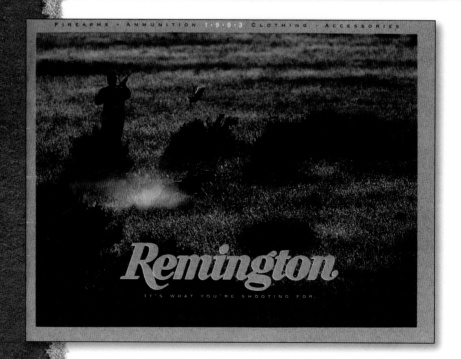

MODEL 870™ WINGMASTER®
CANTILEVER SCOPE MOUNT DEER GUN

MODEL 870™ BRUSHMASTER®
DEER GUN

ing. The first Model 870 in this configuration was built on the standard frame, a shaved version of the 12-gauge frame. The gun normally weighed 6½ pounds, and the 3-inch Magnum version, especially with a ventilated rib barrel, tended to weigh around 6¾ pounds. The new, scaled frame 20-gauges were much lighter than their 12-gauge counterparts, and the 3-inch magnum version, even with a ventilated rib barrel, weighed about a half a pound less than the same gun in the larger gauge. Some pump gunners didn't like the lighter version, because they said it kicked too much, but others didn't mind the extra recoil and bought the scaled-frame version.

Before the use of steel shot was mandated for waterfowling, there were quite a few duck hunters who used the 20-gauge in the 3-inch chambering, not just for shooting over decoys, but even for pass shooting! The late Francis Sell, a gun writer who was a regular contributor to the *Gun Digest*, was known for his promotion of the 3-inch Magnum 20-gauge in the 1960s and 70s. Sell did quite a bit of long-range waterfowling with the magnum 20-gauge. Thanks to the praise sung by him and other writers, both the standard-frame and the scaled-frame 20-gauge magnum 870s sold well.

Times changed, of course, and eventually Remington phased out the standard-frame 20s. Sales figures from its time in production showed that the vast majority of 20-gauge buyers chose the scaled-frame guns. But, with the steel shot requirement applied nationwide, it was discovered that the 3-inch 20-gauge hull just didn't pack enough shot to make

MANY WINGMASTERS HAVE BEEN PASSED ON TO A NEW GENERATION OF OWNERS...TWICE.

A gun doesn't become this sought-after without a lot of good reasons. Some Wingmaster® owners say it points well, it's easy to maintain, or it looks good. But one word always crops up in Wingmaster® discussions: dependable. And if you want one thing in a shotgun, that has to be it. Wingmasters are so dependable, many of them are now being carried by a third generation of owners – proof enough of the designed-in durability and quality that has made this all-American shotgun the wingshooter's favorite for over four decades. A Wingmaster® also feels good in your hands. The balance is right, and

the stock dimensions let the gun shoulder smoothly. The target-type twin-bead sights quickly tell your eye that your head is down on the gun where it should be. And after the first shot, the twin action bars allow you to cycle the fore-end swiftly and smoothly in any weather without twisting or binding. Our new light contour barrel lets you point fast and swing smoothly, and Rem™ Chokes let you tailor pattern performance to any shooting situation. Great strength, pure simplicity, and absolute dependability – qualities that for over 40 years have made the Wingmaster® America's most popular pump action shotgun.

MODEL 870™ WINGMASTER® LC LIGHT CONTOUR

Everything about the Model 870™ Wingmaster® LC is designed to make every shot count. The target-type twin-bead sights quickly tell your eye that your head is down on the gun, and the twin action bars let you cycle the fore-end smoothly in any weather without twisting or binding. The American walnut stock is furnished with satin or high-gloss finish. Light contour Rem™ Choke barrels are available in 26", 28" or 30" lengths. Handles 2¾" and 3" magnum shells interchangeably. Left-hand action available in 28" version. Supplied with Imp. Cyl., Mod., and Full choke tubes. Light contour Wingmasters come in our two-barrel, custom-fitted hard case.

NEW

MODEL 870™ WINGMASTER® CANTILEVER SCOPE MOUNT DEER GUN (20-GA.)

Now, 20-ga. deer hunters can now enjoy the sighting benefits of a Monte Carlo stock and barrel mounted scope. This year, we're making our new fully rifled cantilever scope mount design available in 20-ga. – the perfect match for our new 20-ga. Copper Solid™ sabot slug. Note: Scope and rings not included.

23" BARREL

MODEL 870™ SPECIAL FIELD

You can point fast and shoot quick with this compact, lightweight pump gun designed for the special demands of upland hunting in close cover. Available in 12- and 20-gauge with an English-style, straight-gripped, satin-finished walnut stock, new 23" barrel, slimmed and shortened fore-end, and Rem™ Choke tubes.

NEW

MODEL 870™ WINGMASTER® CANTILEVER SCOPE MOUNT DEER GUN (12-GA.)

For 1994, we have improved the design of our cantilever scope mount: the cantilever arm is shorter in length and has a thicker cross section for maximum rigidity. It doesn't lose zero, even after the effects of repeated recoil. It comes with a 20" long, fully-rifled barrel with 1 in 35" twist for optimum slug stabilization. Sling swivel studs and camo sling are included. Note: Scope and rings not included.

MODEL 870™ BRUSHMASTER® DEER GUN

A 10-pointer will only give you one chance, so don't take a chance on your gun. With its 20" Rem™ Choke barrel and rifle sights, you can point and shoot faster than a buck can bolt. Available in right-and left-hand versions.

KEEPING PACE WITHOUT CHANGING

Not much changed photograph-wise for the waterfowling 870s in the annual Remington catalogs—a color photo transitions to a sepia-toned background, a few headlines are rewritten. Then again, perhaps Remington's marketing writers were living the life of the gun: if it ain't broke, don't fix it.

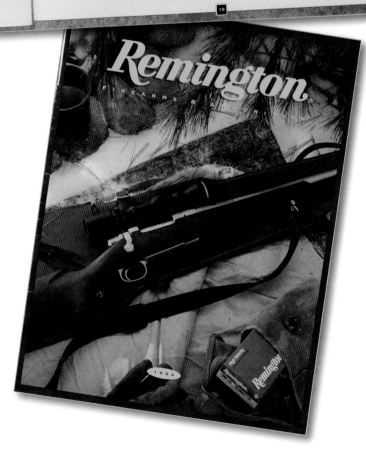

The scaled-frame 20-gauges got a mixed reception. Some loved the fast swing, while others complained the light little gun kicked too much with heavy waterfowling shotshell loads.

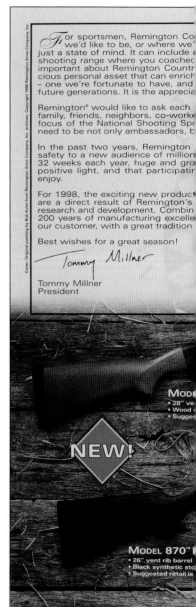

NEW!

MOD
• 28" ve
• Wood
• Sugges

MODEL 870™
• 26" vent rib barrel
• Black synthetic sto
• Suggested retail is

ALL THINGS MAGNUM

Remington didn't miss a beat, when it came to satisfying the American lust for all shotguns magnumed to the max, a trend fueled in large part by waterfowl hunters.

it completely feasible in the duck blind. Today, of course, with our newer and improved shot cups and loadings in steel and other nontoxic alternatives and faster powders, this has changed yet again. But this is now and that was then, and back then, the lack of effective steel shot loads in 3-inch Magnum 20-gauge hurt the sales of both ammunition and guns.

When the nationwide, steel shot-only law went into effect for waterfowl, Remington was one of the few gun makers that didn't have to make any changes to speak of to its guns. Remington announced that the barrels on their shotguns were perfectly safe for steel shot use, as long as it was specifically *not* choked Full and the choking on the barrel was kept to a Modified or less. Simple enough—owners of

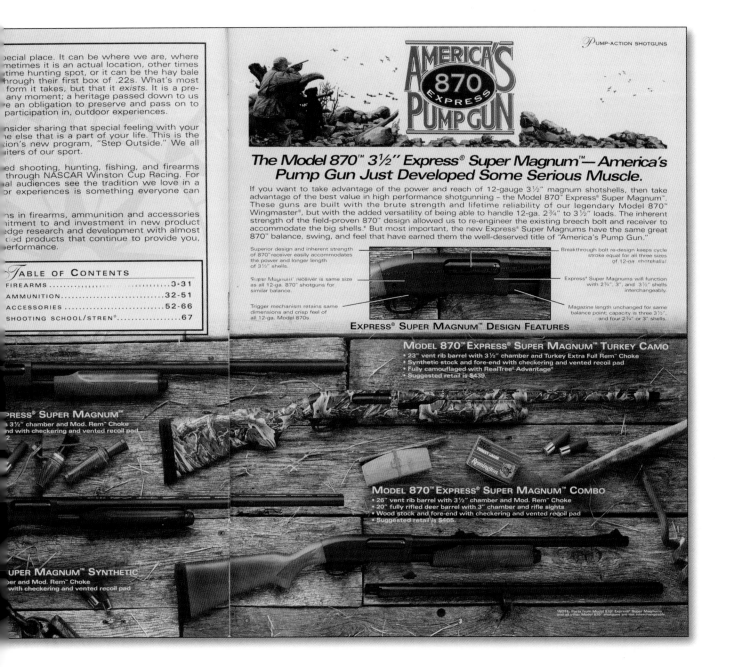

the reliable old Model 870s either simply bought another barrel with more open boring or had the boring opened up on the barrels they had and continued to shoot their favorite duck guns. Either way, it was a much cheaper proposition than buying a new gun, and owners of the Model 870s didn't have to give up the shotguns they were used to and shot well. The same thing can not be said of owners of Winchester Model 12s.

There have been numerous changes to the Model 870 waterfowling guns since the first 870s left the factory, all of these changes being cosmetic in nature. The first change started to take place in 1985, when Remington introduced the Model 870 SP Special Purpose Magnum with a choice of Full-choked 26- or 30-inch barrel. The gun wore a sheenless finish on all exposed metal surfaces, and even the finish on the wood was subdued. As Remington advertised it, this gun was designed specifically for waterfowl and turkey, depending on the barrel length. This turned out to be the first step in making a specialized gun for waterfowling only.

A few short years later, Remington announced the Model 870 Express, an economy version with a matte finish and low-luster hardwood stock. It was

870 EXPRESS
SUPER MAGNUM

ECONOMY AND PERFORMANCE
FOR VIRTUALLY EVERY HUNTING NEED

You can't find a better combination of versatility, economy and performance than our Model 870™ Express® Super Magnum™ shotguns. They handle 2¾", 3" and 3½" 12-gauge shells interchangeably, come at our budget-friendly "Express" prices, and are built on our famous Model 870™ actions. Each version is like having three shotguns in one, with the Combo expanding it to four!

MODEL 870™ EXPRESS®
SUPER MAGNUM™ TURKEY CAMO

MODEL 870™ EXPRESS®
SUPER MAGNUM™ SYNTHETIC

The big winner when you buy any of these shotguns is your wallet. You get the proven action of a Model 870™ — the most durable, best-selling shotgun in history, and still the world's most effective pump gun design. It costs you less because we didn't dress it up like a fancy wall-hanger. It's the toughest, most dependable, hardest-hitting

And the non
exactly what

However

Express® shotgun is the lifetime longevity and proven strength of a smooth-shucking Model 870™. You get the same rugged receiver machined from a solid bar of steel, the same non-binding twin action bars, and the same strong lock-up. That long-barrel

the-hands balance, and smooth natural-pointing qualities of all Remington® Model 870™ pump shotguns.

Start with the practical economy of our Model 870™ Express® and add the exceptional versatility of a 12-gauge, 3½" Super Magnum™ action, and you have the unchallenged "best buy" of any shotgun currently produced. Consider that these shotguns can handle any 12-gauge ammunition made — from heavy-payload 12-gauge, 3½" magnum shells all the way down to light 2¾" field or clay target loads. And the special bolt design in these guns retains the same length of cycle stroke for all shells.

In standard Model 870™ Express® Super Magnum™ shotguns, you

28

SPECIAL PURPOSE
WATERFOWL
GUNS

SHOTGUNS OF UNMATCHED RELIABILITY
WITH UNSURPASSED REACH AND POWER

Remington® Special Purpose Waterfowl guns give you a choice of the three most proven and reliable actions of their type. These include full 10-gauge magnum power from our unequalled Model SP-10™ Magnum, the sure-functioning flexibility of our Model 11-87™ autoloader with 2¾" or 3" magnum shells, and the exceptionally versatile performance of our Model 870™ SPS™ Super Magnum™ pump-action with 12-gauge 2¾", 3" and 3½" shells.

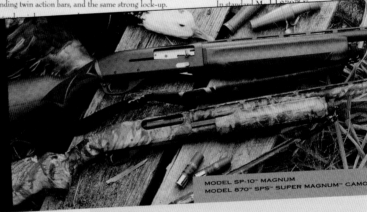

MODEL SP-10™ MAGNUM
MODEL 870™ SPS™ SUPER MAGNUM™ CAMO

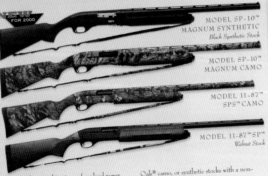

MODEL SP-10™
MAGNUM SYNTHETIC
Black Synthetic Stock

MODEL SP-10™
MAGNUM CAMO

MODEL 11-87™
SPS™ CAMO

MODEL 11-87™ SP™
Walnut Stock

Besides their combinations of payload power and versatility, our three **Special Purpose** Waterfowl guns offer you a variety of options in both stock material and finish for every preference or need. Among these are satin-finished American walnut, synthetic covered with Mossy

Oak® camo, or synthetic stocks with a non-reflective black finish. Barrels and receivers have either matching camo or non-reflective matte finishes. See the chart at right for options and specifications.

SHOTGUN DIMENSIONS / AVERAGE WEIGHTS

Model	★SP-10™ Magnum Synthetic†	SP-10™ Magnum†	SP-10™ Magnum Camo†	870™ SPS™ Super Magnum Camo	11-87™ SPS™	11-87™ SPS™ Camo	11-87™ SP™
Gauge	10	10	10	12 (3½")	12	12	12
Mag. Capacity	2	2	2	3 (3½") 4 (2¾" & 3")	4	4	4
BBL Lengths/ Order No.	26"/4822	30"/4808 26"/4812	26"/4809	28"/4952	28"/5269 26"/5271	26"/9662	28"/9905 26"/9906
Barrel Type	Vent Rib Rem™ Choke	Vent Rib Rem™ Choke	Vent Rib Rem™ Choke	Vent Rib Rem™ Choke	Vent Rib Rem™ Choke	Vent Rib Rem™ Choke	Vent Rib Rem™ Choke
Sights	Twin Bead	Twin Bead	Twin Bead	Twin Bead	Twin Bead	Twin Bead	Twin Bead
Metal Finish	Matte Non-Reflective	Matte Non-Reflective	Mossy Oak® Break-Up Camo	Mossy Oak® Break-Up Camo	Matte Non-Reflective	Mossy Oak® Break-Up Camo	Matte
Overall Length	47½"	51½" (30" BBL) 47½" (26" BBL)	47½"	46" (26" BBL)	48¼" (28" BBL) 46" (26" BBL)	46"	48¼" (28" BBL) 46" (26" BBL)
Length of Pull	14"	14"	14"	14"	14"	14"	14¼"
Drop (Comb)	1½"	1½"	1½"	1½"	1½"	1½"	1½"
Drop (Heel)	2½"	2½"	2½"	2½"	2½"	2½"	2½"
Stock Material	Black Synthetic	American Walnut	Camo-Covered Synthetic	Camo-Covered Synthetic	Black Synthetic	Camo-Covered Synthetic	American Walnut
Stock Finish	Matte	Satin	Mossy Oak® Break-Up Camo	Mossy Oak® Break-Up Camo	Matte	Mossy Oak® Break-Up Camo	Satin
Avg. Wt. (lbs.)	10¾	11 (30" BBL) 10¾ (26" BBL)	10¾	7¼	8¼ (28" BBL) 8¼ (26" BBL)	8¼	8¼ (28" BBL) 8¼ (26" BBL)

★ New For 2000

†These Model SP-10™ shotguns supplied with Full and Mod Rem™ Choke tubes.
Important Note: Critical components – including the barrel, bolt assembly and trigger plate assembly of the Remington Model SP-10™ and other manufacturers' 10-gauge shotguns – are not interchangeable.
Note: All Model 870™ Super Magnums have 3½" chambers except Deer barrel, which has 3" chamber. Super Magnums can shoot 2¾", 3", and 3½" shells interchangeably.

20

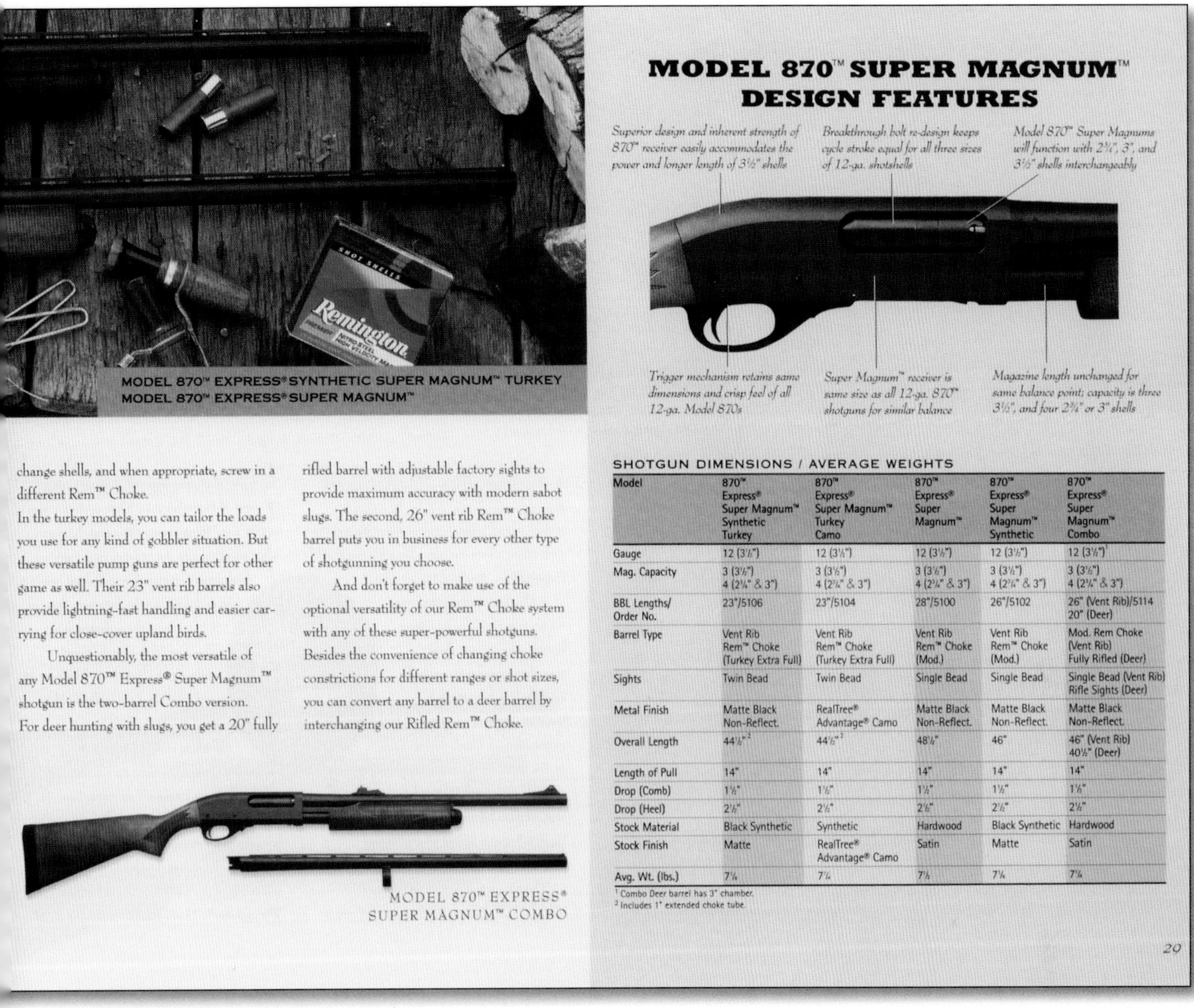

MODEL 870™ EXPRESS® SYNTHETIC SUPER MAGNUM™ TURKEY
MODEL 870™ EXPRESS® SUPER MAGNUM™

MODEL 870™ SUPER MAGNUM™ DESIGN FEATURES

Superior design and inherent strength of 870™ receiver easily accommodates the power and longer length of 3½" shells

Breakthrough bolt re-design keeps cycle stroke equal for all three sizes of 12-ga. shotshells

Model 870™ Super Magnums will function with 2¾", 3", and 3½" shells interchangeably

Trigger mechanism retains same dimensions and crisp feel of all 12-ga. Model 870s

Super Magnum™ receiver is same size as all 12-ga. 870™ shotguns for similar balance

Magazine length unchanged for same balance point; capacity is three 3½", and four 2¾" or 3" shells

change shells, and when appropriate, screw in a different Rem™ Choke.

In the turkey models, you can tailor the loads you use for any kind of gobbler situation. But these versatile pump guns are perfect for other game as well. Their 23" vent rib barrels also provide lightning-fast handling and easier carrying for close-cover upland birds.

Unquestionably, the most versatile of any Model 870™ Express® Super Magnum™ shotgun is the two-barrel Combo version. For deer hunting with slugs, you get a 20" fully rifled barrel with adjustable factory sights to provide maximum accuracy with modern sabot slugs. The second, 26" vent rib Rem™ Choke barrel puts you in business for every other type of shotgunning you choose.

And don't forget to make use of the optional versatility of our Rem™ Choke system with any of these super-powerful shotguns. Besides the convenience of changing choke constrictions for different ranges or shot sizes, you can convert any barrel to a deer barrel by interchanging our Rifled Rem™ Choke.

MODEL 870™ EXPRESS® SUPER MAGNUM™ COMBO

SHOTGUN DIMENSIONS / AVERAGE WEIGHTS

Model	870™ Express® Super Magnum™ Synthetic Turkey	870™ Express® Super Magnum™ Turkey Camo	870™ Express® Super Magnum™	870™ Express® Super Magnum™ Synthetic	870™ Express® Super Magnum™ Combo
Gauge	12 (3½")	12 (3½")	12 (3½")	12 (3½")	12 (3½")[1]
Mag. Capacity	3 (3½") 4 (2¾" & 3")	3 (3½") 4 (2¾" & 3")	3 (3½") 4 (2¾" & 3")	3 (3½") 4 (2¾" & 3")	3 (3½") 4 (2¾" & 3")
BBL Lengths/ Order No.	23"/5106	23"/5104	28"/5100	26"/5102	26" (Vent Rib)/5114 20" (Deer)
Barrel Type	Vent Rib Rem™ Choke (Turkey Extra Full)	Vent Rib Rem™ Choke (Turkey Extra Full)	Vent Rib Rem™ Choke (Mod.)	Vent Rib Rem™ Choke (Mod.)	Mod. Rem Choke (Vent Rib) Fully Rifled (Deer)
Sights	Twin Bead	Twin Bead	Single Bead	Single Bead	Single Bead (Vent Rib) Rifle Sights (Deer)
Metal Finish	Matte Black Non-Reflect.	RealTree® Advantage® Camo	Matte Black Non-Reflect.	Matte Black Non-Reflect.	Matte Black Non-Reflect.
Overall Length	44½"[2]	44½"[2]	48½"	46"	46" (Vent Rib) 40½" (Deer)
Length of Pull	14"	14"	14"	14"	14"
Drop (Comb)	1½"	1½"	1½"	1½"	1½"
Drop (Heel)	2½"	2½"	2½"	2½"	2½"
Stock Material	Black Synthetic	Synthetic	Hardwood	Black Synthetic	Hardwood
Stock Finish	Matte	RealTree® Advantage® Camo	Satin	Matte	Satin
Avg. Wt. (lbs.)	7¼	7¼	7½	7¼	7¼

[1] Combo Deer barrel has 3" chamber.
[2] Includes 1" extended choke tube.

29

meant to be a less costly alternative to the regular Model 870 Wingmaster, but was also intended for waterfowling, where rough environments necessitated a gun that could take a beating.

From the first appearance of the Special Purpose 870, different variations of waterfowling guns began to appear almost every year, reaching a point where there are now nearly innumerable choices. The Model 870 is available in several different types of camouflage patterns on synthetic stocks and forearms. All guns now have sling swivels, a trend that was started by duck and turkey hunters. American shotgunners, as a rule, do not like sling swivels on their shotguns; in the 1960s and '70s one rarely saw a

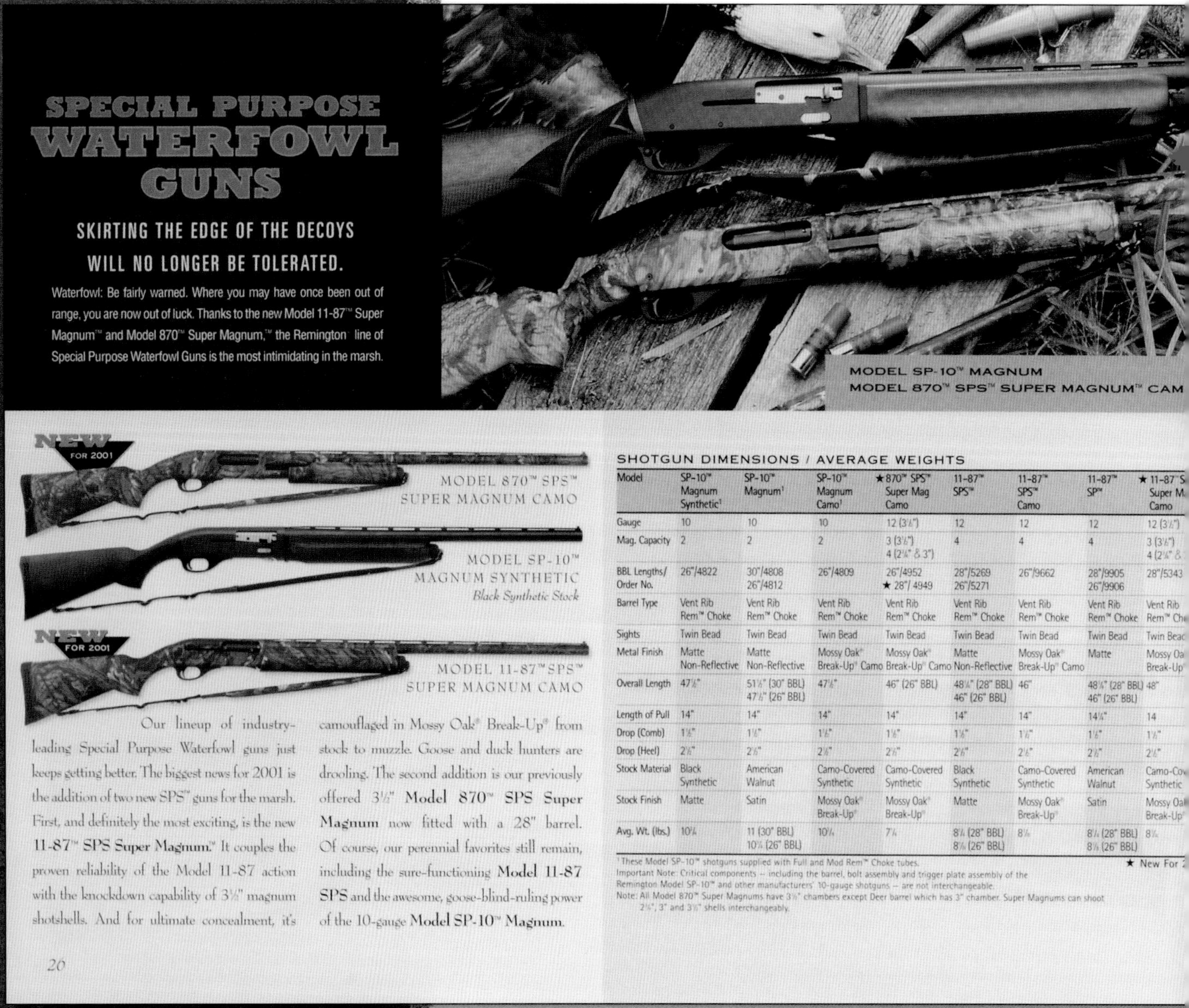

SPECIAL PURPOSE WATERFOWL GUNS

SKIRTING THE EDGE OF THE DECOYS WILL NO LONGER BE TOLERATED.

Waterfowl: Be fairly warned. Where you may have once been out of range, you are now out of luck. Thanks to the new Model 11-87™ Super Magnum™ and Model 870™ Super Magnum,™ the Remington line of Special Purpose Waterfowl Guns is the most intimidating in the marsh.

MODEL SP-10™ MAGNUM
MODEL 870™ SPS™ SUPER MAGNUM™ CAM

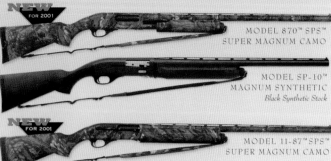

NEW FOR 2001

MODEL 870™ SPS™
SUPER MAGNUM CAMO

MODEL SP-10™
MAGNUM SYNTHETIC
Black Synthetic Stock

NEW FOR 2001

MODEL 11-87™ SPS™
SUPER MAGNUM CAMO

Our lineup of industry-leading Special Purpose Waterfowl guns just keeps getting better. The biggest news for 2001 is the addition of two new SPS™ guns for the marsh. First, and definitely the most exciting, is the new 11-87™ SPS Super Magnum.™ It couples the proven reliability of the Model 11-87 action with the knockdown capability of 3½″ magnum shotshells. And for ultimate concealment, it's camouflaged in Mossy Oak® Break-Up® from stock to muzzle. Goose and duck hunters are drooling. The second addition is our previously offered 3½″ Model 870™ SPS Super Magnum now fitted with a 28″ barrel. Of course, our perennial favorites still remain, including the sure-functioning Model 11-87 SPS and the awesome, goose-blind-ruling power of the 10-gauge Model SP-10™ Magnum.

SHOTGUN DIMENSIONS / AVERAGE WEIGHTS

Model	SP-10™ Magnum Synthetic[1]	SP-10™ Magnum[1]	SP-10™ Magnum Camo[1]	★ 870™ SPS™ Super Mag Camo	11-87™ SPS™	11-87™ SPS™ Camo	11-87™ SP™	★ 11-87™ S Super Ma Camo
Gauge	10	10	10	12 (3½″)	12	12	12	12 (3½″)
Mag. Capacity	2	2	2	3 (3½″) 4 (2¾″ & 3″)	4	4	4	3 (3½″) 4 (2¾″ &
BBL Lengths/ Order No.	26″/4822	30″/4808 26″/4812	26″/4809	26″/4952 ★ 28″/ 4949	28″/5269 26″/5271	26″/9662	28″/9905 26″/9906	28″/5343
Barrel Type	Vent Rib Rem™ Choke	Vent Rib Rem™ Choke	Vent Rib Rem™ Choke	Vent Rib Rem™ Choke	Vent Rib Rem™ Choke	Vent Rib Rem™ Choke	Vent Rib Rem™ Choke	Vent Rib Rem™ Choke
Sights	Twin Bead	Twin Bead	Twin Bead	Twin Bead	Twin Bead	Twin Bead	Twin Bead	Twin Bead
Metal Finish	Matte Non-Reflective	Matte Non-Reflective	Mossy Oak® Break-Up† Camo	Matte Break-Up† Camo	Matte Non-Reflective	Mossy Oak® Break-Up† Camo	Matte	Mossy Oa Break-Up
Overall Length	47½″	51¼″ (30″ BBL) 47½″ (26″ BBL)	47½″	46″ (26″ BBL)	48¼″ (28″ BBL) 46″ (26″ BBL)	46″	48¼″ (28″ BBL) 46″ (26″ BBL)	48″
Length of Pull	14″	14″	14″	14″	14″	14″	14¼″	14
Drop (Comb)	1½″	1½″	1½″	1½″	1½″	1½″	1½″	1½″
Drop (Heel)	2½″	2½″	2½″	2½″	2½″	2½″	2½″	2½″
Stock Material	Black Synthetic	American Walnut	Camo-Covered Synthetic	Camo-Covered Synthetic	Black Synthetic	Camo-Covered Synthetic	American Walnut	Camo-Cov Synthetic
Stock Finish	Matte	Satin	Mossy Oak® Break-Up®	Mossy Oak® Break-Up®	Matte	Mossy Oak® Break-Up®	Satin	Mossy Oak Break-Up
Avg. Wt. (lbs.)	10¼	11 (30″ BBL) 10¾ (26″ BBL)	10¼	7¼	8¼ (28″ BBL) 8⅛ (26″ BBL)	8⅛	8¼ (28″ BBL) 8⅛ (26″ BBL)	8⅛

[1] These Model SP-10™ shotguns supplied with Full and Mod Rem™ Choke tubes.
Important Note: Critical components -- including the barrel, bolt assembly and trigger plate assembly of the Remington Model SP-10™ and other manufacturers' 10-gauge shotguns -- are not interchangeable.
Note: All Model 870™ Super Magnums have 3½″ chambers except Deer barrel which has 3″ chamber. Super Magnums can shoot 2½″, 3″ and 3½″ shells interchangeably.
★ New For 2

20

Remington.
This is Remington Country FIREARMS • AMMUNITION • ACCESSORIES 2001

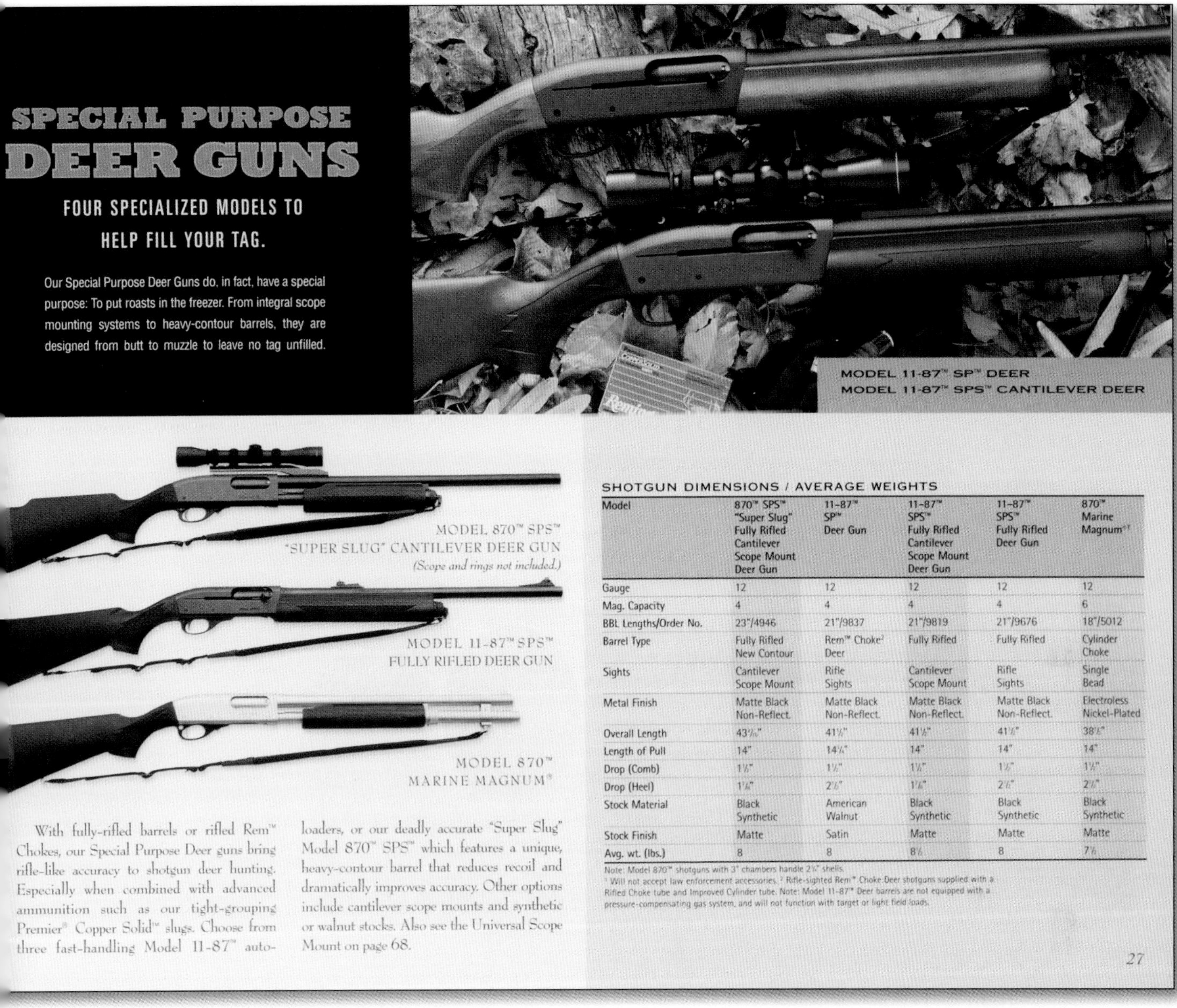

SPECIAL PURPOSE DEER GUNS

FOUR SPECIALIZED MODELS TO HELP FILL YOUR TAG.

Our Special Purpose Deer Guns do, in fact, have a special purpose: To put roasts in the freezer. From integral scope mounting systems to heavy-contour barrels, they are designed from butt to muzzle to leave no tag unfilled.

MODEL 11-87™ SP™ DEER
MODEL 11-87™ SPS™ CANTILEVER DEER

MODEL 870™ SPS™ "SUPER SLUG" CANTILEVER DEER GUN
(Scope and rings not included.)

MODEL 11-87™ SPS™ FULLY RIFLED DEER GUN

MODEL 870™ MARINE MAGNUM®

With fully-rifled barrels or rifled Rem™ Chokes, our Special Purpose Deer guns bring rifle-like accuracy to shotgun deer hunting. Especially when combined with advanced ammunition such as our tight-grouping Premier® Copper Solid™ slugs. Choose from three fast-handling Model 11-87™ autoloaders, or our deadly accurate "Super Slug" Model 870™ SPS™ which features a unique, heavy-contour barrel that reduces recoil and dramatically improves accuracy. Other options include cantilever scope mounts and synthetic or walnut stocks. Also see the Universal Scope Mount on page 68.

SHOTGUN DIMENSIONS / AVERAGE WEIGHTS

Model	870™ SPS™ "Super Slug" Fully Rifled Cantilever Scope Mount Deer Gun	11-87™ SP™ Deer Gun	11-87™ SPS™ Fully Rifled Cantilever Scope Mount Deer Gun	11-87™ SPS™ Fully Rifled Deer Gun	870™ Marine Magnum®1
Gauge	12	12	12	12	12
Mag. Capacity	4	4	4	4	6
BBL Lengths/Order No.	23"/4946	21"/9837	21"/9819	21"/9676	18"/5012
Barrel Type	Fully Rifled New Contour	Rem™ Choke[2] Deer	Fully Rifled	Fully Rifled	Cylinder Choke
Sights	Cantilever Scope Mount	Rifle Sights	Cantilever Scope Mount	Rifle Sights	Single Bead
Metal Finish	Matte Black Non-Reflect.	Matte Black Non-Reflect.	Matte Black Non-Reflect.	Matte Black Non-Reflect.	Electroless Nickel-Plated
Overall Length	43 3/16"	41 1/2"	41 1/2"	41 1/2"	38 1/2"
Length of Pull	14"	14 1/4"	14"	14"	14"
Drop (Comb)	1 1/2"	1 1/2"	1 1/2"	1 1/2"	1 1/2"
Drop (Heel)	1 7/8"	2 1/2"	1 7/8"	2 1/2"	2 1/2"
Stock Material	Black Synthetic	American Walnut	Black Synthetic	Black Synthetic	Black Synthetic
Stock Finish	Matte	Satin	Matte	Matte	Matte
Avg. wt. (lbs.)	8	8	8 1/4	8	7 1/2

Note: Model 870™ shotguns with 3" chambers handle 2¾" shells.
[1] Will not accept law enforcement accessories. [2] Rifle-sighted Rem™ Choke Deer shotguns supplied with a Rifled Choke tube and Improved Cylinder tube. Note: Model 11-87™ Deer barrels are not equipped with a pressure-compensating gas system, and will not function with target or light field loads.

27

duck hunter with a shotgun on a sling. Today, it seems everyone wants a sling on their duck gun.

Today's Remington Model 870 waterfowl gun is nothing like the shotguns that were seen in the 1960s and '70s, or even the '80s and '90s! Mechanically, of course, they are exactly the same—same trigger group with the easy to maintain fire control, the same breech block, the same easy to exchange barrels, and the smooth twin action bars. But the 870 is now available in three different chambers in 12-gauge, the standard 2¾-inch, the 3-inch Magnum, and the newer 3½-inch Super Magnum. A typical 870 waterfowl gun, a Super Magnum, will have a dull, non-reflective finish on the metal work and either a dully finished wooden stock or one that's synthetic. You could get it even more specialized by getting one with a camouflage coat that matches the camouflage you wear in the blind! All of them, of course, will not only have interchangeable choke tubes for different shot ranges and loads, but can be carried slung over the shoulder with a padded sling. The Remington Model 870 Waterfowl gun has come a long way from those early plain Jane versions.

The pump gun may not have been invented by an American, but it has become an "American" shotgun. Among pump guns, no other gun epitomizes the "all-American duck gun" characteristics

MODEL 1100™

THE AUTOLOADER THAT LAUNCHED IT ALL.

If there was a "hall of fame" for shotguns, the Remington® Model 1100™ would undoubtedly be one of the first guns voted in. It's the best-selling autoloader of all time. What more needs to be said?

MODEL 1100™ SYNTHETIC FR/CL
MODEL 1100™ SYNTHETIC

More than 39 years ago, the Model 1100™ forever changed the way American shooters viewed autoloading shotguns. It was the first autoloader to combine the repeat-shot versatility of early-century models with the sleek, modern lines and handling qualities of revered double-barrels. It's been a field-proven favorite ever since. In fact, many veteran hunters who have now migrated to the new Model 11-87™ grew up shooting a Model 1100. And on many occasions, they still do. Its superb balance, handling, lifetime durability and light recoil are the foundation of the Remington® autoloading legacy. Today, the Model 1100 is still going strong — and is available in versions suited for everything from doves to deer.

MODEL 1100™ LT-20
SYNTHETIC FR/RS
20-Gauge, Fully Rifled, Rifle Sights

MODEL 1100™
SYNTHETIC FR/CL
12-Gauge Fully Rifled Cantilever Deer Gun (Scope and rings not included.)

MODEL 1100™
SYNTHETIC
12- and 20-Gauge

SHOTGUN DIMENSIONS / AVERAGE WEIGHTS

Model	1100™ Synthetic	1100™ Synthetic Fully Rifled Cantilever Scope Mount Deer Gun	1100™ LT-20 Synthetic Fully Rifled Rifle Sighted Deer Gun	1100™ LT-20 Youth Synthetic Gun	1100™ LT-20 Youth Synthetic Turkey Camo
Gauge	12, 20	12	20	20	20 (Magnum)
Mag. Capacity	4	4	4	4	4
BBL Lengths/ Order No.	28" 12-ga./25369 26" 20-ga./25371	21"/25363	21"/25365	21"/25367	21"/25379
Barrel Type	Vent Rib Rem™ Choke (Mod. Only)	Fully Rifled	Fully Rifled	Vent Rib Rem™ Choke (Mod. Only)	Vent Rib Rem™ Choke (Full Only)
Sights	Single Bead	Cantilever Scope Mount	Rifle Sights	Single Bead	Twin Bead
Metal Finish	Matte Black Non-Reflect.	Matte Black Non-Reflect.	Matte Black Non-Reflect.	Matte Black Non-Reflect.	Matte Black Non-Reflect.
Overall Length	48" (12-ga.) 46" (20-ga.)	41½"	41"	40½"	40½"
Length of Pull	14"	14"	14"	13"	13"
Drop (Comb)	1½"	1½"	1½"	1½"	1½"
Drop (Heel)	2½"	1½"	2½"	2½"	2½"
Stock Material	Black Synthetic	Black Synthetic	Black Synthetic	Black Synthetic	Camo-Covered Synthetic
Stock Finish	Matte	Matte	Matte	Matte	RealTree® Advantage® Camo
Avg. Wt. (lbs.)	7 (12-ga.) 6¼ (20-ga.)	7½	7	6¾	6¾

¹ 3" Magnum is set up to handle heavy 20-ga. shotshells and will not function satisfactorily with target and field loads.

22

DOWN AND DIRTY

The plethora of camo patterns and synthetic stocks makes any 870 waterfowl version you choose more than able to take on hard knocks in boats and blinds, the foul weather that waterfowl often come with, and the mud and splatter and claw marks your Labrador leaves behind. This is one tough gun.

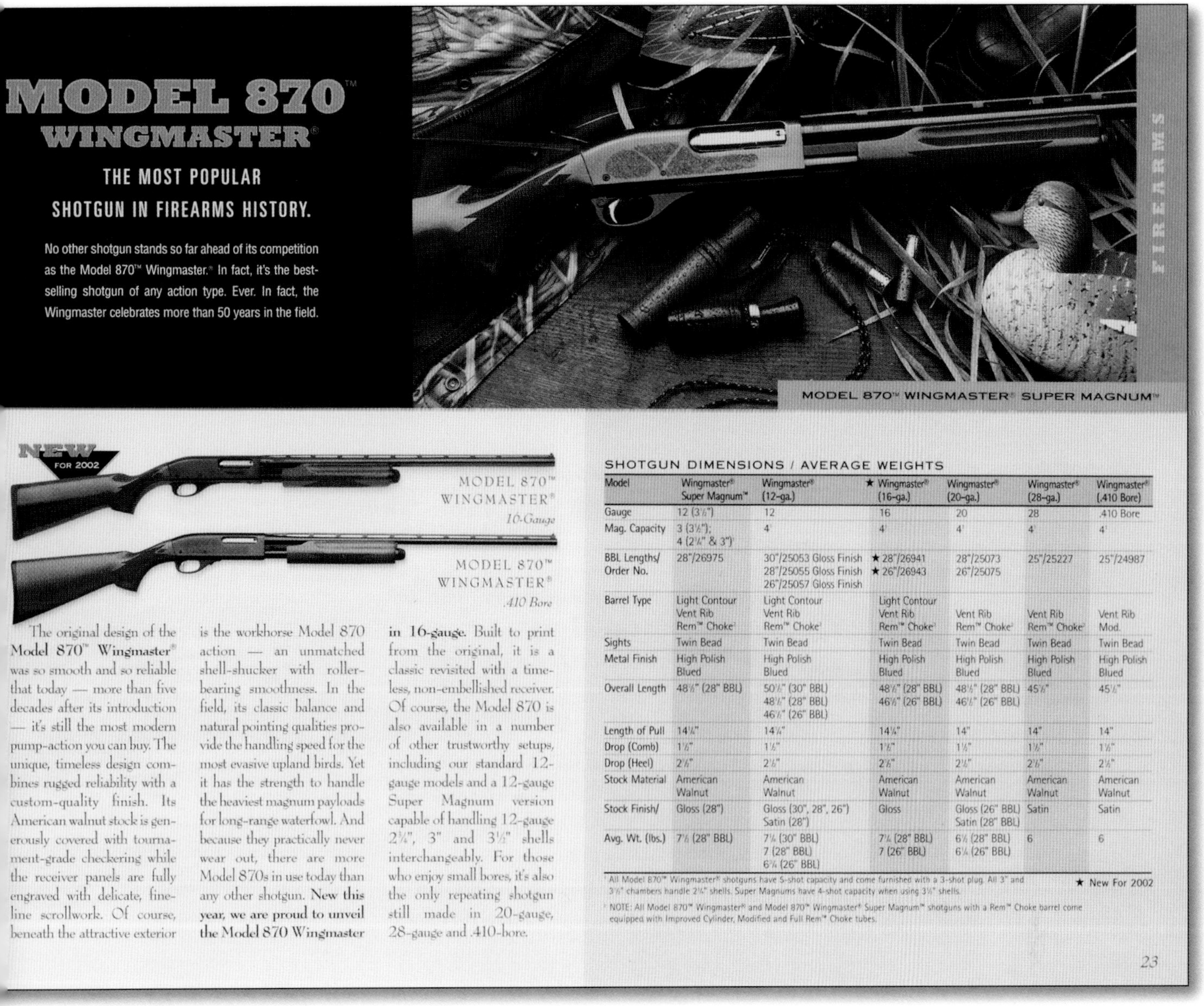

MODEL 870™ WINGMASTER®

THE MOST POPULAR SHOTGUN IN FIREARMS HISTORY.

No other shotgun stands so far ahead of its competition as the Model 870™ Wingmaster.® In fact, it's the best-selling shotgun of any action type. Ever. In fact, the Wingmaster celebrates more than 50 years in the field.

FIREARMS

MODEL 870™ WINGMASTER® SUPER MAGNUM™

NEW FOR 2002

MODEL 870™ WINGMASTER® *16-Gauge*

MODEL 870™ WINGMASTER® *.410 Bore*

The original design of the **Model 870™ Wingmaster®** was so smooth and so reliable that today — more than five decades after its introduction — it's still the most modern pump-action you can buy. The unique, timeless design combines rugged reliability with a custom-quality finish. Its American walnut stock is generously covered with tournament-grade checkering while the receiver panels are fully engraved with delicate, fine-line scrollwork. Of course, beneath the attractive exterior is the workhorse Model 870 action — an unmatched shell-shucker with roller-bearing smoothness. In the field, its classic balance and natural pointing qualities provide the handling speed for the most evasive upland birds. Yet it has the strength to handle the heaviest magnum payloads for long-range waterfowl. And because they practically never wear out, there are more Model 870s in use today than any other shotgun. **New this year, we are proud to unveil the Model 870 Wingmaster in 16-gauge.** Built to print from the original, it is a classic revisited with a timeless, non-embellished receiver. Of course, the Model 870 is also available in a number of other trustworthy setups, including our standard 12-gauge models and a 12-gauge Super Magnum version capable of handling 12-gauge 2¾", 3" and 3½" shells interchangeably. For those who enjoy small bores, it's also the only repeating shotgun still made in 20-gauge, 28-gauge and .410-bore.

SHOTGUN DIMENSIONS / AVERAGE WEIGHTS

Model	Wingmaster® Super Magnum™	Wingmaster® (12-ga.)	★ Wingmaster® (16-ga.)	Wingmaster® (20-ga.)	Wingmaster® (28-ga.)	Wingmaster® (.410 Bore)
Gauge	12 (3½")	12	16	20	28	.410 Bore
Mag. Capacity	3 (3½"); 4 (2¾" & 3")[1]	4[1]	4[1]	4[1]	4[1]	4[1]
BBL Lengths/ Order No.	28"/26975	30"/25053 Gloss Finish 28"/25055 Gloss Finish 26"/25057 Gloss Finish	★ 28"/26941 ★ 26"/26943	28"/25073 26"/25075	25"/25227	25"/24987
Barrel Type	Light Contour Vent Rib Rem™ Choke[2]	Light Contour Vent Rib Rem™ Choke[2]	Light Contour Vent Rib Rem™ Choke[2]	Vent Rib Rem™ Choke[2]	Vent Rib Rem™ Choke[2]	Vent Rib Mod.
Sights	Twin Bead	Twin Bead	Twin Bead	Twin Bead	Twin Bead	Twin Bead
Metal Finish	High Polish Blued	High Polish Blued	High Polish Blued	High Polish Blued	High Polish Blued	High Polish Blued
Overall Length	48½" (28" BBL)	50½" (30" BBL) 48½" (28" BBL) 46½" (26" BBL)	48½" (28" BBL) 46½" (26" BBL)	48½" (28" BBL) 46½" (26" BBL)	45½"	45½"
Length of Pull	14⅜"	14⅜"	14⅜"	14"	14"	14"
Drop (Comb)	1½"	1½"	1½"	1½"	1½"	1½"
Drop (Heel)	2½"	2½"	2½"	2½"	2½"	2½"
Stock Material	American Walnut	American Walnut	American Walnut	American Walnut	American Walnut	American Walnut
Stock Finish/	Gloss (28")	Gloss (30", 28", 26") Satin (28")	Gloss	Gloss (26" BBL) Satin (28" BBL)	Satin	Satin
Avg. Wt. (lbs.)	7½ (28" BBL)	7¼ (30" BBL) 7 (28" BBL) 6¾ (26" BBL)	7¼ (28" BBL) 7 (26" BBL)	6½ (28" BBL) 6¼ (26" BBL)	6	6

[1] All Model 870™ Wingmaster® shotguns have 5-shot capacity and come furnished with a 3-shot plug. All 3" and 3½" chambers handle 2¾" shells. Super Magnums have 4-shot capacity when using 3½" shells.

★ New For 2002

[2] NOTE: All Model 870™ Wingmaster® and Model 870™ Wingmaster® Super Magnum™ shotguns with a Rem™ Choke barrel come equipped with Improved Cylinder, Modified and Full Rem™ Choke tubes.

23

of the rugged, dependable machines they are then does the Remington Model 870. To be sure, there are gun snobs out there who will turn up their noses at pump guns and consider them unacceptable as sporting arms. But they are a minority, for it truly is the pump gun, the Remington 870 pump gun in particular, that comes to mind when most think of waterfowl guns.

I recall, back in the mid-1970s, when I used to work at Chico State University, I met my friend Don Black, who also worked at the university. Don had not been a shotgunner before he arrived in the Chico area. He was from Redding, California, up by the Mount Shasta region, and he was a deer hunter. Most folks up in that part of country are deer hunters, not bird hunters. However, having moved to the Chico area, Don decided to take up duck hunting and had purchased an inexpensive used and somewhat beat up Western Field pump gun. But, after going duck hunting a few times and seeing what others were shooting, he told me he was embarrassed to be seen with the cheap "Monkey Ward" shotgun. ("Monkey Ward" was the somewhat endearing, somewhat slanderous nickname for the now defunct retail chain Montgomery Ward, a store much like Sears and Wal-Mart and which often sold products on the economical side of things.) Don told me he had decided to buy a decent gun to replace the Western Field. I asked him what he was going to get and

— REMINGTON —
Shotguns

It says something when a bunch of game wardens are all using the same shotgun for their personal hunting—and it's *not* their issue gun. Such was the love of the game officials at Gray Lodge WMA for the Model 870.

NO. 8·1   ~ MODEL 870 ~   SIRO TOFFOLON
                                                               OCT ~ 76

ART FOR THE FIELD

The engraver's sketch for a waterfowler's heritage piece, drawn in ink before the chisel meets the metal of an 870's receiver.

he replied, "A Remington Model 870." When I asked him why he'd chosen that one, he said it was because his duck hunting friends who shot pump guns all shot the 870. Don was true to his conviction and ended up getting an 870 with a 30-inch Full-choke barrel. I remember well one particular day, when we shot snows and specklebellies at a place called Web Foot Duck Club, in Colusa, California. We shot a pile of birds and Don did himself proud with that 870!

In the mid- to late 1970s, I used to frequent California's Gray Lodge Wildlife Management Area, about an hour north of Sacramento, during the waterfowl season. I had been hunting there so frequently that I'd become acquainted with all the game wardens who worked there, and several times I hunted with some of them on their days off. They were invariably very accomplished duck hunters, and most of them used the Remington 870. At first I thought those were the guns issued to them by Gray Lodge. But, when I asked one of them, he told me that it was his personal shotgun and that all of them purchased their own shotguns and simply preferred the 870s—and not because they got any sort of a special deal or a discount. Like everyone else, they just went to a gun store and bought the guns off the rack. Their choice was based on what they witnessed at Gray Lodge every day and what they heard about the different guns when they talked to the waterfowl hunters who frequented the place. That particular warden I had a conversation in which he told me everyone was in agreement that the 870 was the best choice, the best gun not just for the price, but the best gun in general.

BEEFED UP

There's no escaping the American waterfowler's desire for the biggest 12-gauge shells. Remington keeps pace all day long with the 3½-inch chambered Super Magnum Model 870s.

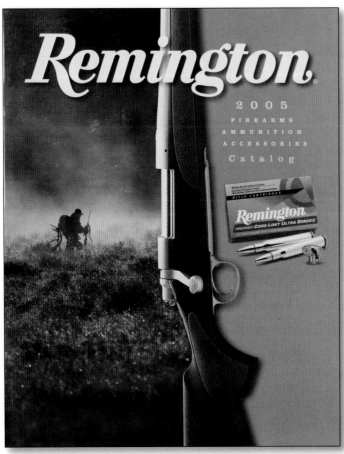

Some of my game warden friends at Gray Lodge bought their 870s with a second barrel, a short one that they swapped to for use as a home-defense gun and also to carry with them in their duty vehicles when they patrolled the grounds. Also, some of them hunted deer and used the short, rifle-sighted barrels for that pursuit. One warden I knew filled his deer tag every year with his 870 (he always got a nice buck, probably not surprising, since he knew where the good bucks were hanging around!) Later, during the pheasant and duck season, he put on the longer barrel and shot his share of birds. I guess these guys did get a lot for their money. Of course there were those who shot other makes, the Brownings and Winchesters, and not just Remington 870s, but also the Remington 1100s, but by and large, the 870 appeared to be the most popular shotgun among the game wardens at Gray Lodge.

WATER OFF A DUCK'S BACK

One of the incarnations newest to the waterfowl lineup of 870s has been a truly tough laminate stock that looks as good as it is durable. Add to that the ever-shifting number of camouflage patterns, and there's no duck or goose habitat a wader-wearing wingshooter can't take on.

122

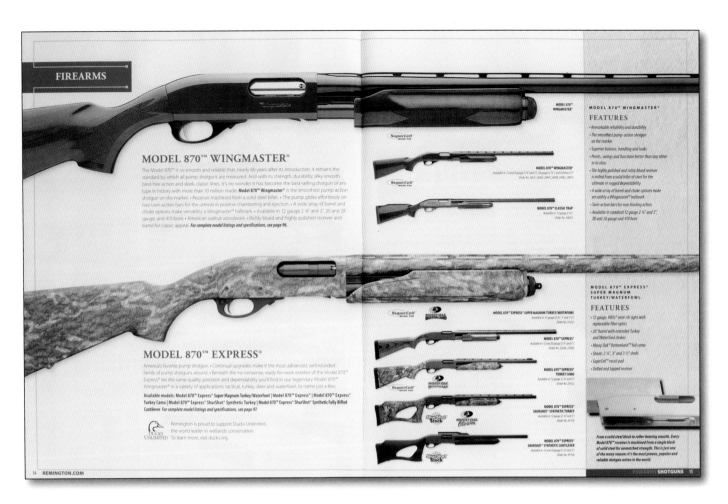

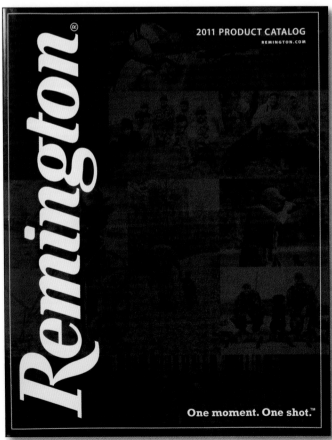

The 870 Express was originally introduced as a less costly alternative to the Wingmaster. It still is, but lacking nothing but a high-polish bluing job and a shiny stock, it epitomizes the work-horse shotgun wterfowlers demand.

FUNCTION OVER FORM

It's clear from this Remington ad that it doesn't matter what finish you choose. Each and every one will hold up and shoot when you want it to.

BACKED BY TRADITION,
HELPING ENSURE THE FUTURE.

MODEL 870™ WINGMASTER®

MODEL 11-87™ SPORTSMAN® CAMO

MODEL 552™ RIMFIRE BDL™ SPEEDMASTER®

INTRODUCING THE NEW **NRA EDITION** FIREARMS BY REMINGTON.

Three firearms forged in nearly 200 years of gunmaking excellence – the Model 870™ Wingmaster,® Model 552™ BDL™ Rimfire Speedmaster® and the Model 11-87™ Sportsman® Camo – are now available in a special edition officially licensed by the National Rifle Association. It's a way to own the finest while supporting the NRA and its programs. All are emblazoned with the NRA logo on the receiver and authenticated with NRA serial numbers.

Owning a Remington has always been a matter of pride. It's now a way of helping ensure the future of our hunting and shooting tradition as well.

OFFICIAL
NRA
LICENSED
PRODUCT

Remington
C O U N T R Y
©2006 REMINGTON ARMS COMPANY, INC.
www.remington.com/nra

A portion of the proceeds from the sale of each firearm is donated to the NRA.

1100 & 870 SP MAGNUMS

NOW, AMERICA'S FAVORITE SHOTGUNS ARE TAILORED FOR SERIOUS WATERFOWL AND TURKEY HUNTERS.

Remington

INTRODUCING THE REMINGTON 1100 AND 870 "SPECIAL PURPOSE" MAGNUMS.

Here's the answer to the special needs of the hunter who patiently shivers in a duck blind or pursues the wily, bearded spook of the forest. These demanding hunting sports require that the hunter be invisible to the game. So Remington is offering two new shotguns with low visibility—the Remington Model 870 and 1100 SP Magnums.

But low visibility is only part of the story. Remington reliability and Magnum performance are prime features. They help give the extra reach for those challenging shots often taken for these birds.

Special features ensure reliable performance, corrosion resistance and extended life. Barrels and receivers are Parkerized—a special metal finishing process that results in a non-reflective flat finish that is highly resistant to rust and corrosion.

Stocks and fore-ends are treated with a low luster satin finish that penetrates the wood, for extra protection and moisture resistance.

A camouflaged, padded Cordura® nylon sling is supplied with both models. Both guns are chambered for 3" Magnum shotshells and offer a choice of 26" or 30" Full choke barrels. And the bores on these barrels are chrome plated—tough, smooth and durable.

All of these features are in addition to the ones that have made Model 1100 and 870 the most popular sellers for decades.

Waterfowl or turkey, auto-loader or pump—whatever the action, the answer is Remington 1100 or 870 SP Magnums.

Buy DUCK STAMPS 50th Anniversary

Gauge	Barrel Length & Choke	Overall Length	Avg. Wt. (lbs.)	Total Shell Capacity	Order Number
Model 870 SP Magnum					
12	26" Full	50"	7¾	5	6986
12	30" Full	46"	7¾	5	6984
Model 1100 SP Magnum					
12	26" Full	50"	7½	5	5325
12	30" Full	46"	7½	5	5359

Remington
DUPONT

Remington is a trademark registered in the U.S. Patent and Trademark Office.

E-71702

REMINGTON INTRODUCES THE MODEL 1100 AND 870 SP MAGNUMS

Two new Remington shotguns specially designed for waterfowl or turkey hunting.

Parkerized action and barrels plus satin finish hardwood stock and fore-end eliminate reflections. Camouflage Cordura nylon sling blends with background cover.

Chambered for 3" Magnum shotshells. Both guns are available with 26" or 30" Full choke barrels.

(DEALER NAME AND ADDRESS)

Use this ad slick to tell your customers you have the new 1100 and 870 SP Magnums from Remington.

Printed in U.S.A.

A TRIBUTE TO THE DUCKS

The Ducks Unlimited model wasn't the only special edition. This highly engraved model was offered through the collector's organization America Remembers.

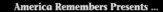

AMERICA'S
FAVORITE
PUMP SHOTGUN.

MORE THAN THE BEST EVER MADE, A RITE OF PASSAGE. For many, our Model 870™ Express® is the first and last shotgun they ever buy — for good reason. It's built on the smoothest, most dependable, most proven pump action in history. With 9 million sold, the Model 870™ has stood as the standard for more than 50 years. We're proud to make them, but prouder that so many generations have made them America's favorite.

MODEL 870™ EXPRESS®

MODEL 870™ EXPRESS®
The ultimate in strength, reliability and silky-smooth action, available in a wide range of models and gauges.

Features: Sleek, swift-pointing design / Receiver milled from a solid billet of steel / Smooth twin action bars / Updated wood laminate, synthetic and camo versions available / 3" and 3 1/2" chambers

LOAD UP ON SAVINGS with Model 870 Express rebate, 8/1/07 – 12/31/07. Visit www.remington.com/FallPromo or see store for details.

up to
$**30**
BACK

©2007 REMINGTON ARMS COMPANY, INC.

Remington®
COUNTRY

www.REMINGTON.com/870Express

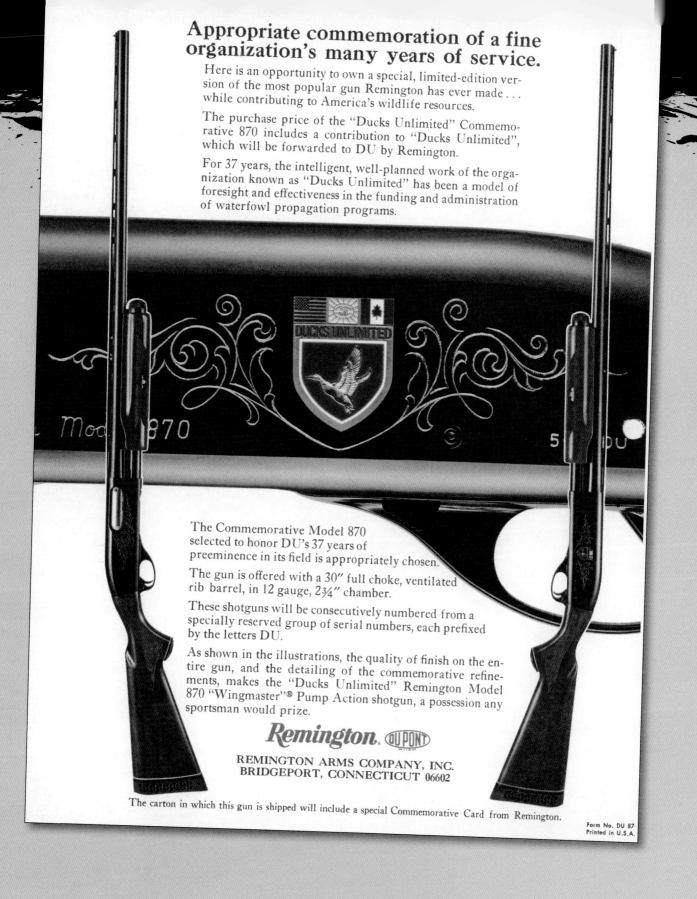

Appropriate commemoration of a fine organization's many years of service.

Here is an opportunity to own a special, limited-edition version of the most popular gun Remington has ever made . . . while contributing to America's wildlife resources.

The purchase price of the "Ducks Unlimited" Commemorative 870 includes a contribution to "Ducks Unlimited", which will be forwarded to DU by Remington.

For 37 years, the intelligent, well-planned work of the organization known as "Ducks Unlimited" has been a model of foresight and effectiveness in the funding and administration of waterfowl propagation programs.

The Commemorative Model 870 selected to honor DU's 37 years of preeminence in its field is appropriately chosen.

The gun is offered with a 30″ full choke, ventilated rib barrel, in 12 gauge, 2¾″ chamber.

These shotguns will be consecutively numbered from a specially reserved group of serial numbers, each prefixed by the letters DU.

As shown in the illustrations, the quality of finish on the entire gun, and the detailing of the commemorative refinements, makes the "Ducks Unlimited" Remington Model 870 "Wingmaster"® Pump Action shotgun, a possession any sportsman would prize.

Remington. DUPONT

REMINGTON ARMS COMPANY, INC.
BRIDGEPORT, CONNECTICUT 06602

The carton in which this gun is shipped will include a special Commemorative Card from Remington.

Form No. DU 87
Printed in U.S.A.

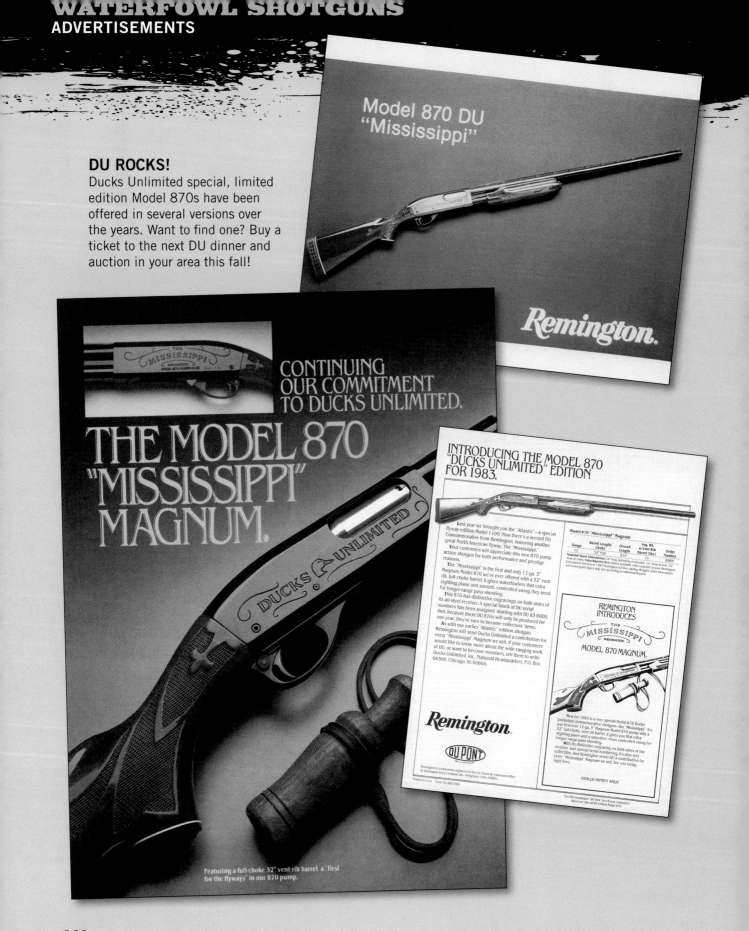

DU ROCKS!

Ducks Unlimited special, limited edition Model 870s have been offered in several versions over the years. Want to find one? Buy a ticket to the next DU dinner and auction in your area this fall!

Model 870 DU "Mississippi"

Remington.

CONTINUING OUR COMMITMENT TO DUCKS UNLIMITED.

THE MODEL 870 "MISSISSIPPI" MAGNUM.

Featuring a full-choke 32" vent-rib barrel, a "first for the flyways" in our 870 pump.

INTRODUCING THE MODEL 870 "DUCKS UNLIMITED" EDITION FOR 1983.

Last year we brought you the "Atlantic"—a special flyway-edition Model 1100. Now there's a second DU Commemorative from Remington, honoring another great North American flyway. The "Mississippi."

Your customers will appreciate this new 870 pump action shotgun for both performance and prestige reasons.

The "Mississippi" is the first and only 12-ga. 3" Magnum Model 870 we've ever offered with a 32" vent rib, full-choke barrel. It gives waterfowlers that extra sighting plane and smooth, controlled swing they need for longer-range pass shooting.

This 870 has distinctive engravings on both sides of its all-steel receiver. A special block of DU serial numbers has been assigned, starting with DU 83 6000. And, because these DU 870s will only be produced in one year, they're sure to become collectors' items.

As with our earlier "Atlantic" edition shotgun, Remington will send Ducks Unlimited a contribution for every "Mississippi" Magnum we sell. If your customers would like to know more about the wide-ranging work of DU, or want to become members, tell them to write Ducks Unlimited, Inc. National Headquarters, P.O. Box 66300, Chicago, Ill. 60666.

Model 870 "Mississippi" Magnum

Gauge	Barrel Length/ Choke	Overall Length	Avg. Wt. w/Vent Rib Barrel (lbs.)	Order Number
12	32" Full	52½"	7½	6990

Nominal Stock Dimensions 14" long (including recoil pad) 2½" drop at heel, 1⅝" drop at comb. Extra Barrels With choice available, refer customer to your Remington Extra Barrel Selector or 1983 Remington full-line catalog. Weights, stock dimensions and wood-grain figure may vary according to individual firearm.

Remington.

DU PONT

Remington is a trademark registered in the U.S. Patent & Trademark Office by Remington Arms Company, Inc., Bridgeport, Conn. 06601.

Printed in U.S.A. Form No. AM 7000

REMINGTON INTRODUCES

THE MISSISSIPPI MODEL 870 MAGNUM.

New for 1983 is a very special Model 870 Ducks Unlimited commemorative shotgun—the "Mississippi." It's our first-ever 12-ga. 3" Magnum Model 870 pump with a 32" full-choke, vent rib barrel. It gives you that extra sighting plane and a smoother, more controlled swing for longer-range pass shooting.

With its distinctive engraving on both sides of the receiver, and special serial numbering, it's also very collectible. And Remington sends DU a contribution for every "Mississippi" Magnum we sell. See one today.

(DEALER IMPRINT AREA)

Use this newspaper "ad slick" to tell your customers about our special DU-edition Model 870.

America Remembers and Ducks Unlimited Present . . .
The Ducks Unlimited Tribute Shotgun

Right side of receiver shows a flock of graceful mallards soaring North to their traditional breeding grounds. To the right of the scene is the ever-popular Ducks Unlimited logo. The receiver is polished and decorated in 24-karat gold, and the artwork is featured in 24-karat gold with a rich blackened patinaed background to elegantly highlight the gold artwork. Elegant scrollwork frames the artwork and adds the finishing touch to this museum-quality Tribute.

Left side of receiver features three scenes of mallards, North America's most recognized waterfowl species, in their wetland habitat. The center features a pair of mallards on a pond with cattails in the background beneath a banner identifying this as the "Ducks Unlimited Tribute." Flanking the center image you will find a scene with a drake taking flight and a scene with a hen preparing to land.

An Important First For Collectors And Waterfowlers

Through the tireless efforts of Ducks Unlimited, leader in wetlands conservation, our knowledge and respect for the preservation of North American waterfowl has grown dramatically over the years. It was in the 1930s when the threat of declining bird populations inspired the idea for Ducks Unlimited, and the organization was formed to restore the waterfowl population and protect their habitat. Their results have been extremely successful, and so today, outdoorsmen and wildlife lovers alike are able to continue to enjoy the grace and beauty of America's abundant waterfowl.

Founded in 1937, Ducks Unlimited has become the world's largest private waterfowl and wetlands conservation organization with over one million supporters. DU has contributed to the conservation of more than nine million acres of prime wildlife habitat. From the very beginning, DU has been a volunteer-based non-profit organization with one message – to protect, restore, and enhance the habitat of North America's waterfowl.

Now, for the very first time, Ducks Unlimited and America Remembers have teamed to issue an exclusive Tribute honoring America's waterfowl with the "Ducks Unlimited Tribute Shotgun." The Tribute is a handsomely decorated Remington Model 870 Wingmaster 12-gauge shotgun,

the best selling American shotgun in history. Combining performance and reliability with sleek, classic lines, the 870 Wingmaster has been a favorite of sportsmen since the early days of Ducks Unlimited.

The Tribute magnificently captures the beauty of North American waterfowl in their natural setting. Craftsmen specifically commissioned for this Tribute by America Remembers decorate each shotgun in 24-karat gold with a special blackened patinaed background for maximum detail and contrast, and the Tribute is available exclusively from America Remembers. The hand-polished walnut stocks feature the Ducks Unlimited logo on both sides.

Only 300 Available

The Ducks Unlimited Tribute Shotgun will be the envy of many an outdoorsman and collector, but only 300 will have the opportunity to own one. Order now, and you can be certain to add this truly important "first" to your collection. We will arrange to ship the Tribute to a licensed dealer of your choice. If for any reason you are less than satisfied with your shotgun, you may return it in original condition within 30 days for a full and courteous refund.

Description: Barrel Length: 28 Inches • Gauge: 12
Choke: Rem Chokes (Full, Improved Cylinder, Modified)

"Each Ducks Unlimited Tribute Shotgun is produced and sold under license from Ducks Unlimited, Inc. - leader in wetlands conservation" OAHL, Inc.

CHAPTER EIGHT

DEER AND TURKEY SHOTGUNS

THUMBS UP FOR THUMBHOLES
Turkey hunters first made the thumbhole stock popular, but the stock's inherent steadiness lends itself well to aiming with a slug gun like this current Model 870.

SCOPED OUT
The cantilever scope mount is ideal for deer and turkey hunters, as it accommodates both glass optics and red dot sights. Remington's placement of the mount on the barrel also provides for variable adjustment in eye relief.

HIDING IN PLAIN SIGHT
This all-camo 870 has turkey dinner written all over it. It comes equipped with fiber optic rifle sights and a Monte Carlo-style cheekpiece that gives a good cheek weld while keeping the sights lined up.

THE MODEL 870 "DEER SHOTGUN," or slug gun, made its first appearance in 1959, when Remington introduced its Model 870 RSS Rifle Slug Special. It was simply a 26-inch barreled Model 870 with rifle sights. Everything else was the same as the standard Model 870 AP or ADL, depending on which version one purchased— there were no sling swivels or any provisions for

scope mounting. In 1961, Remington announced the introduction of the Model 870 Brushmaster with a 20-inch rifle sighted barrel, and it was the same gun as the longer barreled Rifle Slug Special, just with a shorter barrel. The Model 870 "deer or slug" gun continued in this manner for more than two decades. Then, in 1978, the new, scaled-frame Model 870 LW-20 Lightweight

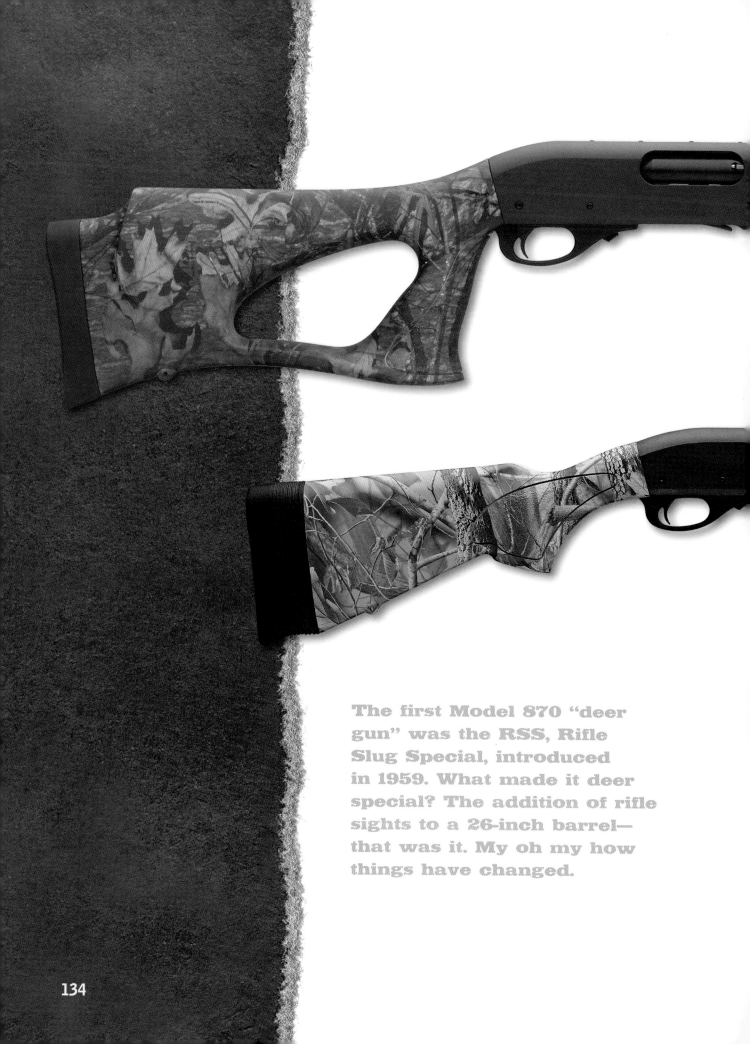

The first Model 870 "deer gun" was the RSS, Rifle Slug Special, introduced in 1959. What made it deer special? The addition of rifle sights to a 26-inch barrel—that was it. My oh my how things have changed.

MIX IT UP
All camo or no camo, thumbhole stock or traditional, extended chokes or flush tubes. Whichever way you want your turkey or deer 870, Remington has it.

Deer Gun was offered. The 20-gauge version of the Deer Gun had been available earlier in the standard frame, but now it was also available in the smaller, lighter gun.

The first major change to deer variants of the Model 870 occurred in 1986, when Remington announced the new Model 870 SP Special Purpose Deer Gun. This model had a dull, non-reflective finish on the metal and a satin finish on the wood. The short, 20-inch barrel had rifle sights, as well as the new Rem Choke system, and the gun had sling swivels and came with a padded camouflaged sling. From this point on, the Model 870 Deer Gun continued to evolve into the several versions that one finds today in Remington's catalog and on retailer's shelves. The cantilever scope mount version first ap-

peared in 1991, and from then on, all different sorts of models began to appear with synthetic stocks and various camouflage finishes, as well as fiber optic sights.

The production and debut of more accurate ammunition and the utilization of rifling in shotgun slug gun barrels had a profound effect on shotgun deer guns. No longer was the slug gun a short-distance gun with questionable accuracy, a reputation attached to many of yesteryear's slug guns. The slug gun had now become a *viable* deer gun, as good as some of the older rifle calibers! With a good sighting system or a scope, the slug gun now is a 100-plus-yard deer gun!

One of the side effects of the development of better rifle slug ammunition and the rifling in shotgun barrels, which increased the range

Before turkey and deer shotguns came to be the task-specific tools we know them to be today, it's important to remember that, back in the day, both bucks and birds were regularly shot with buckshot!

and accuracy of slug guns dramatically, was the creation of a slug gun that was lighter and easier to handle than the old standby, the 12-gauge. The 20-gauge rifle slug gun has now become a very effective deer slayer, something that was simply not possible a few decades ago. Today's 20-gauge slug gun can put all its slugs in a pie plate-size area at 150 yards, still with enough energy to knock down any deer. Remington was not about to miss the bus on this new phenomena and was one of the first to put out a Model 870 Deer Gun in 20-gauge, one with a rifled barrel that was light and easy to carry, yet had the accuracy and power to kill deer at extended ranges.

I have personally never owned or hunted with a shotgun specifically designed for deer hunting, such as the Remington Model 870 Brushmaster or the Special Purpose Deer Gun. I have handled and shot them, but never owned or hunted with one. However, I did hunt with my 870 AP model, which

I used for everything else. Stoked with 00 Buck-shot, I felt ready to tackle any big-game animal that came my way. My gun was a regular shotgun for bird hunting that had a 28-inch fixed-choke Modified barrel—then again, *everyone* at that time simply used their favorite bird gun loaded with buckshot if they were going after big game with a shotgun. I did not in any way feel under-gunned or improperly armed pursuing big game with my regular bird gun, and heck, everyone else was doing the same thing! In fact, the thought of having a specially made shotgun for big-game hunting was incomprehensible to me and most anyone else at that time. A shotgun with slugs accurate beyond 100 yards? Unthinkable, unbelievable, never gonna happen. Like many others, to me a shotgun was at best about a 75-yard gun with slugs, and more like under 60 yards for buckshot. Like I said, I did not in any way feel handicapped or under-gunned, but we all new the limits.

They may have gotten a slow start, but 870s tweaked to be deer-specific are legion now. Models just for gobblers, on the other hand, got a late start in Remington's marketing department, partly because wild turkey populations were in dire straights for many decades.

Remington. PRESS RELEASE

OCTOBER 24, 1996

FOR IMMEDIATE RELEASE
Contact: Bill Wohl
910/548-8577 [Press Only]
800/537-2278 [Press Only]

NEW MODEL 870™ EXPRESS™ 12- AND 20-GAUGE COMBO SETS WITH FULLY RIFLED DEER BARRELS

For 1997, Remington® is offering new 12- and 20-gauge combo sets with fully rifled deer barrels. Remington's Model 870™ Express™ shotguns have long been one of the best values available to field shotgunners. These shotguns offer all the strength, durability and performance features of a Model 870™ pump gun at a highly affordable cost.

Model 870™ Express™ Combo shotgun sets provide an even greater value by providing the versatility of two barrels with the same gun. In 1997, Remington is offering new 12- and 20-gauge, dual-barrel Model 870™ Express™ Combos for all-around field and slug hunting. Included will be a 26-inch vent rib field barrel with a modified Rem™ Choke and a 20-inch fully rifled deer barrel with adjustable factory sights. All exposed metal surfaces have a non-glare, black matte finish. The non-reflective hardwood stock includes cut checkering and a recoil pad. With the addition of other selected Rem™ chokes, this combination permits the low cost, versatile application of one shotgun to every type of field hunting – upland, waterfowl and deer.

This new Model 870 Express™ Combo will be available at a suggested retail price of $421.00 in both 12- and 20-gauge.

# # #

Color and B&W photos available on request.

REMINGTON MODEL 870 SPS CAMO (SPECIAL PURPOSE SYNTHETIC, MOSSY OAK BREAK UP)

VARIATIONS ON A THEME
The top 870 here is intended for turkey, with a single front fiber optic sight and an extended choke tube. The laminate stock version below has a full set of rifle sights and a rifled barrel, making it a wonderful choice for slug hunters going after deer.

It is important to bear in mind that, back in the day, deer and other game were *regularly* shot with buckshot, especially in the southeastern part of the U.S. Just read some of the stories about deer hunting written by such classic writers as Archibald Rutledge or Nash Buckingham. Both men used their standard bird guns loaded with 00 buckshot, and it was one of the reasons the 16-gauge was so popular in the southeast during that era. The 16 was big enough to handle buckshot for deer and at the same time made a fine bird gun! Adding to the prevailing logic, my friends and I actually considered it an *advantage* to use a pump gun with buckshot, since it provided more than the two shots of the other convention of the day, the double.

I must admit that, despite my optimistic outlook on using a shotgun with buckshot, the gods or goddesses of hunting did not smile upon me when I was pursuing big game with such a rig. I never even got a glimpse of the game I was after, let alone a shot! But many millions of other hunters have, of course, had success hunting big game with a shotgun, and the Remington Model

870 in particular, in its various deer gun versions, have contributed significantly to the success of these hunters through the years, ever since the first Brushmaster appeared on the scene, in 1961.

The variety and combinations of different kinds of Deer Guns offered in the Model 870 today is staggering. Considering that it had such a humble beginning, back in 1955, as simply a short-barreled version of the standard shotgun, it is almost mind boggling as to the combinations of barrel lengths and finishes available today. No, the Model 870 Deer Gun of today is definitely not your grandfather's old Rifle Slug Special!

Comparatively, on the other end of the shotguns intended for big game, the Model 870 Turkey gun had a rather late start. In fact, specialized turkey shotguns as a whole have only really been a fairly recent introduction. One has to keep in mind that the wild turkey population in America once was not anywhere near what it is today and has been for the last couple of decades, and what few birds there were had their populations concentrated mainly in the southeastern states. At one point in the early part of the twentieth

Remington.
IT'S WHAT YOU'RE SHOOTING FOR

PRESS RELEASE

FOR IMMEDIATE RELEASE
Contact: William A. Wohl, Sr.
302/774-5048

October 22, 1993

REMINGTON® INTRODUCES TWO NEW 20 GAUGE FULLY RIFLED CANTILEVER DEER SHOTGUNS

To complement the introduction of new 20 gauge Copper Solid™ Sabot Slugs, Remington® has introduced fully rifled 20 gauge shotguns that feature a re-designed cantilever system.

The Remington Model 1100™ LT-20 Fully Rifled Cantilever Deer Gun and the Model 870™ LW (Lightweight) 20 Gauge Fully Rifled Cantilever Deer Gun utilize the Remington's rigid cantilever system that provides multiple mounting locations to permit easy adjustment of eye relief. The new scope rail design accepts one inch Weaver-style scope rings, and is attached to a base that is brazed to the shotgun barrel.

These fully rifled 20 gauge barrels are designed for optimum performance with Remington's new 20 gauge Copper Solid Sabot Slug, and are 21″ in length on the Model 1100 and 20″ in length on the Model 870 LW.

The shotguns feature a polished blue metal finish on all exposed metal work and have a satin finished American walnut stock. The Monte Carlo stock design assists the shooter in proper sighting with scope optics, and the stock is complete with recoil pad and cut checkering. These new Deer Guns come with sling swivel studs, and a Cordura® sling with QD (quick detach) swivels.

The Model 1100 LT-20 Fully Rifled Cantilever Deer Gun will have a suggested retail price of $652.00. The Model 870 LW 20 Gauge Fully Rifled Cantilever Deer Gun carries suggested retail price of $532.00. Both shotguns are expected to be available in the secon quarter of 1994.

# # #

SUPER SLUG

While the pump-action on any 870 is just like every other Remington pump-action, in the Super Slug, the barrel is pinned to the bottom of the receiver to control vibration and provide, according to Big Green, "rifle-like, shot-to-shot consistency." It'll shoot accurately at distances way beyond it's older brother (below).

REMINGTON® MODEL 870™ WINGMASTER® FULLY RIFLED
CANTILEVER PUMP ACTION DEER GUN
Newly Designed Rigid Cantilever System (Scope Not Included)
American Walnut Stock, Cordura® Sling, 20" Barrel

century, the turkey population was so low in America that there was no open season in the vast majority of states.

Turkey populations across the country have rebounded and reached the today's levels only after some very careful management and long closed seasons. Once populations were reestablished and thriving, and hunting seasons were once again implemented, you might think that guns just for turkey hunting would have become *de rigueur*. But that wasn't the case. Hunters, at least initially and as recently as a

mere 20 years ago, just didn't see a need for a specialized turkey shotgun in the past. Most simply used their normal upland or waterfowl guns when they went turkey hunting. A good illustration of the "state of the turkey gun" back in those days is the cover photo of a book that was called The *Upland Hunter's Bible*, a softcover tome published in the 1960s by Stoeger's and written by Dan Holland. The cover photo showed the author and a friend returning from a turkey hunt. The author is seen carrying his favorite upland gun, a light

SP SHOTGUNS: HOW TO MAKE A BIG IMPRESS

MODEL 11-[...] SP CANTILEVER SCOPE MOUNT DEER GUN*

*W*hether you're calling a wily Tom or still-hunting a nervous whitetail, Remington Special Purpose shotguns will give you great performance — without giving you away. Their stocks and fore-ends have a non-reflective finish that minimizes light reflection. Barrels and receivers also are specially treated with a black matte finish that resists rust and corrosion. Even the detachable sling that comes with every SP is made of rugged Cordura® nylon in a hard-to-see camo pattern. All "SP" shotguns come with sling swivel studs.

New for 1991 are hard-wearing synthetic stocks, and a turkey barrel that's perfect for close quarters. Also, all SP guns for 1991 feature target-type twin bead sights on vent rib barrels.

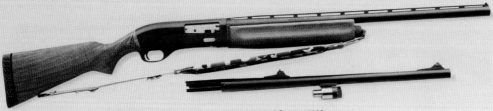

MODEL SP-10™ MAGNUM

The Model SP-10™ could well be a goose's worst nightmare — and a waterfowler's best friend. The world's only gas-operated semi-automatic 10-gauge, it delivers up to 34% more pellets in the target area than a standard 12-gauge. Yet its unique gas operating system softens and spreads out recoil to less than most 12-gauge Magnums. So you can stay on target from first shot to last.

MODEL SP-10™ TURKEY COMBO

Contains the Model SP-10™ with 26" or 30" vent rib barrel, plus an extra 22" rifle-sighted barrel for turkey hunting. Includes Mod., Full, and Extra-Full Turkey Rem™ Choke tubes.

*Scope not included

WITHOUT BEING NOTICED.

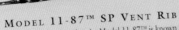

MODEL 11-87™ SP VENT RIB
...tures the pressure compensating gas system that the Model 11-87™ is known for... shoots heavy 3" Magnums
3/4" field loads interchangeably. Cut checkered American walnut stock and fore-end. Available in 26" or
28" vent rib barrels with Rem™ Choke tubes and twin bead sights.

MODEL 11-87™ SP SYNTHETIC
...ble in two versions: the "SPS" with synthetic stock and fore-end, and choice of 26" or 28" vent rib barrels with
...bes; or the "SPS-T" (Special Purpose Synthetic-Turkey). This version comes with a 21" vent rib turkey barrel (pictured)
...and includes an Extra-Full Rem™ Choke Turkey tube. Black sling furnished with both versions.

MODEL 870™ SP VENT RIB
The ultimate in low-visibility pump guns. Available with your choice of 26" or 28" vent rib barrels,
with twin bead sights and Rem™ Choke tubes. Cut checkered American walnut stock and fore-end.

MODEL 870™ SP SYNTHETIC
Available as the "SPS" (Special Purpose Synthetic), which comes with either 26" or 28" vent rib barrels
...Choke tubes; or the "SPS-T" ("Special Purpose Synthetic-Turkey"), which features a 21" vent rib turkey barrel (pictured)
with an Extra-Full Rem™ Choke Turkey tube. Black sling furnished with both versions.

MODEL 870™ SP CANTILEVER SCOPE MOUNT DEER GUN
...deer hunter who likes the positive feel of a pump with the sighting advantages of a Monte Carlo stock and a barrel-mounted scope.*
...mes with Rifled and Improved Cylinder Rem™ Choke tubes for slugs or buckshot, cantilever mount, and 1" scope rings.

...NGTON'S CANTILEVER SCOPE MOUNT: THE VISIBLE DIFFERENCE.
...are built with take-down barrels for maximum versatility. With Remington's Cantilever Scope Mount system, the mount is attached directly to the
...barrel instead of the receiver, which means your gun stays sighted-in — no matter how many times you change barrels.

* Scope not included

11

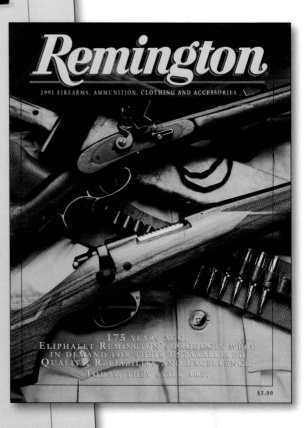

SLUG IT OUT
Remington's Special
Purpose line of 870s
designed for deer
hunters was in full swing
in this 1991 catalog.

COUNT 'EM IF YOU CAN

How many 870 deer guns can you count in this 1994 catalog? With the number of extra barrels available, the number is almost infinite.

GENUINE REMINGTON FACTO

With a simple barrel change, you can use your Reming
to grouse, and white-wings to whitetails. The same s
Sporting Clays, small game, upland, waterfowl and de
than that. We offer the widest selection of genuine A
extra barrels in the business. All made right along
our shotguns when they are new. If you want to get the be
shotgun, always insist on original Remington equipment
extra barrels and accessories available through your Rem

A GREAT VALUE FOR MODEL 110

If you have a favorite Model 1100™ that you want to use with stee
1100™ Steel Shot barrel. It's specially designed to function with tod
handle both 2 ¾" and 3" magnums interchangebly. Note: This barr
nums when fitted on a non-magnum Model 1100™, as this will cause e

SPECIAL PURPOSE SHOTGUNS

WHEN YOU HAVE TO WORK HARDER FOR THE GAME.

Remington's Special Purpose shotguns are for the hunter that has to work a little harder for
his gobbler, buck, or limit of waterfowl. To help out, we've given our Special Purpose
shotguns hard-working features like synthetic stocks, cantilever deer barrels, and the most
comprehensive line of camo finishes in the business – a must when you're matching wits with
an old Tom, a nervous buck, or a flight of gun-shy Canadas. And every Remington Special
Purpose shotgun comes with sling swivel studs and a padded sling of rugged Cordura® nylon.

OUR

SP black oxide

MODEL 870™ SPS WITH FULLY RIFLED
CANTILEVER SCOPE MOUNT DEER BARREL

NEW

The long range big game shooting system that can help you bring that trophy a little closer.
Comes with our new cantilever scope mount – the cantilever arm is shorter and thicker in cross section for
maximum rigidity, and won't lose zero, even after repeated recoil. To position your eye properly, we've
also given the cantilever SPS stock a Monte Carlo comb profile. Note: Scope and rings not included.

MODEL 11-87™ / 870™ SPS WITH REM CHOKE™
CANTILEVER SCOPE MOUNT DEER BARREL

NEW

The Model 11-87™ or 870™ SPS (pictured) has the same great sighting system as the fully rifled version above,
but with the flexibility of Rem™ Choke tubes. Ideal for use with buckshot at close range, or with our new 1 in 24"
twist, 3 ½" Rifled Rem™ Choke for increased accuracy with slugs. Supplied with an Improved Cylinder and new
Extended Rifled Rem™ Choke tube. Stock has Monte Carlo comb profile. Note: Scope and rings not included.

If you're a deer hunt
sights, then the Model
hunting. Everything about
accurate shot in close qu
es,

MO
For you deer hunte
Model 870™ SPS – BG Camo
durability, Mossy Oak® Bottom
Super Full Rem™ Chokes f

20

BARRELS

...nything from gobblers
...sed for Skeet, Trap,
...k for more flexibility
...ctory accessory and
...at are shipped with
...ut of your Remington
...r a full listing of all

Model 1100" Steel Shot, 30" Vent Rib

...answer: our Model
... steel loads, and will
...d with 3" lead mag-
...se the life of the gun.

Model SP-10" Magnum, 22" Deer

TARGET BARRELS

Model 11-87" Premier", 26" Skeet

We offer 12 specifications of Skeet and Trap barrels, including 20-, 28-, and .410-bore
Skeet barrels for Model 1100" and 870" small-gauge guns.

Model 11-87" Premier", L-H, 30" Light Contour

LEFT-HAND EXTRA BARRELS

Model 11-87" Premier", L-H, 26" Skeet

There are 12 left-hand extra barrels in Light Contour, Deer, and Skeet and Trap
specifications. For Model 11-87", 870", and 1100".

Model SP-10" Magnum, 26" Vent Rib

Model 870" Wingmaster", 30" Light Contour

VENT RIB FIELD BARRELS

Model 870" Wingmaster", 26" Vent Rib

...ave extra vent rib field barrels available for our Model SP-10", 11-87", 870", and 1100" shotguns in
...ths from 21" to 30", in blued and Special Purpose finishes, and in standard and new Light Contour
...es for Model 11-87" and 870". All current Remington field barrels are steel-shot compatible. There
...is also a wide selection of small-gauge extra barrels available for the Model 1100" and 870".

SHORT BARRELS: 21"– 26"

...ort barrels are used in heavy cover where easy handling and a fast, smooth swing are important. Usually an
...such as Improved Cylinder is used for small game, and a rifled Rem" Choke tube for use with rifled slugs.

MEDIUM BARREL: 28"

...for small game hunting in open fields where game may flush at farther distances, and a longer sighting plane is
...This is the most popular shotgun barrel length because it provides more flexibility for general purpose hunting.

LONG BARREL: 30"

...is length is usually used for pass shooting ducks and geese. It provides...
...and is slightly heavier, which make...

FITTING STANDARD BA...

...on our new Light Contour shotgun...
...a standard vent rib or deer barrel c...
...wood opened up by a competent gun...
...e Division by writing to: Arms Ser...

...SE FINISHES KEEP YOU OUT OF SIGHT.

...ssy Oak" Greenleaf"

Mossy Oak" Bottomland"

MODEL 11-87" SPS WITH CANTILEVER SCOPE MOUNT DEER BARREL

This year we've given the
Model 11-87" (pictured at
left) and Model 870" (below,
left) SPS guns our re-designed,
long-range cantilever scope
mount deer barrel available in
both fully rifled and Rem"
Choke versions that utilize our
new longer-length, 3 ½" rifled
tube. When the fully rifled
barrel is combined with our
new Copper Solid" sabot
slugs, this system can take
deer cleanly out to 125 yds.
The cantilever arm is shorter
in length and has a thicker
cross section for maximum
rigidity – it won't lose zero,
even after repeated recoil. To
position your eye properly,
we've also given the cantilever
SPS stock a Monte Carlo
comb profile. Note: Scope
and rings not included.

NEW

...' / 870" SPS DEER

...aditional sight picture of a slug barrel with open
...Model 870" SPS Deer gun is made for your style of
...ay to throw 'em to your shoulder and get off a quick.
...e short to swing fast, and fully rifled for accuracy,
... Copper Solid" sabot slugs.

...0" SPS – BG CAMO

...r turkey, the Model 11-87" (pictured) or
...big game shotgunning systems: synthetic stocks for
...open sights for speed, and I. C. Rifled, and Turkey
...up the gun for buckshot, slugs, or turkey loads.

Remington special purpose shotguns – matching the gun to the game.

MODEL 11-87™ SPS DEER GUN
WITH CANTILEVER SCOPE MOUNT

The name "Special Purpose" on a select group of Remington shotguns reveals their intent – hard-working tools to better match the needs of specialized applications. While retaining all the proven operating features of each gun, they incorporate practical variations for deer, waterfowl or turkey hunting – like synthetic stocks, cantilever deer barrels, and a variety of background-blending camo finishes. The Model 11-87™ SPS Cantilever Deer Gun at right is a prime example. A strong, abuse-absorbing synthetic stock with Monte Carlo comb is non-reflective. The gun's sturdy scope mount guarantees permanent zero and point of impact from the impressive accuracy of a fully-rifled barrel. Like all Remington Special Purpose shotguns, it comes with sling swivel studs and a padded sling of rugged Cordura® nylon. (Note: Scope and rings not included.)

Remington.
COUNTRY

MODEL 870™ SPS WITH FULLY-RIFLED
CANTILEVER SCOPE MOUNT DEER BARREL

...he shooting system that can help you bring that trophy a little closer, by reaching out with amazing slug accuracy ...d barrel. Comes with our highly rigid cantilever scope mount that won't lose zero, even after repeated recoil. ... properly, we've also given the synthetic stock a Monte Carlo comb profile. (Note: Scope and rings not included.)

MODEL 11-87™ / 870™ SPS
WITH REM CHOKE™ CANTILEVER SCOPE MOUNT DEER BARREL

...del 11-87™ or 870™ SPS (pictured) have the same great sighting system as the fully-rifled version above, ...e flexibility of Rem™ Choke tubes. Ideal for use with buckshot at close range, or with our new 1 in 35" twist, ...Rem™ Choke for increased accuracy with slugs. Supplied with an Improved Cylinder and our Extended Rifled ...Rem™ Choke tube. Stock has Monte Carlo comb profile. (Note: Scope and rings not included.)

24

The Remington "One System" – The Perfect Integration of Shotgun and Slug Performance

)nly an integrated firearms and ammunition manufacturer like Remington could simultaneously develop and combine the most advanced technology of those elements into its unique "One System" of unmatched slug shooting performance. Our Model 11-87™ and Model 870™ cantilever scope nount shotguns permit the rigid support of superior optics for pinpoint sighting. And their fully-rifled barrels produce the gyroscopic, in-flight stability required by slugs for maximum accuracy. When these are matched with the near-perfect concentricity and ballistic balance of our Premier™ Copper Solid™ sabot slugs, the result is the One System of unequaled deer slug accuracy and game-stopping effectiveness. From the start, the two, shotgun and ammunition, were made for each other – and for you.

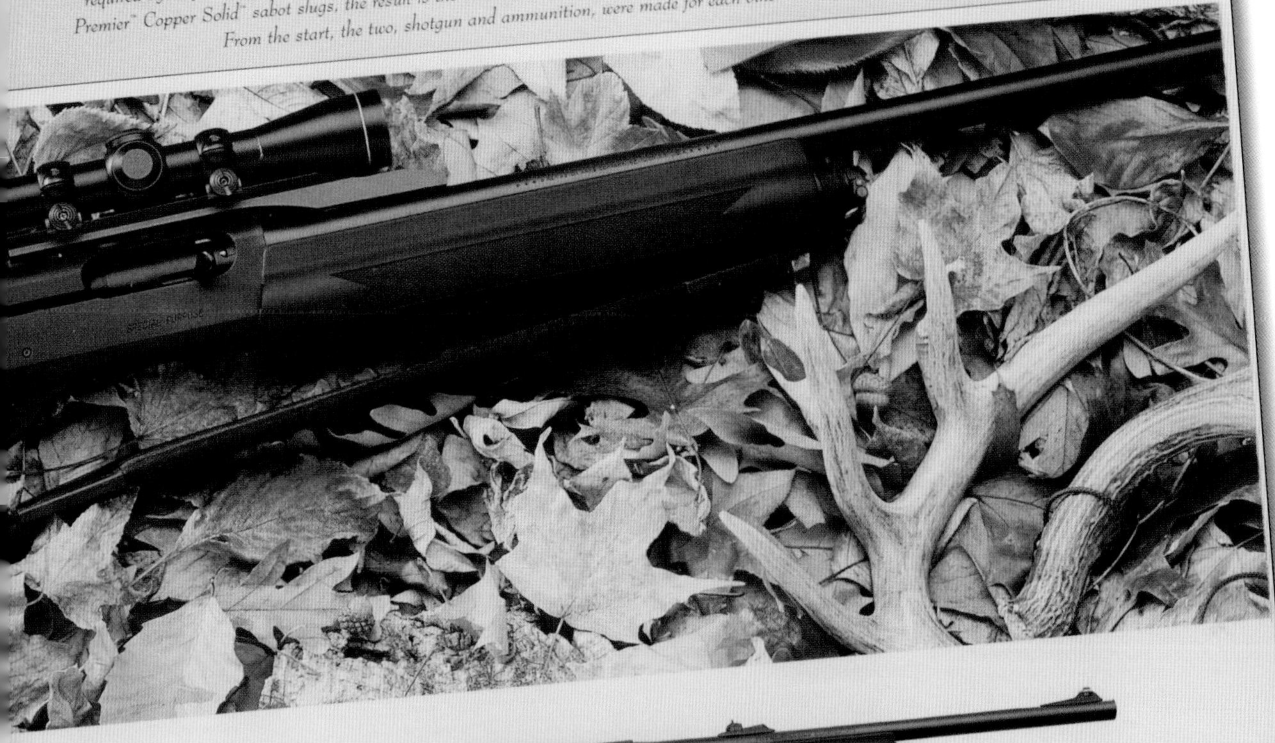

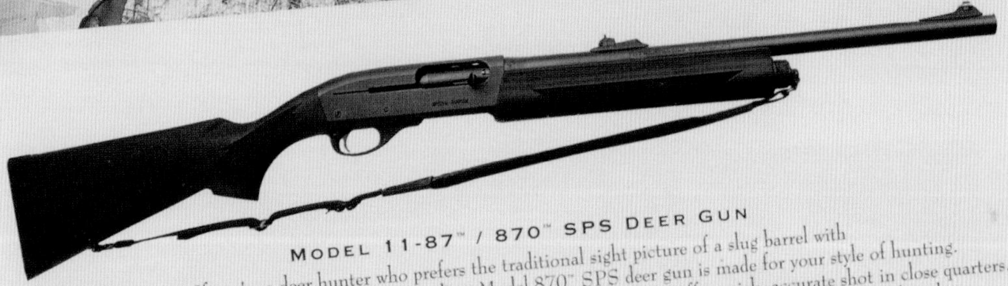

Model 11-87™ / 870™ SPS Deer Gun

If you're a deer hunter who prefers the traditional sight picture of a slug barrel with open sights, then the Model 11-87™ (pictured) or Model 870™ SPS deer gun is made for your style of hunting. Everything about these guns makes it easy to throw 'em to your shoulder and get off a quick, accurate shot in close quarters. The barrels are short to swing fast, and fully rifled for accuracy, especially with our new Copper Solid™ sabot slugs.

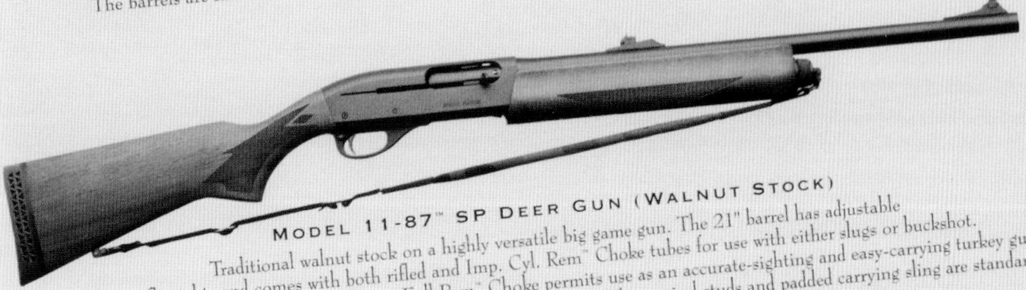

Model 11-87™ SP Deer Gun (Walnut Stock)

Traditional walnut stock on a highly versatile big game gun. The 21" barrel has adjustable rifle sights and comes with both rifled and Imp. Cyl. Rem™ Choke tubes for use with either slugs or buckshot. The addition of an optional, Turkey Extra Full Rem™ Choke permits use as an accurate-sighting and easy-carrying turkey gun. Non-reflective wood and metal finish provide effective concealment. Sling swivel studs and padded carrying sling are standard.

25

The Model 870™ Wingmaster® — A Veteran That's Still Ahead of its Time.

If the Model 870™ Wingmaster® were introduced today, it would be hailed as a major advance in pump action shotgun design — the ultimate in strength, durability, silky-smooth action and sleek, classical lines. Yet this remarkable shotgun has been around for almost half a century and has become the best-selling shotgun of *any* action type in history, with over six million made. Most of these owners are first-time users, still shooting their original 870™. That should tell you something.

Just ask Rudy Etchen, one of this century's greatest competitive shotgunners. In 1950, Rudy took a brand new Model 870™ and broke the first registered 100 straight ever at trap doubles with a pump gun — at the Grand American Trap Championships. In 1982 — 32 years later — he repeated the feat with the same gun. He's still shooting it. Rudy's not sure how many hundreds of thousands of shells he's shucked through his Wingmaster®. But, as Bob Brister recently wrote, "About the only thing 'Mr. Pumpgun' Rudy Etchen hasn't been able to do with his 46-year-old Remington 870™ is wear it out."* The same thing can be said about every Model 870™ — the proof is that many of them are now in the hands of a third generation.

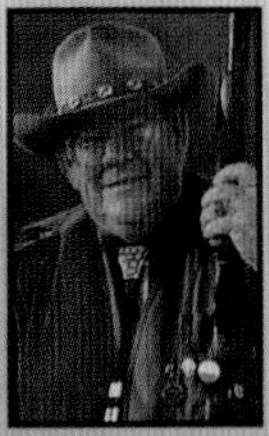

Rudy Etchen

* "Pumping Steel," by Bob Brister, Field & Stream, August, 1995.

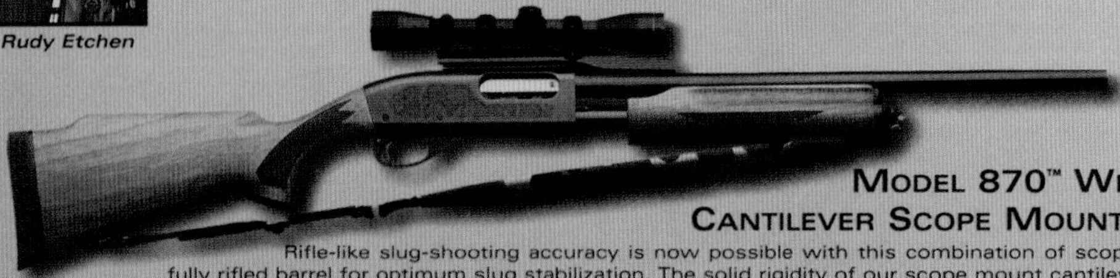

Model 870™ Wingmaster® Cantilever Scope Mount Deer Gun

Rifle-like slug-shooting accuracy is now possible with this combination of scope sights and 20" fully rifled barrel for optimum slug stabilization. The solid rigidity of our scope mount cantilever arm preserves constant, unchanging zero, even after the punishing effects of repeated recoil. Yet a quick barrel change converts it to a standard field gun. The receiver is attractively engraved with scrollwork and whitetail deer on side faces. Sling swivel studs and camo sling are included. *Note: Scope not included.*

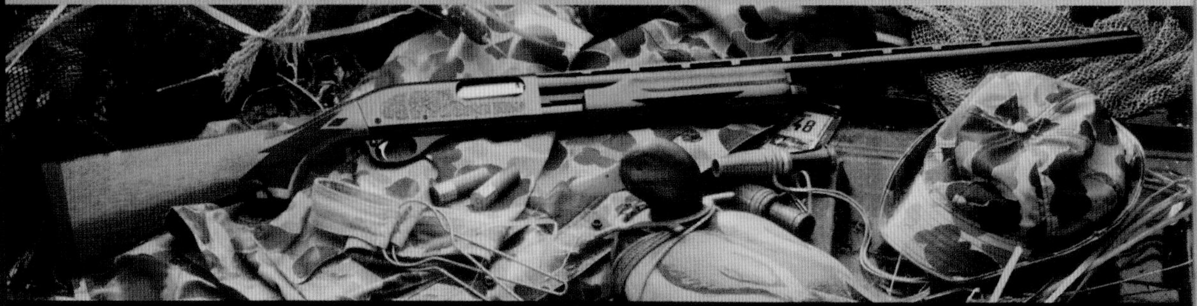

A Handsome Workhorse

Despite its reputation for ruggedness, we can dress up "Old Reliable" into an absolute beauty, like the LC (Light Contour) version above. Clean, slim lines; fine American walnut with a satin or gloss finish; richly blued metal luster; a receiver generously engraved with refined, artistic scrollwork. Yet total versatility results from its interchangeable Rem™ Choke system and ability to handle all 2¾" and 3" Magnum shells. Light contour barrels make it move like a magic wand. Choose from 12-ga. barrel-length options of 26", 28" and 30". Also in 20-ga. with 26" or 28" barrels.

Gun Dimensions / Average Weights

	Barrel Length	Overall Length	Avg. Wt.(lbs)	Length of Pull	Drop (Comb)	Drop (Heel)
12-ga. Wingmaster® LC	30"	50 ½"	7 ¼	14"	1½"	2 ½"
	28"	48 ½"	7	14"	1½"	2 ½"
	26"	46 ½"	6 ¾	14"	1½"	2 ½"
Fully Rifled Cantilever Deer Gun	20"	40 ½"	8	14 ½"	1⅜"	1 ⅞"
20-ga. Wingmaster®	28"	48 ½"	6 ½	14"	1½"	2 ½"
	26"	46 ½"	6 ½	14"	1½"	2 ½"

NEW

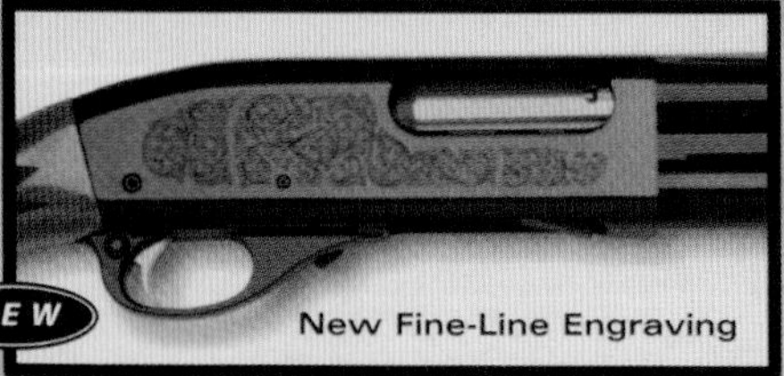

New Fine-Line Engraving

The Peerless® — Everything A Great Over & Under Should Be.

...ess® is everything a great over & under should be — a "Best Buy" that's beautiful in
...and loaded with design features you won't find in over & under field guns costing twice
...ese include superb handling qualities based on modest weight and perfect, between-the-
...ce. Add to that the aesthetics of attractive design, with clean, classic lines and a shallow
...rels are topped with an 8mm-wide vent rib with target-style twin bead sights, have
...cing cones and are furnished with Imp. Cyl., Mod., and full Rem™ chokes.

...AN BEAUTY

...and clean, instantly pleasing to the eye, and giving a hint of its excellent balance. A richly-toned American
...rotected by Remington's tough, high-gloss finish, with sharp, positive checkering on both pistol grip and
...osed metal carries our highly-polished, deep-lustre bluing. In barrel-length options of 26", 28" and 30",
...m 7¼ to 7½ lbs. Comfortable finger grooves on a fore-end tapering slightly towards the front provides
...nce and fast handling. A gold-plated, single selective mechanical trigger guarantees fast follow-up shots.

...Peerless® Design Features

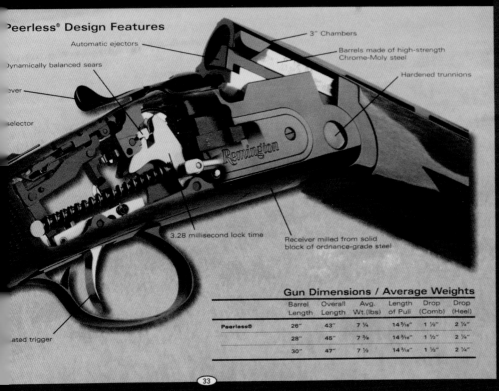

- Automatic ejectors
- ...Dynamically balanced sears
- ...ever
- ...selector
- 3" Chambers
- Barrels made of high-strength Chrome-Moly steel
- Hardened trunnions
- Remington
- 3.28 millisecond lock time
- Receiver milled from solid block of ordnance-grade steel
- ...ated trigger

Gun Dimensions / Average Weights

	Barrel Length	Overall Length	Avg. Wt.(lbs)	Length of Pull	Drop (Comb)	Drop (Heel)
Peerless®	26"	43"	7 ¼	14 ⁵⁄₁₆"	1 ½"	2 ¼"
	28"	45"	7 ⅜	14 ⅜"	1 ½"	2 ¼"
	30"	47"	7 ½	14 ⁵⁄₁₆"	1 ½"	2 ¼"

33

CLASSIC NO MATTER WHAT

How classic is the Wingmaster moniker? Well, you can put it on a slug gun catalog page right next to a page advertising what Remington hoped to be its other next classic, the Peerless over/under.

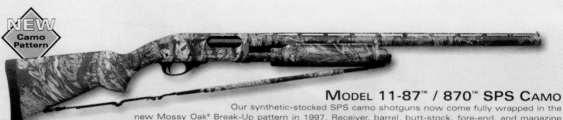

NEW Camo Pattern

MODEL 11-87™ / 870™ SPS CAMO

Our synthetic-stocked SPS camo shotguns now come fully wrapped in the new Mossy Oak® Break-Up pattern in 1997. Receiver, barrel, butt-stock, fore-end, and magazine cap are all completely camouflaged, as is the exposed magazine tube on the Model 870"(pictured). Both guns have 26" vent rib barrels with Improved Cylinder, Modified, and Full Rem™ Choke tubes, and come with sling swivel studs and padded Cordura® sling. Suggested retail for the 11-87™ is $557, and $496 for the 870™.

Model 11-87™ / Model 870™ Special Purpose Synthetic — All Black Matte Finish

	Gauge	Barrel Type/Length	Rem™ Choke(s) Supplied	Finish
11-87" SPS	12	Vent Rib / 26" or 28"	I.C., Mod., & Full	All Black Matte
11-87" /870" SPS Deer	12	Rifle Sighted / 21" 11-87", 20" 870"	Fully Rifled barrel, no choke tube	All Black Matte
11-87" /870" SPS-T	12	Vent Rib / 21"	I.C. & Turkey Super Full	All Black Matte
11-87" /870" SPS	12	Cantilever Scope mount / 21" 11-87", 20" 870"	Fully Rifled barrel, no choke tube	All Black Matte

Model 11-87™ / Model 870™ Special Purpose Synthetic — Camo Finishes

	Gauge	Barrel Type/Length	Rem™ Choke(s) Supplied	Camo Pattern	
11-87" SPS Camo	12	Vent Rib / 26"	I.C., Mod., & Full	Mossy Oak® Break-Up	★
11-87" /870" SPS-T Camo	12	Vent Rib / 21"	I.C. & Turkey Super Full	RealTree® X-tra	★

Note: 21" Model 11-87™ turkey and deer barrels are not pressure-compensated. Not for use with target or light field loads.

★ New For 1997

MODEL SP-10™ MAGNUM

MODEL SP-10™ MAGNUM CAMO

America's only gas-operated 10-gauge shotgun. It's the perfect gun for high-flying honkers and the toughest turkey shots, delivering up to 34% more pellets in the target area than a standard 12-gauge, yet with less recoil than many 12-gauge Magnums. Available with 26" or 30" vent rib, Rem™ Choke barrels. The American walnut stock has a satin finish, and all exposed metal has a nonreflective matte finish. Also available is the SP-10™ Magnum Camo with a fast-pointing 23" vent rib turkey barrel, covered this year in new Mossy Oak® Break-Up camouflage. Interchangeable Rem™ Chokes include Turkey Extra Full, Full and Modified. Includes sling swivel studs and padded Cordura® sling. Suggested retail for SP-10™ Magnum is $1,054, and $1,145 for the SP-10™ Magnum Camo.

NEW Camo Pattern

MODEL 11-87™ / 870™ SPS-T

The totally nonreflective black matte finish on stocks and metal surfaces of our Model 11-87™ and Model 870™ (pictured) SPS-T turkey guns makes them look like just another tree branch. Twin beads on their fast-pointing 21" vent rib barrels will help you line up quickly on a long-bearded Tom. And our Turkey Super Full Rem™ Choke delivers the dense patterns that will ensure a Thanksgiving dinner. Add a Rifled Rem™ Choke tube, and you can turn these rugged, synthetic-stocked shotguns into sharp-shooting deer guns as well. Includes sling swivel studs and padded Cordura® sling. Suggested retail for the 11-87™ is $684, and $425 for the 870™.

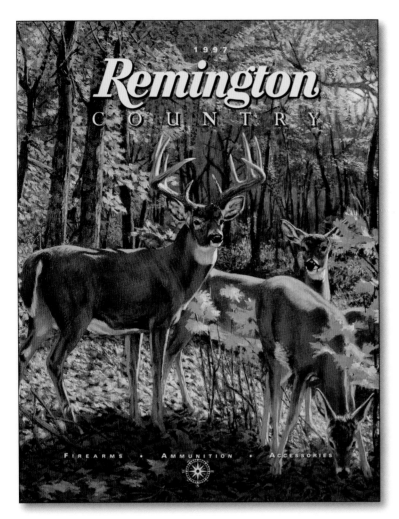

English side-by-side, and his friend, who was also toting a large tom turkey that he had shot, carried a Winchester Model 21 side-by-side.

The upland gun as turkey gun goes back even further, naturally, back even before the 1960s, back to even pre-World War II-era. Again, going back to the two southern gentlemen who were such prolific writers, Archibald Rutledge and Nash Buckingham, both were accomplished turkey hunters. There are many wonderful turkey hunting stories that were written by them, and in each one they describe the shotgun that they used as just their normal bird gun.

If you look at the old *Gun Digest* from the 1960s or even 1970s, you won't find many guns listed as "turkey shotguns." The only guns that were specifically identified as guns for turkey in those days were usually some European combination gun, an over/under with a rifle barrel in a light caliber like the .22 Hornet and a shotgun barrel choked Full. Indeed, not even turkey calls and other related equipment, although available, were all that common in those days. Most turkey hunters simply carried whatever shotgun they owned, and while some certainly tried various home customizations for the pursuit of the big bird, straight from the factory, there wasn't much in the way of specialized turkey guns.

As the turkey population exploded across the country and more and more states had open seasons, a cult-like following for the sport began to develop, and it was then that specialized guns for ol' Tom started to appear. The first Model 870 "turkey gun," if you could call it that, was the Model 870 SP Special Purpose Magnum, which was introduced in 1985. It came with two barrels, a 30-inch Full choke and a 26-inch Full choke. All metal parts were dull-finished, and the wood had a satin-like finish, rather than the standard glossy RKW treatment. The gun also came with sling

The first Remington "turkey gun," if you could call it that, was the 1985 Model 870 SP Special Purpose Magnum. What was so special? Two barrels came with the gun, a 30-inch and a 26-inch, both Full choked. It also came with sling swivels and a sling!

The Model 870™ Express® — The All-American Pump Gun That's All Business.

Our Model 870™ Express® is America's pump gun. It brings performance-oriented hunters the best of both worlds — beneath its no-nonsense, ready-for-work exterior lie the same quality of materials, precision manufacture, and lifetime reliability as in our standard Model 870™ Wingmaster®, the pump gun without peer. But it also delivers these to shooters at a truly economical price. As a result, not only is it the best value version of the best-selling shotgun ever designed, it's the best value in shotguns, period. And it earns this position with a variety of choices that span the spectrum of shotgunning applications.

NEW!

MODEL 870™ EXPRESS® TURKEY CAMO

For 1998, we've covered the synthetic stock and fore-end of our Model 870™ Express® Turkey gun in RealTree® Advantage® camo to help you stay invisible to the prying eyes of a wary gobbler. Like all Express® shotguns, it includes the concealment advantages of a nonreflective flat finish on exposed metal. Available in 12-gauge, with 21" vent rib turkey barrel. A Turkey Extra Full Rem™ Choke tube provides the dense patterns necessary for effective coverage of the vital head and neck area of a big gobbler. Suggested retail is $372.

NEW!

MODEL 870™ EXPRESS® YOUTH TURKEY CAMO

For young "Jakes" or smaller-framed hunters who want a hard-working turkey gun tailored just for their needs, we offer the Model 870™ Express® Youth Turkey gun with a 1" shorter synthetic stock and fore-end covered in RealTree® Advantage® camo to keep you hidden. This 20-ga. Express® comes with a 21" vent rib turkey barrel and Full Rem™ Choke tube. Suggested retail is $372.

MODEL 870™ EXPRESS® TURKEY

A perfect turkey gun with the concealment advantages of our non-glare Express® wood and metal finishes. Available in 12-gauge, with 21" vent rib turkey barrel that carries easily beneath overhanging branches and minimizes movement on a stand. A Turkey Extra Full Rem™ Choke tube provides the exceptionally dense patterns needed for taking a cautious Tom. Suggested retail is $319.

MODEL 870™ EXPRESS®

You can't buy a better shotgun than a Model 870™ Express®, because it's built on the action of the best-selling, most tested shotgun ever made — the legendary Model 870™ Wingmaster®. Just as strong, just as reliable, and just as durable — with an action that cycles just as smoothly. Offered with a wide selection of barrel configurations, a Rem™ Choke system, and in 12-, 20-, 28-ga. and .410 bore. All wood and metal surfaces have a nonreflective, non-revealing finish. The 12-ga., shown here, is offered with your choice of 26" or 28" barrel with Mod. Rem™ Choke. Suggested retail is from $305.

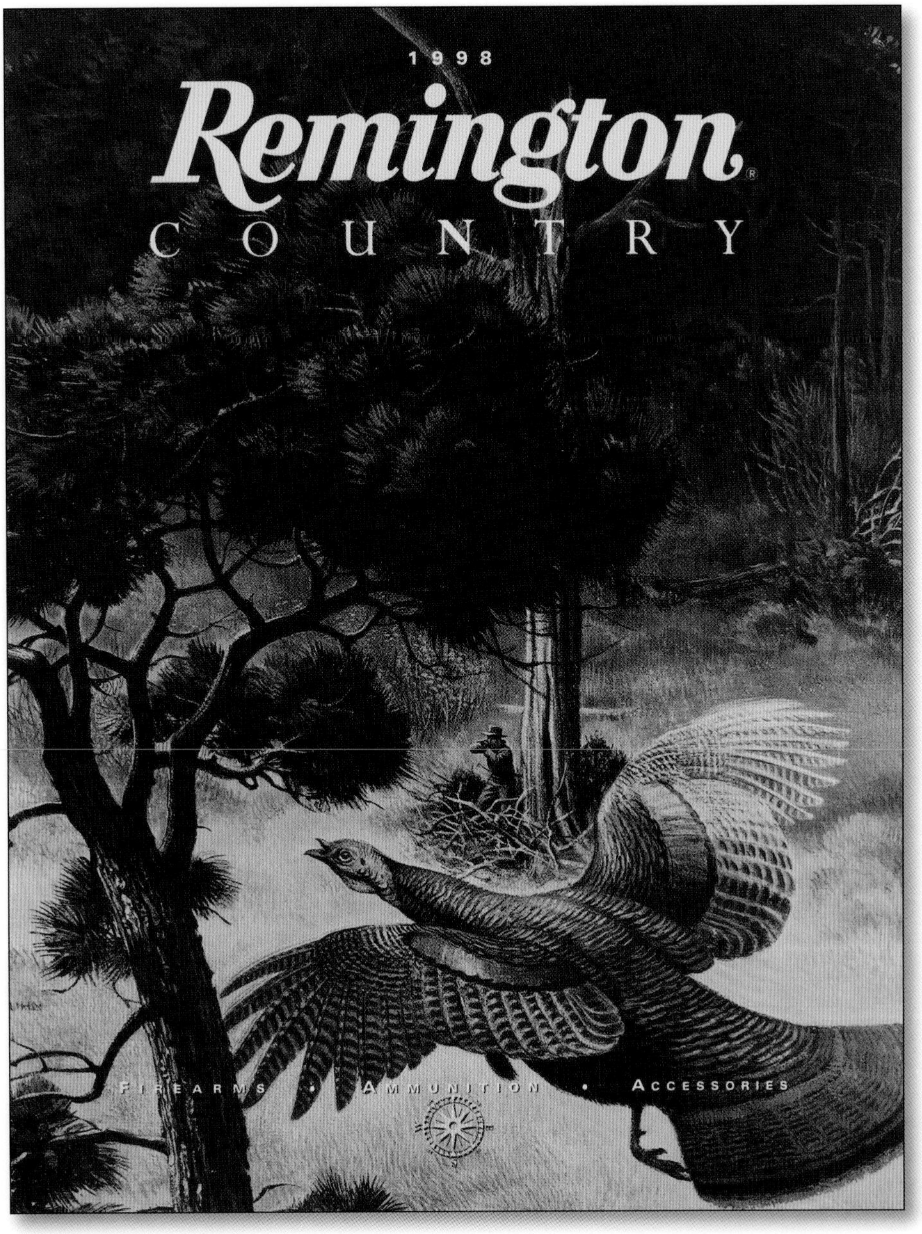

LOOK IN THE SKY, IT'S A BIRD! Turkey guns got off to a slow start at Remington. But, by 1998, the grand game bird was gracing the company's catalog cover, and the inside of the same volume is crammed with 870 turkey-"only" guns.

swivels and a camouflaged sling and was billed as a perfect combination gun for waterfowl and turkey—supposedly waterfowl with the long barrel and turkey with the shorter length. Although it was perfectly serviceable for either application, it was still a compromise. It was neither a pure waterfowl shotgun nor a specialized turkey shotgun. It was obvious to die-hard turkey hunters that a better solution would be to combine the short and lightweight elements of the Deer Gun with some tweaking to better suit turkey hunting.

While hunters were catching on quickly, it took several more years before Remington came out with a turkey specific shotgun, the Model 870 Express Turkey. Actually, it was turkey specific only in name, for what Remington had done was use the same platform to also come out with the Model 870 Cantilever Scope Mount Deer and the

SPECIAL PURPOSE TURKEY GUNS

COVERT COMBINATIONS OF PAYLOAD, PRECISE SIGHTING AND PATTERN POWER

Matching wits with a wild gobbler takes total concealment, not a hint of movement, precise sighting and dense, heavy patterns once you pull the trigger. Remington® SP Turkey Guns offer the widest selection of features specifically designed to help you transport a tasty tom from the field to the freezer, and new sighting options further improve the odds of a wild-game family feast.

MODEL SP-10™
MAGNUM
TURKEY CAMO

MODEL 11-87™
SPS-T™ CAMO

MODEL 870™ SPS-T™
SUPER MAGNUM™ CAMO

Remington® turkey guns have a special purpose – to convert one of those feathered forest phantoms into a family dinner. No game species is warier than the wild turkey. But no other turkey guns are better designed to help you win the

we've added two new sighting systems to improve your chances of putting your pattern on the bird, and putting the bird in the

different brightness settings. TruGlo® fiber-optic rifle sights provide precision line-up of a light-amplifying blaze orange front sight into a notched rear sight flanked by two light-gathering green beads.

Remington offers the broadest selection of versatile turkey gun options in existence. That selection includes eight different guns and four different models. Utilizing Leupold's LG-35 Red Dot sights with our integrated cantilever mounts the pump-action, **Model 870™ SPS-T™ Super Magnum™ Camo** (see chart 1, column 1, at right) with the widest selection of 12-gauge loadings ever possible in a single shotgun. The same Leupold® LG-35 Red Dot system is also available on our

24

AND THE BEAT OF TURKEY WINGS GOES ON

It seems Remington offers at least one or two new turkey guns each year. This 2000 catalog touts mounts for red dot optics on its camoed 870s.

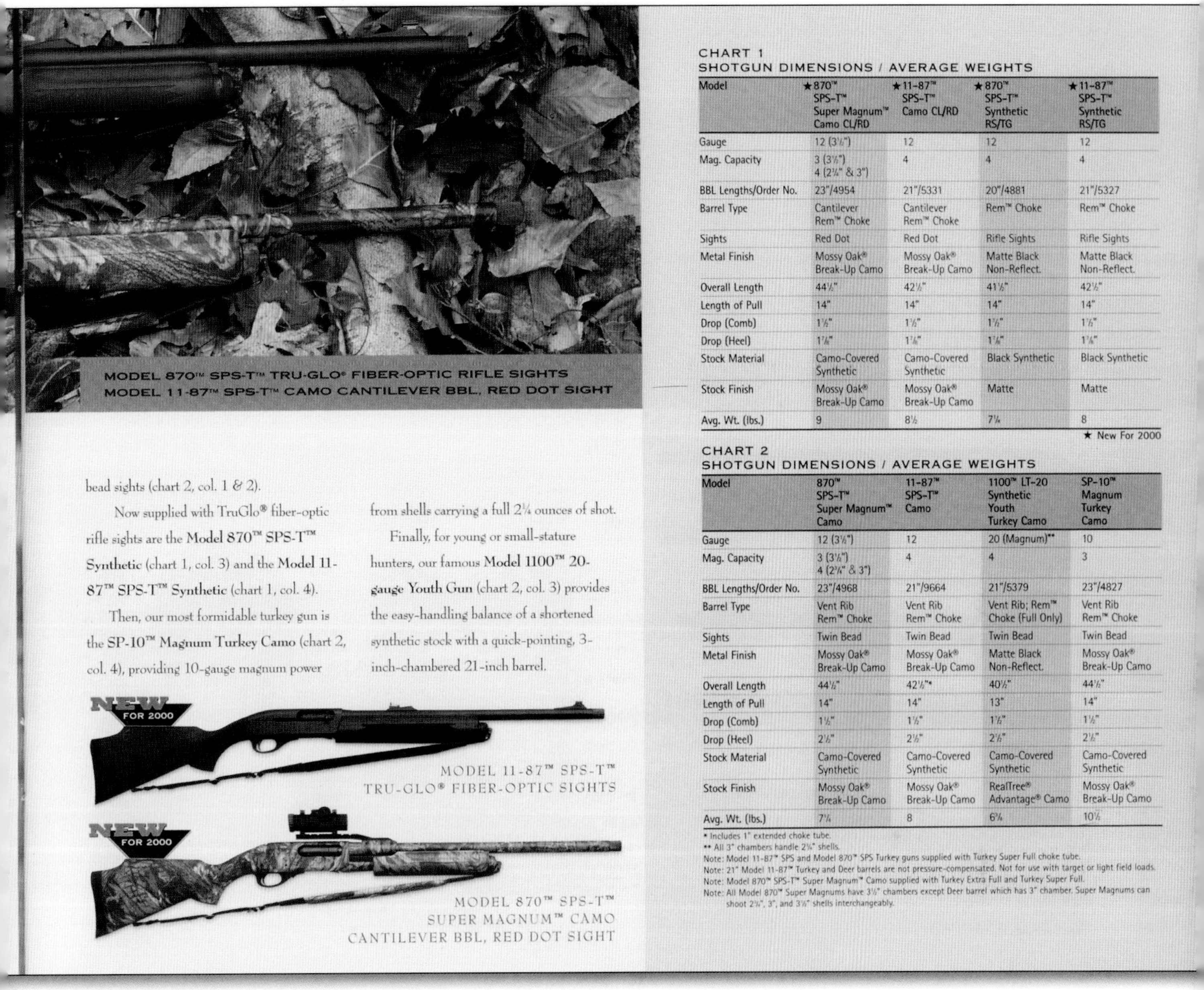

MODEL 870™ SPS-T™ TRU-GLO® FIBER-OPTIC RIFLE SIGHTS
MODEL 11-87™ SPS-T™ CAMO CANTILEVER BBL, RED DOT SIGHT

bead sights (chart 2, col. 1 & 2).

Now supplied with TruGlo® fiber-optic rifle sights are the Model 870™ SPS-T™ Synthetic (chart 1, col. 3) and the Model 11-87™ SPS-T™ Synthetic (chart 1, col. 4).

Then, our most formidable turkey gun is the SP-10™ Magnum Turkey Camo (chart 2, col. 4), providing 10-gauge magnum power from shells carrying a full 2¼ ounces of shot.

Finally, for young or small-stature hunters, our famous Model 1100™ 20-gauge Youth Gun (chart 2, col. 3) provides the easy-handling balance of a shortened synthetic stock with a quick-pointing, 3-inch-chambered 21-inch barrel.

NEW FOR 2000

MODEL 11-87™ SPS-T™
TRU-GLO® FIBER-OPTIC SIGHTS

NEW FOR 2000

MODEL 870™ SPS-T™
SUPER MAGNUM™ CAMO
CANTILEVER BBL, RED DOT SIGHT

CHART 1
SHOTGUN DIMENSIONS / AVERAGE WEIGHTS

Model	★870™ SPS-T™ Super Magnum™ Camo CL/RD	★11-87™ SPS-T™ Camo CL/RD	★870™ SPS-T™ Synthetic RS/TG	★11-87™ SPS-T™ Synthetic RS/TG
Gauge	12 (3½")	12	12	12
Mag. Capacity	3 (3½") 4 (2¾" & 3")	4	4	4
BBL Lengths/Order No.	23"/4954	21"/5331	20"/4881	21"/5327
Barrel Type	Cantilever Rem™ Choke	Cantilever Rem™ Choke	Rem™ Choke	Rem™ Choke
Sights	Red Dot	Red Dot	Rifle Sights	Rifle Sights
Metal Finish	Mossy Oak® Break-Up Camo	Mossy Oak® Break-Up Camo	Matte Black Non-Reflect.	Matte Black Non-Reflect.
Overall Length	44½"	42½"	41½"	42½"
Length of Pull	14"	14"	14"	14"
Drop (Comb)	1½"	1½"	1½"	1½"
Drop (Heel)	1⅞"	1⅞"	1⅞"	1⅞"
Stock Material	Camo-Covered Synthetic	Camo-Covered Synthetic	Black Synthetic	Black Synthetic
Stock Finish	Mossy Oak® Break-Up Camo	Mossy Oak® Break-Up Camo	Matte	Matte
Avg. Wt. (lbs.)	9	8½	7¼	8

★ New For 2000

CHART 2
SHOTGUN DIMENSIONS / AVERAGE WEIGHTS

Model	870™ SPS-T™ Super Magnum™ Camo	11-87™ SPS-T™ Camo	1100™ LT-20 Synthetic Youth Turkey Camo	SP-10™ Magnum Turkey Camo
Gauge	12 (3½")	12	20 (Magnum)**	10
Mag. Capacity	3 (3½") 4 (2¾" & 3")	4	4	3
BBL Lengths/Order No.	23"/4968	21"/9664	21"/5379	23"/4827
Barrel Type	Vent Rib Rem™ Choke	Vent Rib Rem™ Choke	Vent Rib; Rem™ Choke (Full Only)	Vent Rib Rem™ Choke
Sights	Twin Bead	Twin Bead	Twin Bead	Twin Bead
Metal Finish	Mossy Oak® Break-Up Camo	Mossy Oak® Break-Up Camo	Matte Black Non-Reflect.	Mossy Oak® Break-Up Camo
Overall Length	44½"	42½"*	40½"	44½"
Length of Pull	14"	14"	13"	14"
Drop (Comb)	1½"	1½"	1½"	1½"
Drop (Heel)	2½"	2½"	2½"	2½"
Stock Material	Camo-Covered Synthetic	Camo-Covered Synthetic	Camo-Covered Synthetic	Camo-Covered Synthetic
Stock Finish	Mossy Oak® Break-Up Camo	Mossy Oak® Break-Up Camo	RealTree® Advantage® Camo	Mossy Oak® Break-Up Camo
Avg. Wt. (lbs.)	7¼	8	6¾	10¼

* Includes 1" extended choke tube.
** All 3" chambers handle 2¾" shells.
Note: Model 11-87™ SPS and Model 870™ SPS Turkey guns supplied with Turkey Super Full choke tube.
Note: 21" Model 11-87™ Turkey and Deer barrels are not pressure-compensated. Not for use with target or light field loads.
Note: Model 870™ SPS-T™ Super Magnum™ Camo supplied with Turkey Extra Full and Turkey Super Full.
Note: All Model 870™ Super Magnums have 3½" chambers except Deer barrel which has 3" chamber. Super Magnums can shoot 2¾", 3", and 3½" shells interchangeably.

Model 870 Express Rifle Sighted Deer Gun at the same time. All three guns were basically identical except for their sighting systems. These took place in 1991, when turkey hunting was beginning to really hit its stride in America.

As with the Deer Gun, the turkey-specific Model 870s have since sprouted like weeds. There are all sorts of versions today, including pistol-grip styles that can be fired using only the trigger hand, while the other hand operates a call. Camouflage finishes and synthetic stocks are standard now, and a turkey hunter has a choice of camouflage patterns to better accommodate the country where the hunting will take place, a choice unthinkable only two decades before.

As mentioned earlier, the Model 870 turkey guns are an outgrowth of the Model 870 deer guns. Then again, that seems to be the case with just about all the shotgun manufacturers in this country. The pump shotgun made for rifle slug shooting is a distinctly American product, as is the pump gun made for turkey hunting. Considering that there are no deer hunting traditions in the world like there are in America, and no country

REMINGTON
YOUTH GUNS

MATCHED TO SMALLER SHOOTER SIZE AND EVERY SHOOTING CHALLENGE

Remington Youth Guns are serious guns, the very best we make, for serious shooting challenges. They are standard models simply shortened in length to provide comfortable balance and fit for smaller-stature shooters, either youngsters or adults. There are no compromises in their quality and no limitations on their performance capabilities. In rifle or shotgun form, they provide custom fit, without the custom cost.

MODEL 700™ ADL™ YOUTH SYNTHETIC

MODEL 700™ ML YOUTH

MODEL 1100™ YOUTH SYNTHETIC TURKEY CAMO

MODEL 1100™ YOUTH SYNTHETIC

high-quality rifle or shotgun from Remington®.

From our standpoint, it was no big deal. We simply cut back our standard stocks to a shorter, 13-inch length-of-pull, produced these on a regular production basis, and matched them to some of our best rifles and shotguns. You can buy them over the counter — with no premium in price and no custom alterations.

Remember, too, that for young beginners, these can be lifetime guns. When necessary, stocks can be lengthened or easily...

Although we call it our "Y...

game .308 Win. The other is our com Model Seven™ bolt-action – offered choice of the .223 Remington this year), the .243 Win., recoiling .260 Reming the 7mm-08 Reming described by some ex "the best all-around deer cartridge in Ame We haven't overlooked stature black-powder sh ther. For them w lt-action Mode

een-the-hands b g qualities of an horter stock. F e've balanced end with a sh p them from

34

SPECIAL PURPOSE
DEER GUNS

ZEROED-IN ACCURACY THAT LETS YOU PUT THE SLUG WHERE YOU'RE AIMING

Remington's state-of-the-art Special Purpose Deer guns bring rifle-like accuracy to deer hunting with a shotgun. It starts when you combine our fully rifled barrels or rifled Rem™ Chokes with our tight-grouping Copper Solid™ slugs. Adjustable rifle sights or a scope used on our cantilever mounts then permit zeroing in your shotgun to know exactly where your slug will hit at any reasonable range.

MODEL 11-87™ SP™ DEER
MODEL 11-87™ SP5™ CANTILEVER DEER

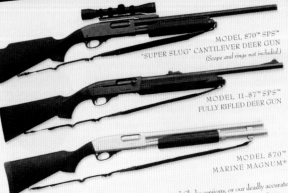

MODEL 870™ SPS™ "SUPER SLUG" CANTILEVER DEER GUN
(Scope and rings not included.)

MODEL 11-87™ SPS™ FULLY RIFLED DEER GUN

MODEL 870™ MARINE MAGNUM®

SHOTGUN DIMENSIONS / AVERAGE WEIGHTS					
Model	870™ SPS™ "Super Slug" Fully Rifled Cantilever Scope Mount Deer Gun	11-87™ SP™ Deer Gun	11-87™ SPS™ Fully Rifled Cantilever Scope Mount Deer Gun	11-87™ SPS™ Fully Rifled Deer Gun	870™ Marine Magnum®¹
Gauge	12	12	12	12	12
Mag. Capacity	4	4	4	4	6
BBL Lengths/Order No.	23"/4946	21"/9837	21"/9819	21"/9676	18"/5012
Barrel Type	Fully Rifled New Contour	Rem™ Choke² Deer	Fully Rifled	Fully Rifled	Cylinder Choke
Sights	Cantilever Scope Mount	Rifle Sights	Cantilever Scope Mount	Rifle Sights	Single Bead
Metal Finish	Matte Black Non-Reflect.	Matte Black Non-Reflect.	Matte Black Non-Reflect.	Matte Black Non-Reflect.	Electroless Nickel-Plated
Overall Length	43½"	41½"	41½"	41½"	38½"
Length of Pull	14"	14½"	14"	14"	14"
Drop (Comb)	1½"	1½"	1½"	1½"	1½"
Drop (Heel)	1¾"	2½"	1¾"	2½"	2½"
Stock Material	Black Synthetic	American Walnut	Black Synthetic	Black Synthetic	Black Synthetic
Stock Finish	Matte	Satin	Matte	Matte	Matte
Avg. wt. (lbs.)	8	8	8½	8	7¼

Note: Model 870™ shotguns with 3" chambers handle 2¾" shells. ² Rifle-sighted Rem™ Choke Deer shotguns supplied with a Rifled Choke tube and Improved Cylinder tube. Note: Model 11-87™ Deer barrels are not equipped with a pressure-compensating gas system, and will not function with target or light field loads. ¹ Will not accept law enforcement accessories.

156

Our Special Purpose Deer guns are superbly equipped to help you fill your tag. Choose from options that include sophisticated sighting equipment, synthetic or walnut stocks, a choice of three Model 11-87™ autoloaders in fully rifled and

Rem™ Choke versions, or our deadly accurate "Super Slug" Model 870™ SPS with its unique heavy barrel contour that improves accuracy dramatically and tames recoil.

27

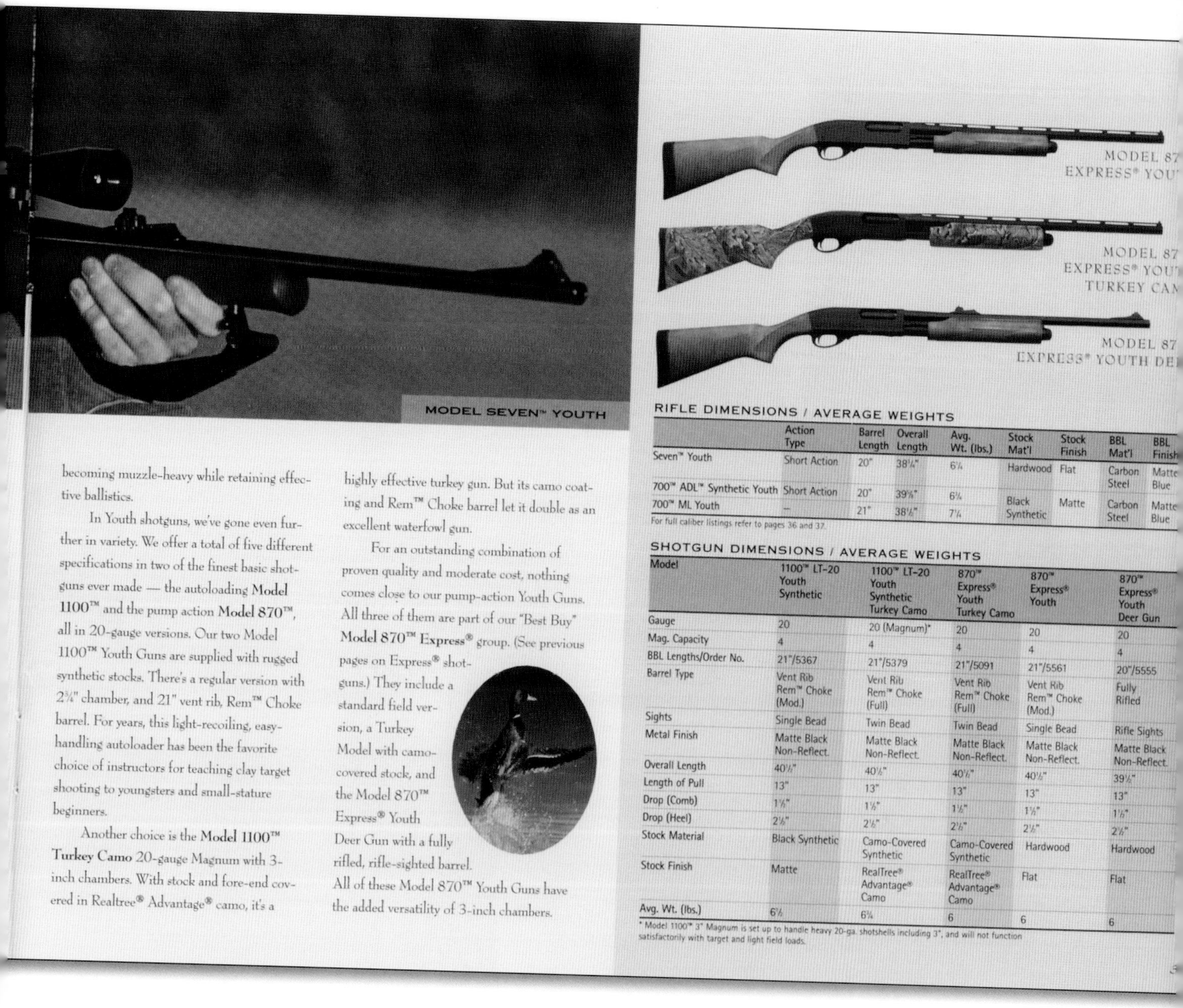

MODEL SEVEN™ YOUTH

MODEL 87
EXPRESS® YOU

MODEL 87
EXPRESS® YOU
TURKEY CAM

MODEL 87
EXPRESS® YOUTH DE

RIFLE DIMENSIONS / AVERAGE WEIGHTS

	Action Type	Barrel Length	Overall Length	Avg. Wt. (lbs.)	Stock Mat'l	Stock Finish	BBL Mat'l	BBL Finish
Seven™ Youth	Short Action	20"	38¼"	6¼	Hardwood	Flat	Carbon Steel	Matte Blue
700™ ADL™ Synthetic Youth	Short Action	20"	39½"	6¼	Black Synthetic	Matte	Carbon Steel	Matte Blue
700™ ML Youth		21"	38½"	7¼				

For full caliber listings refer to pages 36 and 37.

SHOTGUN DIMENSIONS / AVERAGE WEIGHTS

Model	1100™ LT-20 Youth Synthetic	1100™ LT-20 Youth Synthetic Turkey Camo	870™ Express® Youth Turkey Camo	870™ Express® Youth	870™ Express® Youth Deer Gun
Gauge	20	20 (Magnum)*	20	20	20
Mag. Capacity	4	4	4	4	4
BBL Lengths/Order No.	21"/5367	21"/5379	21"/5091	21"/5561	20"/5555
Barrel Type	Vent Rib Rem™ Choke (Mod.)	Vent Rib Rem™ Choke (Full)	Vent Rib Rem™ Choke (Full)	Vent Rib Rem™ Choke (Mod.)	Fully Rifled
Sights	Single Bead	Twin Bead	Twin Bead	Single Bead	Rifle Sights
Metal Finish	Matte Black Non-Reflect.	Matte Black Non-Reflect.	Matte Black Non-Reflect.	Matte Black Non-Reflect.	Matte Black Non-Reflect.
Overall Length	40½"	40½"	40½"	40½"	39½"
Length of Pull	13"	13"	13"	13"	13"
Drop (Comb)	1½"	1½"	1½"	1½"	1½"
Drop (Heel)	2½"	2½"	2½"	2½"	2½"
Stock Material	Black Synthetic	Camo-Covered Synthetic	Camo-Covered Synthetic	Hardwood	Hardwood
Stock Finish	Matte	RealTree® Advantage® Camo	RealTree® Advantage® Camo	Flat	Flat
Avg. Wt. (lbs.)	6½	6¼	6	6	6

* Model 1100™ 3" Magnum is set up to handle heavy 20-ga. shotshells including 3", and will not function satisfactorily with target and light field loads.

becoming muzzle-heavy while retaining effective ballistics.

In Youth shotguns, we've gone even further in variety. We offer a total of five different specifications in two of the finest basic shotguns ever made — the autoloading **Model 1100™** and the pump action **Model 870™**, all in 20-gauge versions. Our two Model 1100™ Youth Guns are supplied with rugged synthetic stocks. There's a regular version with 2¾" chamber, and 21" vent rib, Rem™ Choke barrel. For years, this light-recoiling, easy-handling autoloader has been the favorite choice of instructors for teaching clay target shooting to youngsters and small-stature beginners.

Another choice is the **Model 1100™ Turkey Camo** 20-gauge Magnum with 3-inch chambers. With stock and fore-end covered in Realtree® Advantage® camo, it's a highly effective turkey gun. But its camo coating and Rem™ Choke barrel let it double as an excellent waterfowl gun.

For an outstanding combination of proven quality and moderate cost, nothing comes close to our pump-action Youth Guns. All three of them are part of our "Best Buy" **Model 870™ Express®** group. (See previous pages on Express® shotguns.) They include a standard field version, a Turkey Model with camo-covered stock, and the Model 870™ Express® Youth Deer Gun with a fully rifled, rifle-sighted barrel. All of these Model 870™ Youth Guns have the added versatility of 3-inch chambers.

KIDS LIKE 'EM, TOO!

Remington was quick to catch on to the trend of turkey hunting as a great way to introduce children to the sport, a trend that continues today. The 2000 catalog had plenty of turkey, deer, and general shooting guns proportioned specifically for the younger, shorter, next generation of outdoor sportsmen and -women.

that offers such widespread opportunity for deer hunting, it is not surprising that America would be the originator of shotguns designed specifically for that pursuit. And, when it comes to turkey hunting and turkey guns, it is even more so. It is only natural, then, that America's oldest gun maker, Remington, should be producing so many versions of both deer and turkey shotguns. And what better gun is there to use as the vehicle for so many versions of deer and turkey guns then the Remington Model 870, America's most popular shotgun!

SPECIAL PURPOSE TURKEY GUNS

SPRING FEVER? MAY WE RECOMMEND SOMETHING IN MAXIMUM STRENGTH?

Featuring our Model 870™ Super Magnum™ and new 11-87 Super Magnum,™ the Remington® line of Special Purpose Turkey Guns is ready to administer the finest known cure for Spring Fever: A heavy dose of lead.

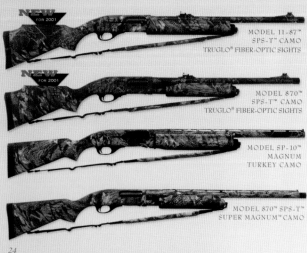

NEW FOR 2001
MODEL 11-87™ SPS-T™ CAMO TRUGLO® FIBER-OPTIC SIGHTS

NEW FOR 2001
MODEL 870™ SPS-T™ CAMO TRUGLO® FIBER-OPTIC SIGHTS

MODEL SP-10™ MAGNUM TURKEY CAMO

MODEL 870™ SPS-T™ SUPER MAGNUM™ CAMO

No species of game is warier than the wild turkey. Fortunately, no turkey guns are better made than the ones you see here. What's more, Remington® offers the broadest selection of turkey guns in existence. And this year, we add six new versions to our industry-leading lineup. Perhaps the most noteworthy of these is the new 11-87 **Super Magnum™ SPS-T.™** This is the gun serious turkey hunters have been waiting for — combining legendary Model 11-87® reliability with the unrivaled knockdown power of 3½″

capability. Other new Special Purpose Turkey guns include a **Model 11-87 SPS-T** with 21″ barrel and cantilever scope mount; a **Model 11-87 SPS-T** with 21″ barrel and Truglo® fiber-optics sights; a **Model 870™ SPS-T** with 20″ barrel and Truglo fiber-optic sights; a youth **Model 870 SPS-T** with 20″ barrel and Truglo fiber-optic sights; and a powerful new **Model 870 Super Magnum SPS-T** with 23″ barrel and cantilever scope mount. All new Special Purpose turkey guns feature weather-defying

synthetic stocks and are ▢ Mossy Oak® Break-Up.® I ▢ not new this year, we'd ▢ mention our most for ▢ gun: The Model SP- ▢

NEW FOR 2001

NEW FOR 2001

24

Remington®

This is Remington Country FIREARMS • AMMUNITION • ACCESSORIES | 2001

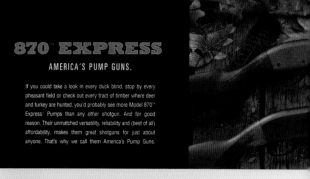

870™ EXPRESS

AMERICA'S PUMP GUNS.

If you could take a look in every duck blind, stop by every pheasant field or check out every tract of timber where deer and turkey are hunted, you'd probably see more Model 870™ Express® Pumps than any other shotgun. And for good reason. Their unmatched versatility, reliability and (best of all) affordability, makes them great shotguns for just about anyone. That's why we call them America's Pump Guns.

MODEL 870™ EXPRESS® SUPER MAGNUM™ TURKEY CAMO

MODEL 870™ EXPRESS® SUPER MAGNUM™ SYNTHETIC

MODEL 870™ EXPRESS® SUPER MAGNUM™ COMBO

MODEL
THE O ▢

Looking ▢
hunting part ▢
Shake han ▢
Model 870 ▢
Its 3½″ shell ▢
long-range ▢
patterns to ▢
most decoy- ▢
But because ▢
2½″ loads t ▢
changeably, ▢
unrivaled in ▢
even comes c ▢
heavy 3½″ lo ▢
shooting lig ▢
doves withou ▢
the same ac ▢

MODEL 870™ SUPER MAGNUM® DESIGN FEATURES:

Superior design and inherent strength of 870 receiver easily accommodate the power and longer length of 3½″ shells

Breakthrough bolt re-design keeps cycle strokes equal for all three sizes of 12-ga. shotshells

Model 870 Super Magnums will function with 2½″, 3″, and 3½″ shells interchangeably

Trigger mechanism retains same dimensions and crisp feel of all 12-ga. Model 870s

Super Magnum™ receiver is same size as all 12-ga. 870™ shotguns for similar balance

Magazine length unchanged for same balance point; capacity is three 3½″ and four 3″ or 5″ shells

30

158

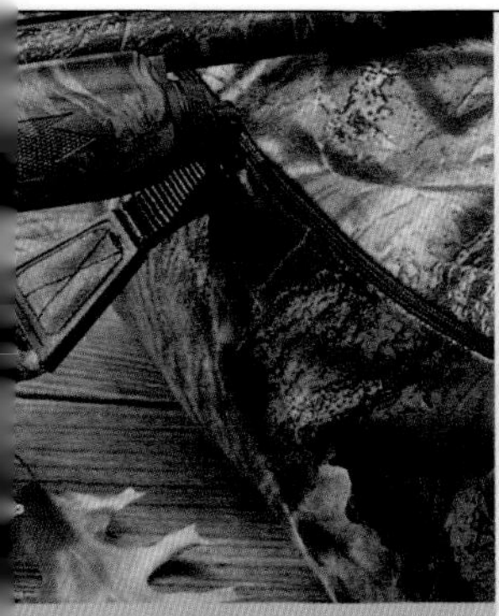

™ SPS-T™ SUPER MAGNUM™ CAMO

Turkey Camo. It's the one gun for hunters truly obsessed with long-range reach and longbeard-busting knockdown power. For specialized turkey choke tubes, see page 68.

MODEL 11-87™ SPS-T™
SUPER MAGNUM™ CAMO
TRUGLO® FIBER-OPTIC SIGHTS

MODEL 870™ SPS-T™
SUPER MAGNUM™ CAMO
WITH CANTILEVER

SPECIAL PURPOSE TURKEY / SUPER MAGNUMS
SHOTGUN DIMENSIONS / AVERAGE WEIGHTS

Model	★ 870™ SPS-T™ Super Magnum™ Synthetic Camo CL/RC	870™ SPS-T™ Super-Magnum Synthetic Camo	★ 11-87™ SPS-T™ Super Magnum™ Synthetic Camo RS/TG	SP-10™ Magnum Turkey Camo
Gauge	12 (3½")**	12 (3½")**	12 (3½")**	10
Mag. Capacity	3 (3½") 4 (2¾" & 3")	3 (3½") 4 (2¾" & 3")	3 (3½") 4 (2¾" & 3")	3
BBL Lengths/Order No.	23"/4957	23"/4968	23"/5353	23"/4827
Barrel Type	Cantilever Rem™ Choke	Vent Rib Rem™ Choke	Rem™ Choke	Vent Rib Rem™ Choke
Sights	–	Twin Bead	Tru-Glo®	Twin Bead
Metal Finish	Mossy Oak® Break-Up® Camo	Mossy Oak® Break-Up® Camo	Mossy Oak® Break-Up® Camo	Mossy Oak® Break-Up® Camo
Overall Length	44½"	44½"	43"	44½"
Length of Pull	14"	14"	14"	14"
Drop (Comb)	1½"	1½"	1½"	1½"
Drop (Heel)	1¼"	2½"	2½"	2½"
Stock Material	Camo-Covered Synthetic	Camo-Covered Synthetic	Camo-Covered Synthetic	Camo-Covered Synthetic
Stock Finish	Mossy Oak® Break-Up® Camo	Mossy Oak® Break-Up® Camo	Mossy Oak® Break-Up® Camo	Mossy Oak® Break-Up® Camo
Avg. Wt. (lbs.)	7½	7¼	8¼	10¾

★ New For 2001

SPECIAL PURPOSE TURKEY
SHOTGUN DIMENSIONS / AVERAGE WEIGHTS

Model	★ 11-87™ SPS-T™ Synthetic Camo RS/TG	★ 11-87™ SPS-T™ Synthetic Camo CL/RC	11-87™ SPS-T™ Synthetic Camo	★ 870™ SPS-T™ Synthetic Camo RS/TG
Gauge	12	12	12	12
Mag. Capacity	4	4	4	4
BBL Lengths/Order No.	21"/5323	21"/5341	21"/9664	20"/4883
Barrel Type	Rem™ Choke	Cantilever Rem™ Choke	Vent Rib Rem™ Choke	Rem™ Choke
Sights	Truglo®	–	Twin Bead	Truglo®
Metal Finish	Mossy Oak® Break-Up® Camo	Mossy Oak® Break-Up® Camo	Mossy Oak® Break-Up® Camo	Mossy Oak® Break-Up® Camo
Overall Length	42½"	42½"	42½"	41½"
Length of Pull	14"	14"	14"	14"
Drop (Comb)	1½"	1½"	1½"	1½"
Drop (Heel)	2½"	2½"	2½"	1¼"
Stock Material	Camo-Covered Synthetic	Camo-Covered Synthetic	Camo-Covered Synthetic	Camo-Covered Synthetic
Stock Finish	Mossy Oak® Break-Up® Camo	Mossy Oak® Break-Up® Camo	Mossy Oak® Break-Up® Camo	Mossy Oak® Break-Up® Camo
Avg. Wt. (lbs.)	8	8½	8	7¼

** All 3" and 3½" chambers handle 2¾" shells.

★ New For 2001

Note: Model 11-87™ SPS and Model 870™ SPS Turkey guns supplied with Turkey Super Full choke tube.
Note: 21" Model 11-87™ Turkey and Deer barrels are not pressure-compensated. Not for use with target or light field loads.
Note: Model 870™ SPS-T™ Super Magnum™ Camo supplied with Turkey Extra Full and Turkey Super Full.
Note: All Model 870™ Super Magnums have 3½" chambers except Deer barrel which has 3" chamber. Super Magnums can shoot 2¾", 3" and 3½" shells interchangeably.

25

WHERE BEFORE THERE WERE NONE

Wild turkeys in the U.S. were once in serious decline. Concentrated recovery efforts have made the wild turkey's comeback one of the most well-respected wildlife management projects in this country's history. Remington's 870 turkey guns started out the same way as the birds themselves, *slooowww*, but now it seems there's nearly a gun for every bird out there!

EXPRESS® SYNTHETIC SUPER MAGNUM™ TURKEY
EXPRESS® SUPER MAGNUM™

RESS® SUPER MAGNUM™
AT CAN DO IT ALL.

-anything
ou down?
mington®
Magnum™
naximum
nd dense
d on the
gobblers.
rom light
ns inter-
m that's
ump gun
shooting
terfowl to
t-darting
it all with
d feel of

our original Model 870™ (the most popular pump gun in history). Finally, we can't forget to mention what may be the most appealing thing about the Express Super Magnum: It comes at a very affordable price. Many workhorse models are available, including stock choices of flat-finished hardwood, durable black synthetic or popular camo finishes. To get the most versatile of any Model 870 Express Super Magnum, choose the two-barrel Combo. For deer hunting with slugs, you get a 20" fully-rifled barrel with adjustable factory sights and a standard 26" vent-rib Rem™ Choke barrel for just about any other shotgunning imaginable. Also check out our factory upgrade kits on page 68.

MODEL 870™
EXPRESS® TURKEY CAMO

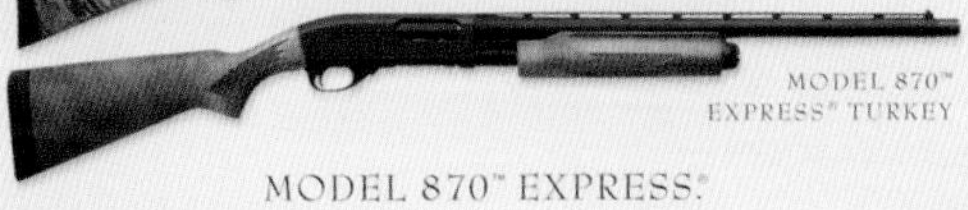

MODEL 870™
EXPRESS® TURKEY

MODEL 870™ EXPRESS®
THE ECONOMICAL, ALL-AMERICAN SLIDE-ACTION.

This is the shotgun that has bagged more game than most guns will ever see. And although it's definitely a no-frills firearm, don't think for a minute that the Express® is anywhere near "cheap." Far from it. Express shotguns feature the same durability and reliability of the legendary Model 870™ Wingmaster.®

So while you may pay a very economical price for a **Model 870 Express**, you're not, by any means, getting short-changed. And with 14 different versions available, you're sure to find a setup for whatever you hunt, wherever you hunt. For factory accessories including our 12- and 20-gauge upgrade kits, see page 68.

MODEL 870™ EXPRESS® SUPER MAGNUM™
SHOTGUN DIMENSIONS / AVERAGE WEIGHTS

Model	870™ Express® Super Magnum™ Synthetic Turkey	870™ Express® Super Magnum™ Turkey Camo	870™ Express® Super Magnum™	870™ Express® Super Magnum™ Synthetic	870™ Express® Super Magnum™ Combo
Gauge	12 (3½")	12 (3½")	12 (3½")	12 (3½")	12 (3½")[1]
Mag. Capacity	3 (3½") 4 (2¾" & 3")	3 (3½") 4 (2¾" & 3")	3 (3½") 4 (2¾" & 3")	3 (3½") 4 (2¾" & 3")	3 (3½") 4 (2¾" & 3")
BBL Lengths/ Order No.	23"/5106	23"/5104	28"/5100	26"/5102	26" (Vent Rib)/5114 20" (Deer)[1]
Barrel Type	Vent Rib Rem™ Choke (Turkey Extra Full)	Vent Rib Rem™ Choke (Turkey Extra Full)	Vent Rib Rem™ Choke (Mod.)	Vent Rib Rem™ Choke (Mod.)	Mod. Rem™ Choke (Vent Rib) Fully Rifled (Deer)
Sights	Twin Bead	Twin Bead	Single Bead	Single Bead	Single Bead (Vent Rib) Rifle Sights (Deer)
Metal Finish	Matte Black Non-Reflect.	RealTree® Advantage® Camo	Matte Black Non-Reflect.	Matte Black Non-Reflect.	Matte Black Non-Reflect.
Overall Length	44½"	44½"	48½"	46"	46" (Vent Rib) 40½" (Deer)
Length of Pull	14"	14"	14"	14"	14"
Drop (Comb)	1½"	1½"	1½"	1½"	1½"
Drop (Heel)	2½"	2½"	2½"	2½"	2½"
Stock Material	Black Synthetic	Synthetic	Hardwood	Black Synthetic	Hardwood
Stock Finish	Matte	RealTree® Advantage® Camo	Satin	Matte	Satin
Avg. Wt. (lbs.)	7½	7¼	7½	7½	7½

[1] Combo Deer barrel has 3" chamber.

MODEL 870™ EXPRESS® SHOTGUN DIMENSIONS / AVERAGE WEIGHTS

Model	870™ Express® (12-ga.)	870™ Express® (20-ga.)	870™ Express® Synthetic	870™ Express® Turkey Camo[1]	870™ Express® Turkey	870™ Express® Synthetic Fully Rifled Deer Gun	870™ Express® Deer
Gauge	12	20	12	12	12	12	12
Mag. Capacity	4	4	4	4	4	4	4
BBL Lengths/ Order No.	28"/5568 26"/5569	28"/5583 26"/5582	28"/5587 26"/5589	21"/5089	21"/5573	20"/5097	20"/5565 20"/5575
Barrel Type/ Order No.	Vent Rib Rem™ Choke (Mod.)	Vent Rib Rem™ Choke (Mod.)	Vent Rib Rem™ Choke (Mod.)	Vent Rib Rem™ Choke (Extra Full)	Vent Rib Rem™ Choke (Extra Full)	Fully Rifled	Imp. Cyl. Choke/5565 Fully Rifled/5575
Sights	Single Bead	Single Bead	Single Bead	Twin Bead	Twin Bead	Rifle Sights	Rifle Sights
Metal Finish	Matte Black Non-Reflect.	Matte Black Non-Reflect.	Matte Black Non-Reflect.	Matte Black Non-Reflect.	Matte Black Non-Reflect.	Matte Black Non-Reflect.	Matte Black Non-Reflect.
Overall Length	48½" (28" BBL) 46½" (26" BBL)	48½" (28" BBL) 46½" (26" BBL)	48½" (28" BBL) 46½" (26" BBL)	42½"	42½"**	40½"**	40½"
Length of Pull	14"	14"	14"	14"	14"	14"	14"
Drop (Comb)	1½"	1½"	1½"	1½"	1½"	1½"	1½"
Drop (Heel)	2½"	2½"	2½"	2½"	2½"	1¼"	1¼"
Stock Material	Wood	Wood	Black Synthetic	Camo-Covered Syn.	Wood	Black Synthetic	Wood
Stock Finish	Flat	Flat	Matte	RealTree® Advantage® Camo	Flat	Matte	Flat
Avg. wt. (lbs.)	7½ (28" BBL) 7¼ (26" BBL)	6½ (28" BBL) 6¼ (26" BBL)	7½ (28" BBL) 7¼ (26" BBL)	7¼	7¼	7	7¼

[1] Stock and fore-end in Advantage® camo.

Model	870™ Express® Left Hand	870™ Express® Combo (12-ga.)	870™ Express® Combo (20-ga.)	870™ Express® HD	870™ Express® Youth	870™ Express® Youth Turkey Camo[1]	870™ Express® Youth Deer Gun
Gauge	12	12	20	12	20	20	20
Mag. Capacity	4	4	4	4	4	4	4
BBL Lengths/ Order No.	28"/5577	28" (Vent Rib)/5571 26" (Vent Rib)/5578 20" (Imp. Cyl. Deer or Fully Rifled Deer)	28" (Vent Rib)/5585 26" (Vent Rib)/5597 20" (Imp. Cyl. Deer or Fully Rifled Deer)	18"/5549	21"/5561	21"/5091	20"/5555
Barrel Type	Vent Rib Rem™ Choke (Mod.)	Vent Rib Rem™ Choke (Mod.) I.C. Deer or Fully Rifled Deer	Vent Rib Rem™ Choke (Mod.) I.C. Deer or Fully Rifled Deer	Cylinder Choke	Vent Rib Rem™ Choke (Mod.)	Vent Rib Rem™ Choke (Full)	Fully Rifled
Sights	Single Bead	Single Bead (Vent Rib) Rifle Sights (Deer BBL)	Single Bead (Vent Rib) Rifle Sights (Deer BBL)	Single Bead	Single Bead	Twin Bead	Rifle Sights
Metal Finish	Matte Black Non-Reflect.	Matte Black Non-Reflect.	Matte Black Non-Reflect.	Matte Black Non-Reflect.	Matte Black Non-Reflect.	Matte Black Non-Reflect.	Matte Black Non-Reflect.
Overall Length	48½"	48½", 46½" (Vent Rib) 40½" (Deer BBL)	48½", 46½" (Vent Rib) 40½" (Deer BBL)	38½"	40½"	40½"	39½"
Length of Pull	14"	14"	14"	14"	13"	13"	13"
Drop (Comb)	1½"	1½"	1½"	1½"	1½"	1½"	1½"
Drop (Heel)	2½"	2½"	2½"	2½"	2½"	2½"	2½"
Stock Material	Hardwood	Hardwood	Hardwood	Black Synthetic	Hardwood	Camo-Covered Syn.	Hardwood
Stock Finish	Flat	Flat	Flat	Matte	Flat	RealTree® Advantage® Camo	Flat
Avg. Wt. (lbs.)	7½	7½ (Vent Rib) 7¼ (Deer BBL)	6½ (Vent Rib) 6¼ (Deer BBL)	7¼	6	6	6

[1] Stock and fore-end in Advantage® camo.

31

— SPRING FEVER? —
May We Suggest
Something in Maximum Strength?

Above: Model 870™ SPS-T™ 20-Gauge Camo

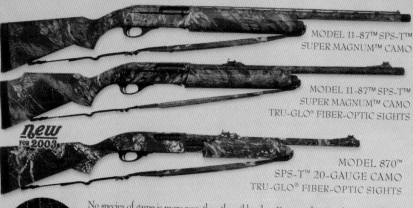

MODEL 11-87™ SPS-T™
SUPER MAGNUM™ CAMO

MODEL 11-87™ SPS-T™
SUPER MAGNUM™ CAMO
TRU-GLO® FIBER-OPTIC SIGHTS

new FOR 2003

MODEL 870™
SPS-T™ 20-GAUGE CAMO
TRU-GLO® FIBER-OPTIC SIGHTS

MODEL 11-87™ SPS-T™:
- Soft recoiling gas operation.
- Comes in both standard 3" 12-gauge and 3½" 12-gauge Super Magnum.
- Full Mossy Oak® Break-Up® camouflage.
- Barrels are Rem™ Choked from the factory.
- Supplied with Turkey Super Full choke tube.
- Equipped with sling swivel studs and matching padded camo sling.
- Available in 21" and 23" barrel lengths.
- Cantilever scope rail, twin bead sights and Tru-Glo® fiber-optic rifle sights also available.
- Fitted with Remington's new high-performance R3™ recoil pad.

See page 34 for complete specifications.

No species of game is more wary than the wild turkey. Fortunately, no turkey guns are better made than the ones you see here. What's more, Remington® offers the most expansive selection of turkey guns in existence and is constantly innovating. Case in point — this year we offer the Model 870™ SPS-T™ 20-gauge. Matched with our 20-gauge Premier® Hevi•Shot® turkey loads this camo-clad beauty is perfect for anyone looking to head into the woods with a lighter load delivering superb handling without sacrificing the magnum power. Add that to a list that includes the Model 11-87™ Super Magnum™ SPS-T™ camo with 23" barrel and Tru-Glo® fiber-optic rifle sights and the Model 11-87 SPS-T Super Magnum with 23" vent-rib barrel.

MODEL 870™ SPS-T™
- Ultra reliable Model 870™ pump action.
- Supplied with Turkey Super Full choke tube.
- Full Mossy Oak Break-Up camouflage.
- Comes in Standard 3" 12-gauge, 3½" 12-gauge Super Magnum and, new for 2003, 20-gauge Magnum.
- Available in 20" and 23" barrel lengths.
- Cantilever scope rail, youth version, twin bead sights and Tru-Glo® fiber-optic rifle sights are also available.
- Fitted with Remington's new high-performance R3™ recoil pad.

See page 34 for complete specifications.

NEW 20-GAUGE 870™ SPS-T™ WITH TRU-GLO® FIBER-OPTIC SIGHTS
There's more than one way to take a gobbler. The low recoil and light handling 20-gauge shotgun has become a favorite of those on the leading edge of creative turkey hunting. With the advent of the newer 20-gauge magnum turkey loads and the reliability of the time-honored Model 870™ action this is an ideal choice for a Spring morning in the woods. An Extended Turkey Super Full choke tube and a weather-defying, ultra-light synthetic stock in Mossy Oak's New Break-Up® pattern fitted with Remington's new high-performance R3™ recoil pad completes the package.

24

SPECIAL PURPOSE WATERFOWL

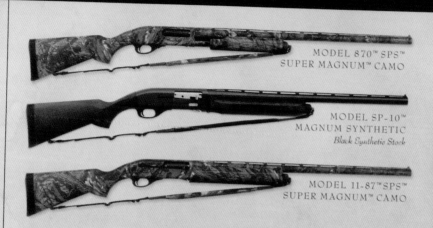

MODEL 870™ SPS™
SUPER MAGNUM™ CAMO

MODEL SP-10™
MAGNUM SYNTHETIC
Black Synthetic Stock

MODEL 11-87™ SPS™
SUPER MAGNUM™ CAMO

S™ /
SPS™

HOTGUNS:
pump-action and
urations.
e fully camouflaged in
k-Up.®
ls available.
swivel studs and
sling.
roved Cylinder,
Rem™ Chokes.
gton's new
R₃™ recoil pad.

EATURES:
pular gas-operated

e power will handle any
y hunting situation.
r Remington's new
ot® waterfowl loads.
b barrels.
n is fully covered in
Up.®
swivels and

camo stock versions
Remington's new high-
coil pad.

plete specifications.

It's just plain hard to beat our industry-leading lineup of Special Purpose Waterfowl guns. The 11-87™ SPS™ Super Magnum™ couples the proven reliability of the Model 11-87 action with the knockdown capability of 3½" magnum payloads. And for ultimate concealment, it's camouflaged in Mossy Oak® Break-Up® from stock to muzzle. If you prefer a slide action, you can choose the equally impressive 3½" Model 870™ SPS Super Magnum. Of course, our perennial favorites still remain, including the sure-functioning, 12-gauge Model 11-87 SPS and the goose-blind-ruling power of the 10-gauge Model SP-10™ Magnum.

SPECIAL PURPOSE DEER AND MARINE MAGNUM®

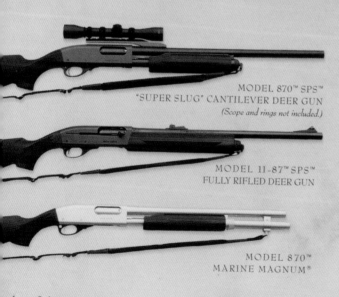

MODEL 870™ SPS™
"SUPER SLUG" CANTILEVER DEER GUN
(Scope and rings not included.)

MODEL 11-87™ SPS™
FULLY RIFLED DEER GUN

MODEL 870™
MARINE MAGNUM®

rrels or rifled Rem™ chokes, our
er guns bring rifle-like accuracy
nting. Choose from three fast-
-87™ autoloaders, or our deadly
ug" Model 870™ SPS™ which

features a unique, heavy-contour barrel that reduces recoil and dramatically improves accuracy. Other options include cantilever scope mounts and synthetic or walnut stocks. Also see the Universal Scope Mount on page 70.

MODEL 870™ S
MODEL 11-87™
DEER SHOTGU

• Comes in 3" Magn
• Highly accurate slu
  both Model 870™ a
• Model 11-87 SPS™
  rifled barrel, either
  mount or rifle sight
• Model 870™ SPS c
  rifled barrel with ca
• Fitted with Reming
  high-performance R

MODEL 870™ MA
MAGNUM® FEAT

• 18" cylinder bore, be
• Synthetic stock and
• Fully plated with cor
  electroless nickel.
• Sling swivel studs.
• 7-shot magazine.
• Fitted with Remington
  high-performance R₃ ecoil pad.

See page 34 for complete specifications.

GOBBLERS TO THE MAX

The waterfowler's desire for 3- and 3½-inch 12-gauge shells pales in comparison to the all-consuming craving turkey hunters have for these magnum rounds.

25

MODEL 870™ EXPRESS® SUPER MAGNUM™

— THE WORLD'S MOST DEPENDABLE —
Pump Shotgun In
Super Magnum™ Strength.

Above: Model 870™ Express® Super Magnum™ Turkey Camo

Because it handles everything from light 2³/₄" loads to heavy 3¹/₂" magnums interchangeably, you've got a shotgun that's unrivaled in versatility. No other pump gun even comes close. You can go from shooting heavy 3¹/₂" loads at high-passing waterfowl to shooting light 2³/₄" loads at fast-darting doves without a hitch. And it does it all with the same action stroke, balance and feel of our original Model 870™ (the most popular pump gun in history). Finally, we can't forget to mention what may be the most appealing thing about the Express® Super Magnum™ It comes at a very affordable price. Many workhorse models are available, including stock choices of flat-finished hardwood, durable black synthetic or popular camo finishes. To get the most versatile of any Model 870 Express Super Magnum, choose the two-barrel Combo.

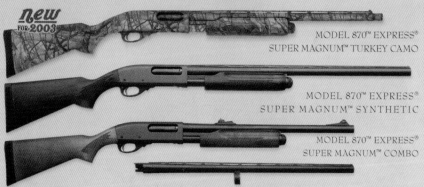

**MODEL 870™ EXPRESS®
SUPER MAGNUM™ TURKEY CAMO**

**MODEL 870™ EXPRESS®
SUPER MAGNUM™ SYNTHETIC**

**MODEL 870™ EXPRESS®
SUPER MAGNUM™ COMBO**

For deer hunting with slugs, you get a 20" fully-rifled barrel with adjustable factory sights and a standard 26" vent-rib Rem™ Choke barrel for just about any other shotgunning imaginable.

**MODEL 870™ EXPRESS®
SUPER MAGNUM™ FEATURES:**

- Will function 2³/₄", 3" and 3¹/₂" shells interchangeably.
- Superior design and inherent strength of America's favorite pump shotgun, the Model 870.™
- Super Magnum™ receiver same size as all 12-gauge Model 870 shotguns for same balance point.
- Innovative bolt design keeps cycle stroke equal for all 3 sizes of 12-gauge shotshells.
- Magazine capacity is three 3¹/₂" shells and four 2³/₄" and 3" shells.
- Available in wood, synthetic and camou-flaged versions as well as a combo package, which features both a vent rib and rifle-sighted deer barrel for maximum versatility.
- New for 2003 is the addition of a new high-quality camo pattern, Skyline® Excel.™
See page 35 for complete specifications.

MODEL 870™ SUPER MAGNUM® DESIGN FEATURES:

Superior design and inherent strength of 870™ receiver easily accommodates the power and longer length of 3¹/₂" shells

Breakthrough bolt re-design keeps cycle stroke equal for all three sizes of 12-ga. shotshells

Model 870™ Super Magnums will function with 2³/₄", 3", and 3¹/₂" shells interchangeably

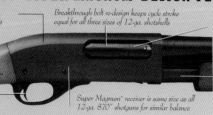

Trigger mechanism retains same dimensions and crisp feel of all 12-ga. Model 870s

Super Magnum™ receiver is same size as all 12-ga. 870™ shotguns for similar balance

Magazine length unchanged for same balance point; capacity is three 3¹/₂", and four 2³/₄" or 3" shells

26

YOUTH FIREARMS

MODEL 870™ EXPRESS® YOUTH SHOTGUNS FEATURE:

- Offered in 12-,16- and 20-gauge versions.
- 20″ barrel youth deer gun with fully rifled barrel and rifle sights, camo stock and fore-end. Also available in youth turkey gun with Skyline® Excel™ camo and 16-gauge synthetic youth variations.
- All feature Rem™ Choke barrels and come with Rem Choke modified tubes.
- Perfect length, weight and balance for smaller-stature shooters.
- Model 870™ action is the reliability standard for pump shotguns around the world.

new FOR 2003

MODEL 870™
EXPRESS® YOUTH
TURKEY CAMO

MODEL 870™
EXPRESS® YOUTH SYNTHETIC
16-Gauge

MODEL 870™
EXPRESS® YOUTH DEER

new FOR 2003

MODEL 1100™
YOUTH SYNTHETIC
TURKEY CAMO

MODEL 1100™
YOUTH SYNTHETIC LT-20

MODEL 1100™ YOUTH SYNTHETIC 20-GAUGE FEATURES:

- Ideal fit and handling for smaller-stature shooters and hunters.
- 13″ length of pull and 21″ vent rib Rem™ Choke barrel for perfect weight and balance.
- Camouflaged version sports a stock and fore-end in Skyline® Excel™ camo.
- Comes with Rem™ Choke modified choke tube.
- Low-recoil gas operation.

FIREARMS

SHOTGUN DIMENSIONS / AVERAGE WEIGHTS

Model	1100™ LT-20 Youth Synthetic	★1100™ LT-20 Youth Synthetic Turkey Camo	870™ SPS-T™ Youth RS/TG Synthetic Turkey Camo	870™ Express® Youth Synthetic	★870™ Express® Youth Turkey Camo	870™ Express® Youth	870™ Express® Youth Deer Gun
Gauge	20	20 (Magnum)¹	12	16	20	20	20
Mag. Capacity	4	4	4	4	4	4	4
BBL Lengths/Order No.	21″/25367	★21″/25245	20″/24873	23″/25203	★21″/25175	21″/25561	20″/25555
Barrel Type	Vent Rib Rem™ Choke (Mod.)	Vent Rib Rem™ Choke (Full)	Rem™ Choke (Super Full)	Vent Rib Rem™ Choke (Mod.)	Vent Rib Rem™ Choke (Full)	Vent Rib Rem™ Choke (Mod.)	Fully Rifled
Sights	Single Bead	Twin Bead	Truglo® Fiber Optic Rifle	Single Bead	Twin Bead	Single Bead	Rifle Sights
Metal Finish	Matte Black Non-Reflect.	Matte Black Non-Reflect.	Mossy Oak® Break-Up®	Matte Black Non-Reflect.	Matte Black Non-Reflect.	Matte Black Non-Reflect.	Matte Black Non-Reflect.
Overall Length	40½″	40½″	40½″	42½″	40½″	40½″	39¼″
Length of Pull	13″	13″	13″	13″	13″	13″	13″
Drop (Comb)	1½″	1½″	1½″	1½″	1½″	1½″	1½″
Drop (Heel)	2½″	2½″	2½″	2½″	2½″	2½″	2½″
Stock Material	Black Synthetic	Camo-Covered Synthetic	Camo-Covered Synthetic	Black Synthetic	Camo-Covered Synthetic	Hardwood	Hardwood
Stock Finish	Matte	Skyline® Excel™ Camo	Mossy Oak® Break-Up®	Matte	Skyline® Excel™ Camo	Flat	Flat
Avg. Wt. (lbs.)	6½	6½	7¼	6¼	6	6	6

¹ Model 1100™ 3″ Magnum is set up to handle heavy 20-ga. shotshells including 3″, and will not function satisfactorily with target and light field loads.
² NOTE: 870™ Express® is 2¾″ chambered.

★New for 2003

RIFLE DIMENSIONS / AVERAGE WEIGHTS

	Action Type	Barrel Length	Overall Length	Avg. Wt. (lbs.)	Stock Mat'l	Stock Finish	BBL Mat'l	BBL Finish
Model Seven™ Youth	Short Action	20″	38¼″	6¼	Hardwood	Flat	Carbon Steel	Matte Blue
700™ ADL™ Synthetic Youth	Short Action	20″	39⅛″	6¼	Black	Matte	Carbon	Matte

For full caliber listings refer to page 32.

31

DEER AND TURKEY **SHOTGUNS** | **163**

MODEL 870™ SPECIAL PURPOSE TURKEY

SPRING FEVER? MAY WE SUGGEST SOMETHING IN MAXIMUM STRENGTH.

No species of game is more wary than the wild turkey. Fortunately, no turkey guns are better made than the ones you see here. Truth is, Remington® offers the most expansive selection of turkey guns in the industry. That's because we know, for every specific circumstance, there's a specific gun.

Take the Model 870™ SPS-T™ 20-gauge, for example. Matched with our 20-gauge magnum turkey loads this camo-clad beauty is perfect for anyone looking to head into the woods with a lighter gun delivering superb handling without sacrificing the magnum power.

New for 2005, our Model 870 SP-T™ Super Magnum Thumbhole comes fully covered in Mossy Oak® Obsession® camo. Equipped with our R3® recoil pad and a 23" TRUGLO® adjustable rifle sight barrel, the SP-T Super Magnum Thumbhole model offers superior handling for precise shot placement.

MODEL 870™ SPS-T™ AND SP-T™ FEATURES:

- The Model 870™ SPS-T™ comes in a Mossy Oak® Break-Up® camo
- The Model 870™ SP-T™ Super Magnum™ Thumbhole comes in a Mossy Oak® Obsession® camo
- Ultra reliable Model 870 pump action
- Supplied with Turkey Super Full Choke Tube (0.665")
- Comes in Standard 3" 12-gauge, 3½" 12-gauge Super Magnum™ and 20-gauge Magnum™ (Non-thumbhole model only)
- Twin bead sights or TRUGLO® fiber-optic rifle sighted barrel
- Fitted with Remington's high-performance R3® recoil pad

Model 870™ SP-T™
Super Magnum Thumbhole

For complete model listings and specifications see page 84.

SPECIAL PURPOSE WATERFOWL

ALL ARRIVING FLIGHTS ARE ABOUT TO BE GROUNDED.

The Remington® line of Special Purpose Waterfowl guns – they'll never know what hit 'em. An effective waterfowl gun must be able to resist the elements and continue to work reliably and efficiently. That's why Remington makes a complete line of Special Purpose Shotguns built to handle all types of waterfowl and the environments they live in.

Well rounded, and packed with features, the Model 11-87™ SPS™ Waterfowl is as reliable as they come. Or, if you prefer a pump-action, you might take a look at the equally impressive Model 870™ SPS™ Super Magnum.™ Of course, there's always the perennial favorite, the 12-gauge Model 11-87 SPS and new for 2005, the Mossy Oak® Obsession® 10-gauge Model SP-10™ Magnum.™ To you, these are the ultimate waterfowl guns. To ducks and geese? Air traffic control – with an attitude.

MODEL 870™ SPS™ & MODEL 11-87™ SPS™ WATERFOWL SHOTGUNS FEATURE:

- Available in both pump-action and autoloading configurations
- Camo versions are fully camouflaged in Mossy Oak® Break-Up® or Mossy Oak® New Shadowgrass™
- 26" and 28" barrels available
- Comes with sling swivel studs and padded sling
- Equipped with Improved Cylinder, Modified and Full Rem™ Chokes
- Fitted with Remington's high-performance R3® recoil pad

Model 870™ SPS™
Super Magnum™ Camo

Model 11-87™ SPS™
Waterfowl Camo
12-Gauge

For complete model listings and specifications see page 84.

new for 2005

Model 870™ SP-T™
Super Magnum Thumbhole

Model 870™ SPS-T™
12-Gauge Camo

R_3

new for 2005

100 YEARS
AUTOLOADING SHOTGUNS
2005
CENTENNIAL
Remington

Model SP-10™
Magnum™ Camo

Model 11-87™ SPS™
Super Magnum™ Camo

R_3

MODEL SP-10™ FEATURES:

- New for 2005, camouflage version is fully covered in Mossy Oak® Obsession®
- America's most popular gas-operated 10-gauge shotgun
- Awesome 10-gauge power will handle any waterfowl or turkey hunting situation
- Perfect platform for Remington's 10-gauge Hevi•Shot® waterfowl loads
- 26" camouflage and 30" satin finish wood, both with vent rib barrels
- All come with slin...
- Camo stock w...
  high-perform...

For complete model listings

SPECIAL PURPOSE MARINE MAGNUM®

Perhaps the perfect all-purpose 12-gauge utility shotgun, the Model 870™ Marine Magnum® is built to last. With an electroless nickel plating covering its entire metal surface, including the inside of the barrel and receiver, the Model 870 Marine Magnum resists corrosion in even the harshest environments. Its synthetic stock features generous checkering for easy and secure handling and a high-performance R3® recoil pad for less kick. Comes with 18" cylinder barrel with single-bead front sight, six-round magazine, padded Cordura sling, and swivel studs.

R_3

Remington
2005
FIREARMS
AMMUNITION
ACCESSORIES
Catalog

Remington

INVESTING IN OUR FUTURE.

We've gone the extra step to redesign some of our standard, premium-grade stocks for a shorter length-of-pull – then fitted them to some of our finest, most proven rifles and shotguns. All Youth rifles we make are counter-balanced with a shorter 20" (22" on long action offerings) barrel and all Youth shotguns with a 21" (20" for youth deer gun) barrel to keep them from becoming muzzle-heavy while also retaining effective ballistics. Two centerfire rifle choices are available. The first is our compact Model Seven™ bolt action chambered for 260 Remington, and a synthetic model, chambered for 223 Remington, 243 Win and 7mm-08 Remington. The other is our legendary Model 700.™ The Model 700 SPS™ Youth Synthetic is available in a short action synthetic stock configuration, chambered for either 243 Win or 308 Win, and the SPS Youth Synthetic long action is chambered for either 270 Win or 30-06 and is specifically designed to take advantage of our new Managed-Recoil™ ammunition. All synthetic stocked youth rifles feature the R3® recoil pad.

In Youth shotguns, in addition to existing offerings in the Model 870™ Express line, we're featuring three new pump shotgun offerings this year – the Model 870™ Wingmaster® Jr., the Model 870™ Express® Jr. NWTF Jakes Gun – both with shorter 12" length of pull stocks and 18 ³/₄" barrels, as well as a Model 870™ Express Synthetic Youth Combo featuring a 21" vent rib barrel and a 20" fully rifled barrel.

The all-new Model 11-87™ Sportsman Youth shotgun brings 20-gauge 2 ³/₄" and 3" capability to the youth autoloading shotgun line. Now smaller stature shooters can benefit from full range capability in a soft recoiling gas autoloading shotgun. Like its pump-action counterparts, the Model 11-87™ Sportsman Youth features a one-inch shorter length-of-pull stock and a 21" vent rib, Rem™ Choke barrel. Although we call it our Youth firearm line, the rifles and shotguns here are ideal for more than just young shooters. They're also perfect for any hunter needing a shorter overall length of pull.

The Limited Edition Model 870™ Express® Jr. comes with a Team NWTF medallion in the stock. For every special edition Model 870 sold, a portion of the proceeds will be donated to the National Wild Turkey Federation.

new for 2005
Model 870™ Express® Jr.
NWTF Edition

new for 2005
Model 870™ Wingmaster® Jr.

new for 2005
Model 11-87™ Sportsman™ Youth Synthetic

Model 870™ Express® Youth Synthetic
(Youth Turkey Camo also available)

Model 870™ Express® Youth Deer

MODEL 870™ EXPRESS® JR. SHOTGUNS FEATURE:

- Limited Edition Team NWTF medallion in stock
- 12" Jakes length of pull – full 1" shorter than youth
- Stock and fore-end camouflaged in Skyline® Excel®
- All feature Rem™ Choke barrels and come with Rem Choke full tubes
- Perfect length, weight and balance for smaller-stature shooters
- Model 870 action is the reliability standard for pump shotguns around the world

MODEL 870™ EXPRESS® YOUTH SHOTGUNS FEATURE:

- Offered in 12-, 16- and 20-gauge versions
- 20" barrel youth deer gun with fully rifled barrel and rifle sights, camo stock and fore-end. Also available in youth turkey gun with Skyline® Excel® camo and 16-gauge synthetic youth variations
- All feature Rem™ Choke barrels and come with Rem Choke modified tubes
- Perfect length, weight and balance for smaller-stature shooters
- Model 870 action is the reliability standard for pump shotguns around the world
- New for 2005 – Synthetic Youth Deer/Field Combos

28

FIREARMS

new for 2005

Model 870™ Express® Jr.
NWTF Edition

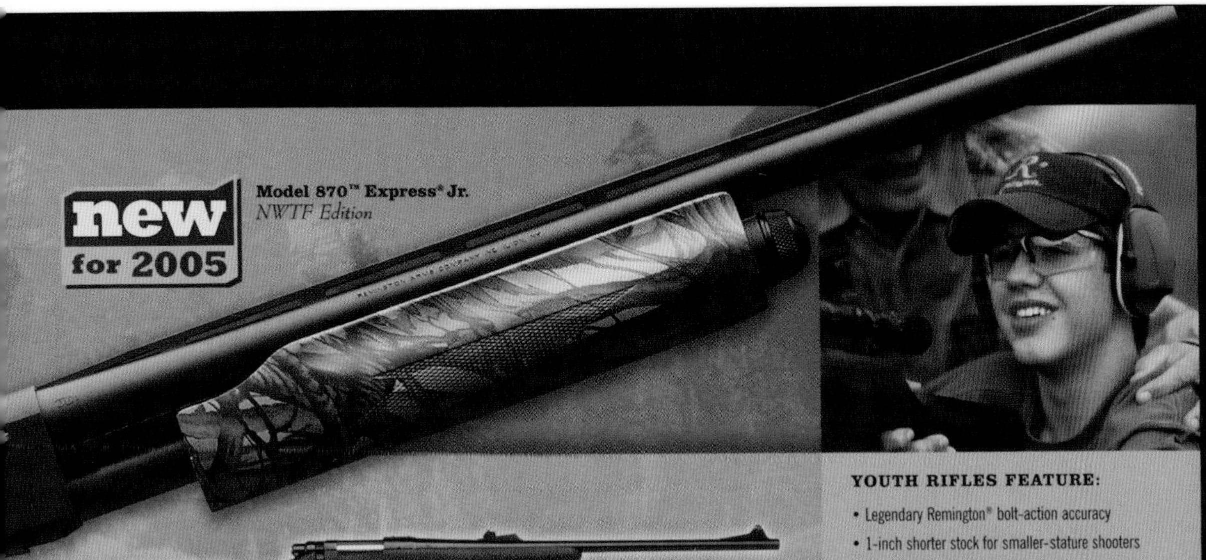

Model Seven™ Youth Synthetic

Model 700™ SPS™ Youth Synthetic

YOUTH RIFLES FEATURE:

- Legendary Remington® bolt-action accuracy
- 1-inch shorter stock for smaller-stature shooters
- Receiver machined from ordnance grade steel
- Three-rings-of-steel (bolt, barrel and receiver) surround the cartridge head for strongest lock-up
- R3® recoil pad on synthetic stock rifles
- Hammer forged barrel with blued finish
- Hinged floorplate magazines
- Sling swivel studs
- Iron sights standard (Model Seven™ only)

FOR FULL CALIBER LISTINGS AND OFFERINGS REFER TO PAGE 82.

RIFLE DIMENSIONS / AVERAGE WEIGHTS

Model	Action Type	Barrel Length	Overall Length	Avg. Wt. (lbs.)	Stock Mat'l	Stock Finish	BBL Mat'l	BBL Finish
Model Seven™ Youth	Short Action	20"	38 3/4"	6 1/4	Hardwood	Satin	Carbon Steel	Polished Blue
Model Seven™ Youth Synthetic	Short Action	20"	38 1/4"	6 1/4	Synthetic	Matte	Carbon Steel	Matte
700™ SPS™ Youth Synthetic	Short Action	20"	38 5/8"	6 3/4	Synthetic	Matte	Carbon Steel	Matte
700™ SPS™ Youth Synthetic	Long Action	22"	39 5/8"	7 1/4	Synthetic	Matte	Carbon Steel	Matte

SHOTGUN DIMENSIONS / AVERAGE WEIGHTS

Model	new 870™ Express Jr. NWTF Edition	new 870™ Wingmaster® Jr.	new 11-87™ Sportsman™ Youth Synthetic	870™ Express® Youth Turkey Camo	870™ Express® Youth	870™ Express® Youth Deer Gun	new 870™ Express® Youth Synthetic Combo
Gauge	20	20	20	20	20 / 16[1]	20	20
Mag. Capacity	4	4	4	4	4	4	4
BBL Lengths/Order No.	18 3/4"/26470	18 3/4"/26460	21"/29891	21"/25175	21"/25561 (20-ga.) 23"/25203 (16-ga. Syn.)	20"/25555	21"/25659 20"/25659
Barrel Type	Vent Rib Rem™ Choke (Full)	Vent Rib Rem™ Choke (IC, Mod, Full)	Vent Rib Rem™ Choke (Mod)	Vent Rib Rem™ Choke (Full)	Vent Rib Rem™ Choke (Mod.)	Fully Rifled	Vent Rib Rem™ Choke and Fully Rifled Deer
Sights	Single Bead	Twin Bead	Single Bead	Twin Bead	Single Bead	Rifle Sights	Single Bead (Vent Rib) Rifled Sights (Deer BBL)
Metal Finish	Matte Black Non-Reflect.	High Polish Blued	Matte Black Non-Reflect.	Matte Black Non-Reflect.	Matte Black Non-Reflect.	Matte Black Non-Reflect.	Matte Black Non-Reflect.
Overall Length	37 1/4"	37 1/4"	40 1/2"	40 1/2"	40 1/2"	39 1/2"	40 1/2"
Length of Pull	12"	12"	13"	13"	13"	13"	13"
Drop (Comb)	1 1/2"	1 1/2"	1 1/2"	1 1/2"	1 1/2"	1 1/2"	1 1/2"
Drop (Heel)	2"	2"	2 1/4"	2 1/4"	2 1/4"	2 1/4"	2 1/4"
Stock Material	Camo-Covered Synthetic	American Walnut	Synthetic	Camo-Covered Synthetic	Hardwood or Black Synthetic	Hardwood	Synthetic
Stock Finish	Skyline® Excel™ Camo	Hi-Gloss	Black	Skyline® Excel™ Camo	Flat	Flat	Black
Avg. Wt. (lbs.)	6	6	6 1/2	6	6	6	6

[1] 16-gauge Synthetic (order #5203) features a 23" vent rib barrel, overall length is 42 1/2".

29

MODEL 870™
WINGMASTER®

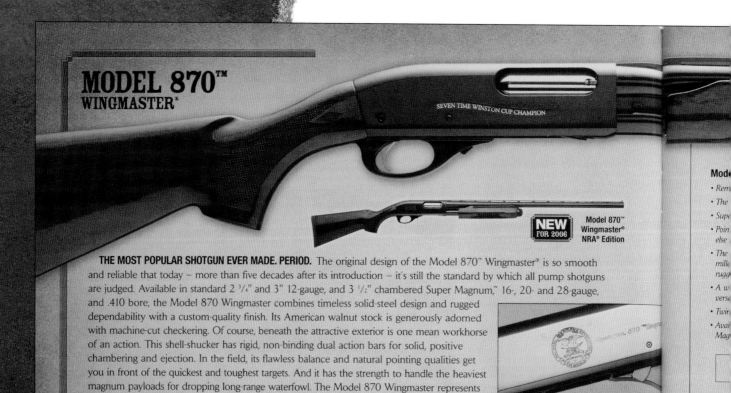

Model 870™
Wingmaster®
NRA® Edition

THE MOST POPULAR SHOTGUN EVER MADE. PERIOD. The original design of the Model 870™ Wingmaster® is so smooth and reliable that today – more than five decades after its introduction – it's still the standard by which all pump shotguns are judged. Available in standard 2 ³/₄" and 3" 12-gauge, and 3 ¹/₂" chambered Super Magnum,™ 16-, 20- and 28-gauge, and .410 bore, the Model 870 Wingmaster combines timeless solid-steel design and rugged dependability with a custom-quality finish. Its American walnut stock is generously adorned with machine-cut checkering. Of course, beneath the attractive exterior is one mean workhorse of an action. This shell-shucker has rigid, non-binding dual action bars for solid, positive chambering and ejection. In the field, its flawless balance and natural pointing qualities get you in front of the quickest and toughest targets. And it has the strength to handle the heaviest magnum payloads for dropping long-range waterfowl. The Model 870 Wingmaster represents pump-gun perfection and practically never wears out. Perhaps that's why there are more of them in use today than any other shotgun.

Special NRA® Edition

MODEL 870™ SPECIAL PURPOSE

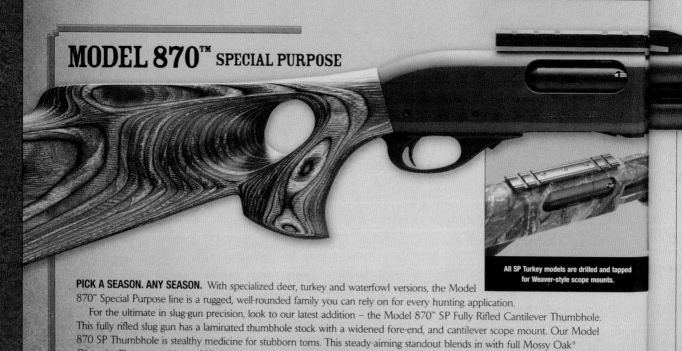

All SP Turkey models are drilled and tapped for Weaver-style scope mounts.

PICK A SEASON. ANY SEASON. With specialized deer, turkey and waterfowl versions, the Model 870™ Special Purpose line is a rugged, well-rounded family you can rely on for every hunting application.

For the ultimate in slug-gun precision, look to our latest addition – the Model 870™ SP Fully Rifled Cantilever Thumbhole. This fully rifled slug gun has a laminated thumbhole stock with a widened fore-end, and cantilever scope mount. Our Model 870 SP Thumbhole is stealthy medicine for stubborn toms. This steady-aiming standout blends in with full Mossy Oak® Obsession™ camo and has a 23" barrel with Truglo® fiber-optic rifle sights. An R3® Recoil Pad helps cancel kick.

The new Model 870 SPS-T 12-gauge Super Magnum features the concealment of Mossy Oak Obsession camo and handles 2 ³/₄" to 3 ¹/₂" loads. Its 23" barrel has twin beads.

NEW FOR 2006

Model 870™ Wingmaster®
Dale Earnhardt Edition
20-gauge

master® Features:

y and durability

-action shotgun on the market

ndling and looks

nctions better than anything

and richly blued receiver is
llet of steel for the ultimate in

rel and choke options make
ster® hallmark

non-binding action

l 12-gauge, 3 ¹/₂" Super
28-gauge and 410 bore

odel listings and
see page 88.

DALE EARNHARDT LIMITED-EDITION SHOTGUN. *For the fourth and final year, legends merge in Remington® Country. We're proud to unveil the 2006 Dale Earnhardt Limited-Edition Shotgun – a 20-gauge Model 870™ Wingmaster.® Consistent, dominating performance was Earnhardt's hallmark, and it's also what makes the Wingmaster such a fitting tribute to one of NASCAR's greatest. The last edition to this commemorative lineup features a 26" light contour barrel, a richly finished American walnut stock and a polished blued receiver we used as a canvas for some stunningly detailed artwork. It's engraved with Dale's likeness highlighted by a 24-karat gold signature and a "Seven Time Winston Cup Champion" banner. Beauty meets proven function in this fine collector's piece. And a portion of the proceeds from each sale goes to the Dale Earnhardt Foundation.*

Model 870™ Wingmaster®
12-gauge

Model 870™ Wingmaster®
.410 Bore

HOLY STOCKS!
Thumbhole stocks
provide solid support
in awkward positions,
something turkey
hunters often find
themselves in.
Remington makes
sure its 870 turkey
hunters are thusly well
equipped.

NEW FOR 2006

Model 870™
Special Purpose
Thumbhole
Fully Rifled Cantilever

al Purpose Features:

ifle-like shot placement
e stock design

r reduces recoil
ever barrel
gs

Model 870™ SPS-T™
Super Magnum

NEW FOR 2006

Model 870™ SPS™
Super Magnum Camo

NEW FOR 2006

Model 870™ SP-T™
Super Magnum™
Thumbhole

odel listings and
see page 88.

MODEL 870™
SPECIAL PURPOSE

SuperCell® RECOIL PAD

ShurShot™ Stock

SPECIALLY DESIGNED
FOR LONGER SHOTS
AT BIGGER GAME.

The most dependable slide action of all time in three advanced designs that will go the distance with deadly precision, whether your target is a big red head or the crease behind a buck's shoulder. All feature our new SuperCell™ recoil pad, which dramatically reduces felt recoil through a potent matrix of shock-dissipating cells. The turkey shotguns are fully covered in Realtree® APG™ HD™ camo and deliver 3 ½" Super Magnum™ payloads with lethal authority at the longest ranges. Now featuring our new ShurShot™ synthetic pistol-grip stock, the updated **Model 870™ SPS™ ShurShot Synthetic Turkey** offers both right-and left-handed hunters the pinnacle of lightweight shooting comfort and handling ease. With this stock in your grip, repositioning for the shot is quick and efficient, plus the position of your hand naturally diffuses recoil. The 23" barrel offers awesome maneuverability, while the fully adjustable TruGlo® fiber-optic sights and an extended Wingmaster HD™ Turkey Rem™ Choke maximize pattern placement.

Recoil suppression and adaptability are hallmarks of the **Model 870 Super Magnum MAX Gobbler™** thanks to its Knoxx® SpecOps™ pistol-grip stock. Length of pull is adjustable, so you can customize the fit to your shooting style. This highly advanced stock also incorporates state-of-the-art recoil-dampening technology – with dual shock-absorbing springs – to tame 3 ½" super magnum thunder. Other features include a swift-pointing 23" barrel with bright, fully adjustable Williams® fiber-optic Fire Sights™ for precision, and an included Turkey Super-Full Rem™ Choke.

The **Model 870 SPS ShurShot Synthetic Fully Rifled Cantilever** shotgun puts exceptional accuracy and swift handling characteristics in the hands of left- and right-handed deer hunters. With its cantilever mount, adding optics couldn't be easier, and its fully rifled 23" barrel maximizes reach with today's high-performance slug loads. The stock and fore-end are dressed in Realtree® Hardwoods HD.™ When it's time to add a sling, the swivel studs are built-in for your convenience.

XTREME CONDITIONS
SHOTGUNS

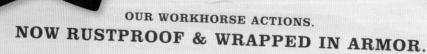

MODEL 870™
MARINE M...
Available in ...

For co...
listings...
see pa...

OUR WORKHORSE ACTIONS.
NOW RUSTPROOF & WRAPPED IN ARMOR.

The primary design premise of our Model 870™ and Model 11-87™ actions is dependability – add the tremendous corrosion and abrasion resistance of our proprietary TriNyte® Corrosion Control System, and they're virtually invincible. Fact is, these are the most durable, reliable shotguns on land or sea. All have electroless-nickel-coated internals and a plated trigger group for dramatically enhanced resistance to fouling and oxidation. Plus, the same sleek lines and swift pointing characteristics you love about Remington® shotguns.

Built on the most trusted slide action of all time, the **Model 870 XCS Marine Magnum®** is the new standard for all-weather reliability. It has a Black TriNyte coating, a tactical-style SpeedFeed® I stock, 7-round capacity and an 18" cylinder bore. The stock's shell holder keeps up to four extra rounds at your fingertips.

Our Premier Dealers have four Xtreme Conditions Shotguns to choose from. The 12-gauge **Model 870 XCS Super Magnum** and **Model 11-87 XCS Super Magnum** with TriNyte PVD coatings, black synthetic SpeedFeed® I shell-holding stocks. The **Model 870 XCS Super Magnum Waterfowl** and **Model 11-87 XCS Super Magnum Waterfowl** have all the same great features plus Mossy Oak® Duck Blind™ camo stocks and fore-ends.

16

NYTE
ROSION
L SYSTE...

MODEL 870™ SPS™
SHURSHOT™ SYNTHETIC TURKEY
Available in: 12 gauge (2 ½", 3" and 3 ½")

apg HD **NEW**

REALTREE hardwoods HD **NEW**

ShurShot Stock

MODEL 870™ SPS™
SHURSHOT™
SYNTHETIC CANTILEVER
Available in: 12 gauge (2 ½" and 3")

apg HD

MODEL 870™ SPS™ SUPER MAG MAX GOBBLER™
Available in: 12 gauge (2 ½", 3" and 3 ½")

SpecOps™ stock
...l-compensation
...atically reduces
...d muzzle jump.

Recoil-dampening springs

LOP adjustment

MODEL 870™ SPS™ SHURSHOT™ SYNTHETIC TURKEY FEATURES

- 23" rifle-sighted barrel
- TruGlo® fiber optic sights
- Wingmaster HD™ extended Rem™ Choke (Turkey)
- Receiver drilled and tapped for scope mounts (Weaver Rail #429M)
- Realtree® APG™ HD™ camo
- Black sling included
- Molded in rear sling swivel stud and front stud included in magazine cap
- Featuring Remington's new SuperCell® recoil pad technology

A truly ambidextrous design, the ShurShot™ pistol grip stock delivers lightweight comfort, steady shooting and rapid handling for both right- and left-handed shooters.

FLEXIBILITY

Taking a cue from the tactical crowd, adjustable folding stocks have also become popular with the big-game 870 crowd, their design often being more maneuverable in tight places.

Also available in Mossy Oak® Duck Blind® stock and fore-end

Premier

MODEL 870™ XCS
SUPER MAGNUM
Available in: 12 gauge (2 ½", 3" and 3 ½")

Also available in black synthetic stock and fore-end

Premier

MODEL 11-87™ XCS
SUPER MAGNUM WATERFOWL
Available in: 12 gauge (2 ½", 3" and 3 ½")

For complete model listings and specifications, see pages 92-93.

... Corrosion Control System (Patent pending). Consisting of electroless
...d proprietary PVD, this armor-tough, multi-layer coating is the world's
...ective barrier against rust and abrasion for firearms, yet is only a fraction
...an hair in thickness. The only thing you'll notice is the near invincibility.

MODEL 870™ XCS FEATURES

- TriNyte® Corrosion Control System on barrel and receiver creates an armor-tough barrier against rust and abrasion
- Its Model 870™ action is the rugged standard for dependability and smooth operation
- 18" cylinder bore, bead-sighted barrel
- 2-shot magazine extension – 7-shot capacity
- SpeedFeed® I stock with shell holder keeps 2-4 extra rounds at your fingertips
- Corrosion-resistant trigger group with plated components
- Sling swivel studs

Remington®

2008 CATALOG
FIREARMS, AMMUNITION & ACCESSORIES

MODEL 870™
WINGMASTER®

AS TIMELESS AND DEPENDABLE
AS YOUR LOVE FOR THE SOUND OF WINGS.

Sure as autumn arrives, the Model 870™ Wingmaster® rises to meet another day in the upland fields and woods of America. The Model 870 is so smooth and reliable that today – nearly 60 years after its introduction – it's still the standard by which all pump shotguns are measured. With a receiver machined from a solid billet of steel, it is the model of enduring strength. True to its original design, the pump glides with silky surety on two twin action bars for the utmost in positive chambering and ejection. These characteristics, along with its flawless balance and natural pointing qualities have made the Model 870 the best-selling, most trusted shotgun of all time – of any action type, from any manufacturer. As the most aesthetically refined representative of our prestigious pump-action family, the Model 870 Wingmaster is a true American icon.

Available in 12 gauge 2 ¾" and 3", 20 and 28 gauge, and .410 bore, it has a custom-quality finish and handsome American walnut woodwork. The receiver and barrel are richly blued and highly polished for classic appeal. We also offer a broad selection of barrel and choke options to fit your application. Our Premier Dealers can step the aesthetic appeal up a notch with a version featuring a high-gloss claro walnut stock and fore-end, as well as a handsome pheasant and duck scene embellishment engraving on the receiver.

MODEL 870™ WINGMASTER®
Available in 12 and 20 gauge (2 ½" and 3") 28 gauge (2 ½") and .410 bore (3")

MODEL 870™
EXPRESS®

AMERICA'S FAVORITE
PUM SHOTGUN.

Its solid, dependable action makes it America's favorite, and our continual upgrades make it the most advanced, well-rounded family of pump shotguns around. Along with its continually evolving designs, this shotgun's superiority is a matter of rugged dependability, great pointing characteristics and versatility. In fact, the Model 870™ has been the standard for slide-action performance for almost 60 years.

Our new **Model 870 Express® ShurShot™ Synthetic Turkey** is optimized for big birds with the revolutionary ShurShot synthetic pistol-grip stock. It's contoured to accommodate both right- and left-handed shooters, while offering an incredibly steady-aiming platform that [...] felt recoil. The 21" barrel adds to its superb maneuverability, and the Turkey [...] Oak® Obsession™ coverage on the stock [...]

With our **Model 870** [...]
incredible stability and [...]

MODEL 870™ EXPRESS® SHURSHOT™ SYNTHETIC TURKEY
Available in 12 gauge (2 ½" and 3")

MODEL 870™ EXPRESS®
Available in 12 and 20 gauge (2 ½" and 3")

MODEL 870™ EXPRESS® SYNTHETIC
with 7-round capacity
Available in 12 and 20 gauge (2 ½" and 3")

MODEL 870™
SPECIAL PURPOSE

PERFECTING THE ART OF
FLATTENING BIGGER GAME
AT LONGER RANGES.

Introducing the most dependable slide action of all time in three advanced designs that will go the distance with deadly precision, whether your target is the crease behind a buck's shoulder or a big red head. We've built the industry's finest rifled slug guns for years, but our new 12-gauge **Model 870 SPS™ ShurShot™ Synthetic Super Slug** advances deer-leveling technology to farther reaches and smaller group sizes than ever before possible. Even more so when paired with high-performance ammunition like our Premier AccuTip sabot slugs. Because barrel stability is key to extended-range accuracy, this shotgun's barrel is of extra-heavy, 1" diameter configuration and measures a full 25 ½". It's also pinned to the receiver to control vibration for rifle-like, shot-to-shot consistency. Five longitudinal flutes keep weight and heat buildup to a minimum while bolstering barrel rigidity. Six Parabolic Ultragon™ rifling grooves with a 1-in-35" twist optimize slug flight. But much more than just the ultimate accuracy-enhancing barrel design, this shotgun provides the rock-steady aim and outstanding pointability of our ambidextrous ShurShot pistol-grip synthetic stock. New on the Super Slug stock for 2009, rubberized overmolding at the pistol grip and extended fore-end offer a sure hold in adverse conditions. For unmatched shooting comfort, we added the SuperCell™ recoil pad. The receiver is drilled and tapped, and the included Weaver rail makes adding optics a cinch. Sling swivel studs are built in.

The **Model 870 SPS ShurShot Synthetic Fully Rifled Cantilever** is an outstanding long-range rig with a fully rifled 23" barrel equipped with a cantilever mount. Its Realtree® Hardwoods HD™ ShurShot stock delivers the best in both stability and maneuverability, and has sling swivel studs built-in.

Our **Model 870 SPS ShurShot Synthetic Turkey** is fully covered in Realtree APG™ HD™ camo and delivers 3 ½" Super Magnum™ payloads with lethal authority at the longest ranges. It features our ShurShot™ synthetic pistol-grip stock and 23" barrel for awesome maneuverability. The fully adjustable TruGlo® fiber-optic sights and an extended Wingmaster HD™ Turkey Rem™ Choke maximize pattern placement.

Four 3-shot groups @ 100 yards with Model 870 Super Slug using Premier® AccuTip Bonded Sabot Slug 12-gauge ammunition.

172

SPOT ON

If you had any doubt that the slug gun has come a long way,
then you'd best take a look at this 2009 catalog page for
the Super Slug. Now *those* are groups to get the job done.

NEW MODEL 11-87™ OFFERINGS

NEW SEMI-AUTO WORKHORSES
FOR FIELD, WOODS AND WATER.

World-famous Model 11-87™ speed, mild recoil and reliability in three new configurations. Choose from the classic appeal of our **Model 11-87™ Sportsman® Field**, our completely updated **Model 11-87 Sportsman Super Magnum Synthetic** and **Model 11-87 Sportsman Super Magnum Waterfowl** featuring overmolded grips, HiViz® sights and more, and the long-range lethality of the **Model 11-87 Sportsman Super Magnum ShurShot® Turkey.**

NEW MODEL 870™ OFFERINGS

GET PUMPED
FOR SPECIAL APPLICATIONS.

America's favorite pump action is once again setting the standard for performance in a host of applications. This year, we're proud to introduce the **Model 870™ Express® Tactical A-TACS® Camo**, the **Model 870 SPS™ Super Magnum Turkey/Predator w/Scope**, the **Model 870 Express Turkey Camo** and the **Model 870 Express Super Magnum Turkey/Waterfowl.**

The awesome versatility of 3 ½" Super Mag capability in a dual-purpose bird-slaying platform.

MOSSY OAK BOTTOMLAND

MODEL 870™ EXPRESS®
SUPER MAG TURKEY/WATERFOWL
(Page 16)

NEW

SuperCell™ RECOIL PAD

8

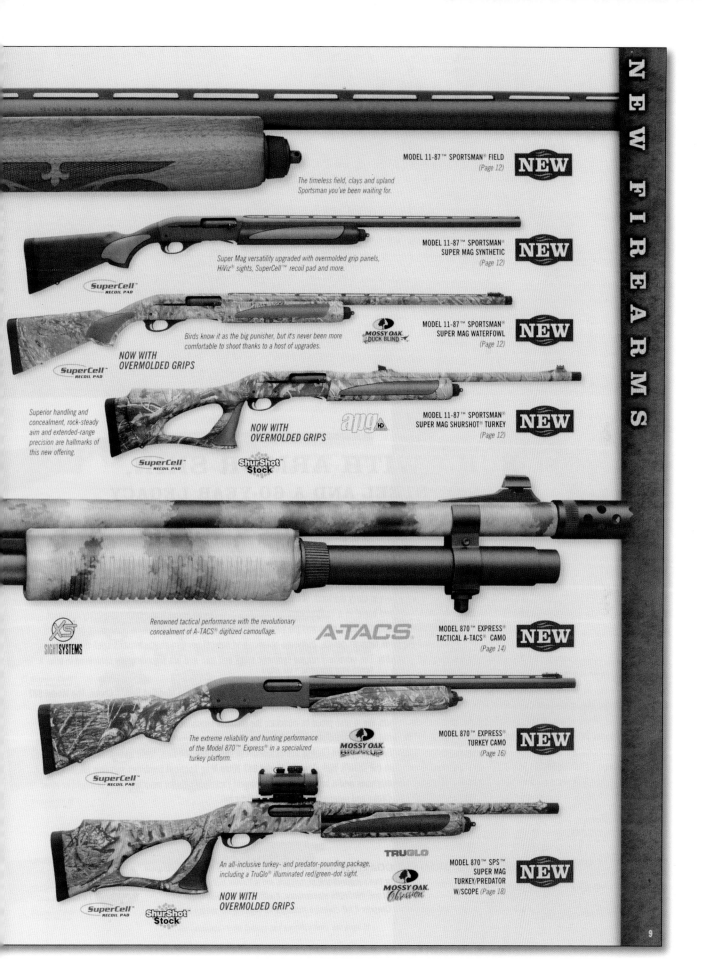

MODEL 11-87™ SPORTSMAN® FIELD
(Page 12)

The timeless field, clays and upland
Sportsman you've been waiting for.

NEW

**MODEL 11-87™ SPORTSMAN®
SUPER MAG SYNTHETIC**
(Page 12)

Super Mag versatility upgraded with overmolded grip panels,
HiViz® sights, SuperCell™ recoil pad and more.

SuperCell™ RECOIL PAD

NEW

**MODEL 11-87™ SPORTSMAN®
SUPER MAG WATERFOWL**
(Page 12)

Birds know it as the big punisher, but it's never been more
comfortable to shoot thanks to a host of upgrades.

MOSSY OAK DUCK BLIND

NOW WITH
OVERMOLDED GRIPS

SuperCell™ RECOIL PAD

NEW

**MODEL 11-87™ SPORTSMAN®
SUPER MAG SHURSHOT® TURKEY**
(Page 12)

Superior handling and
concealment, rock-steady
aim and extended-range
precision are hallmarks of
this new offering.

NOW WITH
OVERMOLDED GRIPS

apg HD

NEW

SuperCell™ RECOIL PAD

ShurShot™ Stock

**MODEL 870™ EXPRESS®
TACTICAL A-TACS® CAMO**
(Page 14)

Renowned tactical performance with the revolutionary
concealment of A-TACS® digitized camouflage.

XS SIGHTSYSTEMS

A-TACS®

NEW

**MODEL 870™ EXPRESS®
TURKEY CAMO**
(Page 16)

The extreme reliability and hunting performance
of the Model 870™ Express® in a specialized
turkey platform.

MOSSY OAK BREAK-UP

NEW

SuperCell™ RECOIL PAD

**MODEL 870™ SPS™
SUPER MAG
TURKEY/PREDATOR
W/SCOPE** (Page 18)

An all-inclusive turkey- and predator-pounding package,
including a TruGlo® illuminated red/green-dot sight.

TRUGLO

MOSSY OAK Obsession

NEW

SuperCell™ RECOIL PAD

ShurShot™ Stock

NOW WITH
OVERMOLDED GRIPS

9

MODEL 870™
SPECIAL PURPOSE

NEW

NOW WITH OVERMOLDED GRIPS TRUGLO

MOSSY OAK Obsession

MODEL 870™ SPS™ SUPER MAGNUM TURKEY/PREDATOR W/SCOPE
Available in: 12 gauge (2½", 3" and 3½")
(Order No. 81062)

MOSSY OAK Treestand Super Slug

MODEL 870™ SPS™ SHURSHOT® SYNTHETIC SUPER SLUG
Available in: 12 gauge
(2¾" and 3")
(Order No. 82101)

MODEL 870™ SPS™ SHURSHOT® SYNTHETIC TURKEY
Available in: 12 gauge (2¾", 3" and 3½")
(Order No. 81061)

See pages 92–93 for ShurShot® stocks and Wingmaster HD™ Choke Tubes.

For complete model listings and specifications, see page 101.

PERFECTING THE ART OF
FLATTENING BIGGER GAME
AT LONGER RANGES.

Introducing the most dependable slide action of all time in three advanced designs that will go the distance with deadly precision, whether your target is the crease behind a buck's shoulder, a wily coyote or a big red head. The **Model 870™ SPS™ Super Magnum Turkey/Predator w/scope** is an all-inclusive, all-camo package put together with devastating implications for birds at extended range and predators that close the distance. Along with the ambidextrous freedom and handling ease of our ShurShot® pistol-grip stock with grip-enhancing overmolds, it features a highly maneuverable 20" barrel and a TruGlo® red/green selectable illuminated sight mounted atop its pre-installed Weaver-style rail. It handles 2 ¾", 3" and 3 ½" 12-gauge rounds interchangeably. A black padded sling and Wingmaster HD™ Turkey/Predator Rem™ Choke are included.

Our 12-gauge **Model 870™ SPS™ ShurShot® Synthetic Super Slug** advances deer-leveling technology to farther reaches and smaller group sizes than ever before. The 25 ½" extra-heavy, 1"-diameter barrel is pinned to the receiver to control vibration for rifle-like shot-to-shot consistency. For optimal slug flight, the barrel is a full 25 ½" long and features six Parabolic Ultragon™ rifling grooves with a 1-in-35" twist. You also get the rock-steady aim and awesome control of our ShurShot synthetic pistol-grip synthetic stock. Receiver is drilled and tapped with Weaver rail included. Our **Model 870 SPS ShurShot Synthetic Turkey** features our ShurShot synthetic pistol-grip stock and a compact 23" barrel. The fully adjustable TruGlo® fiber-optic sights and an extended Wingmaster HD Turkey Rem Choke maximize pattern placement.

COMPETITION
SHOTGUNS

MODEL 1100™ PREMIER SPORTING SERIES
Available in: 12, 20, 28 gauge (2½") and 410 bore (3")
(Order No. 82842, 82846, 82854, 82858)

MODEL 1100™ SPORTING SERIES
Available in: 12, 20, 28 gauge (2¾") and 410 bore (3")
(Order No. 29215, 25289, 29583, 29549)

MODEL 1100™ COMPETITION
Available in: 12 gauge (2¾")
(Order No. 26819)

MODEL 1100™ CLASSIC TRAP
Available in: 12 gauge (2¾")
(Order No. 25333)

MODEL 870™ CLASSIC TRAP
Available in: 12 gauge (2¾")
(Order No. 24857)

CONFIDENCE
IS OFFICIALLY TANGIBLE.

No shotguns have won more titles or are better equipped for the high-volume regimen of today's elite shooters. Prepare to see record scores crushed at a rapid rate by our latest upgrade to the lineup – the new **Model 1100™ Premier Sporting** series. Featuring nickel receivers with intricate fine-line embellishments and gold accents, they're as aesthetically impressive as they are sweet to point and shoot. Gold triggers and a custom Premier Sporting hard case complete the package. The Premier is offered alongside our original **Model 1100 Sporting** shotguns. Both the Model 1100 Sporting and Sporting Premier series offer discriminating shooters 12, 20, 28 and 410 options with semi-fancy American walnut stocks and fore-ends, vent-rib Rem™ Choke barrels and four Briley™ extended chokes as standard equipment.

Our **Model 1100 Competition** is super-tuned for the competitive scene. By overboring the 30" barrel and lengthening the forcing cones, we improved shot-to-shot pattern consistency and made what was one of the softest-recoiling actions in the world even easier on your shoulder. The receiver and all internal parts feature a nickel-Teflon® finish for the smoothest, most reliable cycling ever. It's optimized for 2 ¾" target loads and field loads. Its optional adjustable comb can be fine-tuned to your shooting preference, and the barrel has a 10mm target-style rib. All this transforms an already legendary design into an unstoppable force at the range.

Generations of die-hard competitors have made our **Model 1100 Classic Trap** and famous **Model 870™ Classic Trap**. From 16s to the very back line, they continue to shoot their way to the top of major events every year.

For complete model listings and specifications, see page 101.

ALMOST NO COMPETITION

The Remington 870 has become so ubiquitous as a hunting gun that Remington's premier competition shotguns are riding in a decided second place in the page arrangement of the 2010 catalog.

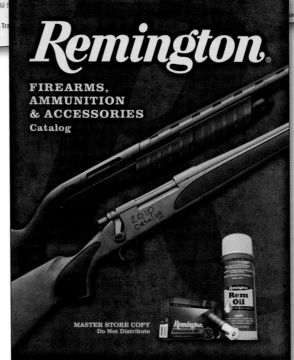

Remington.

FIREARMS,
AMMUNITION
& ACCESSORIES
Catalog

2010 Catalog

Rem Oil

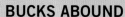
BUCKS ABOUND
This highly engraved Deer Hunter Tribute limited edition 870 was available for a short time through America Remembers. Almost too pretty to shoot, don't you think?

New For '61

◀ **THE MODEL 870**
"Brushmaster"
12 GA. SHOTGUN

Another new gun from Remington that combines the game getting features of both rifle and shotgun . . . carbine styled, for the ever growing group that demands this type gun.

Study and use the listed features and your sales of another Remington "first" will prove the popularity and acceptance of the lighter, shorter, faster "Brushmaster" by the man who hunts rugged country.

Price: $109.70

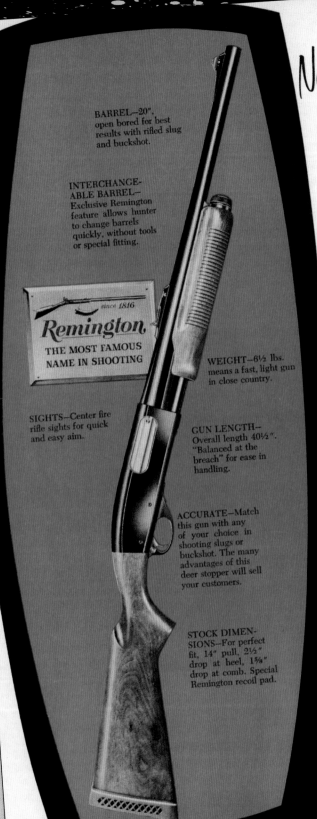

BARREL—20", open bored for best results with rifled slug and buckshot.

INTERCHANGEABLE BARREL— Exclusive Remington feature allows hunter to change barrels quickly, without tools or special fitting.

since 1816
Remington
THE MOST FAMOUS NAME IN SHOOTING

WEIGHT—6½ lbs. means a fast, light gun in close country.

SIGHTS—Center fire rifle sights for quick and easy aim.

GUN LENGTH— Overall length 40½". "Balanced at the breach" for ease in handling.

ACCURATE—Match this gun with any of your choice in shooting slugs or buckshot. The many advantages of this deer stopper will sell your customers.

STOCK DIMENSIONS—For perfect fit, 14" pull, 2½" drop at heel, 1⅝" drop at comb. Special Remington recoil pad.

THE
MODEL 760 CDL

Built to real game getting measurements, the "CDL" model incorporates all features made famous in the past year by the 760C, plus deluxe features that add that "extra" look. The same fast handling, well balanced features are prominent in the M760 CDL deluxe carbine — and shooters will acclaim both its handling qualities and good looks.

Calibers: 280 Remington, 270 Win., 308 Win., and 30/06.

Price: $137.25

Remington **DU PONT**

REMINGTON ARMS COMPANY, INC., BRIDGEPORT 2, CONN.

In Canada: Remington Arms of Canada, Ltd.
38 Queen Elizabeth Blvd.
Toronto 18, Ontario

FORM NO. AA 12 • PRINTED IN U.S.A.

178

REMINGTON

THE BIG NEWS FOR '61

Since Remington entered the highly competitive "Carbine" market sales have proven that shooters want Remington high powered carbine rifles.

And for those shooters who want a carbine in an auto-loading action, here it is . . . . the MODEL 742C "WOODSMASTER," the *only* autoloading carbine available chambered for high powered cartridges.

Remington

BARREL—18½" tapered Remington gun steel. Short length for easier handling, easier travel.

RUGGED—The M742C will take the roughest country, stand up under real punishment.

LIGHT WEIGHT— Only 7 lbs.! This is a gun any hunter can carry all day.

ACCURATE—When accuracy counts. This gun has famous built-in Remington accuracy.

THE MODEL 742 CARBINE

MODEL 742C "CARBINE" 30/06 Caliber hammerless, solid frame, side ejection, autoloading. Cross bolt safety. Receiver drilled and tapped for telescope mounts. Stock dimensions: pull 13½", drop at comb 1¼", drop at heel 2", weight 7 lbs. Length overall 37".

Price: $138.50

MODEL 742 CDL "DELUXE" Same specifications as 742C plus—deluxe checkered stock and forend; decorative grip cap, sling swivels. Receiver inscribed with game scenes.

Price: $154.45

STOCK—All purpose type, specially designed for shooter who wants both iron and telescopic sights.

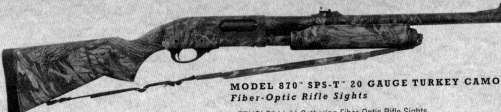

Our New Guns Are So Dull, They Won't Turn A Single Head.

Probably only serious turkey hunters will appreciate the rugged beauty in these new Remington 1100 and 870 SP (Special Purpose™) Magnums. The non-glare finishes on all visible parts help you remain invisible to the wariest of eyes.

The barrels, receivers, even the bolts and carrier assemblies have been bead-blasted and protected with a dull gray Parkerized finish.

The subdued oil coating on the hardwood stocks and fore-ends resists reflecting light. It also penetrates the wood to protect it from moisture.

The bore and chamber are chrome-plated for additional corrosion protection. Moving parts are polished by our "vibra-honing" process to work smoothly and reliably right out of the box.

That's true for all of our world famous 1100 auto-loaders and 870 "Wingmaster" pumps. Over 7 million of them have been field tested by sportsmen during the past 35 years. And proven many times over for dependability, pointability and value.

You'll find the SP Magnums in 12 gauge only with vent rib, 3" chambers and Full choke barrels. Choose either 30" for the longer sighting plane. Or 26" for faster handling in tight quarters. Recoil pads and a padded camouflage sling of "Cordura" nylon are included.

Next time you hunt turkey, take along the new SP Magnum and see how attractive a dull gun can be— out there in Remington Country.

New Model 870 SP Magnum

New Model 1100 SP Magnum

Remington Country

Call 1-800-THE-GUNS for your nearest Remington dealer. And pick up your free catalog of the world's largest line of sporting arms and ammunition.

Remington. DU PONT

Remington and Wingmaster are trademarks registered in the U.S. Patent and Trademark Office. Special Purpose is a trademark of Remington Arms Company, Inc., Wilmington, Del. 19898. Cordura is a trademark of E.I. du Pont de Nemours & Company, Inc., Wilmington, Del. 19898.

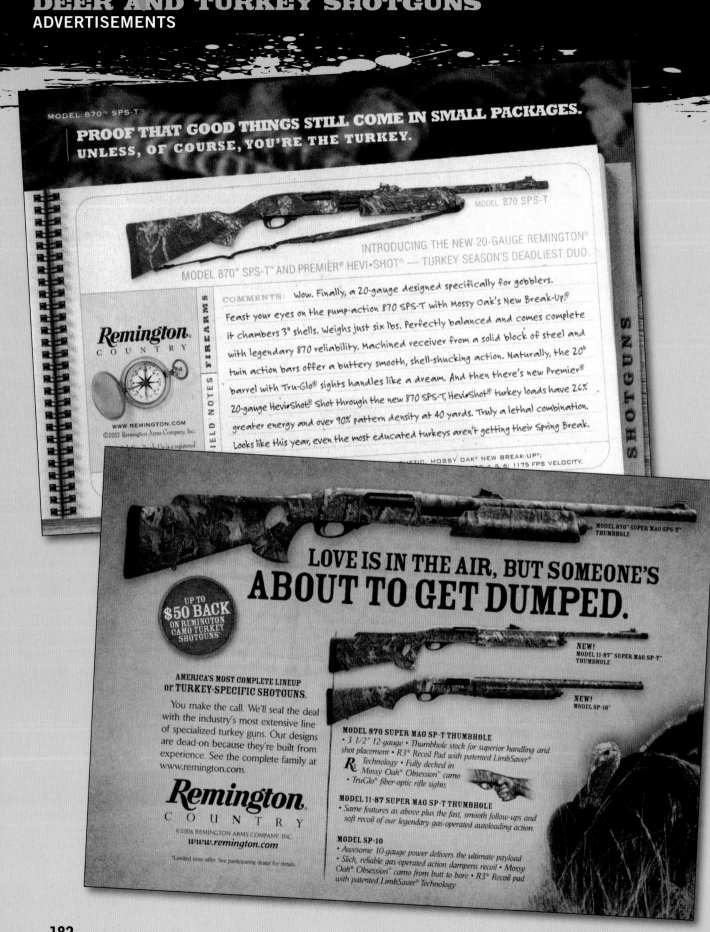

2008 SHOT SHOW
FIREARM SPECIALS

Model 11-87™ Sportsman™ Super Mag ShurShot™ Predator

FEATURES

- Model 11-87™ Sportsman™ Super Mag ShurShot™ Predator/Turkey
- Industry first—Predator designated shotgun—High Capacity Mag.
- Realtree® Max-1 HD™ full camo
- 3-shot magazine tube extension – holds 8 rounds total
- Drilled & tapped receiver w/23" TruGlo® rifle-sighted barrel
- Wingmaster HD™ optimized Rem® Choke Predator/Turkey tube
- Three (3) pound "competition" spring on trigger assembly
- NEW SuperCell™ recoil pad technology

Gauge	Action Type	Barrel Length	Barrel Type	Overall Length	Average Weight	Order #	MSP
12	Auto	23"	RS-TG	43"	8 lbs.	83605	$699

Model 870™ Express® Magnum ShurShot™ FR-RS

FEATURES

- Model 870™ Express® ShurShot™ Full Camo FR-RS "Deer Gun"
- Industry first – Pinned barrel design – Enhanced Rifle like accuracy
- Full Camo Realtree® Hardwoods™ coverage in a slug gun
- 20" Fully Rifled-Rifle Sighted barrel
- Receiver Drilled & Tapped for ease of optics mounting
- Includes new Extended fore-end and ShurShot™ stock
- Three (3) pound "competition" spring on trigger assembly
- NEW SuperCell™ recoil pad technology

Gauge	Action Type	Barrel Length	Barrel Type	Overall Length	Average Weight	Order #	MSP
12	Pump	20"	FR-RS	40"	7 ½ lbs.	81122	$469

Remington®
COUNTRY
www.REMINGTON.com

Remington Arms Company, Inc.
870 Remington Drive • Madison, NC 27025 • 800-243-9700

CHAPTER NINE

POLICE AND MILITARY SHOTGUNS

NO OTHER SHOTGUN is found more often in the racks of the police patrol vehicles and in the hands of S.W.A.T. team members in the United States, than the Remington Model 870. To some extent, the same thing can also be said of other countries, and it is most certainly true of North America, where both U.S. and Canadian law enforcement agencies, for the most, part use the Remington Model 870 as their tactical shotgun. In addition to North America, here's a partial listing of countries that have and still use the 870: Canada, England, Australia, New Zealand, Israel, Japan, South Korea, Germany, Italy, Spain, Belgium, Sweden, Switzerland, Netherlands, Poland, Norway, Finland, Thailand, Philippines, Panama, Colombia, Paraguay, Uruguay, Jamaica, Haiti, U.A.E, Saudi Arabia, Jordan, Egypt, Turkey, Afghanistan, Iraq, Oman, Djibouti. That's 35 countries, and it isn't even the complete list! For example, I have seen the "Pumas," Ecuadorian Army Special Forces, armed with 870s, as I have Mexico's special anti-narcotics units operating in Baja California, and Sonora. (Those Mexican police departments close to the U.S. border often make arrangements to purchase 870s directly from U.S. dealers, not the Remington factory.) Once you start breaking down the vast number of specialty law enforcement units who employ their 870s daily as they go about their duties, there's no telling how many other countries use the Model 870.

The Model 870's production of more than 10 million to this date is indeed a remarkable number in that no other shotgun has ever been produced in such large numbers. However, this incredible run probably couldn't have been reached without the help of manufacture and sales of the police/military versions of the shotgun. Granted, the vast majority of the Model 870s produced and sold are sporting versions, but the contribution of the police/military versions can lay claim to a large portion of that more than 10 million number that have so far been made and sold.

One could argue and say that Remington's aggressive marketing and its sheer size as a large gun manufacturer allows it to sell the Model 870 all over the world, to

GET A BADGE
No, unless you work for
Uncle Sam or carry a state or
county badge, the 870 MCS
Breaching shotgun is not
for you. Still, it's incredibly
interesting to see just how
specialized the creators at
Remington can make their
hallmark shotgun.

**THE FACTS MA'AM,
JUST THE FACTS**
That's what the basic "riot" gun
was, just the facts. This form of
the 870 has ridden in a lot of
squad cars over the years.

compete with other makers on favorable terms. But that
wouldn't be entirely correct. Certainly, Remington is a
very large arms maker and the company does have an
aggressive marketing program worldwide, but the Model
870 would not be so readily purchased by other countries
if it were not a superior product. There are many other
tactical-style shotguns on the market made both in the
U.S. and abroad, many of which are priced much lower

SPECIALIZED

As creative as Remington has been when it comes to customizing the 870 for trap shooters, turkey hunters, or waterfowlers, what they do for military and law enforcement ranks defines specilization.

than the Remington Model 870. Yet, when given a choice, the vast majority of police departments and militaries around the world select the 870. For example, France purchases and uses the Model 870 for its police and military, yet France has its own manufacturer that makes pump guns. Obviously, the French police and military find the Remington Model 870 to be superior to whatever is being produced domestically. The same thing can be said of Belgium, whose arms making giant, the famed Fabrique Nationale, makes pump guns, yet the Belgian army and most of the country's police departments use the 870. Italy, too, has its own Beretta pump gun, among others of solid reputation, but just as Belgium has, most of the police departments in Italy and the army prefer the Remington Model 870. Likewise, again, Filipino gun makers produce several types of inexpensive pump shotguns that are popular in America, especially among cowboy action shooters, but the Philippines military and most police forces prefer the Remington Model 870, just as so many other do.

The Model 870 is used by just about every major national special operations military and law enforcement organization in the world. This includes the U.S. Army Special Forces (Green Berets) and the U.S. Navy SEALS, despite the fact that most of the U.S. military uses a shotgun of another make that was chosen by Pentagon. (Does it seem odd that two of the toughest sectors of our military use the 870 gun, but another was chosen for so much of the rest of our ranks?) Of the foreign countries, the UK's 22nd SAS, Australian SAS, New Zealand SAS, Germany's GSG9, and France's GIGN are all users of the 870. In fact, the British 22nd SAS has been using the Model 870 since 1969, and Remington received a contract that same year to make a special version, the Mk-1, for the U.S.'s own Marine Corps. There are many other spe-

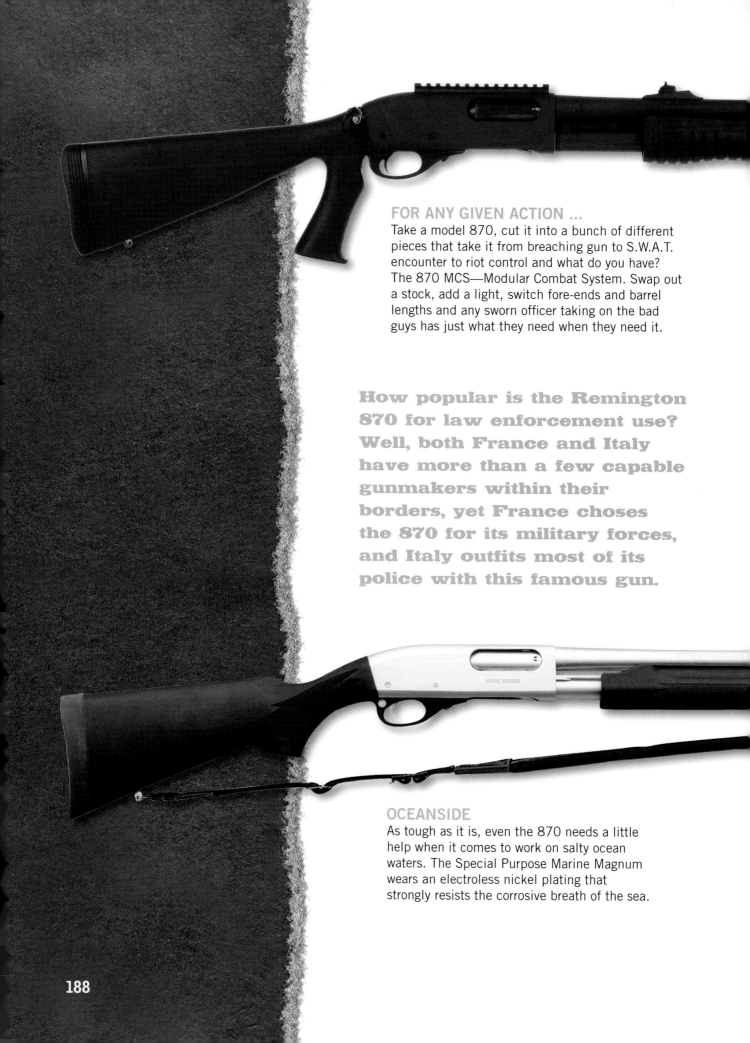

FOR ANY GIVEN ACTION ...

Take a model 870, cut it into a bunch of different pieces that take it from breaching gun to S.W.A.T. encounter to riot control and what do you have? The 870 MCS—Modular Combat System. Swap out a stock, add a light, switch fore-ends and barrel lengths and any sworn officer taking on the bad guys has just what they need when they need it.

How popular is the Remington 870 for law enforcement use? Well, both France and Italy have more than a few capable gunmakers within their borders, yet France choses the 870 for its military forces, and Italy outfits most of its police with this famous gun.

OCEANSIDE

As tough as it is, even the 870 needs a little help when it comes to work on salty ocean waters. The Special Purpose Marine Magnum wears an electroless nickel plating that strongly resists the corrosive breath of the sea.

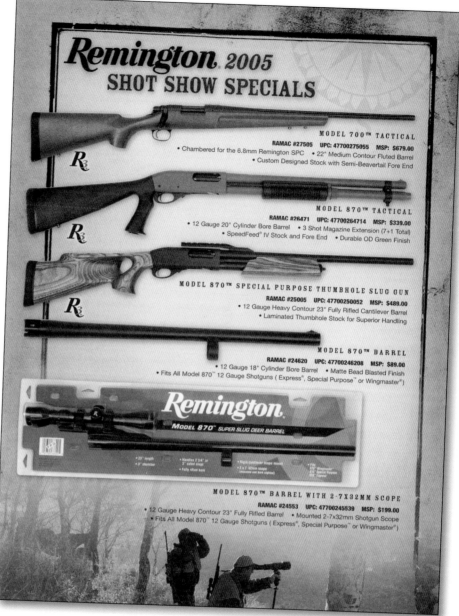

GAME ON!
The tactical grip and olive drab stock on the 870 in the middle of this recent catalog page is aimed at the hot new sport of 3-gun.

cial operations units in the world that use the 870, and so, like the law enforcement list, such a compilation would be very long, much longer than we have room for here!

Although the 1990s were, perhaps, the most important years in the development of various tactical versions of the Model 870, as we've mentioned before, it all started with the very "plain Jane" version, the Model 870 R (the "R" stands for "Riot"), going back to the beginning of Model 870's original appearance on the market. It was offered right from the start, in 1950, although it didn't get the kind of coverage that

READY FOR THE CHALLENGE—*ANY* CHALLENGE

This is the MCS—Modular Combat System—for the Model 870. Three stocks, three barrels, two magazine tubes, accessory mounts, and Remington's REM LOC quick-change stock system allow officers and military personnel to customize their shotgun to meet ever-changing circumstances in the field, everything from a full-stock breaching gun (below) to a gun better suited to a potential shootout with an extended magazine and a longer barrel (bottom) and everything in between. It's an ingenious design that demonstrates Remington's forward-thinking attitude toward firearms design.

other models received. In fact, the Model 870 R made its debut without any fanfare and with barely an announcement at all from Remington's front office. Maybe that's because it just wasn't all that different than its siblings. After all, the so-called Model 870 Riot was nothing more than the standard Model 870 AP, the original plain version with an un-checkered stock and corn cob pump fore-end with its ring tail grooves, but outfitted with a 20-inch Cylinder-bored barrel. That was it, just a barrel change. Otherwise, everything else was exactly as it was on the field version of the Model 870 AP.

The Remington Model 870 R stayed the same for quite some time. The only alteration that took place was that a barrel with rifled sights was eventually offered as an alternative to the plain bead barrel. The debut of the Model 870 R with rifled sights coincided with Remington's introduction of the Model 870 RSS Rifle Slug Shotgun, in 1959, demonstrating Remington's economy and efficiency of using parts across the model lines to create additional and

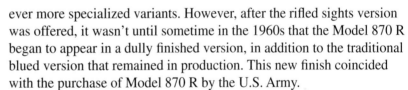

ever more specialized variants. However, after the rifled sights version was offered, it wasn't until sometime in the 1960s that the Model 870 R began to appear in a dully finished version, in addition to the traditional blued version that remained in production. This new finish coincided with the purchase of Model 870 R by the U.S. Army.

The biggest changes in the tactical versions of the Model 870 started to take place in the 1980s and really got going in the next decade. There were many aftermarket synthetic stocks with pistol grips that became popular with law enforcement agencies back in the 1980s. Remington, though, was slow to recognize the trend, as the guns coming out of its factory continued to be the few basic standard Model 870 Rs it had been offering for more than the last 20 years. It really wasn't until the 1990s that Remington got into making 870s with pistol grips and folding stocks, along with other specialized tactical-oriented features.

So, while Remington had been what some might say was resistant to changing the 870 R, at least during the '80s, in the decade before the century change, the company came to fully realize that there was a huge market for these tactical shotguns. No longer were the plain old riot-type guns good enough, the newest generation of users wanted a more updated "black gun," one that could have flashlight and laser attachments, folding stocks or stocks similar to those on assault rifles, and a host of other features that would make the gun ready for combat, home-defense, and even the soon to explode sport of 3-gun competition. Remington has tried to meet all of these demands and has continued to churn out different variations on the theme.

MODEL 870™
EXPRESS^x

Model 870™ Express®
Super Magnum™

NEW FOR 2006

Model 870™ Express®
Super Magnum™
Mossy Oak® Shadowgrass®

AMERICA'S FAVORITE PUMP SHOTGUN HAS A NEW LOOK. Its solid, ultra-dependable action makes it America's favorite, and the new laminated wood stock places it among the best looking and most weather resistant as well. If you could throw the lid off every duck blind, stop by every pheasant field and check out every tract of timber where deer and turkey are hunted, you'd probably see more Model 870™ Express® pumps than any other shotgun. It's been the standard for slide-action performance for more than 50 years. And because it's available in a Super Magnum version that handles everything from light 2 ¾" loads to heavy 3 ½" magnums, it's the standard for versatility as well.

This extensive lineup covers virtually any application in any neck of the woods or wetlands you're hunting – from the vent-rib do-alls to specialized deer, turkey and waterfowl models. You even have an array of stock choices, including the new laminated wood version, durable black synthetic and popular camo finishes.

Its versatility, reliability and, perhaps best of all, affordable pricing, make it a shotgun anyone can own. We're proud to make them, but even prouder of the fact you've made them America's Pump Guns.

TACTICAL SHOTGUNS

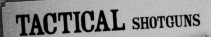

YOUR LINEUP OF DEFENSE. Handling speed, demand when the stakes are at their highest. ary Model 870™ and Model 1100™ actions. eir lives to every day, they excel in close onal defense. Offered in 12-gauge with synthetic stocks, and matte olive drab barrels el 870™ stock choices include the Speedfeed® IV stock or the with a spring-loaded cam for recoil reduction and fast follow-ups ith your choice of an 18" barrel with a two-shot magazine extension s version has an 18" barrel. All have fixed improved cylinder chokes. Model 1100™ Tactical shotgun is available with a Speedfeed IV pistol Speedfeed IV model has an 18" barrel with a two-shot extension. 22" barrel and a four-shot extension, perfect for 3 gun competitions.

reliability and devastating power – everything you Our rugged new tactical shotguns are built on the Based on the same designs law-enforcement personn quarters and are the ultimate choice for competition R3® recoil pads with patented LimbSaver® technology, and receivers.

Knoxx Industries SpecOps™ adjustable length of pull – both feature full pistol grips. Speedfeed IV model or a 20" barrel with a three-shot extension.

grip stock or standard black synthetic stock an Standard synthetic stocked version is equipped

FROM ZERO TO SIXTY

Remington was actually reluctant to change its original riot gun 870 R. Today that attitude has changed drastically—and for the better.

Model 870™ Express®

NEW FOR 2006

Wood models now available in all-new laminate

Model 870™ Express®
Super Magnum™ Turkey Camo
(Standard version also available)

NEW FOR 2006

Model 870™ Express®
Super Magnum™ Synthetic
(Standard version also available)

Model 870™ Express®
Fully Rifled Cantilever

Model 870™ Express®
Cantilever Deer Gun
(Scope not included)

Model 870™ Express®
Super Magnum™ Combo

Model 870™ Express® Super Magnum™ Features:

- Will function 2 ¾", 3" and 3 ½" shells interchangeably
- Superior design and inherent strength of America's favorite pump shotgun, the Model 870™
- Super Magnum receiver same size as all 12-gauge Model 870 shotguns for same balance point
- Innovative bolt design keeps cycle stroke equal for all 3 lengths of 12-gauge shotshells
- Magazine capacity is three 3 ½" shells and four 2 ¾" and 3" shells
- Available in wood laminate, synthetic and camouflaged versions as well as a combo package, which features both a vent rib and rifle-sighted deer barrel for maximum versatility

For complete model listings and specifications, see page 88-89.

Model 870™ Tactical
with SpecOps™ stock

Model 870™ Tactical

Model 870™ Tactical
with SpecOps™ stock

Model 1100™ Tactical

Tactical Shotgun Features:

- Optimized for close-quarters handling speed – the ultimate choice for personal protection or competition
- Built on pump Model 870 and autoloading Model 1100 actions for superior reliability
- 12-gauge with matte olive drab receivers & barrels
- R3® recoil pads with patented LimbSaver® Technology to reduce felt recoil
- Both actions available with synthetic Speedfeed IV full pistol-grip stock
- Model 870 available with a tough, lightweight Knoxx Industries SpecOps™ stock featuring a recoil-absorbing spring-loaded cam and adjustable length of pull (12" to 16")
- Fixed chokes – improved cylinder on Model 870 and Model 1100, Rem® Choke on 22" Model 1100
- 2-, 3- or 4-shot extensions based on barrel length for maximum firepower

For complete model listings and specifications, see page 89.

17

Although the 1990s were the break-out years for the various tactical versions of the 870, it wasn't until we were firmly into the new century, in 2004, that a revolutionary new concept was applied to the 870 system and the Model 870 MCS was developed. The Modular Combat Shotgun (MCS) was developed largely due to the ideas brought by an employee new to Remington at the time, and now the current Director of International Military/Law Enforcement Sales, a man named Michael Haugen. Haugen convinced Remington to develop a radically different system, one based on his experience

MODEL 870™ XCS
MARINE MAGNUM®

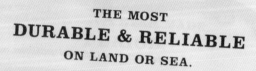

THE MOST
DURABLE & RELIABLE
ON LAND OR SEA.

The original Model 870™ Marine Magnum® set the standard for all-weather reliability, and our latest upgrade to its design launches it beyond the capabilities of any shotgun out there. Featuring the extreme corrosion and abrasion resistance of our proprietary Black TriNyte® Corrosion Control System, the new 12-gauge Model 870™ XCS (Xtreme Conditions Shotgun) Marine Magnum will serve and protect in the most extreme conditions on earth. For even more rugged endurance, all internal metal parts are coated with electroless nickel, and the trigger group is plated to resist fouling and oxidation.

The tactical-style SpeedFeed® I stock and R3® recoil pad with LimbSaver® technology work in conjunction to tame the recoil of even the most potent 2 ³/₄" or 3" magnum rounds. The stock is equipped with a shell holder to keep up to four extra rounds at your fingertips. Match these features with a 7-round capacity and 18" cylinder bore barrel, and you have the ultimate special-purpose firearm. Anywhere, anytime — count on it.

MODEL 870™
SPECIAL PURPOSE

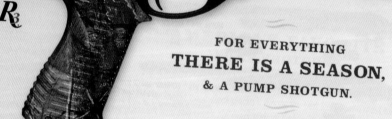

FOR EVERYTHING
THERE IS A SEASON,
& A PUMP SHOTGUN.

With specialized deer, turkey and waterfowl versions, the Model 870™ Special Purpose line is a rugged, well-rounded family you can rely on for every hunting application.

The new Model 870 Super Magnum™ MAX Gobbler™ is a masterpiece of long-range precision and shooting comfort. Its Knoxx® SpecOps™ pistol-grip stock has an adjustable length of pull and incorporates state-of-the-art recoil-dampening technology to tame the 3 ¹/₂" magnum thunder. Other features include a 23" barrel with bright, fully adjustable Williams® fiber-optic Fire Sights™ and full coverage in new Realtree® APG™ HD™ camo. Included is a Turkey Super-Full Rem™ Choke.

For slug precision, the Model 870™ SP Fully Rifled Cantilever Thumbhole is fully rifled with a laminated thumbhole stock, widened fore-end, and cantilever scope mount. Our Model 870 SP™ Thumbhole is a steady-aiming standout that blends in with full Mossy Oak® Obsession™ camo. It has a 23" barrel with Truglo® fiber-optic rifle sights. The Model 870 SPS-T™ 12-gauge Super Magnum features a 23" barrel with twin beads, the concealment of Mossy Oak Obsession camo and handles 2 ³/₄" to 3 ¹/₂" loads. Other 870 SPS™ models include our Special Purpose Super Magnum Synthetics, fully camouflaged in Mossy Oak Obsession and available in a 12 gauge with your choice of 26" or 28" barrel.

14

WEATHER BE GONE
In 2007, the shiny Marine 870 got a makeover to the more subtle Black TriNyte Corrosion Control System and the gun had the letters XCS added to it for "Xtreme Condition Shotgun."

NEW

MODEL 870™ XCS
MARINE MAGNUM®

MODEL 870™ XCS
MARINE MAGNUM®
Available in 12 gauge (2 ¾" and 3")

R3

NEW

For complete model listings and specifications, see page 91.

TriNyte® Corrosion Control System (Patent pending). Consisting of electroless nickel and proprietary PVD, this armor-tough, multi-layer coating is the world's most effective barrier against rust and abrasion for firearms, yet is only a fraction of a human hair in thickness. The only thing you'll notice is the near invincibility. Available in a variety of finish colors.

TN
TRINYTE
CORROSION
CONTROL SYSTEM

FEATURES

- TriNyte® Corrosion Control System on barrel and receiver creates an armor-tough barrier against rust and abrasion
- Its Model 870 action is the rugged standard for dependability and smooth operation
- 18" cylinder bore, bead-sighted barrel
- 2-shot magazine extension — 7-shot capacity
- SpeedFeed® I stock with shell holder keeps 2-4 extra rounds at your fingertips
- Corrosion-resistant trigger group with plated components
- Durable synthetic stock and fore-end
- Sling swivel studs
- R3® recoil pad with LimbSaver® technology

apg HD

The new MAX Gobbler™ comes fully decked in the photo realism of new Realtree® APG™ HD.™

NEW

MODEL 870™ SPS™ SUPER MAG
MAX GOBBLER™
Available in 12 gauge (2 ¾", 3" and 3 ½")

MODEL 870™ SUPER MAG
SP-T™ THUMBHOLE
Available in 12 gauge (2 ¾", 3" and 3 ½")

MOSSY OAK.
Obsession

MODEL 870™ SPS-T™
SUPER MAG
Available in 12 gauge (2 ¾", 3" and 3 ½")

MOSSY OAK.
Obsession

R3

MODEL 870™ SP™
THUMBHOLE CANTILEVER
Available in 12 gauge (2 ¾" and 3")

For complete model listings and specifications, see page 90.

MODEL 870™ SPS™ SUPER MAG MAX GOBBLER™
FEATURES

- Knoxx® SpecOps™ stock provides adjustable LOP and state-of-the-art recoil dampening
- Williams® Fire Sights™ fiber-optic sight system for fast target acquisition and accuracy
- Fitted with Remington's high-performance R3® recoil pad with LimbSaver® technology
- New Realtree® APG™ HD™ camo
- Drilled and tapped for Weaver-style rail

Recoil-dampening
springs

LOP adjustment

The Knoxx® SpecOps™ stock features a recoil-compensation system that dramatically reduces felt recoil and muzzle jump.

15

TACTICAL
SHOTGUNS

R_3

MODEL 870™ TAC-3
Available in 12 gauge (2 ¾" and 3")

MAKE THE RIGHT
TACTICAL DECISION.

They're the choice of many top law enforcement agencies, and for good reasons. Time-tested and extremely reliable, Remington Model 870™ and Model 1100™ tactical shotguns combine legendary quality with a level of flexibility that only comes with experience in the field.

The all-black lineup of Model 870 tactical shotguns will feature three different choices in tactical stocks, 18" to 20" barrels, and two- or three-shot magazine tube extensions. Load them up with even the most potent magnum loads, the Knoxx® SpecOps™ stocks are capable of taming even the harshest recoil.

All Model 870s are 12 gauge, 2 ¾" and 3" chambered. Model 1100s are chambered for 2 ¾" rounds and are available with 18" or 22" barrels with 2- or 4-shot magazine tube extensions. Every model in this lineup features a black oxide finish, a black synthetic tactical-style fore-end, and R3® recoil pads (except folding stock) and sling swivel studs installed.

MODEL 870™ TAC-2 FS
Available in 12 gauge (2 ½" and 3")

R_3

R_3

TACTICAL
RIFLES

PRECISION SHOOTING
WITH A TACTICAL EDGE.

When it comes to tactical firearms, there's no more trusted name in the game than Remington.® This year, we unveil our new line of tactical rifles, including the popular Model 700™ XCR and the Model 7615™ pump rifle. Remington tactical rifles offer the perfect solution for long-range precision shooters or for those looking for the reliability and tactical flexibility of a pump carbine.

A long-time favorite of both the military and tactical police units, the Model 700 offers the legendary accuracy and unfailing performance you've come to expect. New for 2007, our Model 700 XCR Long Range Tactical Rifle, features a 416 stainless steel barreled action with Black TriNyte® PVD coating, providing a diamond-hard layer of defense against the elements. Its new tactical Bell & Carlson stock comes in OD green with black webbing and features a full-length aluminum bedding block, tactical beaver-tail fore-end and a recessed thumb-hook feature for optimum "off the bench" shooting performance. The barrel features wide tactical-style barrel fluting for rapid cooling.

In tactical situations that call for a carbine flexibility with pump-action speed and dependability, there's the Model 7615. This unique carbine-style rifle is ideally suited for the tactical target shooter and is considered a great alternative to the AR-15. It's Knoxx® SpecOps™ NRS™ (Non Recoil Suppressing) adjustable stock allows the shooter to set the rifle to its most effective length for superior handling no matter the situation. The Model 7615 Tactical Rifle comes in a parkerized finish and includes a 10-round detachable magazine box and sling swivel studs.

For complete model listings and specifications, see pages 94 & 96.

20

FEATURES

- Model 870s are 12 gauge, 2 3/4" and 3" chambered, and are available in 18" or 20" barrels with 2- or 3-shot magazine tube extensions
- Model 1100s are 12 gauge, 2 3/4" chambered, and are available in 18" or 22" barrels with 2- or 4-shot magazine tube extensions
- Blasted black oxide finish with black synthetic tactical-style fore-ends
- All stocks include sling swivel studs and a Remington® R3® recoil pad with LimbSaver® technology (folding stocks excluded)

NEW MODEL 870™ TAC-2
Available in 12 gauge (2 3/4" and 3")

NEW MODEL 870™ TAC-3 FS
Available in 12 gauge (2 3/4" and 3")

NEW MODEL 1100™ TAC-4
Available in 12 gauge (2 3/4")

NEW MODEL 1100™ TAC-2
Available in 12 gauge (2 3/4")

Knoxx® SpecOps™ folding stock with recoil reduction.

...lete model listings and specifications, see page 91.

MODEL 700 TACTICAL
FEATURES

- Includes tactical precision shooting features for long-range target shooting and hunting
- New Tactical Bell & Carlson stock in OD Green w/black webbing
- Full-length aluminum bedding block, tactical beavertail fore-end and recessed "thumbhook" behind pistol grip for off-the-bench shooting performance
- Black TriNyte® Corrosion Control System over 416 stainless steel for uncompromised strength and corrosion/abrasion resistance
- 26" varmint-contour 416 stainless steel barreled action with dish-style target crown, drilled and tapped for scope mounts
- Hinged floorplate magazine
- Dual front swivel studs and rear stud
- Barrel is free-floating with LTR-style fluting

NEW MODEL 700™ XCR TACTICAL LONG RANGE RIFLE

MODEL 700™ XCR TACTICAL LONG RANGE RIFLE
Available in 223 Remington, 300 Win Mag, 338 Win

NEW MODEL 7615™ TACTICAL RIFLE
Available in 223 Remington

...EL 7615 TACTICAL
...ATURES

...ue carbine-style rifle is the perfect alternative ...ing arm choice to the AR-15
...ound detachable magazine box
...kerized finish
...xx® SpecOps™ NRS™ (Non Recoil Suppressing) stock
...ndard 7600 synthetic fore-end with sling swivel studs

21

"TAC"-DRIVING TACTICALS
There are now almost as many tactical versions of the 870 as there are sporting.

as a Special Forces (Green Beret) soldier of more than 17 years.

There is no other shotgun system quite like the Remington's Model 870 MCS, and its design allows the company to sell the system to countries that have adopted other makes for their daily use tactical shotgun. The 870 MCS system can be changed from a short, pistol-gripped 10-inch barreled "breaching" shotgun to a longer barreled version with a buttstock designed for other applications, or it can include screw-in chokes or a rail system for attaching laser devices and lighting systems. It is a very flexible, multifunctional system that no other maker produces.

Another system that is utilized by the military and police is called the ARS or Accessory Rail System. In this system, an even shorter version of the 870 breaching gun is attached via a rail to the lower portion of the M-16 rifle or the M-4 carbine. However, this makes for an extremely heavy weapon, and while it is not the most popular way of using the 870 for military and police ap-

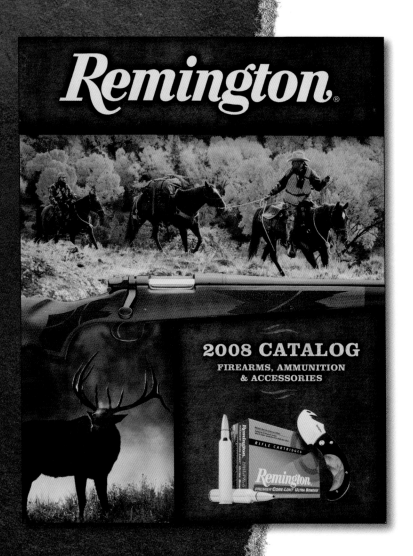

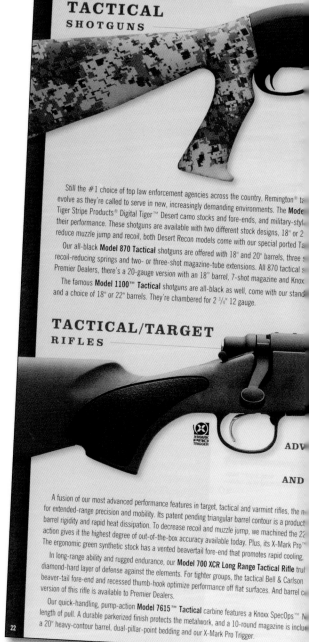

plications, it does have its place in an arsenal designed to address specific tactical situations.

The Remington Model 870 MCS is light years away from the original 870 R that was used in the 1960s and '70s. But it is still an 870, the most desirable combat shotgun around, and The MCS as a stand-alone tactical shotgun is an extremely popular choice among our military and law enforcement ranks, especially the Special Forces troops.

For those who are old enough to have served during Vietnam, especially in the infantry, the short-barreled "riot" shotgun would not be a stranger to you. The U.S. Army and Marine Corps learned very quickly that, in the thick jungles of Vietnam, a shotgun could be a very effective and potent

NEW LOOK AT
'RICA'S MOST
'RUSTED
ICAL SHOTGUN.

rugged, ultra-dependable and continually
esert Recon series shotguns are equipped with
-coated metalwork for looks as distinctive as
or three-shot magazine-tube extensions. To
m™ Choke tube.

ding a Knoxx® SpecOps™ folding stock with
ered for 2 3/4" and 3" 12-gauge rounds. For

oxx SpecOps SpeedFeed® IV pistol-grip stock

MODEL 870™ TAC SFIV DESERT RECON — **NEW**

MODEL 870™ TAC DESERT RECON — **NEW**
Available in 12 gauge (2 1/2" and 3")

MODEL 870™ FOLDING STOCK (with 7-shot extension)
Available in 12 gauge (2 1/2" and 3")

Also available w/pistol grip stock

MODEL 1100™ TAC-4
Available in 12 gauge (2 1/2")

For complete model listings and specifications, see page 94.

The Tactical Extended Rem Choke is designed for optimum performance and recoil reduction. It also aids in reducing muzzle rise for consistent shot placement.

MODEL 870™ DESERT RECON
FEATURES

• SpeedFeed I (shell holding) stock on 12 gauge, 18" 2-shot extension model
• SpeedFeed IV (pistol grip style) stock on 12 gauge, 20" 3-shot extension model
• Tiger Stripe Products® Digital Tiger™ TSP Desert Camo on stock and fore-end
• Military-style "Olive-Drab" powder coat finish on barrel and receiver
• Special ported "Tactical" Extended Rem™ choke tube
• Front bead sights on both models
• Drilled and tapped receivers

MODEL 700™ VTR™ — **NEW**
Available in: 204 Ruger, 22-250 Remington, 223 Remington, 308 Win

EW TECHNOLOGIES,
T GROUPS
G RIGHTS BUILT-IN.

armint-Target Rifle (VTR™) is optimized
R&D focused on reduced weight, enhanced
gral muzzle brake. Our famous Model 700
e ultimate in crispness and shot control.
old accents provide a firm gripping surface.
s. It's Black TriNyte® PVD coating creates a
-length aluminum bedding block. The tactical
with wide tactical-style fluting. A compact

uppressing) stock with an adjustable
s the **Model 700 SPS Tactical**. It has

MODEL 700™ XCR TACTICAL LONG RANGE RIFLE
Available in: 223 Remington, 300 Win Mag, 308 Win

MODEL 700™ XCR COMPACT TACTICAL RIFLE — **NEW**
Available in: 223 Remington, 308 Win

MODEL 700™ SPS TACTICAL RIFLE
Available in: 223 Remington, 308 Win

MODEL 7615™ TACTICAL RIFLE
Available in: 223 Remington

For complete model listings and specifications, see pages 97-99.

MODEL 700™ VTR™
FEATURES

• Green stock with black overmold grips
• Target/Match 1 in 9" twist (223 Remington)
• Target/Match 1 in 12" twist (308 Win)
• 22" barrel with integrated muzzle brake design and triangular barrel contour to enhance accuracy (patent pending)

Integral Muzzle Brake

Triangular Barrel Contour

23

weapon on patrols. Initially, the riot shotgun saw service with guards patrolling the chain link perimeter fences of the air fields and other such installations, and from there it didn't take long for the infantry to discover its usefulness for similar duty in the jungle. There was always at least one soldier or marine that carried a shotgun on those patrols.

The most common shotguns employed during Vietnam were made by various companies and while they were mostly good guns, they were also relics of the past, the typical "trench" pieces. There were Winchester Model 12s, Ithaca Model 37s, Remington Model 31s, and even the ancient Winchester Model 97s with exposed hammers. I believe that the most common shotguns were those made by Stevens. These were all excellent shotguns that certainly had proven themselves in the game fields and in combat both in World War I and II, as well as in the Korean War. So, in Vietnam, the Remington Model 870 was the new kid on the block, one that had yet to be tested in combat and had not yet experienced widespread use. In 1965, when the escalation of the war in Vietnam began in earnest and U.S. combat troops arrived in

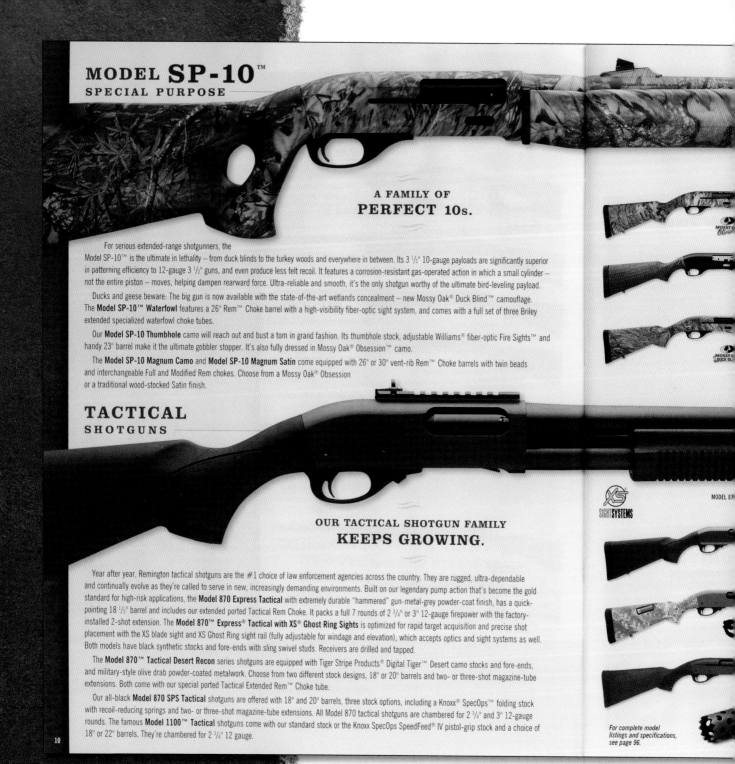

MODEL SP-10™
SPECIAL PURPOSE

A FAMILY OF
PERFECT 10s.

For serious extended-range shotgunners, the Model SP-10™ is the ultimate in lethality – from duck blinds to the turkey woods and everywhere in between. Its 3 ¹/₂" 10-gauge payloads are significantly superior in patterning efficiency to 12-gauge 3 ¹/₂" guns, and even produce less felt recoil. It features a corrosion-resistant gas-operated action in which a small cylinder – not the entire piston – moves, helping dampen rearward force. Ultra-reliable and smooth, it's the only shotgun worthy of the ultimate bird-leveling payload.

Ducks and geese beware: The big gun is now available with the state-of-the-art wetlands concealment – new Mossy Oak® Duck Blind™ camouflage. The **Model SP-10**™ **Waterfowl** features a 26" Rem™ Choke barrel with a high-visibility fiber-optic sight system, and comes with a full set of three Briley extended specialized waterfowl choke tubes.

Our **Model SP-10 Thumbhole** camo will reach out and bust a tom in grand fashion. Its thumbhole stock, adjustable Williams® fiber-optic Fire Sights™ and handy 23" barrel make it the ultimate gobbler stopper. It's also fully dressed in Mossy Oak® Obsession™ camo.

The **Model SP-10 Magnum Camo** and **Model SP-10 Magnum Satin** come equipped with 26" or 30" vent-rib Rem™ Choke barrels with twin beads and interchangeable Full and Modified Rem chokes. Choose from a Mossy Oak® Obsession or a traditional wood-stocked Satin finish.

TACTICAL
SHOTGUNS

OUR TACTICAL SHOTGUN FAMILY
KEEPS GROWING.

Year after year, Remington tactical shotguns are the #1 choice of law enforcement agencies across the country. They are rugged, ultra-dependable and continually evolve as they're called to serve in new, increasingly demanding environments. Built on our legendary pump action that's become the gold standard for high-risk applications, the **Model 870 Express Tactical** with extremely durable "hammered" gun-metal-grey powder-coat finish, has a quick-pointing 18 ¹/₂" barrel and includes our extended ported Tactical Rem Choke. It packs a full 7 rounds of 2 ³/₄" or 3" 12-gauge firepower with the factory-installed 2-shot extension. The **Model 870™ Express® Tactical with XS® Ghost Ring Sights** is optimized for rapid target acquisition and precise shot placement with the XS blade sight and XS Ghost Ring sight rail (fully adjustable for windage and elevation), which accepts optics and sight systems as well. Both models have black synthetic stocks and fore-ends with sling swivel studs. Receivers are drilled and tapped.

The **Model 870™ Tactical Desert Recon** series shotguns are equipped with Tiger Stripe Products® Digital Tiger™ Desert camo stocks and fore-ends, and military-style olive drab powder-coated metalwork. Choose from two different stock designs, 18" or 20" barrels and two- or three-shot magazine-tube extensions. Both come with our special ported Tactical Extended Rem™ Choke tube.

Our all-black **Model 870 SPS Tactical** shotguns are offered with 18" and 20" barrels, three stock options, including a Knoxx® SpecOps™ folding stock with recoil-reducing springs and two- or three-shot magazine-tube extensions. All Model 870 tactical shotguns are chambered for 2 ³/₄" and 3" 12-gauge rounds. The famous **Model 1100™ Tactical** shotguns come with our standard stock or the Knoxx SpecOps SpeedFeed® IV pistol-grip stock and a choice of 18" or 22" barrels. They're chambered for 2 ³/₄" 12 gauge.

For complete model listings and specifications, see page 96.

MODEL 870

XS SIGHT SYSTEMS

MOSSY OAK

MOSSY OAK DUCK BLIND

COURSE OF FIRE
There are plenty of tactical Model 870s available for those without badges and uniforms. Some are designed for home-defense, while others are semi-customized for action-shooting sports like 3-gun competition.

MODEL SP-10™
THUMBHOLE
Available in: 10 gauge (3 ½")

MODEL SP-10™
MAGNUM CAMO
Available in: 10 gauge (3 ½")

MODEL SP-10™
MAGNUM SATIN
Available in: 10 gauge (3 ½")

MODEL SP-10™
WATERFOWL
Available in: 10 gauge (3 ½")

...el listings and specifications, see page 95.

FEATURES

- America's most popular gas-operated 10-gauge shotgun
- Awesome 10-gauge power will handle any waterfowl or turkey hunting situation
- Model SP-10 Thumbhole comes with Williams® fiber-optic Fire Sights™ on a 23" barrel
- Camouflage versions fully covered in Mossy Oak® Obsession™ or Duck Blind™
- All come with sling swivels and padded sling

The thumbhole stock redistributes recoil and gives you a rock-solid grip for increased accuracy.

NEW

...L with Ghost Ring Sights
...ble in: 12 gauge (2 ½" and 3")

...EW

MODEL 870™ EXPRESS® TACTICAL
with Grey Powder Coat Finish
Available in: 12 gauge (2 ½" and 3")

MODEL 870™ TAC
DESERT RECON
Available in: 12 gauge (2 ½" and 3")

MODEL 1100™ TAC-4
Available in: 12 gauge (2 ½")

The Tactical Extended Rem Choke is designed ...optimum performance and recoil reduction. It also ...reducing muzzle rise for consistent shot placement.

MODEL 870™ EXPRESS® TACTICAL WITH GHOST RING SIGHTS
FEATURES

- 18 ½" tactical barrel with XS® front blade sight RC Tactical (ext/ported tube)
- XS Ghost Ring sight Rail (mounts to receiver)
- Sight is fully adjustable for windage and elevation
- Front blade sight works in conjunction with Ghost Ring to quickly and accurately acquire target
- Tactical style fore-end
- 2-shot magazine extension
- Receiver drilled and tapped for scope mounts (XS Picatinney rail with ghost ring included)

11

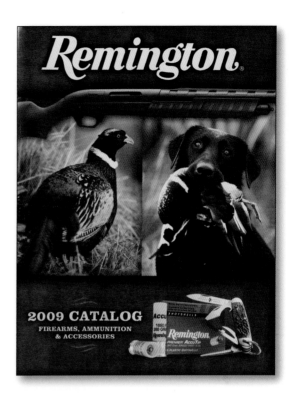

Remington®

2009 CATALOG
FIREARMS, AMMUNITION
& ACCESSORIES

were the newer Remington 870s. Although there weren't that many around at first, as their use increased and spread, the 870s quickly gained a reputation for being very dependable and easy to take apart and clean and maintain.

Those military units involved in carrying out frequent patrols came to value shotguns in general very much, but soon began to differentiate between various makes that were available and define their preferences. For those who rarely if ever engaged in firefights and simply had shotguns because they were issued, it really didn't matter to them what make they carried. But for those who engaged the enemy often, the Remington 870 became the top choice, its easy take-down system one of the reasons for this preference. In an environment as hot and humid as were the jungles of Vietnam, the weapons had to be cleaned constantly in order to ensure their function. The Remington 870 was by far the easiest to disassemble and clean of all the available makes. The other reasons were, of course, the durability and the dependability of the 870, even when compared to other popular brands with the same kinds of features. But the fact that the

large numbers, the Remington 870 was only 15 years old. The Pentagon, which is notoriously slow in adapting new tools of the trade, was still using World War II-era equipment in some cases, and its choice of shotguns for duty in Vietnam fell into that category. However, because there was a shortage of shotguns, new shotguns were bought and, in many cases, they

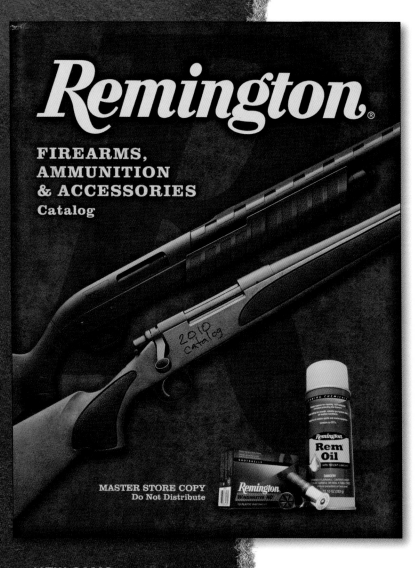

NEW CAMO

Remington procured the A-TAC—Advanced Tactical—camo pattern for use on the Model 870 and other tactically oriented firearms in the 2010 catalog.

870 was easy to maintain, added more to its popularity among troops.

I know for a fact that, in the U.S. Army Special Forces, which literally made its living running long-range patrols during Vietnam, the Remington 870 was decidedly the preferred shotgun. The typical A Detachments (today they are called ODAs or Operational Detachment Alpha), were informally called "A Teams," back in the day, and were usually located in some isolated area. Such a detachment's soldiers were left to mostly fend for themselves, though they were also somewhat supported by a team of RVNSF (Republic of Vietnam Special Forces) called LLDBs, for Luc Luong Dac Biet, which was the name for Vietnamese Special Forces, as well as by indigenous troops, the CIDGs

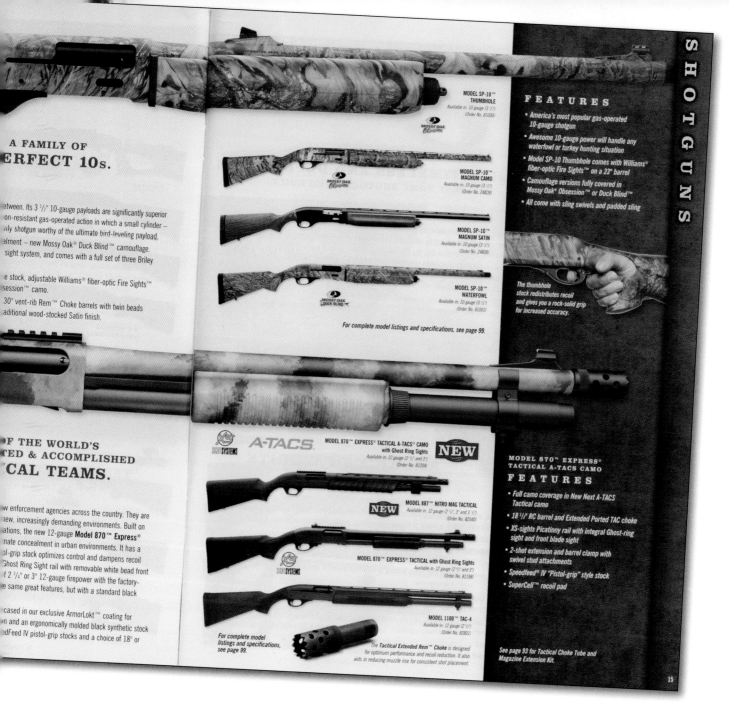

A FAMILY OF ~ERFECT 10s.

~tween. Its 3 ½" 10-gauge payloads are significantly superior
~on-resistant gas-operated action in which a small cylinder —
~ily shotgun worthy of the ultimate bird-leveling payload.

~lment — new Mossy Oak® Duck Blind™ camouflage.
~sight system, and comes with a full set of three Briley

~e stock, adjustable Williams® fiber-optic Fire Sights™ —
~session™ camo.

~30" vent-rib Rem™ Choke barrels with twin beads
~aditional wood-stocked Satin finish.

**MODEL SP-10™
THUMBHOLE**
Available in: 10 gauge (3 ½")
(Order No. 81000)

**MODEL SP-10™
MAGNUM CAMO**
Available in: 10 gauge (3 ½")
(Order No. 24828)

**MODEL SP-10™
MAGNUM SATIN**
Available in: 10 gauge (3 ½")
(Order No. 24808)

**MODEL SP-10™
WATERFOWL**
Available in: 10 gauge (3 ½")
(Order No. 81001)

For complete model listings and specifications, see page 99.

FEATURES

- America's most popular gas-operated 10-gauge shotgun
- Awesome 10-gauge power will handle any waterfowl or turkey hunting situation
- Model SP-10 Thumbhole comes with Williams® fiber-optic Fire Sights™ on a 23" barrel
- Camouflage versions fully covered in Mossy Oak® Obsession™ or Duck Blind™
- All come with sling swivels and padded sling

The thumbhole stock redistributes recoil and gives you a rock-solid grip for increased accuracy.

~F THE WORLD'S ~TED & ACCOMPLISHED ~CAL TEAMS.

~w enforcement agencies across the country. They are
~new, increasingly demanding environments. Built on
~ations, the new 12-gauge **Model 870™ Express®**
~mate concealment in urban environments. It has a
~ol-grip stock optimizes control and dampens recoil
~Ghost Ring Sight rail with removable white bead front
~f 2 ¾" or 3" 12-gauge firepower with the factory-
~e same great features, but with a standard black

~cased in our exclusive ArmorLokt™ coating for
~n and an ergonomically molded black synthetic stock
~edFeed IV pistol-grip stocks and a choice of 18" or

**MODEL 870™ EXPRESS® TACTICAL A-TACS® CAMO
with Ghost Ring Sights**
Available in: 12 gauge (2 ½" and 3")
(Order No. 81204)

NEW

MODEL 887™ NITRO MAG TACTICAL
Available in: 12 gauge (2 ½", 3" and 3 ½")
(Order No. 82540)

NEW

MODEL 870™ EXPRESS® TACTICAL with Ghost Ring Sights
Available in: 12 gauge (2 ½" and 3")
(Order No. 81198)

MODEL 1100™ TAC-4
Available in: 12 gauge (2 ½")
(Order No. 82801)

For complete model listings and specifications, see page 99.

The Tactical Extended Rem™ Choke is designed for optimum performance and recoil reduction. It also aids in reducing muzzle rise for consistent shot placement.

MODEL 870™ EXPRESS® TACTICAL A-TACS CAMO
FEATURES

- Full camo coverage in New Next A-TACS Tactical camo
- 18 ½" RC barrel and Extended Ported TAC choke
- XS-sights Picatinny rail with integral Ghost-ring sight and front blade sight
- 2-shot extension and barrel clamp with swivel stud attachments
- Speedfeed® IV "Pistol-grip" style stock
- SuperCell™ recoil pad

See page 93 for Tactical Choke Tube and Magazine Extension Kit.

(Civilian Irregular Defense Groups). That is not to say these teams were abandoned by the MACV Saigon, under whose command the U.S. Army Special Forces served. But, the isolated location, usually quite a distance away from other friendly units, made it difficult for these teams to get help quickly. The "scroungers" of these A Teams, therefore, were responsible for locating "special" items, if the team didn't already have them on hand. Top among the wanted items were Remington 870s. The scroungers would usually trade for what they wanted with locally made "war trophies," since the

trading took place with rear echelon troops. Some of the more enterprising team members would contract local villagers to manufacture VC flags, sandals, and other trade goods. Also, the Montagnard tribesmen, who were usually employed by Special Forces teams would make the crossbows and other trinkets for the teams to use in trading. There were no shortage of unique trade goods, and they were certainly useful in acquiring whatever was needed by the team, the most popular of which, at least with the Special Forces troops, was the much sought-after Remington Model 870.

CHAPTER TEN

THE 870 INSIDE AND OUT

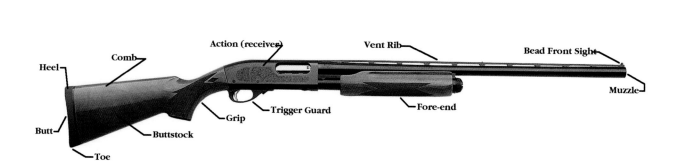

Heel • Comb • Action (receiver) • Vent Rib • Bead Front Sight • Muzzle • Butt • Buttstock • Toe • Grip • Trigger Guard • Fore-end

TO KNOW YOUR GUN is to love your gun. Or maybe that should be the other way around—to love your gun is to *know* your gun. I'm talking about familiarization with your favorite 870, not just as a tool to shoot pheasants, protect the home, play an action-shooting game, or win a round of skeet with, but something on a deeper level. That deeper level I'm speaking of is the basic maintenance that

will keep your 870 as reliable for your grandchildren as it is for you now.

Perhaps a discussion on disassembly of the 870 won't be viewed as necessary by some of the readers of this book. After all, the 870 is such a ubiquitous shotgun that everyone should be familiar with basic things like disassembly for cleaning and minor maintenance. Unfortunately, such is not the case. According to Walt Segovis,

REMINGTON 870

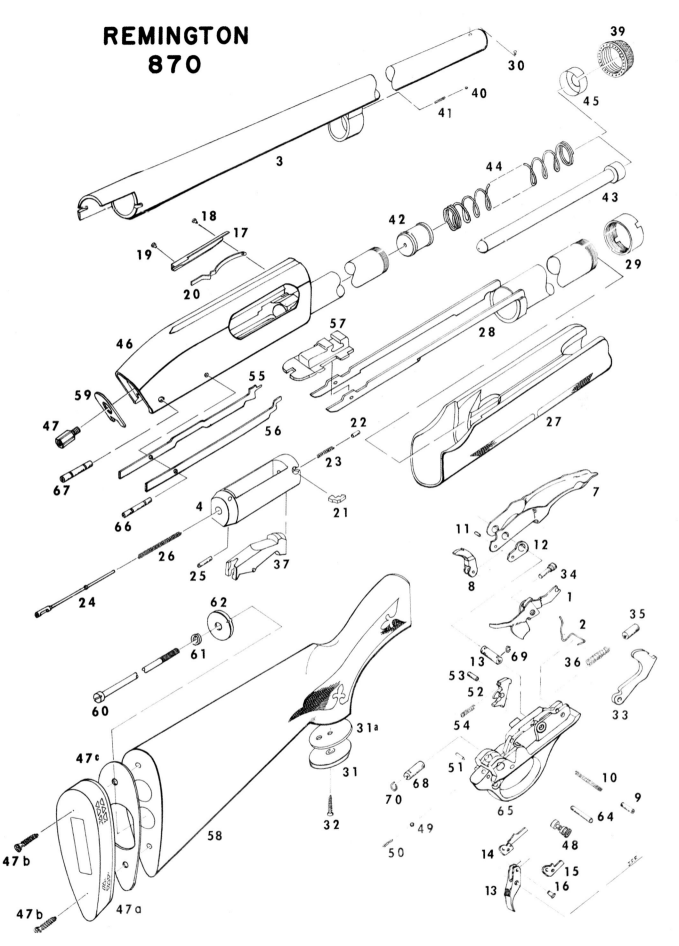

IDENTIFICATION CODE STAMPS – SHOOTERS RIGHT

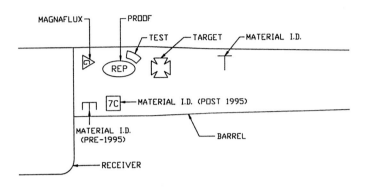

MAGNAFLUX   PROOF
TEST   TARGET   MATERIAL I.D.

REP

7C ◄— MATERIAL I.D. (POST 1995)

MATERIAL I.D.
(PRE-1995)

BARREL

RECEIVER

IDENTIFICATION CODE STAMPS – SHOOTERS LEFT

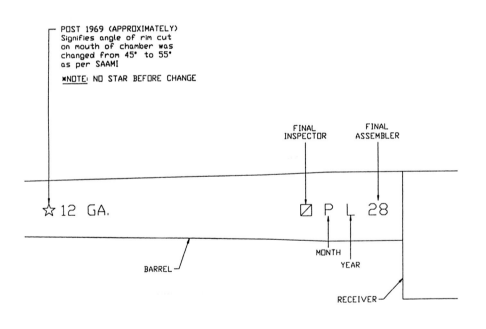

POST 1969 (APPROXIMATELY)
Signifies angle of rim cut
on mouth of chamber was
changed from 45° to 55°
as per SAAMI

*NOTE: NO STAR BEFORE CHANGE

FINAL
INSPECTOR

FINAL
ASSEMBLER

☆ 12 GA.   ☑ P L 28

MONTH

YEAR

BARREL

RECEIVER

NUMBERS AND LETTERS

These are just a few of the dozens of proof marks you
could find on a Remington 870. If you're examining a
used gun or collectible for potential purchase, or even
if you just want to know when your gun was made,
Remington says the best bet is to call and run the
serial number by them.

a gunsmith friend of mine who works in a region where shotgunning is very popular, the vast majority of work he receives before each hunting season is that for simple cleanings! In fact, Walt tells me the most common problems associated with guns that are brought in for repair, guns that, according to their owners are not working properly, is the lack of cleaning. He has shown me some of the guns he's received for repair or cleaning, and it is absolutely mind-boggling how these guns have functioned at all after seeing all the gunk and debris clogged up in their mechanisms. Walt tells me that it is not unusual for him to receive a gun for repair or cleaning that has not seen a cleaning rod or any other type of maintenance other than a wipe with an oily rag on the outside for several decades!

GENERAL MAINTENANCE

Let's assume that you've purchased a new Remington Model 870 and you'd like to improve upon the habits of Walt's general customer base. To begin, it doesn't matter which version you bought, since all 870s take down the same way. But let's say you've bought your new 870 just before the opening of dove season. You wipe off the grease or other rust preventative that was put on at the factory, run a patch through the barrel to remove any excess grease there, then take it out on the opening day and shoot up a couple of boxes of No. 8s. (And by the way, you should always clean a newly purchased gun before shooting it for the first time. It's just plain common sense and safety practice. You never know what could have been lodged in the barrel or in other part of the gun as part of the packaging and shipping process. So, be sure to clean the gun first before taking it out to shoot or, at the very least, run a patch through the barrel.)

The national average of shots fired to bring down a single dove is supposed to be somewhere around four to five shots per bird. Assuming that you are an average shot and got your 10, 12, or 15 bird limit (depending on the limit in your region), you've fired about two to three boxes of ammunition. I'm here to tell you,

the gun definitely needs cleaning after burning up that much ammunition.

Thank goodness you purchased the Remington Model 870, for it's one of the simplest and easiest pump-action shotguns to disassemble for cleaning. It is precisely this feature that Remington had constantly used to promote the 870 in its advertising during the early years. No other pump shotgun to this date is as easily field stripped for cleaning as the Remington 870. So, without any further explanation, let's get right to the basic field stripping that all Model 870 owners should be familiar with and accustomed to performing.

If you bought your gun still in the box, it probably came to you disassembled into two parts, with the barrel and the receiver separated. So, you already knew how to put it together, since you had to do that in order to take it out dove shooting. Now you're home, doves in hand, and the gun well dirtied. Let's get to it.

First and foremost, let's make sure that the gun is unloaded. We can assume that everyone knows how to check that. Then, move the slide handle (pump handle) rearward until the action is open. (If the purpose of disassembly is to only remove the barrel, then it won't be necessary to move the slide handle.) At this point, unscrew the magazine cap located at the end of the magazine tube. This can be most easily accomplished by first setting the butt of the gun on the floor, holding the gun upright, muzzle pointing away from you and preferably towards a ceiling or another safe direction. Once the magazine cap has been unscrewed and removed, simply lift the barrel off the action of the gun. The barrel is now ready for cleaning, a good scrubbing with a copper brush and solvent first, and then running some patches through the bore until it is shiny and clean and absent of spots or other markings.

You will next need a workbench or, perhaps, a kitchen table, really any flat and solid surface area on which to perform the rest of the disassembly. Assuming that the hammer was cocked when you initially moved the slide handle rearwards, move the slide handle forward again and close the

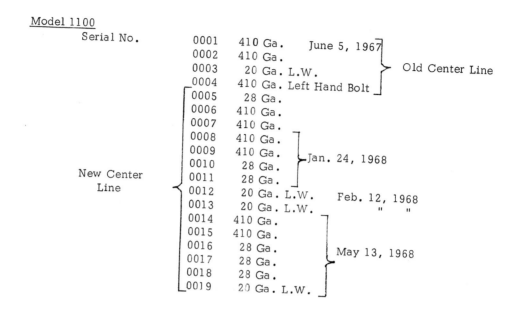

SERIAL NUMBERS

Models 1100 & 870 Model Guns

Model 1100
Serial No.

0001	410 Ga.	June 5, 1967
0002	410 Ga.	
0003	20 Ga. L.W.	
0004	410 Ga. Left Hand Bolt	Old Center Line

} Old Center Line

New Center Line

0005	28 Ga.
0006	410 Ga.
0007	410 Ga.
0008	410 Ga.
0009	410 Ga.
0010	28 Ga.
0011	28 Ga.
0012	20 Ga. L.W.
0013	20 Ga. L.W.
0014	410 Ga.
0015	410 Ga.
0016	28 Ga.
0017	28 Ga.
0018	28 Ga.
0019	20 Ga. L.W.

0008–0011 } Jan. 24, 1968

0012–0013 Feb. 12, 1968 " "

0014–0019 } May 13, 1968

Model 870
Serial No.

New Center Line

0001	410 Ga.	May 19, 1967
0002	28 Ga.	

} Old Center Line

0003	410 Ga.	Dec. 8, 1967
0004	28 Ga.	" "
0005	410 Ga.	
0006	28 Ga.	
0007	410 Ga.	
0008	28 Ga.	
0009	410 Ga.	
0010	28 Ga.	

Note: Dates given are those when serial numbers were engraved --- not dates of completed guns.

CLEnnis:T
Ilion Research Division
6-11-68

SUB-GAUGE SERIES

Model 870s chambered in 28-gauge and .410-bore were a favorite of skeet shooters shooting sub-gauge tournaments in the 1960s. This internal Remington memo details some of the serial numbers on these guns in June 1968.

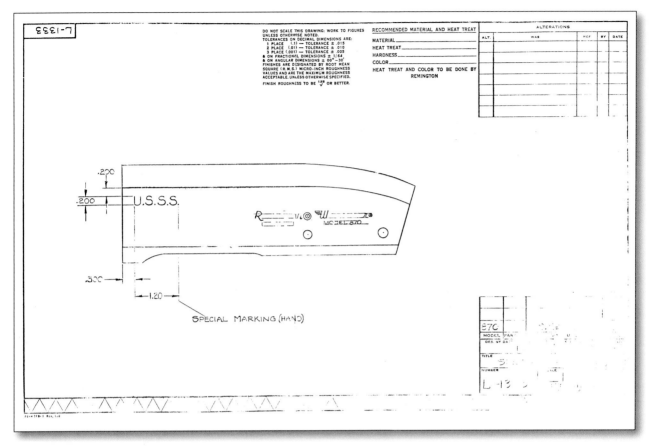

DO NOT SCALE THIS DRAWING; WORK TO FIGURES
UNLESS OTHERWISE NOTED.
TOLERANCES ON DECIMAL DIMENSIONS ARE:
 1 PLACE   (.1) — TOLERANCE ± .015
 2 PLACE   (.01) — TOLERANCE ± .010
 3 PLACE   (.001) — TOLERANCE ± .005
& ON FRACTIONAL DIMENSIONS ± 1/64
& ON ANGULAR DIMENSIONS ± 00° - 30'
FINISHES ARE DESIGNATED BY ROOT MEAN
SQUARE (R.M.S.) MICRO-INCH ROUGHNESS
VALUES AND ARE THE MAXIMUM ROUGHNESS
ACCEPTABLE. UNLESS OTHERWISE SPECIFIED.
FINISH ROUGHNESS TO BE ¹⁄₂⁵ OR BETTER.

RECOMMENDED MATERIAL AND HEAT TREAT

MATERIAL_____
HEAT TREAT_____
HARDNESS_____
COLOR_____
HEAT TREAT AND COLOR TO BE DONE BY
                REMINGTON

.200
.200 U.S.S.S.

R_____◉ W_____®
MODEL 870

.300
1.20
SPECIAL MARKING (HAND)

PARTICULARS

A schematic for the left-hand side of a Wingmaster receiver. This one notes the precise dimensions and placement of the U.S.S.S. stamp.

breech. Next, taking a punch, either push out or tap out the two pins that are holding the trigger housing (trigger plate) group in the receiver. It doesn't matter from which side you push out or tap out the pins, they work either way. Once you have removed the pins, simply lift out the rear end of the trigger housing group. The entire fire-control mechanism will now be in your hand, ready for cleaning and oiling. The mechanism should be very lightly oiled after any debris that is found is removed with a brush. Do *not* oil it heavily as some are prone to do and which is a bad habit that results in attracting more dirt that will eventually gunk up the mechanism.

The next step is to move the slide handle forward while depressing the front end of the

left shell latch located inside the receiver near the open edge of its bottom. The shell latch is a long, flat metal piece that has been pressed into the rear portion of the recess in the receiver. The entire breech block assembly and the slide assembly with its twin action bars should slide out and can be cleaned before reassembly.

The breech block, and the breech face in particular, should be wiped clean. Some residue might require aggressive rubbing or possibly use of a brush. Once the breech block and the breech face are clean, oil them lightly. Wipe the action bars clean and then oil them lightly, as well. The key is to oil lightly. Do *not* drown the mechanisms in oil. It won't make any of it work any better and, instead, just makes the works more

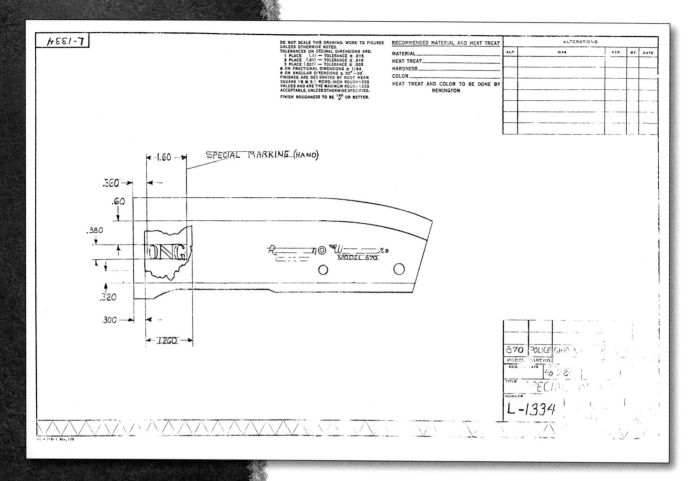

It should come as no surprise that, with more than 10 million Model 870s produced, you're bound to find Remington's serial numbering system somewhat confusing.

prone to gathering dirt and causing problems down the line. At this point you might want to wipe clean the inside cavity of the receiver shell. There may be some unburned powder residue or other debris that needs to be cleaned out before the gun is reassembled. Now the gun is ready to be reassembled, to wit, simply follow the steps for disassembly in reverse.

That is all the disassembly that is needed for a thorough cleaning. Any further disassembly, what some call "detail stripping," is not necessary for regular maintenance, nor is it recommended. Anything beyond the basics described here, unless you are very familiar with guns and their workings, should be left for a qualified gunsmith to handle. Because of the fact that the Remington 870 is so easily field stripped, it gives the impression that the remainder of the parts available for disassembly is equally simple. This just isn't so. Many aspiring amateur gunsmiths attempt

WHEN WAS IT MADE?

If you're like most gun owners, I'm sure you would like to know when your 870 was made. Of course, the year that you purchase a new-in-box gun is no indication at all as to when the gun was made, since it could have been in a warehouse or sitting in the dealer's rack for some time. It would only give you a rough idea, and you can safely guess that it was made within that decade. If you acquired your 870 used, then you don't even have the benefit of guessing, unless, of course, the previous owner did the research and can tell you when that particular gun left the factory.

As with most guns, the serial number is the key to discovering the year of manufacture. However, the number that you will find on the barrel will *not* be helpful, since, like most repeating shotguns, the 870 leaves the factory with mismatched numbers, i.e., the numbers on the barrel will not be the same as on the receiver. It used to be that the numbers matched, especially with guns that had barrels that were difficult to remove, or as was the case with the Winchester Model 12, which had the barrel attached to the magazine tube and the slide handle. But that is not the case with the 870 or other repeaters with easily switchable barrels. So, the serial number that you find on the *receiver* of the gun is the number that will tell you when the gun was made, rather than the number or the year code, as some guns have, on the barrel.

It might not come as a surprise that, with more than 10 million of just this one model produced, that Remington's serial numbering system is somewhat confusing. When I asked Remington what was the simplest and easiest way to determine when a particular Model 870 was made, I was advised that the best course of action was to call them and ask! That being said, let's see if we can scratch out some of the basics.

The initial production of 870s, from 1950, ran from numbers 1,000 to 1,298,983V (until November 26, 1968). After November 26, 1968, the serial numbers had prefix letters and ran from S000,001 to S999,999. But this was only until January 2, 1975, when a new series began with T071,997. The T series ran out in July 1978. Next came the V series, which began with V021,411 and ran out in April 1983, and then we had the W series, which began in July 1983. Now, that sounds simple enough, as each new series began with a new letter and a zero, but the problem in really honing in on dates lies in the fact that the subsequent numbers weren't necessarily in chronological order. Add to that the fact that the 870s also have suffix letters beginning with V for 12-gauge, W for 16-gauge, X for 20-gauge, K for 20-gauge LW/LT, J for 28-gauge, H for .410-bore, M for 12-gauge Magnum, N for 20-gauge Magnum, and U for 20-gauge LT Magnum. Clear as mud, right?

So, although it is possible to track down the date of your 870, it can get confusing, and the best course of action would probably be to call Remington and ask, just as the company advised me. And, to the company's credit, when I talked to them, they said they welcomed calls from 870 owners and would do all they could to help identify the particular gun.

Remington®

Pump Action Shotgun

REMINGTON
870

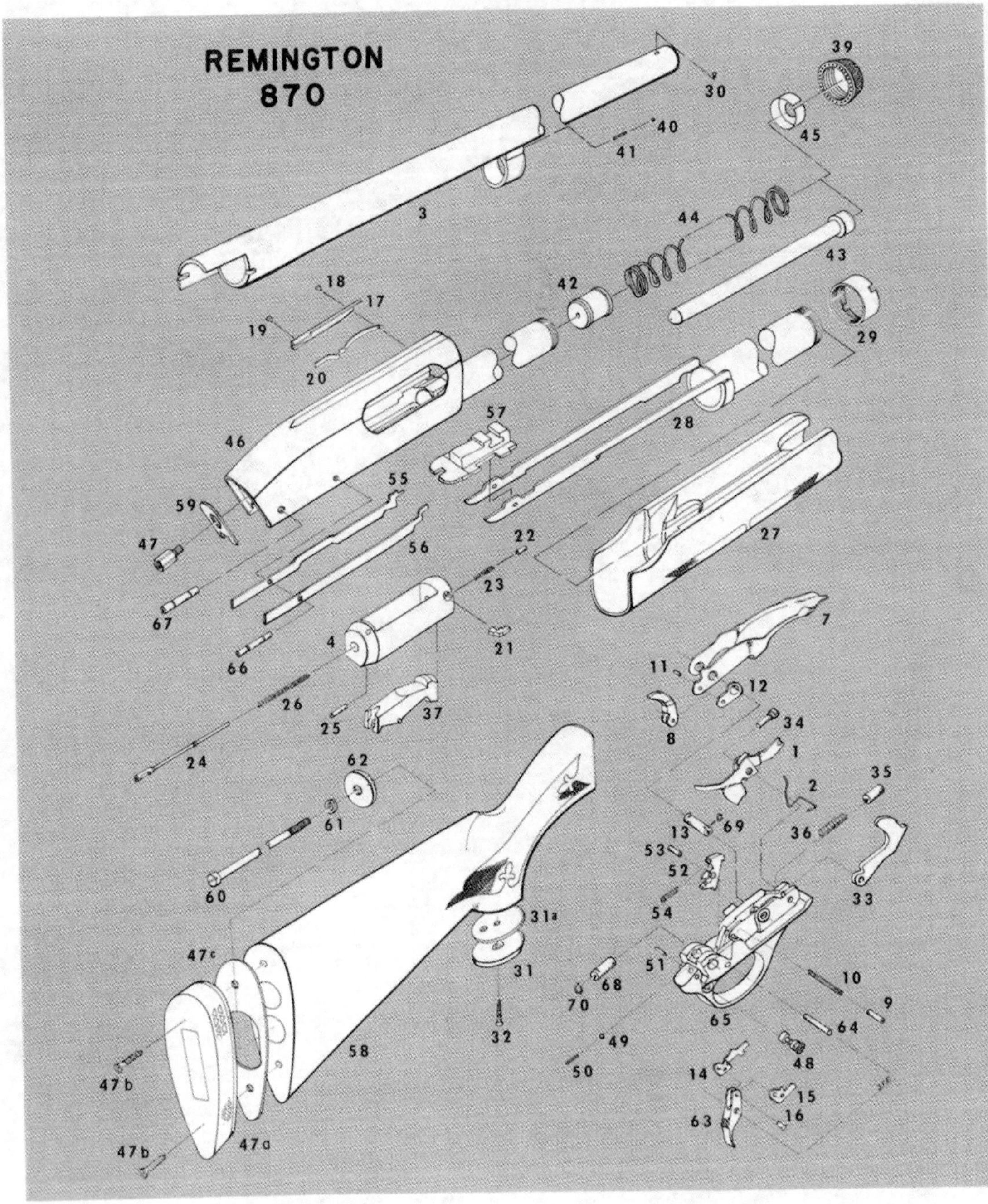

Send all guns for factory service and inquiries on service and parts to
REMINGTON ARMS COMPANY, INC.
Arms Service Division
Ilion, New York 13357

All other inquiries are to be addressed to
REMINGTON ARMS COMPANY, INC.
Bridgeport, Connecticut 06602

SG 7

to go beyond the field stripping and usually end up at some gunsmith's doorsteps holding a shoebox full of parts. So, stay away from detail stripping unless you truly know what you are doing. Besides, for the most part, if well maintained and cleaned regularly, an 870 will last a life time and will never need to be detail stripped beyond the basic disassembly.

Okay, there are always exceptions to the rule, so, if a complete disassembly is something that you must perform and you are familiar with firearms disassembly, you should first get a Remington Model 870 Field Service Manual from Remington Arms or one of the other aftermarket privately written manuals that are available. The Remington Field Service Manual gives detailed instructions on how to disassemble an 870 down to its last screw or bolt. At least with a manual on hand, you will have something to fall back on if you should get stumped by some part that doesn't fit or won't come out.

Beyond general maintenance, let's say that, for whatever reason, you decide to refinish the butt stock and the slide handle. You can actually do so without removing the buttstock parts from the metal, but, if you feel they must be separated, the process can be accomplished easily enough. The slide can be simply removed from the magazine tube as explained before, but the wooden handle does not need to be removed from the metal tubing and the action bars that are attached to the tubing. Simply refinish the fore-arm wood with it attached to the metal components. The butt stock can be completely removed by first taking off the butt plate or the recoil pad, whichever is at the end of the butt stock. Then, using a long shank screwdriver, simply unscrew the through-bolt that attaches the butt stock to the receiver—not exactly a complicated task that requires an engineering degree. Reassembly occurs in reverse.

There is nothing complicated in any of this, as the Remington Model 870 is not a complicated gun. The designers eliminated many of the parts that are usually found on other pump guns, so the gun is easy to clean and maintain.

CHAPTER ELEVEN

PUMP-ACTION PERFECTION.

The Model 870 "Wingmaster". It's just been restyled for its 30th anniversary.

Since 1950, the Model 870 "Wingmaster" has been one hard-working shotgun. More have been sold than any other pump-action shotgun in history. Now, after thirty years and over three million sold, later the most popular pump took by the the Al

AMERICA'S SHOTGUN

IF THERE EVER WAS A SHOTGUN that could be labeled as "America's Shotgun," it is the Remington 870. It is, by far, the most popular and most widely used of all shotguns in America. From its initial appearance in gun dealers' racks, in 1950, it has continued to maintain its popularity among scattergunners and sell like no other shotgun ever made. In 2010, it reached its *ten millionth* production number!

My first exposure to the Remington 870, better known in its earlier years as the Remington "Wingmaster," was through the pages of the outdoor magazine ads of the era, though there were no gun magazines per se, in the early 1950s. It wasn't until the mid- to late 1950s that the first magazines truly dedicated to firearms appeared. *Guns* magazine appeared first, in 1955, followed by *Guns & Ammo*, in 1956. Prior to that, the only gun-specific publication, if you could call it that, was the NRA's *American Rifleman*.

Just as today's market offers 10 to 20 times more shotgun choices to customers than did the 1950s, the selection of shooting and hunting literature today is mind boggling compared to what it was during that same time. The reigning outdoor magazines of the era were the "big three"— *Outdoor Life*, *Field and Stream,* and *Sports Afield*—and, of course, there was the *American Rifleman*. There were the so-called "men's" magazines, such as *True*, *Argosy*, *Saga*, *Stag*, and a few others. No, they did not contain photographs of nude women or other risqué material, as the times were much too tame for that. (There were, however, on occasion, some "daring" art works of scantily clad women, usually portrayed as being "rescued" by heroic men, but never such a portrayal in photographs.) Now, like *National Geographic*, they did publish photographs of naked natives from time to time, but the essence of a men's magazine was very different in those days than it is today. Most of them went under in the 1970s and 80s, this pulp-type genre of adventure magazine with outdoor articles and stories of

adventure, war, etc. They weren't exactly literary journals, though there were a number of surprisingly well-known authors published in these magazines. Upton Sinclair, Edgar Rice Burroughs, and Max Brand, just to name a few, were published in the men's magazines prior to World War II, and post-war, authors such as Kurt Vonnegut Jr., Saul Bellow, and other of their contemporaries published in these magazines. For the most part, they contained light, entertaining stuff, and they carried gun articles and advertising and had gun editors. Remember, this was manly stuff. Some of the gun editors of those magazines were big names in the gun writing business of the day, such as Lucian Carry of *True* and the likes of Pete Kuhloff and Larry Koller.

All the day's gunmakers advertised in the pages of those magazines, and Remington ran some of the largest and most colorful full-page ads. Those touting the 870 usually displayed images of two guns. They headlined the "New" Remington shotguns, one the basic model AP "Standard" with a plain buttstock and corn cob pump handle, and the other the higher grade ADL that Remington labeled as "De Luxe" and described as having a finely checkered stock and a grooved and checkered semi-beavertail forearm. Also, the ADL model was noted to have the top surface of its plain barrel in a matte finish, something that was quite common on shotgun barrels in those days and absolutely impossible to find today. (The last gun maker to maintain this practice was Browning, and even Browning discontinued the plain barrels with a matte top for its A-5s in the 1970s, now some 40 years ago. Too bad, the matte top on the plain barrel was a nice touch.)

In the early ads for the 870, Remington touted its modern features, top among them the fact that the barrels were completely interchangeable within gauge without any fitting. The second feature Remington promoted was that all barrels came with a barrel extension into which the bolt

MODEL 870™ EXPRESS

MAKES A QUICK, CLEAN KILL ON EVERYTHING EXCEPT YOUR WALLET.

MODEL 870 EXPRESS
SUPER MAGNUM SYNTHETIC

THE VERSATILE, AFFORDABLE REMINGTON®
MODEL 870 EXPRESS® AMERICA'S FAVORITE PUMP SHOTGUN.

Remington
C O U N T R Y

WWW.REMINGTON.COM
©2002 Remington Arms Company, Inc.

FIELD NOTES | FIREARMS

COMMENTS: Regardless of the critter, if there's a season for it, the 870's the gun to shoulder. Just like a trusty labrador, it's as reliable as they come. The non-binding twin action bars and solid steel receiver won't lock up in rain, snow or dirt. Available in over three dozen different 12-, 16- and 20-gauge models; magnum or 3 1/2" Super Mag; camo, hardwood or synthetic stocks; matte black metal finish. The balance and feel makes this gun point like no other. It's a darn fine gun no matter what you're after — including a nice price.

NOTE: NEW MODELS FOR 2002 INCLUDE A 16-GAUGE, LIGHT-CONTOUR, VENT RIB; A 28-GAUGE; A 410 BORE AND A 16-GAUGE, SYNTHETIC STOCK IN 28" BARREL FOR ADULTS AND 23" BARREL FOR YOUTHS.

SHOTGUNS

locked. This was a feature found previously only on autoloaders, so the Remington "Wingmaster" was the first pump gun to have the barrel with an extension. Finally, a third feature that Remington claimed was exclusive to its gun was the 870's double action bars. Pump guns of the era, including Remington's biggest competitors in pump shotguns, the Winchester Model 12 and the Ithaca Model 37, had only a single action bar, which sometimes, if improperly fitted or too loose, would bind and cause cycling problems. Remington touted these three features as being exclusively theirs and modern. It appears that many shooters agreed.

My association with the Remington 870 dates back more than a half-century. I began my shotgunning career as a 13-year-old with a rather heavy and clunky 12-gauge shotgun of another make. At the time, my family was living in Tokyo, Japan, where my father was assigned as a civilian employee of the United States Government. My first shotgun was purchased at the Tokyo Main PX, a U.S. Army-run exchange facility. The Main PX carried a lot of firearms, all of the major U.S. makes. Unfortunately, when it came to shotguns, they were almost exclusively 12-gauge models. Smaller-gauge guns were carried by the PXs very rarely, if ever, and I don't recall ever seeing one at that particular PX. So, although I was young and of rather small physical stature, my first shotgun was a full-sized and rather heavy 12-gauge.

I had a miserable first hunting season with that gun, despite the fact that I had prepared myself over the summer by shooting skeet and had became quite an accomplished skeet shot even though my gun was tightly choked. But, on game, I was hopeless. The gun was just too heavy and unwieldy. I couldn't hit anything with it. After that first hunting season, and after much begging and nagging, I convinced my father to sell my shotgun and get me another one, a lighter one. My father, not being a hunter or a shooter, couldn't understand my insistence on getting a lighter gun—to him a shotgun was a shotgun—but much to my relief, he finally relented, and back to the PX we went.

ALWAYS TWO
It was common practice in early Remington ads to promote two guns at one time, usually the plain-Jane AP model alongside the higher grade ADL, which Remington called the "De Luxe."

The lightest gun that was available at the PX was the Remington Model 870—or at least that is, the lightest gun my father was willing to buy. There were some new autoloaders that weighed even less than the Remington, but they cost considerably more. I pleaded. One shotgun in particular, a newly released autoloader of famous make was advertised at 6¼ pounds. I would have gladly robbed a bank or become a mafia hit man to get that gun, if only someone would have offered me a job as a bank robber or a hit man. But it was not to be, and dad wouldn't budge, as the new lightweight autoloader cost almost three times the price of the Remington Model 870. And, so, the Remington was the gun that I got. Destiny, fate—I'm not sure which it was, but the following season I began hunting with that 870, and my luck in the field changed dramatically.

MODEL 870™
WINGMASTER®

THE MOST POPULAR SHOTGUN IN HISTORY
COMMEMORATES OURS.

SuperCell™
RECOIL PAD

One hundred years as the world's foremost innovator of pump-action shotguns is cause for celebration — and our leader is dressed for the occasion. In the field or in a showcase, the 12-gauge **Model 870™ Wingmaster® "100th Anniversary of Pump Action Shotguns" Commemorative Edition** makes a grand entrance with gold inlays and exquisite fine-line accents on the receiver and a striking, high-gloss walnut stock and fore-end featuring our nostalgic fleur-de-lis checkering. For a century, Remington® pump shotguns have reigned supreme over every other. Now owning a piece of the legend is more attractive than ever.

The original **Model 870™ Wingmaster** is so smooth and reliable that today — more than 57 years after its introduction — it's still the standard by which all pump shotguns are judged. Available in 12 gauge 2 ³/₄" and 3", 20 and 28 gauge, and .410 bore, it has the ultra-positive chambering and ejection, flawless balance and natural pointing qualities that have made the Model 870 Wingmaster an American icon. The original Model 870 Wingmaster has a custom-quality finish and handsome American walnut woodwork. Our Premier Dealers can step the aesthetic appeal up a notch with a version featuring a high-gloss claro walnut stock and fore-end, as well as a handsome pheasant and duck scene embellishment engraving on the receiver.

MODEL 870™
EXPRESS®

AMERICA'S
FAVORITE
PUMP SHOTGUN.

Its solid, dependable action makes it America's favorite, and our continual upgrades make it the most advanced, well-rounded family of pump shotguns around. Along with continually evolving designs, this shotgun's superiority is a matter of rugged dependability, great pointing characteristics and versatility. In fact, the Model 870™ has been the standard for slide-action performance for over 57 years.

Our new **Model 870 Express® ShurShot™ Synthetic Turkey** is optimized for big birds with the revolutionary ShurShot synthetic pistol-grip stock. It's contoured to accommodate both right- and left-handed shooters, while offering an incredibly steady-aiming platform that handles like lightning and lessens felt recoil. The 21" barrel adds to its superb maneuverability, and the Turkey Extra Full Rem™ Choke channels maximum payload to the sweet spot. Mossy Oak® Obsession™ coverage on the stock and fore-end keeps you concealed.

With our new **Model 870 Express ShurShot Synthetic Fully Rifled Cantilever**, the buck stops a lot farther out than you ever imagined. It features the incredible stability and comfort of our ambidextrous ShurShot stock and a 23" fully rifled barrel.

The **Model 870 Express Turkey Camo** and the **Model 870 Express Turkey/Deer Combo** utilize our synthetic stocks in Mossy Oak Break-Up.™ Choose the **Model 870 Express Super Magnum** with a 28" barrel and full Mossy Oak Break-Up coverage.

NEW

MODEL 870™ EXPRESS®
SHURSHOT™ SYNTHETIC CANTILEVER
Available in: 12 and 20 gauge (2 ¹/₂" and 3")

14

S H O T G U N S

FEATURES

- Remarkable reliability and durability
- The smoothest pump action shotgun on the market
- Superior balance, handling and looks
- Points, swings and functions better than anything else in its class
- The highly polished and richly blued receiver is milled from a solid billet of steel for the ultimate in rugged dependability
- A wide array of barrel and choke options make versatility a Wingmaster® hallmark
- Twin-action bar for non-binding action
- Available in standard 12 gauge 2 ³/₄" and 3", 20, 28 gauge and .410 bore

For complete model listings and specifications, see page 92.

MODEL 870™ WINGMASTER®
Available in: 12 and 20 gauge (2 ³/₄" and 3"), 28 gauge (2 ³/₄"), and .410 bore (3")

NEW

MODEL 870 WINGMASTER
"100TH ANNIVERSARY OF PUMP ACTION SHOTGUNS" EMBELLISHED RECEIVER
Available in: 12 gauge (3")

MODEL 870™ WINGMASTER®
with Semi-Fancy Claro Walnut
Available in: 12 and 20 gauge (2 ³/₄" and 3")

Premier

MODEL 870™ EXPRESS® SHURSHOT™ SYNTHETIC TURKEY
FEATURES

- 12 gauge, 21" vent-rib bead-sighted barrel
- Standard Express finish on barrel and receiver
- Supplied with a Turkey Extra Full Rem™ Choke
- Synthetic stock with integrated sling swivel attachment
- Mossy Oak® Obsession™ camo stock and fore-end
- Shoots both 2 ³/₄" and 3" shells
- Drilled and tapped receiver for use with Weaver Rail #429M (not included)
- New ShurShot™ synthetic pistol grip stock

MODEL 870™ EXPRESS® SHURSHOT™ SYNTHETIC TURKEY
Available in: 12 gauge (2 ³/₄" and 3")

MOSSY OAK Obsession

NEW

MODEL 870™ EXPRESS®
Available in: 12 and 20 gauge (2 ³/₄" and 3")

MODEL 870™ EXPRESS® SYNTHETIC
Available in: 12 gauge (2 ³/₄" and 3")

Also available in Turkey/Deer combo w/Cantilever and Vent Rib barrels

Premier

MODEL 870™ EXPRESS® SYNTHETIC
with 7-round capacity
Available in: 12 and 20 gauge (2 ³/₄" and 3")

MODEL 870™ EXPRESS® SUPER MAGNUM™
Available in: 12 gauge (2 ³/₄", 3" and 3 ¹/₂")

MOSSY OAK BREAK-UP *Premier*

MODEL 870™ EXPRESS® TURKEY CAMO
Available in: 12 gauge (2 ³/₄" and 3")

Also available in Turkey/Deer combo w/Cantilever and Vent Rib barrels

For complete model listings and specifications, see pages 92-93.

From a solid steel block, to roller-bearing smooth. Every Model 870™ receiver is machined from a single block of solid steel for unmatched strength. Just one of the many reasons it's the most proven, popular and reliable shotgun action in the world.

15

SO MANY
Just a sampling of the cataloged Model 870s from a recent publication, this one the 2008 annual.

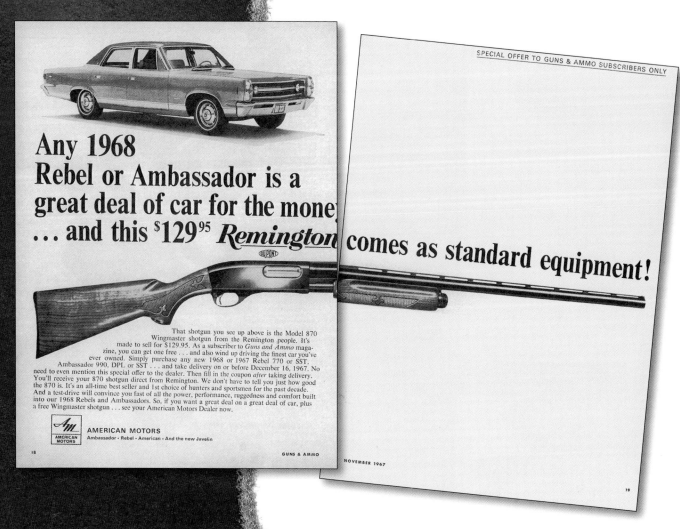

WHAT A DEAL!

Times sure have changed. Anyone in today's politically correct world would be hard-pressed to find an auto dealer putting together a sale that included a gun. A shame, but we can all still enjoy this look back.

Mine was a Remington Model 870 AP "Wingmaster," the plain model with a corn cob pump handle that had ringtail grooves. It had a 28-inch plain barrel that was choked Modified, and the gun weighed 6¾ pounds, just as advertised. It had cost all of $50 at the Tokyo Main PX, about $22 less than what it sold for stateside!

For a skinny 14-year-old—I was around five feet, four inches tall at the time and must have weighed around 100 pounds soaking wet—the gun, although heavy for someone my size, was still manageable and a definite improvement over its predecessor. I shudder to think of all the miles I logged lugging that Remington around over hill and dale as I followed my cocker spaniel Robin in pursuit of game. At the end of the day it was pretty heavy, but still it was light enough that I could shoulder it and shoot it with some degree of proficiency, even at the end of a long day afield.

I am proud to say it was my 870 Wingmaster that was the gun with which I shot all my first game birds. The first I shot with it was an Eastern or Asian turtle dove, which is about the size of a feral pigeon. To this day, I remember that shot as clearly as if it were yesterday. The bird appeared out of nowhere, as I was walking on a narrow footpath with forested hillside on my left and open fields to my right. The bird flew from right to left, crossing my path. I snapped the gun to my shoulder, firing instinctively, and the bird dropped in a shower of feathers. What a thrill!

The next bird I shot was a Japanese green pheasant, one that was a bit of an "iffy" proposition. The pheasant flushed with much cackling and pounding of wings, and I fired my first shot hurriedly—and missed. I cranked off two more shots, as the pheasant sped away, and very luckily connected with the last shot. The pheasant coasted down some distance away, and my faithful cocker Robin retrieved it. I used to have an old black-and-white photograph of me holding up the pheasant by the neck and cradling my Remington Wingmaster in the crook of my left arm, but that photograph is long lost.

My next game bird was a bamboo partridge, which I shot cleanly, and later there was a duck. For the next three years, as I hunted on the main Japanese island of Honshu, and later the smaller southern island of Okinawa, I shot that Remington Model 870 at everything. Before I switched to another shotgun a few years later, I had added quail, woodcock, snipe, rail, and moorhen to the list. In short, I shot all the different species of game birds that I was to shoot for the next 10 years with that first Remington Wingmaster. It was a shotgun that provided me with many "firsts," including my first double on woodcock shot on the island of Okinawa, again with the help of my cocker Robin, who not only flushed the birds, but retrieved them, as well.

I had always been an avid reader of all of the outdoor magazines and eagerly absorbed everything that was written by the gun writers of the day. Jack O'Connor of *Outdoor Life* in particu-

lar was someone in whom I had complete trust. O'Connor always promoted short barrels, 26-inch barrels being standard on his double guns. He recommended that repeaters have 26 inches or less in barrel length. So, before my perfectly good Wingmaster left my possession, I decided to install a Cutts Compensator choke device.

I had the barrel cut back to about 22 inches or so and the bulbous Cutts Compensator was then added. In hindsight, considering that I never used anything but the spreader constriction with that Cutts Compensator, I think I would have been much better served and saved myself some money by simply by cutting the barrel back to about 25 inches and using a straight Cylinder-choked gun. Attaching the Cutts Compensator changed the feel and balance of the gun. It no longer had a nice between-the-hands feel and had, instead, become somewhat nose heavy and clubby. I may not have been a connoisseur of finely balanced guns, but I could still feel the difference in balance and didn't care for the way my gun felt with the Cutts Compensator. Although I continued to shoot quite a bit of game with it, poor balance not withstanding, I didn't like the way it handled, as it no longer had swing I'd come to be so natural with. And so we parted ways. I got rid of it and got another gun and promised myself not to ever install a choke device again.

I got my second Remington Wingmaster about 15 years later. It was a much fancier version than my early AP Standard grade. The wood had what Remington called the RKW finish, a fancy name for glossy polyurethane, and a "vibra-hone" finish on the metal surfaces (not sure exactly what "vibra-hone" means, but it did have a better polish and bluing job than my first gun). It also had the *fleur de lis* pattern of impressed checkering, which I thought looked kind of tacky; I would have preferred a plain, unmarked grip and forearm. I bought the gun used with two barrels, a plain 30-inch Full choke and a plain 28-inch Modified. I had the Modified barrel chopped down to 24 inches and the bead reset and used that for upland. The other 30-inch barrel was for waterfowl.

In hindsight, I probably should have kept the 28-inch Modified barrel and chopped the 30-inch Full barrel. My waterfowling was always done over decoys, and a 30-inch Full choke wasn't really necessary. Still, and despite my alterations, it was probably one of the most versatile guns that I have ever owned. With the 30-inch barrel, it had adequate weight up front and tight choking for extended range shooting when I did, on occasion, take a long shot at ducks. My most memorable long-range shooting with that gun occurred, when I took a couple of shots at very high bunch of snipe passing overhead. The snipe appeared as tiny dots, but I cranked off a pair of shots and scored a rare double on the diminutive birds.

That second 870 of mine weighed around 7½ pounds with the long barrel. With the abbreviated barrel and no choke, it came in around 7 pounds, perhaps a bit less, and was very light up front, an important feature for upland gunning. If it hadn't had such a thick forearm and a recoil pad, I'm sure it would have tipped the scale around 6½ pounds.

I remember one particular September afternoon, when my brother Jim and I, along with a neighborhood teenager Dave, went dove shooting at a ranch just outside of Petaluma, California, where the local doves used to come in to roost. A favorite spot for us to set up was in a grove of pepper trees separated by an opening in the middle that was about 25 to 30 yards wide. The birds would come in skimming over the first grove of trees intent on landing in the second grove, where they roosted. My brother had just gotten a new Remington Model 870 LW 20-gauge and was anxious to try it out. I was shooting an autoloader of another make, while I'd loaned Dave my 870 with the short, Cylinder-bored 24-inch barrel.

Famed gun writer Jack O'Connor once gifted his son one of his favorite guns, a much-loved 16-gauge side-by-side Winchester Model 21. Nice as the gift was, the son preferred his own Model 870 for hunting pheasants.

Because Dave was armed with a gun that had no choke, we posted him in front of the pepper trees, so that he would get a first crack at the incoming birds. My brother and I set up behind the second grove. To make the long story short, the birds started to come in and we began shooting. It was fast and furious shooting, all at relatively close range. When the shooting stopped, we discovered that we had done very well. Dave, in particular, was thrilled, because he had done so well with that short-barreled 870. My brother Jim, too, was very pleased with his new 870 LW 20-gauge. He said that it was lightning fast and operated smoothly and without a hitch.

That was back in 1970. After Dave graduated from high school that year, he enlisted in the Army. When he got out, the first shotgun he purchased was, you guessed it, a Remington Model 870. As far as Dave was concerned, there was no question about the choice, it had to be an 870! Think that dove shoot had made an impression on him?

In the summer of 1988, I bought a Remington Model 870 Wingmaster 12-gauge and took it with me to Ecuador, South America, where I was assigned to work and live for the next four years by the State Department. My first hunting trip with that gun took place in September, when I was invited to go duck shooting at night (night shooting is perfectly legal in Ecuador), at a place called Taura, not far from Guayaquil, where I lived and worked at the American Consulate General. The gun that I had was an early Rem Choked version of the 870, and it was certainly much nicer cosmetically than my previous 870s. It had a pseudo oil finished satin stock and forearm, with nice, attractive cut checkering and none of that tacky pressed *fleur de lis* pattern of the past. The metal had a nice polish and deep bluing, and the 28-inch barrel had a ventilated rib. It also sported a thick, black recoil pad. The gun was nice, though a little heavy.

The place where we were shooting was a large harvested rice field, but apparently there was enough rice around on the ground to entice the ducks to come in and feed. They were mostly the black bellied tree ducks that are called *patillos*, and the fulvous tree ducks called *marias*. (Incidentally, these are Ecuadorian names, not official Spanish-language names.)

The first time I shouldered that gun to actually fire it, I shot at the silhouettes of a pair of *patillos* against the moonlit sky. The gun came up naturally, I shot at the first duck, and then, without even thinking, shucked the pump and shot at the second duck, dropping both stone dead. There was no doubt that the gun pointed and shot well, just like all the 870s I have ever shot. But I never really took to that particular gun. It was just too heavy and lacked the feel of my older 870s. When I finally weighed it, the gun tipped in at 7¾ pounds, for me just too much. Indeed, the gun was much heavier than any of my previous 870s, even the one with 30-inch barrel. So, despite the fact that it shot well, I ended up trading it away.

I have owned, shot, and sold or traded quite a few Wingmasters in my time, and I have never had one that I didn't like, except that one that was too heavy, and that one I liked as a gun, I just didn't like its hefty weight. Truthfully, of the ones I've traded, I've done so not because I didn't like them, but merely because I needed guns to trade and 870s are liked by everyone! It is, truly, everyone's shotgun in America. I know many shooters who own large collections of fine shotguns, yet still seem to gravitate to the Model 870 whenever they decide to do some serious shooting. And when you have the money to shoot something much more expensive, that says a lot about all the 870 represents.

The late Jack O'Connor wrote, in the 1960s, that he'd given his favorite pheasant gun, a custom-stocked 16-gauge Winchester Model 21, to his son Bradford. O'Connor, as his readers know only too well, was a staunch promoter and fan of the Winchester Model 21, a gun that he touted as much as his beloved .270, the rifle caliber that became his trademark. In his opinion, the Winchester Model 21 was the best double-barreled shotgun in the world, better

than a Purdey or other English Best gun. That was how highly he thought of this shotgun. However, his son apparently did not share the same fondness for the Model 21 as had his father. O'Connor said that Bradford, it seems, preferred to use his Remington Model 870 pump for pheasant!

Recently, while dove shooting here in Arizona, I befriended an elderly retired gentleman who shot almost every day of the season. He always shot the same gun, a well-worn vintage Remington Model 870 without a rib or Rem Chokes, just a plain barrel choked Modified, just like my old Wingmaster. He used some horrible looking reloads, usually loaded in the hulls from those cheap promotional dove and quail loads sold in discount stores. I assumed, incorrectly, that he couldn't afford to shoot better ammunition and that his old 870 was the only shotgun that he had. So, you can imagine that I was somewhat surprised when I later learned from a mutual friend who knew the man well that he was actually quite well off and had a large collection of shotguns, including several expensive over/under and auto-loading shotguns. Just goes to show how one should never judge a person by appearance, whether it's their clothing, the ammunition they use, or a gun they shoot. In the case of this old gentleman, he obviously just preferred to shoot his old Model 870. And why wouldn't he? He shot that 870 with practiced smoothness, and quite often his two shots sounded quicker than someone else's double gun or auto-loader.

Another acquaintance of mine and a well-known dealer in fine shotguns used to make frequent trips down to Mexico to shoot white wing doves, before the Mexican laws became stricter and the licenses priced very high. I've seen his very impressive and expensive collection of shotguns, including more than a dozen high-grade Italian over/unders, each one costing as much as a decent car. These guns were all stocked to his measurements in fantastic pieces of Turkish walnut, each a sight to behold. But whenever he went down to Mexico, he always took his beat-up old 870 that, despite its wear (or maybe because of it), had an action as smooth as butter. I assumed that he took the old Remington because he didn't want to risk losing or damaging one of his expensive guns. I even commented to that effect to him one time, when we were chatting about shooting in Mexico. When I said to him that it was a good idea not to take an expensive gun to Mexico and that he was smart to take the old Remington Model 870, he looked at me surprised and said, "Oh, no, I take the 870 because I shoot it better than any other gun I own, and it never breaks down!" Those words, "I shoot it better" and "it never breaks down!" are something you hear quite often associated with the Model 870.

Still another Arizonan, a young deputy sheriff I know, took up shotgunning not too long ago. He started dove and quail hunting with a rather heavy 12-gauge over/under and often complained about not being able to get on the birds fast enough, as well as having to lug around such a weighty gun. Some of the local older and more experienced upland hunters advised him to get a 20- or 28-gauge. They told him that he didn't need a 12-gauge for dove and quail and confirmed to him that he was lugging around unnecessary weight in shotgun and ammunition. The young deputy took the advice of the more experienced hunters to heart and, when he was able to save some overtime pay, bought a 28-gauge Remington Model 870 Express, the economy version of the more expensive Model 870 Wingmaster. The next time I saw him, he was beaming from ear to ear and excitedly recounted to me the tale of his latest quail hunt. He said the gun was light and moved so quickly that he was on the birds in half the time it had taken him with his 12-gauge.

That deputy friend of mine shot a lot of quail and dove for the next couple years with that 28-gauge 870 Express. Then he decided to upgrade to a "better" shotgun, and his obliging wife gave him a new 28-gauge for Christmas, an over/under of decent make that cost double the price of his pump gun. For whatever reason, the new gun did not fit the young deputy, and he just could not shoot it as well as his little 870. After struggling with the new gun for a season, he quietly retired the over/under (he didn't want to sell it and hurt his wife's feelings), and resumed shooting with the old pump gun. He scratched his head and said to me, "I don't know, it sure is a pretty gun, but I can't shoot it like my 870. It just doesn't handle and point as well."

And therein lies the secret of the Model 870. It is not only practically indestructible, but it handles and points naturally for the vast majority of folks who pick it up and shoulder it. Remington hit the jackpot when they designed the stock, for it seems to fit everyone, from the mythical "average" man to those who range both bigger and smaller. There's just something about the shape and angle of the grip and the thickness and height of comb that makes it just fit nearly everyone, and its dimensions were so successful that Remington later carried them over to its legendary Model 1100 auto-loader.

The popularity of the Remington Model 870 is certainly not unique to my home state of Arizona. I remember seeing a documentary, back in the early 1970s, about the Cree Indians in the Hudson Bay region who shot geese for subsistence. It was fascinating to watch them knock down those snows and specs using standard 12-gauge field loads, and not even the so-called "high brass" shells. Oh, and they all shot Remington Model 870s. One hunter, who was more or less the central character of that documentary, made a comment that the hunters didn't like autoloaders, because they tended to jam, and double guns were lacking because the offered only two shots. He said that, in their experience, the Model 870 was, by far, the best. They'd shot other guns in years past, but they just hadn't been as durable, according to him. (It seems that this most featured hunter of the documentary spoke from a position of some authority, as not only was he one of the group of subsistence hunters, he was also apparently the local gunsmith of sorts. Another hunter brought a gun to him that was damaged somehow and would not shoot straight. These guns were treated quite roughly by the native hunters, and apparently the barrel of this particular shotgun had somehow gotten a bit bent. The "gunsmith" took the barrel and tied it tightly with rawhide to a stump. He then tied a piece of rawhide to the end of the barrel and pulled on it to bend the barrel a little. He would bend the barrel a bit, untie it from the stump, put it back on the receiver, and shoot it at a piece of paper attached to another stump. He kept doing it, checking the target, giving the barrel another yank, and so on, until the gun shot straight!)

One of the more unusual, or perhaps I should say unexpected, admirers of the Remington Model 870 is Glen Jensen, who has been an employee of Browning for more than a half century. Jensen is the official Browning historian, and he has been employed by that company since shortly after the end of World War II. Jensen has a very substantial collection of guns, and most of them, as you would expect, are Brownings. But he also has guns from other makers. When I asked him what he thought of the Model 870, he surprised me by saying that he thought it was one of the best shotguns ever made! He proceeded to tell me that he'd purchased one of the very first 20-gauge Model 870s to come off the assembly line in 1950 and has been using it for over 60 years. To put it in his words, he described it as, "A real sweetheart of a shotgun, the best that Remington made, one of the best of all shotguns!" Now *that* is a mighty high compliment coming from someone who is a devout Browning admirer on the order of the old Superposed and A-5. And Jensen didn't hesitate to give his opinion about the Model 870. When I asked him if I could quote him directly, thinking that perhaps he might want to tone down his high praise for the gun made by a competitor of his longtime employer, he responded by saying that he didn't mind at all, repeating, "It is a real sweetheart!"

Everyone has a story about the ruggedness and reliability of the Model 870. There are countless tales about how someone had to use the gun as a crutch or a paddle and still was able to shoot it without a problem. And there are those accounts about recovering a lost gun long submerged in water and covered with mud that functioned without a problem after the muck was hosed off. Find an 870 owner, and there's surely a story to be told along these lines.

Except when it comes to me. I don't have any personal accounts of such incidents. All I can say is that all of my Model 870s have functioned reliably under all conditions. And I have witnessed many occasions where 870s were used extensively in the field and cannot remember seeing or hearing about any problems. No doubt, there were and are instances when this gun has failed, after all, it is but a mechanical device, and all mechanical devices can and do fail from time to time. But, in my experience, I've not seen them, and I've got more than a few years behind the gun.

Although he was already mentioned in the early chapter on Trap and Skeet, no discussion of the Remington Model 870 can take place without at least some additional words about

the "Mr. 870," the amazing Rudy Etchen. There have been books written about Etchen and countless magazine articles appeared through the years in everything from the *American Rifleman*, *Field & Stream*, to *Sports Illustrated*, so I won't try to cover all the ground that has already been more than adequately observed. But his exploits with the Model 870 cannot go unmentioned, since this book is about this gun! Etchen, who died in 2001, was a phenomenal shotgunner who set all sorts of trap and skeet records, as well as live pigeon shooting records. Contrary to some claims that he used his beloved Model 870 for all his shooting, he did use other shotguns, including Parkers for live pigeon shooting and a Remington Model 32 over/under for skeet. But he is best known for his exploits with the Model 870.

As already mentioned in the earlier chapter, in 1950, Etchen, who at the time was a 27-year-old employee of Remington, took one of the very first Model 870 trap guns that came off the assembly line and shot the first ever 100 straight in trap handicap doubles at the Grand. He shot the same gun at trap for the rest of his life and, 32 years later, repeated the 100 straight in doubles at the 1982 Louisiana State Shoot. Etchen claimed that he'd shot more than two *million* rounds through that old Model 870! That's a huge claim, and whether that many rounds were put through his gun is immaterial, for the one thing that's for sure is that he shot it a lot, and for a half a century!

As an individual, Rudy Etchen probably did more to popularize the Model 870 than any other person. Just think about it. The same year that the gun is introduced, he sets a new record at the Grand by breaking 100 straight in handicap trap doubles with this brand new gun—Remington just couldn't have gotten better advertising. From that point on, with Etchen winning trap tournaments with his Remington Model 870 all across the country, sales of the gun took off, reaching toward the position it has today, the most popular and best selling shotgun in America, "America's Shotgun!"

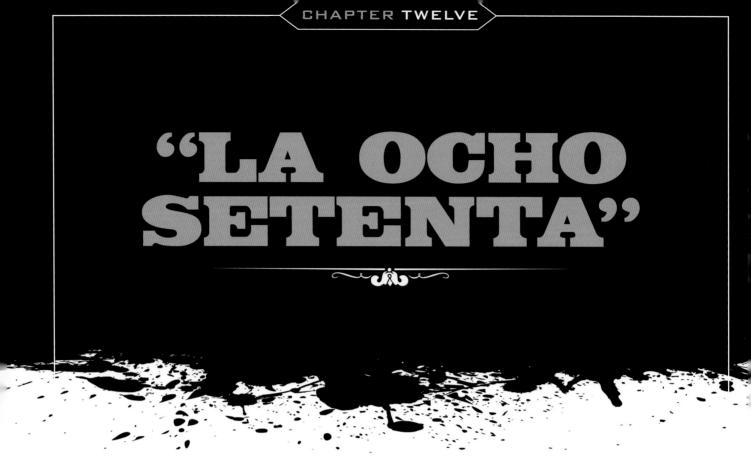

CHAPTER TWELVE

"LA OCHO SETENTA"

ALTHOUGH IMMENSELY popular in America, the Remington Model 870's favor extends well beyond our borders. It has become a universal shotgun, everyman's favorite, regardless of nationality.

As I have already mentioned in the previous chapter on waterfowl shotguns, in the mid-1970s, I used to do a lot of duck shooting in Gray Lodge Wildlife Management Area located just outside of Gridley, California, in Sacramento Valley. Gray Lodge, being a popular public waterfowling area, attracted duck hunters from all over California, but mostly from the northern area of the state. If a survey was ever taken to see what gun the vast majority of duck hunter shot at Gray Lodge during that era, I have no doubt the winner would have been the Remington Model 870, hands down.

Quite often, while waiting to have my number called to enter the shooting areas, I would prowl around the parking lot, talking to other duck hunters, mostly those who had already finished shooting, to ask them about the conditions that day. Among those I regularly encountered were quite a few Russians from San Francisco, who used to come up to shoot on weekends. These were older men, the Russian émigrés who came to America after the Bolshevik Revolution, so most of them were at least in their fifties, and some in their sixties and even seventies. I used to chat with them, ask them about hunting and usually also about their guns. I remember asking one of these Russian duck hunters, I think he was in his sixties, what kind of shotgun he used. He said without hesitation, *vosyem semdyisyat*—that's Russian for eight seventy. I was slightly taken aback, having never heard the Remington Model 870 referred to in Russian that way. He saw my reaction, so he quickly added just one more word—"Remington."

GOOD FRIENDS AND THE 870 GO TOGETHER
The author's good friend Lorenzo Lertora on the right with this 20-gauge Model 870, posing with his hunting partner Daniel Saab after a successful white wing dove shoot in Manabi, Ecuador, in 2009.

The older Russians, especially those who could still remember the Czarist days, were quite familiar with American gun makers. Remington, in particular, was well known to older Russians, since Remington produced a huge number of the Russian service rifle, the Model 1891 Mosin-Nagant, a robust, accurate, and dependable rifle that the Russians fondly referred to it by the nickname *treh-linyeika*. It is, therefore, not surprising that the old Russians would be drawn to a familiar name like Remington, as well as a shotgun that was as robust and dependable as the service rifle they were so familiar with.

From the outside, the Model 870 might seem like an odd choice for these émigrés. Like most Europeans, Russians are primarily double-barrel shotgun aficionados. But unlike the British and some Europeans, Russians have also always been fond of the old Browning A-5, since that gun had been sold in Russia even before the Bolshevik Revolution. At the same time, Russians were exposed to American pump shotguns, specifically

SALUTE THE *SANTA CRUZ*
The author's friend Lorenzo Lertora, a little younger than in the previous page's photo, with his 12-gauge *ocho setenta* and a pile of *santa cruz* pigeons shot on a military banana plantation in Rio Bonito, Ecuador, in 1990.

230

the Winchester Model 97s, since Winchester was also a known brand name, in no small part due to the fact that the Winchester Model 95 lever-action rifle was used by the Russian Army. So, a pump gun wasn't something altogether unfamiliar to Russian hunters. I was to discover later that there were quite a few Russian duck hunters who came to Gray Lodge and shot Remington 870s.

A decade later, when I arrived in Ecuador, South America, I was taken on my first duck hunt in that country by a Dr. Antonio Chedraui, a friend of one of the employees of the Consulate General, in Guayaquil, where I was assigned. He shot a Remington Model 870, so I asked him if he liked his gun. His response was that indeed, he liked his *ocho setenta* very much. A month later, I met and went shooting with another Ecuadorian hunter with whom I'd become very good friends. Lorenzo Lertora was an avid hunter who shot every weekend year round. Ecuador had no hunting season at the time I was assigned there in the years spanning the mid-1980s through early 1990s. Lorenzo had then and has now many shotguns of different make and actions, but he seems to prefer his *ocho setenta* over all. He once said to me that in his opinion, "*La ocho setenta es la major escopeta en el mundo!*"— "The 870 is the best shotgun in the world!" What he meant was not necessarily that it was the finest made or the best made like the very expensive English or European shotguns, of which he has both of very fine quality. What he meant was that, as a utilitarian shotgun, one that he could use anytime and not have to worry about it breaking down, the Remington Model 870 was the best of its kind. Lorenzo's opinion is shared by many, not just in the Americas, but in other parts of the world, as well.

Lorenzo is truly wedded to the Remington Model 870. He started his wingshooting career with a Model 870 and developed into a superb wingshot. I have seen him operate his *ocho setenta* like a maestro, knocking down birds that seemed impossible to hit. I believe he is the best game shot with a pump gun I have seen. He is not a trick shot with clay birds like some

of the magicians who operate pumps with a blur and break fantastic numbers clay pigeons. But I would put him up against any pump gunner on live game. Lorenzo with his *ocho setenta* has no equal as a game shot, in my opinion. I have been so impressed with his hunting prowess using the Model 870 that I even wrote an article about him called "The Pump Gunner," which appeared in the Winter 2011 edition of *Upland Almanac*.

Still another Ecuadorian I knew was a man quite wealthy and an avid hunter. He could have shot any shotgun that he wanted, but he, too, seemed to have a special preference for the Remington Model 870. He had several of these pump guns in 12- as well as in 20-gauge and used them almost exclusively during his hunting excursions. And he was only the second I could mention here, for it was in Ecuador that I first became aware of the Remington Model 870's tremendous popularity and widespread use outside of the United States. Before that, I thought that pump guns in particular were strictly an American thing. My experiences in Ecuador gave me a totally different perspective.

In Paraguay, I met a hunter who loved to shoot perdiz over a pair of Weimaraners he owned. He had a decent collection of shotguns of various makes and actions, including some very unusual Czechoslovakian shotguns. But his favorite was a 20-gauge *ocho setenta* that he claimed was a perfect gun for *perdiz*. It was not the smaller-framed LW version, rather it was the long discontinued standard-frame gun, but he loved it and shot it very well.

I have seen the *ocho setenta* used all over Latin America. In Argentina, in Buenos Aires, in a large gun store, I saw Remington Model 870s priced the same as some Beretta autoloaders. I was surprised by the high price, and when I asked the gun shop owner why the Model 870s were so expensive, he said it was the import duty that raised the price. Apparently, goods from Italy weren't taxed as heavily. I asked him if he sold any Model 870s at such high prices (about double what they sell stateside), and he replied,

"Si senor, la ocho setenta es muy popular."—"Yes sir, the 870 is very popular." I might add that Argentina has a special connection with Beretta, having had strong ties with Italy since the country was founded. Yet, the Argentine armed forces, as well as their National Police use the Remington Model 870s.

In Mexico, the most common pump gun that you will find in the field is the Model 870. Many Mexican hunters who live close to the U.S. border simply cross into the U.S. and secure an import permit from their consulate. This allows them to purchase a shotgun legally from a U.S. gun shop. The vast majority buy the Remington Model 870, because it is inexpensive, yet dependable and durable.

A Mexican quail hunter I know, Ricardo, is a man of very modest means (at the time I met him, he was employed as a handyman at the U.S. Consulate General, in Tijuana). When we met, he was shooting an old pump gun of another make. He used some terrible looking reloads that he used to crank out on an old and outdated Pacific shotshell reloader, a model that had been discontinued some 20 years earlier. There were no parts available for this machine, so whenever something broke down, he simply had to substitute the part with another that was "close enough." Add to that the fact that most of the hulls he used were in such horrible shape that they should have been discarded at least five loadings earlier! Understandably, shooting those reloads would cause his gun to jam from time to time. One time, there was a particularly inopportune malfunction when quail were buzzing all around us. As he desperately tried to clear a jammed cartridge, he said to me wistfully that, as soon as he could put aside enough money, he was going to get an *ocho setenta* and stop having these problems. I seriously doubt that even the usually reliable *ocho setenta* could have handled Ricardo's reloads without a hitch. But, such is the reputation of the Model 870 that Ricardo was convinced his problems would be solved if only he had an *ocho setenta*.

Perhaps to those who are unfamiliar with Spanish, the words *ocho cinco* may have more meaning, after the quirky NFL wide receiver Chad Johnson changed his last name to the number on his jersey, 85. Actually, he should have called himself *ochenta y cinco*, which is correctly "eighty five"; *ocho cinco* is "eight five." But, to Spanish speakers, especially those who shoot, only *ocho setenta* will have meaning. *Ocho cinco* is more of a "Spanglish" kind of a name that will have meaning to NFL fans only (especially since he spells it out without a break as one word, *ochocinco*, when it should be two words!). But I digress.

I have seen Remington Model 870s in use in the field in all corners of the world, from Mexico and South America to North Africa's Egypt and Morocco and on to Greece and Japan. In all these places, the Model 870 seemed to have developed a reputation for reliability, unfailing performance, and unquestioned ruggedness.

In 1993, I was in a jewelry store in Rabat, Morocco, looking at some baubles, when I noticed a photograph on the wall behind the counter that showed a man kneeling on the ground with what appeared to be some birds. I asked the store owner behind the counter if it was a photograph of him, and he smiled broadly in response, showing his shiny gold teeth, and said that indeed it was his photograph. He reached back and handed me the fancy framed photograph of him kneeling in a pose with ducks that he had shot. In his right hand he was holding a Remington 870 with its butt on the ground, right next to the pile of ducks.

"You have a Remington," I said to him.

"*Aiwa*" ("Yes"), he answered, and added in English, with a broad smile, "A Remington 870!"

In 1996, while dove shooting on the outskirts of an oasis in the Egyptian desert, I ran into a Bedouin, mounted on a camel, with a shotgun slung over his shoulder. As he approached me on his "steed," he looked for all the world like a scene out of the movie *Lawrence of Arabia*, you know, the one where Omar Sharif, perched upon a camel, approaches Peter O'Toole (Lawrence) at the waterhole. Anyway, my real-life Bedouin's sling appeared to be just a piece of rawhide that he had tied around the gun's barrel and the grip of the stock. The desert nomad saw that I was a foreigner and

immediately launched into a convoluted form of English that he obviously wanted to practice very much—and it was also obvious that he didn't get much of a chance to practice his English in the middle of the desert! Our so-called "conversation" was somewhat disjointed, since he insisted on speaking in his peculiar English, and it was very hard to understand what he was saying. But I noticed that his shotgun was a much worn Remington Model 870, one of those early plain Jane 870 AP models, so I asked him how he liked it. He grinned broadly, showing an array of badly stained and crooked teeth. He reached back, patted the scarred buttstock of his shotgun affectionately with his hand, and said very clearly, "Good! Very, very good!" And, let me tell you, there was nothing convoluted about that!

In another part of the world, in 1982, while woodcock hunting in northern Greece, outside of Thessaloniki, my friend Grigori Panayotidis and I were accompanied by a local hunter who had a large Braque Français, a French pointer that was reputed to be a woodcock specialist, or at least that is what Grigori told me. However, the "specialist" spent most of the time disappearing and then reappearing after long absences and, at least on that occasion, didn't produce any woodcock. Our local guide, Panos, had an old standard Model 870 AP. He, like all European hunters I encountered, had the gun on a sling. The gun was old and the receiver was silvery from wear, no bluing left on it whatsoever. If you didn't know better, you would have thought it was one of those stainless or chromed "marine" version of the 870. The plain barrel was short, not quite the length of a riot or police shotgun, I'd venture to say about 23 or 24 inches, and it had some sort of a crude sight attached at the end. When I asked him if the gun had originally come with such a short barrel, he said that no, it originally had a longer barrel.

Apparently, when Panos first got the gun, he had to make a trip to Thessaloniki on business, so he took his gun to a gunsmith in town and had the sling swivels attached. But later,

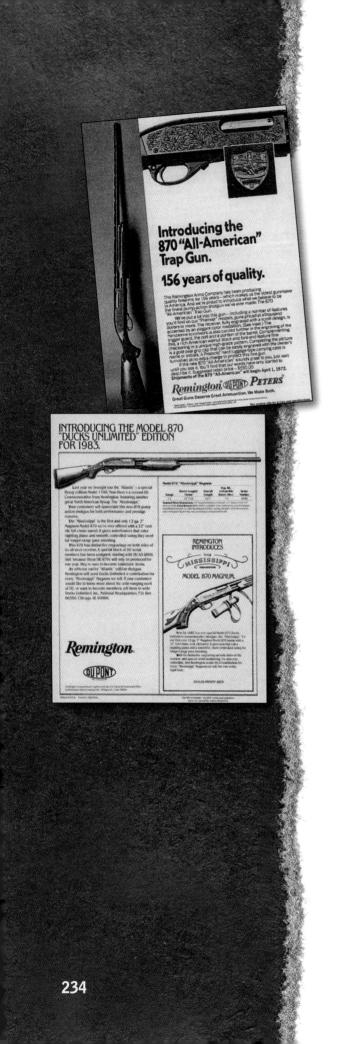

he had an unfortunate accident with the gun and badly damaged the end of the barrel. Rather than making an expensive trip back to the gunsmith in Thessaloniki, he took a hacksaw to it and cut off the damaged barrel end. He had no way of resetting the original bead, so he took what looked like a piece of white plastic and super-glued it on the end. He laughed when I asked him about the unusual front sight. Apparently, he was familiar with the name of "Ithaca Ray Bar" as it refers to a shotgun's front sight, having no doubt learned it from one of the American customers he'd guided who'd possessed an Ithaca shotgun. He laughed again said that his gun had a Greek Ray Bar sight!

Panos told us that he'd bought the gun from an American hunter, a serviceman who was from Athens, and a man whom he'd guided many years earlier. He had never seen a pump gun before and had marveled at its mechanism. He said that he'd very much admired the gun and, at the end of the hunt, the American offered to sell it to him—and let him have the gun for the price of his guiding fee, no doubt as a favor.

Panos was not a man of means and could not afford an expensive gun. He told us that he'd been using an old Damascus-barreled hammer gun of unknown origin before the 870 made its way into his hands. He said that gun had been a bit rickety and he was never too sure if it wouldn't explode every time he fired it. So, getting the Remington 870 was like a gift from heaven. He loved his 870 and said he preferred it over the double-barrel shotguns all his friends carried. My friend Grigori told me that our guide was deadly with his 870, although we never witnessed his shooting on that hunt. I have no doubt that he was good with that gun, because, with its abbreviated length, it had no choke. I noticed that almost invariably, most Greek hunters had tightly choked guns, yet their upland game was primarily woodcock, partridge, and quail, all birds that are shot at close range. So, our man with a Cylinder-bored gun *would* seem deadly with his 870 to anyone who witnessed his shooting, especially to anyone who shot a tightly choked gun.

About two decades earlier and two oceans away, in the late 1960s, while shooting Eurasian turtle doves on the island of Okinawa, I ran into a pair of hunters, both armed with Model 870s that they carried slung over their shoulders. We chatted a while, and they told me that they had been up all night trying to ambush some wild boars that had been raiding a farmer's sweet potato field at night. I asked them if they liked their guns, and they both said that their Model 870s were the best shotguns around, never broke down, and always worked! Many other American brand shotguns were found in the hands of Okinawan hunters in those days. The military exchanges on the island carried a full line of Remington, Winchester, and Browning shotguns. And many servicemen bought these guns as favors for their Okinawan friends, or simply bought them and sold them for a profit, although that was strictly illegal and, thus, a black market proposition. Like I said, another time, another era. Plus, you have to understand that, back then, black marketeering was something that was always around where there was a large military presence.

More recently, just a few years ago, in fact, I met an elderly Japanese gentleman who was in Arizona, where I live now, to watch the "cactus league" spring baseball. Many Japanese are avid baseball fans, and because many of their top players are playing in the major leagues in the U.S., Japanese fans who can afford it come to the U.S. not only during the regular season, but during the spring training season, as well. I met this particular Japanese baseball enthusiast at a large sporting goods store near my house. I was looking at the various shotguns in the store's "gun library" when I noticed the Japanese gentleman also window shopping. He was standing next to me, and we had both been drooling over a particularly handsome over/under with gorgeous wood and beautiful engraving. The price tag on the gun indicated that I would have had to either rob a bank or sell my house to come up with the money to buy it. I commented to the fellow window shopper that although it was a beautiful gun, it was just too rich for my blood. He laughed at my remark

and said that indeed it was a beautiful gun, but it was too expensive for him, too. Then he added, "It won't do anything that my old shotgun won't do. I've hunted with mine for 50 years, and I doubt if this gun would do any better, fancy wood, engraving, and all!"

His remarks raised my curiosity, and I guess it showed on my face. He noticed my unuttered question, chuckled softly, and said, "My old shotgun is a Remington pump gun, nothing fancy, just an old 870 I've hunted with since the 1950s!" Well, that said it all!

The 1950s were the years when Japanese shotgun making had not yet gotten into full swing. To be sure, there were SKB and Miroku double guns, but they were very expensive. Most Japanese hunters bought foreign guns that were available in Japanese gun shops, usually as used guns. Used Remington shotguns were commonplace in Japan at that time. Many of these guns were the ones originally purchased at the U.S. military exchanges by servicemen who'd used them while they were stationed in Japan. The guns were usually sold upon departure as used guns, and they would then end up in the gun racks in gun shops or directly purchased by individuals. It was all perfectly legal, as long as all the proper taxes were paid.

It was obvious that the elderly Japanese baseball fan was financially well off. After all, it was highly unlikely that someone with a modest income would have been able to afford to travel to the U.S. to watch spring baseball, not just once, but every spring, a fact he'd alluded to as we talked. I am sure he could afford a much more expensive shotgun than the old 870, despite his remarks about the pricey over/under we were admiring. But it was obvious he felt the 870 was good enough, and no doubt he was comfortable with it and shot it well. My Japanese shopping compatriot, just as those whose tales I've told before his, only go to prove what a truly remarkable gun is the Remington Model 870, and it highlights why it should be considered as a worldwide favorite and not just America's favorite shotgun.

ODDS AND ENDS

THERE ARE A NUMBER of things that were unique to the Model 870, when it first appeared. As already mentioned, the quick removable and completely interchangeable barrel system, the fire-control (trigger group) mechanism that could be removed with the mere punching out of two pins, and a couple other innovative features made the Model 870 unique for the times. All these have remained through the years, but there were a couple very unusual features that have not survived the test of time.

The first of these was what Remington called the "Vari-Weight" plug system that was offered for the 12-gauge shotgun only. This was, as mentioned in earlier chapters, a metal plug that weighed around ¾-pound and could be inserted into the magazine tube to increase the weight of the gun and move the balance point forward. The early Model 870s, particularly the standard

grade AP models, were fairly light, listed at 6¾ pounds. It was not unusual to get a gun that weighed even a bit less, depending on the density of wood and the barrel length. This was great for upland hunters, who always look for a lighter gun. But, for waterfowlers and clay target shooters, the gun was too light. By adding the Vari-Weight plug, the gun's weight increased considerably and made the gun more nose heavy at the same time, an important feature for both these sportsmen. But Remington quietly dropped the Vari-Weight plug offering, which had come standard with all 12-gauges, in the 1960s, about the time the standard AP model was dropped.

A modified form of the old Vari-Weight plug was revived for the smallbore 28-gauges and .410-bores, when Remington came out with its scaled-frame guns, in 1969. They were first offered as a matched pair of skeet guns and had weights that would attach to the magazine cap to increase forward weight. In actuality, this system had been available much earlier, when Remington introduced its small-framed Model 11-48 autoloader in 28-gauge and .410-bore. When the small-framed 870s came out, Remington simply adopted the same system to the new pump guns. However, as it had been with the 12-gauge, this practice was also stopped after a while.

Another feature offered for small-frame guns, as well as for the Model 870 LW 20-gauge, was the lightweight Honduras mahogany stock and forearm. The small-framed guns stocked as such weighed about a ¼-pound less than the later walnut-stocked guns. No doubt Remington stopped the practice of stocking in mahogany due to cost, but, in doing so, a truly delightful lightweight gun disappeared from the line. Of course, some would argue that a quarter of a pound isn't much and, indeed, it is only about four ounces so involved. However, in a truly lightweight gun, four ounces can make a major difference, and many believe that the old Honduras mahogany stocked small-gauge Model 870s had superior handling qualities compared to the slightly heavier walnut stocked versions. Today, if you can locate one of these small-framed Model 870s with mahogany wood, they will cost at least 25-percent more than the walnut stocked versions.

The Vari-Weight plug system for 12-gauge guns, the external weight device, and the Honduras mahogany wood for the small-framed sub-gauges were unique features of the Model 870 that no other guns from other manufacturer offered. They were useful, and many liked those features. However, it's clear that Remington felt they weren't cost effective, that they weren't popular enough to justify their continuations, and, so, they were dropped.

The elimination of the standard AP model was also based on sales figures. However, there was an element of the plain Jane version that was lost when the ADL model, with its thicker, semi-beavertail forearm, became the standard model for the 870. The old standard Model 870

AP weighed at least a quarter-pound less than the fancier ADL, especially with a plain, rib-less barrel. The gun balanced differently, being barrel-light, and was preferred by most upland hunters. The metal components were finished the same as the ADL, but the stock was without checkering, the forearm was a small, corn cob style, and the barrel was plain, unless the owner specifically ordered a gun with a vent rib. The gun was cheaper than the fancier ADL model and comparable in price with some of the less expensive pump guns that were being sold by Sears and other discount outlets. What you got with the standard AP model was the exact same quality, just with plain wood.

However, as mentioned earlier, the Remington front office was concerned with what it called "good looks," feeling this was something the AP model seemed to lack. Remington brass believed this lack of beauty was the main cause of what they perceived to be lack of sales. Perhaps they were correct, since the discontinuance of the AP model took place before the 870 became the best-selling pump gun in America. But, by eliminating the AP model, Remington effectively eliminated a gun that was lighter and better balanced than any of its other 870 models—at least that's how some 870 shooters feel.

Today, Remington produces the economy versions of the Model 870 Wingmaster as the Express model and the even less expensive Sportsman model. These guns are mechanically the same as the true Wingmaster, but have a rougher finish and are either stocked in hardwood or laminate. These economy-grade guns tend to weigh more, because both the hardwood and the laminated wood are heavier than walnut. Additionally, the rough-coat finish, in some cases, extends to the chamber area of the guns. It is puzzling as to why Remington doesn't plug the chamber area before applying this kind of Parkerizing finish to the barrels. Quite often, the hot, melting plastic of the hulls stick to the chamber area after firing, causing extraction problems. Usually this can be corrected easily enough by polishing out the chamber area, but that should be done at the fac-

CHOKE TUBES AND EXTRA BARRELS

With the variety of Rem™ Choke tubes and extra barrels available for your Remington shotgun, you can participate in a wide range of shooting sports with a single firearm. Rem™ Chokes are high-strength stainless steel screw-in tubes that can be easily changed in the field to provide the correct pattern for whatever you're shooting. And with a simple barrel change, you can use your Remington shotgun for white-wings to whitetails.

New for 1991 are Cantilever Scope Mount barrels for the Model 870™ Wingmaster® and Model 11-87™ Premier™.

Please note the following ammunition recommendations for use with the Model 1100™ Steel Shot barrel. When used with Model 1100™ Magnum shotguns:
- Use 2 3/4" magnum or 3" magnum steel shotshells.
- Use 2 3/4" magnum or 3" magnum lead shotshells.
When used with Model 1100™ non-magnum shotguns:
- Use 2 3/4" magnum or 3" magnum steel shotshells.
- Use 2 3/4" magnum lead shotshells. Do not use 3" magnum lead shotshells in non-magnum Model 1100™ shotguns, as this will cause extra wear and decrease the life of the gun.

MODEL 870™ EXTRA BARRELS WITH 3" CHAMBERS

Model 870™ extra barrels with 3" chambers used on Magnum receivers will handle both 2 3/4" and 3" shells. Use only 2 3/4" shells when these barrels are used on non-magnum receivers.

Length & Choke		Gauge/MSRP 12ga.	20ga.
Field Grade, Vent Rib	30" Rem™ Choke (Wingmaster)	$180.	
	28" Rem Choke (Wingmaster)	180.	$180.
	26" Rem Choke (Wingmaster)	180.	180.
	30" Rem Choke (L-H)(Wingmaster)	198.	
	28" Rem Choke (L-H)(Wingmaster)	198.	
	26" Rem Choke (L-H)(Wingmaster)	198.	
Deer Barrels, Cantilever Scope Mount with Rings	20" Rem Choke	195.★	
	20" Rem Choke (Rifle Sights)	131.	
	20" Rem Choke (L-H) (Rifle Sights)	158.	
	20" Imp. Cyl. (Rifle Sights)	—	104.
SP Deer, Rifle Sights	20" Rem Choke	137.	
SP, Vent Rib	30" Rem Choke	173.	—
	26" Rem Choke	173.	—
Special Field**, Vent Rib	21" Rem Choke	177.	177.
D&F Grades (engraved):		Special Order	

*20-gauge 870 Lightweight barrels will not fit 20-gauge standard 870 guns.
**Special Field barrels will not fit regular Model 870 guns.

MODEL 11-87™ PREMIER™ EXTRA BARRELS WITH 3" CHAMBERS

Length & Choke		12 Ga.
Deer Barrels, Cantilever Scope Mount with Rings	21" Rem Choke	$195.★
	21" Rem Choke (Rifle Sights)	144.
L-H Deer Barrel /Rifle Sights	21" Rem Choke	165.
SP Deer /Rifle Sights	21" Rem Choke	151.
SP Magnum, Vent Rib	30" Rem Choke	183.
	26" Rem Choke	183.
Premier, Vent Rib	30" Rem Choke	183.
	28" Rem Choke	183.
	26" Rem Choke	183.
L-H Premier, Vent Rib (Bradley-type front sight & middle bead)	28" Rem Choke	201.
Premier Skeet Barrel (2 3/4" chamber only)	26" Skeet	183.
	26" Rem Choke	192.
Premier Trap Barrel (2 3/4" chamber only)	30" Trap Full	191.
	30" Rem Choke	200.
	28" Trap Full	191.
	28" Rem Choke	200.

[1] These barrels are not equipped with a pressure compensating gas system.
[2] Manufacturer's suggested retail price
[3] Scope not included

★ NEW FOR 1991

MODEL 870™ EXTRA BARRELS WITH 2 3/4" CHAMBERS

Model 870 extra barrels with 2 3/4" chambers will fit both Magnum and 2 3/4" receivers. Use only 2 3/4" shells in these barrels.

Length & Choke		12	20 Lwt.	28	.410†
Field Grade	25" Full	—	—	$145	$145
	25" Mod.	—	—	145	145
	25" Imp. Cyl.	—	—	145	145
Trap	30" Rem™ Choke	$193	—	—	—
	30" Trap Full	184	—	—	—
	30" Full (L-H)	211	—	—	—
	28" Rem Choke	193	—	—	—
	28" Trap Full	184	—	—	—
Skeet	26" Rem Choke	185	$185	—	—
	25" Skeet	—	—	160	160
D & F Grades (engraved):		Special Order in all gauges			

Rem Choke target barrels have Trap Full, Extra Full and Super Full, or Skeet and Improved Skeet, plus wrench. † .410-bore Field barrels have 3" chambers and will handle both 2-1/2" and 3" shells. .410-bore Skeet barrels have 2-1/2" chambers and will only handle 2-1/2" shells.

MODEL 1100™ EXTRA BARRELS WITH 2 3/4" CHAMBERS

Length & Choke		12	20 (LT-20)	28	.410*
Field Grade, Cantilever Scope Mount with Rings	21" Rem™ Choke	$195.	—	—	—
Field Grade, Deer, Rifle Sights	21" Rem Choke	144.	—	—	—
	21" Rem Choke L-H	158.	—	—	—
	21" Imp. Cyl.	—	$130.	—	—
SP Deer, Rifle Sights	21" Imp. Cyl.	130.	—	—	—
	21" Rem Choke	144.	—	—	—
Special Field, Vent Rib	21" Rem Choke	183.	183.	—	—
Steel Shot Barrel, 12 gauge	30" Rem Choke	187.	—	—	—
	26" Rem Choke	187.	—	—	—
Field Grade, Vent Rib	30" Rem Choke	183.	—	—	—
	28" Rem Choke	183.	183.	—	—
	26" Rem Choke	183.	183.	—	—
	30" Rem Choke (L-H)	201.	—	—	—
	28" Rem Choke (L-H)	201.	—	—	—
	26" Rem Choke (L-H)	201.	—	—	—
	25" Full	—	—	$163.	$163.
	25" Mod.	—	—	163.	163.
	25" Imp. Cyl.	—	—	163.	163.
Trap, Vent Rib	30" Rem Choke	200.	—	—	—
	28" Rem Choke	200.	—	—	—
Skeet, Vent Rib	26" Rem Choke	192.	192.	—	—
	25" Skeet	—	—	176.	176.
Left-Hand, Vent Rib, Trap & Skeet	30" Rem Choke (L-H)	211.	—	—	—
	26" Skeet (L-H)	201.	—	—	—
D & F Grades (engraved):		Special Order			

NOTE: LT-20, 20-gauge Lightweight barrels (4400 Series) will not fit pre-1977 20-gauge Lightweight or standard 20-gauge Model 1100 shotguns. (Refer to parts list for pre-1977 guns.) * .410-bore Field barrels have 3" chambers and will handle both 2-1/2" and 3" shells. .410-bore Skeet barrels have 2-1/2" chambers and will only handle 2-1/2" shells.

EXTRA, EXTRA, READ ALL ABOUT IT!
Even more than two decades ago, Remington had the concept of "user-friendly" firmly in place, with plenty of barrel, choke, and easy swap-out spare parts available.

DON'T USE ANYTHING LESS THAN A REMINGTON PART IN YOUR REMINGTON.

*...well-loved gun is a well-used gun. And the more you use your firearm, the more likely it is that
...'ll eventually need a spare part or two. When that happens, look to the Remington Gun Shop
...a full line of the most popular spare parts for Remington shotguns and rifles. There are seven
...ferent kits, and each is complete with all the components and installation information you need.*

KIT #1:
SHOTGUN BOLT PARTS
...ntains firing pin, spring, and retainer;
...ractor, spring, and plunger; operating
...dle. For Model 870™, Model 1100™,
and Model 11-87™ shotguns.
$20.29 — $26.49

KIT #2:
AUTO-LOADER GAS SEALS
...ontains piston, piston seal, barrel seal,
...d fore-end support. For Model 1100™
...d Model 11-87™ shotguns.
...49 — $28.59

KIT #3:
SHOTGUN MAGAZINE COMPONENTS
Contains magazine
...ap and plug. For Model
...70™, Model 1100™ and
...odel 11-87™ shotguns.
$10.39 — $18.69

KIT #4:
FRONT RIFLE SIGHTS
...ontains ramp and screws, blade,
...and hood. For Models 700™,
Four™, Six™,
7400™, 7600™, 74™,
76™, and 78™ rifles.
$16.39 — $26.99

KIT #5:
REAR RIFLE SIGHTS
Contains ramp and screws, slide, aperture,
windage and elevation screws.
For Models 700™, Four™, Six™, 7400™,
7600™, 552™, and 572™ rifles. $29.99

KIT #6:
REM™ CHOKES
Contains tube of specified choke size.
For all Remington Rem™ Choke Barrels.
$17.59 — $35.95

CHOKE TUBE
12 Gauge
Mod

MAGAZINE COMPONENTS
Model 1100
.410 Bore

GAS SEAL
Model 1100
LT-20, 20 Gauge
Lightweight

Remington® GUN SHOP

Remington® GUN SHOP

M...
Co...
desire...
m...
Re...
cente...

15

A note about older Model 870s on the used gun market. As a general rule of thumb, older model guns, regardless the make, tend to cost less than new guns, unless the "used" gun is in new-in-box, unfired condition and is a discontinued model. Most 870s follow this natural pricing course. The exceptions are the older 28-gauge and .410-bore small-frames. Some of these command *more* than a new gun, especially those wearing stocks of Honduran mahogany.

tory, not by the purchaser of the gun! Of course, not all the Express and Sportsman Model 870s have this problem. As I said, only some of them seem to have the rough chambers. Nevertheless, as rare as it may be, this problem does surface from time to time. As a result, many 870 fans believe Remington would be much better served by simply resurrecting the old AP model, rather than coming up with poorly finished economy versions of it.

I remember when the economy versions of the 870 first appeared on the market. I was in South America at the time, in a country where the 870 had an almost cult following among hunters there. I was duck hunting with a friend once, when we ran into an acquaintance who was shooting one of the new economy version 870s that he had just purchased on his way while on a stopover in Miami. We asked him how he liked his new 870, which seemed to be better suited for duck hunting with its dull finish than did my companion's shiny Model 870 Wingmaster. Our friend responded by saying that he didn't like the new gun. He felt the action felt gritty and didn't operate as smoothly as his old 870 had. I found out later that he got rid of his new 870 and purchased a used one that was of the old style. Now, whether his new 870 really had a "gritty" action or not, I don't know, but he sure seemed to feel his newer gun didn't meet his expectations.

At this point, I would like to make a note about older Model 870s on the used gun market. As general rule of thumb, older model guns, regardless of make, tend to cost less than the newer guns, unless they are in new, unfired condition and are discontinued models. In such cases, a collector might be willing to pay more than the normal price. The 870s on the used gun market are priced accordingly. It is not unusual to find an older 870 (with no Rem Chokes or cut checkering) in 12-, 16-, or 20-gauge in good condition priced around $300. An older AP model usually costs but a couple hundred dollars, while the slightly upgraded ADL or the newer version with impressed checkering will average also around $300. This makes perfect sense. After all, the newer Wingmasters (not the Express or Sportsman) are very nicely finished and offer more versatility with Rem Chokes. This pricing extends to the 20-gauge LW or LT models with a smaller frame. The older guns with impressed checkering and fixed-choke barrels are priced well below the price of newer models.

Strangely, the lower pricing of older models does not extend to the 28-gauge and .410-bore small-frame guns. In fact, it is not unusual to find the older guns with those ugly impressed checkering pattern and fixed-choke barrels selling for more than the newer guns! And, if the small-frame gun happens to have Honduras mahogany wood, then the price is going to be considerably higher (but at least that feature makes a higher price understandable, since mahogany stocked guns are not that common). Otherwise, even the plain models with walnut stocks that have impressed checkering are going to cost as much if not more than a new gun that you can buy in any of the discount stores! I have not been able to determine just why this is taking place.

The sellers of older guns take great pains to advertise their guns as the "first model" small-gauge or "early" small-gauge, etc., as if the early guns had something special about them. Except for those that wore the lighter mahogany stocks, nothing else is different. Whether "first model" or late model, mechanically they are all identical. The only exception would be the barrels. The older guns had fixed chokes, while the newer guns have the Rem Chokes (plus, the newer barrels are slightly heavier). And, as far as finishing is concerned, the newer Wingmasters are far superior, with their deep bluing and cut checkering.

Recently, I saw a fairly worn 28-gauge with a plain barrel (no ventilated rib) sell for as much as a new Wingmaster model. The used gun not only had blue wear and wood that was scratched and dented, but also a rust spot on the side of the receiver, yet it sold for the same price as a new Wingmaster 28-gauge. That's a hard one to figure. Yes, the newer guns are a bit heavier because of thicker barrels, but, on these smaller-frame guns, the weight difference is much less than on the bigger guns. The only

exception would be that those older guns were stocked with Honduras mahogany. Otherwise, I find it hard to accept that anyone would be willing to pay a significant amount more just to have a few ounces less. Could that mahogany just be that much more desirable? Maybe, but be that as it may, that seems to be the trend on pricing the 870s on the used gun market today.

As reliable as the Model 870 is, it is not completely without problems. One problem that recurred quite often, especially with police shotguns, was the jamming of two cartridges under the closed bolt, immediately above the shell carrier. This would "freeze" the action, and the slide can not be moved rearward to eject the empty in the chamber. The culprit is what is called "short stroking." This occurs when the pump handle isn't raked completely to the rear. When this happens, the empty hull in the chamber fails to be ejected, while, at the same time, the fresh round from the magazine is released but cannot complete its cycle up into the chamber.

This is user error, to be certain, and the simple solution to this problem is to make sure to rack the pump completely to the rear. Most pump gunners rarely experience this problem, but there are those who do short stroke the pump in the "heat of the moment" so-to-speak. This is especially common with those who are unfamiliar with firearms, especially pump-action shotguns. To that end, one must remember that many police recruits are unfamiliar with firearms before joining the police department. The police developed an "immediate action drill" to address this issue. When the jam occurs, the police recruits are trained to hold down the action release, slam down the butt of the gun hard to the ground and, at the same time, jerk the pump handle downward vigorously. Usually this will free up the jam. Also, many police Model 870s were modified by gunsmiths to have a slit in the middle of the shell carrier. This allows the insertion of a screw driver or a pen knife to jiggle the stuck round loose.

The immense popularity of the 870 has seen this gun used in almost every conceivable form of shotgunning. Because of that, one would think there would be many customized versions. There tends to be a trend toward this with the tactical games crowd, but, when it comes to bird hunters, customization is rarely seen beyond a few who will spend the money for engraving and upgraded wood.

It took a while, but sometime in the late 1980s, Remington corrected this minor annoying problem by cutting a little tab in the shell carrier, which allows some give to the jammed cartridge. Now if the action is jammed, all you have to do is forcibly cycle the action again and it will loosen the stuck cartridge. Those 870s without this feature can easily be retrofitted, and parts are available from various gun parts suppliers.

The immense popularity of the 870 has seen this gun used in almost every conceivable form of shotgunning. Because of that, one would think there would be many customized versions. But interestingly enough, although there are many customized *tactical* 870s with different stocks and various attachments, one doesn't see many specially modified 870s in the field among bird hunters. There are, of course, many guns that have been custom stocked, but this is most often seen among trap shooters. Trap shooters probably are most prone to tinkering with their shotguns, particularly when it comes to stocks. Too, there are also guns that had been custom engraved, but not many. Overall, as far as modifications done to make the gun more suitable for a particular owner's bird hunting, I haven't seen many.

An exception to this was a gun I saw for sale at a gun shop in Massachusetts, one that was specifically modified for grouse hunting. The owner of the gun shop said that the gun belonged to a local man who was an absolute fanatic about grouse hunting. He said that this particular New England grouse hunter was constantly tinkering with guns, trying to make them better for his favorite wing shooting. He had apparently tried to modify an autoloader as well as a double gun in the past. To modify a pump gun for his grouse shooting, he chose a Remington Model 870.

The gun had obviously started out as a regular Model 870 Wingmaster with a plain barrel. But the changes made that gun unique and unusual, to say the least. First, the barrel was cut back to 24 inches and the bead reset. Then the wood was thinned considerably and the buttstock was cut down to a 13-inch length of pull and hollowed out in the back. Next, the magazine tube was perforated to lighten it—it looked like a heat shield cover on a sub-machine gun! But the most unusual aspect was the receiver that had been shaved and modified to resemble the trimmed receiver of the Remington's autoloader Model 11-96 Euro Lightweight. For those unfamiliar with the Euro model, Remington made the gun for the European market, and it was considerably lighter than the domestic version. The Remington engineers shaved off metal from non-critical areas, so the gun was lightened, but still safe to shoot. This gun's receiver was shaved off exactly like that of the Euro model, yet I saw this gun in 1992, four years *before* Remington put out its Euro Lightweight model. (I wonder if this man somehow had an inside track on Remington designs!) The gun, which was a 12-gauge, I was told weighed 6¼ pounds. It handled wonderfully, lightning fast, making it a very good grouse gun. So, perhaps the modifications were a bit radical, but they were interesting!

No doubt the same thing could have been accomplished with a Model 870 Special Field with a 24-inch barrel and shaved receiver, and there would have been no need to make the magazine tube into Swiss cheese. But then, I'm sure the owner had more fun starting from the ground up and creating his perfect pump gun for grouse. Besides, the gun shop owner said that the gun had been "customized" more than a decade earlier, long before Remington's Special Field models were available.

Incidentally, shaving a receiver isn't something new. Remington had done this before with the 870, although the alteration was almost unnoticeable, not nearly as radical as on the 11-96 Euro model. As mentioned earlier, the 11-48 receivers were made in three sizes, the 12-gauge, 16-/20-gauge, and the later, smaller 28-gauge/.410-bore. The 870's receivers were 12-gauge (same as the 11-48s 16-gauge), 16-gauge, and the 20-gauge (the Standard, not the LW or LT model), which were 16-gauge receivers shaved to make them lighter and a bit smaller. Later, of course, Remington came out with a smaller receiver for the 20-gauge LW and LT models, which have become standard today, and also the 28-gauge/.410-bore receivers, making the 870 also a gun of three receiver sizes.

Remington no longer appears to be carrying the 870 Special Field model as a regular item and it is no longer listed in their catalog. Periodically, a special edition will appear in the Special Field version, such as the special Sam Walton version that was marketed a few years ago. But, as a regular item, the Special Field is no longer carried in the 870, only in the Model 1100.

One of the problems with the old Special Field with 21-inch barrel was that it was too light and whippy up front. It made for a good gun for snap shooting, as with woodcock hunting. But, for most other types of applications, it lacked the inertia up front to be a viable upland gun for longer shots. I believe that if an 870 Special Field was reintroduced, one with a longer barrel of 24 or 25 inches, it would sell.

The late Don Zutz experimented with the Special Field. His was the Model 1100 autoloader, but the idea was the same. It had a 21-inch barrel that Zutz found to be too short and stubby. He said it lacked inertia up front and could not be swung smoothly with any consistency for good shooting. Zutz pronounced the Special Field as a good "snap shooting" gun, good for the likes of woodcock shooting, but not for all upland gunning. Later he replaced the stubby barrel with a longer 26-inch tube and discovered that the gun handled much better!

Unfortunately, for those who may want to switch to a longer barrel on their 870 Special Field, it isn't as simple as just getting a new barrel. Both the 1100 autoloader and the 870 Special Field versions had their magazine tubes shortened. On the normal 870, the barrel loop, or hanger, had to be moved back, so that gun's barrels will not fit on the Special Field, because the Special Field magazine tube will be too short. In case of the 1100, there were no changes made to the barrel for the Special Field except to have it cut to 21 inches. The barrel loop of the 1100 barrel was already set back closer to the receiver than the one on the standard 870 barrel, so no changes were necessary.

Before the Special Field models were dropped by Remington, it did increase the barrel length to

The Model 870 was one of the few pump-action shotguns made in a true left-hand version. Not even the wildly popular Winchester 12 pump got this treatment (nor any of the other Winchester pumps that followed in its wake). Clearly, Remington has always gone the extra mile when it comes to making the 870 an everyman's gun.

23 inches. Don't know exactly why that length was chosen, but I am told that those who tried the slightly longer version found the guns to be an improvement over the older 21-inch guns. Having said all that, there are those who love the old stubby-barreled Special Fields and wouldn't trade them for longer-barreled versions.

I remember a particular individual who swore by his Model 870 Special Field 12-gauge that had an Improved Cylinder fixed-choke barrel. He used it for everything, including duck hunting! I might add that he did a very credible job on ducks with that stubby gun, though, of course, he was shooting over decoys, not pass shooting. Nonetheless, I think his case was an exception. He was a good shot and somehow managed to swing that short-barreled gun to make some intermediate-range shots. However, because he was shooting an Improved Cylinder-choked gun, he held off shooting anything beyond about 35 yards, so maybe that was the trick. Whatever it was, it worked for him. I know *I* would not have been able to hit those ducks with that gun.

The only other truly "specialized" or modified for bird shooting 870 that I saw was quite a few years back, before all these different versions of the 870 began to be offered by the Remington factory. The gun belonged to a waterfowl hunter in California, who was a specialist in pass-shooting geese. He had a special 10-gauge-sized over-bored barrel with lengthened forcing cones that he got from Stan Baker, up in Seattle. (At that time, Stan Baker was considered *the* shotgun barrel guru and did all sorts of custom barrel work. Baker used to have screw-in chokes before anyone else did, even before Briley, and he over-bored shotgun barrels before anyone else really started doing it. Yes, Burt Becker used to over-bore A.H. Fox barrels, back in the 1930s, and there were other shotgun specialists in this country, as well as in England, who did this kind of work. So it wasn't a new concept, but it also wasn't a frequent alteration. Today, many gunmakers over-bore their shotgun barrels before they leave the factory. This is especially popular with competition trap and sporting clays guns.)

All metal work on this particular 870 the duck hunter owned were Parkerized, making the gun look more or less like the current Express or SP models. The wood, too, had been completely redone. The shiny RKW finish and the impressed *fleur de lis* faux checkering had been removed. The wood had a dull, tung oil finish and the grip and the forearm areas hand checkered in about 18 lines per inch. The gun also had sling swivels and a plain black, unpadded nylon sling. This last was pretty unusual in and of itself, as slings were uncommon in those days on shotguns that weren't slug guns for deer. I suppose that, in a sense, it was not much different from today's SP Super Magnum. However, the special Stan Baker barrel is what made this gun different—very different.

The owner of this over-bored 870 was a man who used to specialize in pass-shooting on the "line" in the various California waterfowl refuges, especially at Gray Lodge and Sacramento Wildlife Areas, where goose populations were pretty good; the 10-gauge was not allowed in these areas. It was fascinating to see him knock those snows and specs from incredible heights with his special, customized 870, while his neighbors stood watching with gaping mouths.

Finally, although it was mentioned in the earlier chapter, I feel that it is important to bring up the fact that the Model 870 is made in a true left-handed model, in fact, one of the very first pump-action shotguns to be made this way. It may not seem like such an important feature, but for those who are Southpaws, the fact that the 870 can be purchased in a version specifically *made* for them and not just modified for better adaptability by left-handers is a very important point. The very popular (in its day) Winchester Model 12 pump gun was never made in a left-handed version. (In fact, none of the Winchester pump guns were ever made for left-handed shooters.) Ithaca, with its Model 37, and Browning, with the BPS, can lay claim to being ambidextrous pump guns, but only the Remington 870 is truly available as a dedicated left-hand gun. Truly, Remington came up with a shotgun for everybody, when it designed the 870.

CHAPTER FOURTEEN

THE AGELESS, UBIQUITOUS MODEL 870

10 MILLION AND STILL GOING STRONG

With a detailed engraving of the Remington factory facility in Ilion, New York, the 10-millionth Model 870 pays proper homage to its roots.

870 can truly be called an "age-less" shotgun. As this book goes to press, it is now 62 years old, but it is still as fresh and new in its concept as it was the day the first gun left the factory—and that is something made all the more remarkable by the fact that it has not changed at all! Oh, sure, there have been some surface cosmetic changes. And, too, there are some tactical and turkey guns that, on the outside, appear to have no resemblance to the original Model 870 AP. There are now guns with folding, stocks, telescoping stocks, stocks made of synthetic material, and stocks made of laminated wood. And the surface finishes range from the rough, dull, Parkerized finish such as on the Express models, to more exotic patterns of camouflage to match the clothing a hunter might be wearing, everything from an Advantage Camouflage pattern to Desert Camouflage on the Desert Recon Model. There are also now the screw-in Rem Chokes, which make extra barrels redundant and allow the shooter to have everything from Cylinder to Extra-Extra Full in one barrel. There are fiber optic sights that glow like neon signs in the dark, and rails for red dot sights, scopes, flashlights, and laser sights. Through it all, it is still the same Model 870 with exactly the same fire-control system and the same

dependable, dual action bars that Remington touted in the 1950s. In short, at least mechanically speaking, it has not changed at all. It may have put on different clothing to match the fashions of time, but the heart and soul have remained unphased and unchanged as the same, dependable 870 that has become the No. 1 selling shotgun in America. That, that heart and soul, are what make this gun so remarkable.

Consider the fact that the U.S. Army Special Forces, the U.S. Navy SEALs, the U.S. Marine Corps, the British 22nd SAS, and numerous other military units started using the 870 during the 1960s and are *still* using exactly the same shotgun. True, the newer Model 870 MCS is also used, but the standard 18-inch barreled 870 is still the shotgun of choice for all those specialized units. When you consider that all of Remington's other weapons have undergone numerous changes and upgrades or have been replaced—including the M-16, which may look the same today as it did back in Vietnam, but is, in fact, a remarkably different gun in 2012—it is nothing less than stunning that the 870 has remained the same and is still preferred over all the rest.

Recently, Remington came out with a new pump gun, the ultra-modern Model 887 Nitro Magnum with

an ArmoLokt coating, fiber optic sight, and many other advanced features. It is no doubt an excellent pump gun, especially for waterfowling, where guns are exposed to wet environments and rough treatment. But Remington was very careful to stress that the new introduction was *not* a replacement for the Model 870. Remington, as have some other manufacturers, made that mistake earlier, when it came out with the Model 11-87 autoloader and announced that it was a replacement for the legendary Model 1100—and then never had it happen. It didn't take long for the front office to realize there were still legions of shotgunners who preferred and wanted the Model 1100 and did not particularly care for the newer gun. Remington was not about to make the same mistake with its pump guns, not when it concerned the 870, the best-selling pump gun around the world. So, while there's no doubt the newer 887 Nitro Magnum is an excellent entry as a new twenty-first century waterfowl gun and will grab its share of the market, it is highly unlikely the newer gun will ever reach the overall popularity level of the 870.

The Model 870 is so entrenched in the hearts and minds of pump-gunners world wide, that it has become an ageless shotgun, a shotgun for everyone at all times. As I said in the beginning of this book, most of us here in the states think of the pump-action shotgun as a uniquely American shotgun anyway. While that's not exactly the case, since the action itself wasn't invented by an American, there's still no doubt that the pump gun was refined and developed into the gun that it is today by American gun designers and American gun companies. Additionally, nowhere in the world does the pump shotgun receive such widespread use as it does in America, so, it's not a stretch that it could be, (should be?) considered an American shotgun. Still, the popularity of the Remington Model 870 outside the U.S. borders has made it into an equally popular international shotgun, not just with military and police ranks, but with the Bedouin tribesman that manages to get hold of one, or a villager from northern Greece who works as a woodcock hunting guide during the season, or a wealthy, retired Japanese baseball fan who probably could afford a shotgun that costs as much as a car, but prefers to stick to his old 1950s-vintage 870. The Remington Model 870 has become a modern classic and a favorite of everyone, the definition of ubiquitous.

It took 16 years to reach the first million in production numbers, that year being 1966. The second million mark came in 1973, and the third million only five years later, in 1978. The four million mark was reached in 1984, the five million

FREEDOM GROUP
————FAMILY OF COMPANIES————

To:	All Employees
From:	Ted Torbeck – Chief Executive Officer
Date:	September 22, 2009
Re:	*USA TODAY*® Ad - 10 Millionth Remington® Model 870™ Production

It is my distinct honor and pleasure to report that Remington Arms Company, Inc. has reached yet another milestone in the long history of being America's Oldest Gunmaker. I am happy to announce the production of the 10 Millionth Remington Model 870 pump-action shotgun. Introduced in 1950 and in continuous production since, this iconic firearm stands as the most popular shotgun in firearms history.

To commemorate this momentous occasion and in gratitude to our millions of Model 870 owners, a full-page ad will be featured in the September 24, 2009, *USA TODAY* newspaper. Please pick-up a copy on Thursday and don't forget to share this exciting news with family and friends. There will be limited copies of this issue available at corporate, but we encourage you to pick up your own.

To further commemorate the 10 Millionth Model 870, Remington will be launching several national ad campaigns, an online consumer sweepstakes and an in-store promotion with major retail partners. More details will follow on our website.

I want to personally thank all of you for your support of the Freedom Group Family of Companies and our combined efforts which made the Model 870 what it is today. Your ongoing dedication to quality and innovation will forge the path to the next Remington legend.

GRAND ANNOUNCEMENT
Above is the CEO's announcement, in September 2009, of the Model 870 making it to 10 million in production numbers. At right is the ad the company took out in the *USA Today* newspaper to celebrate the momentous occasion.

in 1990, six million only three years later in 1993, and the seven million mark three years later again, in 1996. Having reached the 10 million mark in 2010, it will probably be only a short while more before the 11 million mark is crossed. That is quite an impressive record. No other shotgun in the world has reached those manufacturing numbers, ever! This ageless gun will no doubt continue on well through this century, and who knows, it may still be around in the next, still being used by some shotgunners who like to shoot those old 870s. It's not such a far-flung idea, after all, there are plenty of guns still in use today that were made in the

No other shotgun in the world has reached the 10 million mark. The ageless Model 870 will no doubt continue on well through this century, and who knows, maybe the next. That's not such a far-flung idea, after all, there are plenty of the guns still in use today that were made in the nineteenth century, even those with Damascus barrels and hammers—and the 870 is a lot stouter than those old-timers.

nineteenth century, particularly the Damascus barreled hammer doubles—and the 870 is a lot stouter and made of better metals than those old-timers.

All across the North American continent and the rest of the world, the Remington Model 870 is in use in the field. Let's just take a sampling of one day. We begin in North America in a place called Colusa, California, where the thick morning fog had completely lifted by eight, just as a camouflage-clad waterfowl hunter attached the last duck of his limit to a bird strap and prepared to leave the blind. He looks up into the gray overcast sky to see skeins of snow geese pass by low overhead, filling the air with a cacophony of that high-pitched yelping they do and sounding much like so many excited women. The hunter lifts his duck strap and slings his camouflage-finished Model 870 Express Super Magnum over his right shoulder and smiles to himself. It had been a great morning.

Halfway across the continent, it is a couple of hours later, almost 10 in the morning, and a pair of hunters have shot the last ringneck flushed by their Lab. With it they had filled their South Dakota limit of pheasants, both via their Remington Model 870s. The older man is carrying an older, much-worn 16-gauge Model 870 AP that is probably as old as he is, while the younger man is carrying a shiny new gun, a Wingmaster with Rem Chokes.

At that exact same instance, an older gentleman in New Hampshire, who has been hunting all morning, has just shot the last grouse needed to fill his limit and, so, he walks out of the cutover he'd been working and onto the road. He seems very content, as he slows his pace for the walk back towards his vehicle, enjoying the feel of the nice heft of the grouse in the game bag of his strap vest. He is cradling his much used and scarred Remington Model 870 20-gauge LW, which he had been shooting for the past 40 years.

South of the border, a stone's throw away from California, in a place near the Mexican town of Tecate and outside a small village called El Hongo, Ricardo is smiling broadly as he calls out to his young German shorthair, "Charlie, *traiga! Traiga*, Charlie!— "Charlie, fetch. Fetch, Charlie! Life has been good these past few years. Ricardo had been able to save enough money on his modest salary to finally buy an ocho setenta. The gun shot beautifully, even though it did sometimes have problems with his reloads that everyone teased him about. His good friend Juan Carlos referred to them as, *"cartuchos mas feo en el mundo!"*—"ugliest cartridges in the world!" And then he had gotten hold of a German shorthair pup that had proven to be a natural, a dog that just pointed and retrieved like a veteran. The pup cost him some money and trade goods (in this case, the trade goods amounted to some manual labor in partial payment to the owner of the litter), but it had been well worth it. He glanced at his shiny *ocho setenta* that he was cradling in his left arm as he stooped down to take the gorgeous valley quail cockbird from Charlie. Yes, life was good, thought Ricardo. He was a bachelor who lived alone, no wife or children, but he had his two most prized worldly possessions right there with him, the *ocho setenta* and Charlie—and he was engaged in his absolutely most favorite past time, quail hunting.

At just about that time, far down south in South America, in the country of Ecuador, Lorenzo has just finished shooting a nice bag of *santa cruz* pigeons (pale-vented pigeons) with his 20-gauge Remington Model 870 Wingmaster. Lorenzo had been trying out new ammunition that he'd acquired, along with a new choke tube he'd bought for the 870. The combination appeared to be working very well indeed. The *santa cruz* had flown very well that day, although not as well as he remembered back in 1990, when he'd shot on a military-run banana plantation, a place called Rio Bonito. Then, of course, he'd shot a 12-gauge 870. He was younger then, and wouldn't have thought of using a 20-gauge. Now the 20 was much more appealing. It was lighter, easier to handle, and had less recoil. Yes, the *ocho setenta*, in whatever gauge, was always his favorite. He had been shooting an *ocho setenta* since he'd first started shooting as a kid, more than 40 years!

Hours earlier, thousands of miles away across the Pacific Ocean, in Japan, at a picturesque location on the Izu Peninsula not far from Tokyo, an elderly man slowly walked back to his car, having shot a limit of *kojiuke* (bamboo partridge) over his aging English setter. The man carried a very old Remington Model 870, one that was made back in the 1950s. It had been obviously well maintained and lovingly cared for by its owner. It was an absolutely plain-Jane model, the Model 870 AP, with a scarred, un-checkered stock and a small, corn cob pump handle. It has a 26-inch plain barrel choked Improved Cylinder. The action on the gun is buttery smooth, almost liquid, and though the metal on the gun had lost most of its bluing long ago, it is spotlessly clean. The man was content and already thinking about the trip he will be making in the spring to watch baseball in Arizona.

Two oceans away, an aging Greek hunter leaves his village outside of Thessaloniki early in the morning and makes his way along a small path towards a wooded hill. He is accompanied by what looks like some sort of a setter mixed breed. Panos smiles as he watches the dog enthusiastically sniffing the path in front of them and thinks back to the days when he had a French Braque, some 30 years earlier. Ironically, the little mutt that he has now is a much better hunter than the pedigreed dog of long ago. He adjusts the sling on his right shoulder so that the old Remington 870 rides a bit more comfortably. The gun is old, very old. Indeed, it was old some 35 years earlier, when he first got it. But it still works perfectly. It had lasted all these years without having any problems whatsoever. Even the piece of white plastic he'd attached with super-glue so many years ago was still in its place. After all the years of hunting the surrounding hills, he still gets excited about the prospect of shooting a couple of *bekazza* (woodcock, in Greek). Yes, Panos thinks to himself, it looks like it will be a good hunt.

Across the Mediterranean, in Egypt, Hassan is trying to sneak up on a small group of mallards that he's spotted in the shallow pond of an oasis near the Western desert. The mallards were a part of the first group of ducks that had arrived from Europe to winter in Egypt and points south. Regardless of what went on in that part of the world, the migrating waterfowl arrived each fall like clockwork, that much he knew he could always count on. There were all sorts of problems in his country and pro-democracy demonstra-

Americans embrace the pump-action as their own, despite the fact the action wasn't invented here. And nowhere else in the world does the pump receive such widespread use as it does in the U.S. Nevertheless, the popularity of the 870 is global, not just with military and law enforcement ranks, but also with a Bedouin tribesman hunting ducks, a Greek sportsman guiding for woodcock, and a retired Japanese businessman swinging to take a bamboo partridge. It is this worldwide fondness for the 870 that has allowed it to become a modern classic and a favorite of everyone.

tions were taking place right then in the capital city of Cairo's Tahrir Square almost daily. People were beaten, arrested, and sometimes killed by the police and soldiers. But, to Hassan the Bedouin, who is completely apolitical, the only thing that matters is that he can get within shotgun range of those ducks. The pro-democracy demonstrations on Tahrir Square might as well be on another planet. In fact, he has never even been to Cairo. He has heard from those who have been there about all the wonderful and strange things Cairo holds, but he has never had any reason or the inclination to see for himself. The only thing that matters to him is daily survival, and right now those ducks are it. If he can get a couple ducks with one shot while they are still on the water, he might get another one when they take off. And, if he got several ducks, that would be, *Insha'Allah*! (Allah willing!), a gift from heaven. His family would eat one duck tonight, and he would sell the rest and make some money, perhaps trade for something his family needed. So, Hassan grips his faithful, old Remington 870 that is battered and scarred and not exactly well maintained. Proper gun maintenance in the harsh desert environment isn't something on top of the list for Hassan. But the gun has always worked, always gone *bang!* even when he loaded it with those awful looking shells that he bought from Ahmed, who loaded them using ancient hand tools while sitting cross-legged on a dirty carpet. It is indeed a mystery how Ahmed determined how much powder and shot to put into his loads, since there was no loading data. Even if there was data that was written down some place, Ahmed couldn't have read it, so it wouldn't have done him any good. But at least they did go *bang!*—most of the time. He is hopeful the ones now in his gun will go that way, as he continues his sneak on the ducks.

***

That is but a miniscule sampling of what can take place in a single day, just a small look at the role the Remington Model 870 plays around the world, throughout the year, a sort of "One Day in the Life of a Remington 870," if I may be allowed to paraphrase the title of Alexander Solzhenitsyn's famous novella. It is nothing less than an amazing shotgun that is found in every corner of the world and used by everyone, rich man, poor man, and in between. It is that which makes it the ageless and ubiquitous 870.

Magnificent Review of a Revered Brand of Firearm

Standard Catalog of®
REMINGTON FIREARMS

700+ Color Photos
More Than 2,000 Collector Values

DAN SHIDELER

A trusted legacy is not easy to come by, and even more difficult to maintain for nearly 300 years - yet that's what Remington has done, and done well.

Remington firearms were the top choice for the pioneers as they settled across America, as well as the soldiers fighting for freedoms in the Civil War. This brand of firearms is on the top of the list of collectors and shooters still today, and in the *Standard Catalog of Remington* you'll learn more about what makes this brand of firearm the one to get.

Add the *Standard Catalog of Remington* to your library of resources today, and it will earn its keep within the first few times you review it.